CSR, Sustainability, Ethics & Governance

Series editors
Samuel O. Idowu, London Metropolitan University, London, United Kingdom
René Schmidpeter, Cologne Business School, Germany

More information about this series at http://www.springer.com/series/11565

Belén Díaz Díaz • Samuel O. Idowu •
Philip Molyneux
Editors

Corporate Governance in Banking and Investor Protection

From Theory to Practice

Springer

Editors
Belén Díaz Díaz
Department of Business Administration
University of Cantabria
Santander, Spain

Samuel O. Idowu
Guildhall Faculty of Business and Law
London Metropolitan University
London, United Kingdom

Philip Molyneux
College of Business Administration
University of Sharjah
Sharjah, United Arab Emirates

ISSN 2196-7075 ISSN 2196-7083 (electronic)
CSR, Sustainability, Ethics & Governance
ISBN 978-3-319-70006-9 ISBN 978-3-319-70007-6 (eBook)
https://doi.org/10.1007/978-3-319-70007-6

Library of Congress Control Number: 2017961126

Cover illustration: eStudio Calamar, Berlin/Figueres

Printed on acid-free paper

This Springer imprint is published by Springer Nature
The registered company is Springer International Publishing AG
The registered company address is: Gewerbestrasse 11, 6330 Cham, Switzerland

Foreword

The corporate governance of financial institutions represents one of the pillars of the reform that has been, and continues to be, implemented in the sector after the financial crisis that has, unfortunately, dominated the last decade. Obviously, before 2008, both the law and various regulatory agencies had been attempting to improve the governance of commercial companies in general and financial institutions in particular, but it is only now in recent years that the importance of the issue has intensified, now with unique characteristics.

First, the soft law phase is over, according to which improvements in governance were entrusted to the voluntary following of good governance codes drawn up by expert commissions, in which the only positive obligation was to explain to what extent their content was being followed. Now it is the laws, regulations, directives and decisions of supervisory bodies that establish how companies should be governed.

Second, there is a certain universalisation of the criteria for good governance, compared to the previous model in which, ultimately, the criteria had to respect the national idiosyncrasies of commercial law. The international scale of the financial crisis meant that governments attempted to deal with these problems in multilateral meetings (such as the G20) and the preparation of standards to be followed was entrusted to supranational institutions, with these standards later to be adopted within national legal frameworks. Therefore, it is bodies such as the Financial Stability Board, the OECD and, within Europe, the European Banking Authority (EBA), the European Securities Markets Authority (ESMA) and the European Central Bank that dictate the criteria that national authorities must submit to, which causes more than a few problems when adapting the national characteristics of many countries to meet these criteria.

Third, concern about the governance of financial institutions has exceeded the initial scope of listed companies. In early studies of corporate governance, there was the *agency problem*, according to which the situation to be resolved was the fact that the effective management of listed companies, with thousands or millions of shareholders, had been left in the hands of a small group of directors, not so much because the legal framework did not provide shareholders with sufficient powers to control directors but because most times the position of shareholders was characterised by its transitory nature and by their identifying of the profitability of their investment with their dividends or the revaluation of their shares, without any genuine concern about the company's governance. Due to these circumstances, which have fortunately now certainly changed through greater activism by shareholders, it became necessary to increase the number of standards or recommendations to guarantee correct corporate governance and the adequate prevention of the interests of minority shareholders, giving independent directors an important role to play in this.

However, as we said, nowadays the standards that regulate the governance of banking companies treat them equally, ignoring the existence or not of minority shareholders, to the extent of finding examples like the requirement for independent directors of unlisted banks, subsidiaries wholly owned by other listed companies, which, logically, have their own independent directors. This is because experience has shown that the interests to be protected are not just those of minority shareholders but also those of depositors and even of taxpayers, whose money, it is repeated time after time, cannot be allowed to become necessary again to resolve financial crises.

In particular, the interest of legislators in the defence of investors and consumers is, justifiably, growing, as reflected throughout this book. The fact is that financial activity has to represent a sign of progress, both for the owners of the institutions that provide it and for the clients that need it.

All the initiatives focused on the improvement of the governance of financial institutions should be applauded, although it should be remembered when preparing them that, nowadays, the line is becoming increasingly blurred between traditional providers of financial services and new operators that, without being organised as banks, are now offering many of these services. In a world in which banks compete for talent with technology companies, or in which international transfers or other payment services are offered by very different types of operators, it must be ensured that capital requirements, governance or prudent supervision standards do not undermine the healthy, effective and equal competition of all agents in the market.

In this regard, it is essential that corporate governance standards be focused on ensuring good corporate governance, with special attention paid to the prudent handling of risks, which is the key to profitability and, therefore, of the sustainability of the sector. Perhaps one of the most important lessons to be learned from the crisis is that those institutions with a sustainable business model, solid corporate governance and prudent risk management have been able to successfully deal with unprecedented adverse economic and financial conditions.

The Santander Group pays special attention to the improvement of its own governance and to any initiative that promotes improvement in the quality of the management of financial institutions. These include initiatives in which the bank has been a pioneer, such as those related to the equality of shareholders' rights (the principle of one share, one vote, one dividend), the promotion of informed participation in shareholder meetings, diversity and balance in the composition of the board of directors and information transparency, especially concerning remunerations.

The *Santander Financial Institute* plays a special role in this work, including actions such as the promotion of this book, which we are convinced will be of great interest, as it provides a holistic analysis of the problem of good governance of financial institutions, describing the features of the problem itself and providing examples of reforms that have been adopted in various countries.

Support for higher education is one of the hallmarks of Banco Santander's corporate social responsibility policy. We now have agreements that support research and education with over one thousand universities around the world. We are very proud to have started this exciting journey at the University of Cantabria, an institution that was established where our bank began its operations 160 years ago and that is making such a great contribution to the economic and social progress of a region that we have such close ties with.

General Secretary and Secretary of the
Board of Directors of Santander Bank,
Madrid, Spain

Jaime Pérez Renovales

Preface

Research in the field of corporate governance (CG) has evolved over the last three decades and the effectiveness of board structures, CEO and Chair features and executive compensation remain at the centre of both policy debates and CG research. The worldwide financial crisis clearly demonstrated to all the inefficiencies of corporate governance structures in the financial services sector, particularly with regard to banks. Bad governance has been considered to be at the hub of the main causes of the devastating crisis that almost brought our world to economic and financial collapse!

Recommendations to improve CG in banks have resulted in the introduction of voluntary Good Governance Codes as well as a range of legislation in nation states worldwide. In the European Union for example, recent regulation focuses on three main issues: credit institution and investment firm remuneration policies (Directive 2010/76/EU), strengthening shareholder rights (Directive 2007/36/EC) and the disclosure of non-financial and diversity information (Directive 2014/95/EU).

Moreover, research on international corporate governance cannot be addressed without taking into account the contributions of La Porta et al. (1997, 1998, 1999) based on the idea that both the laws protecting the rights of investors and their level of effective enforcement are the major drivers of corporate governance development in any country.

Governance in the financial sector has attracted special research attention in the search for better mechanisms that discourage abusive and irresponsible behaviour. In this context, consumer protection issues have also become important features of the financial sector. This became so as a result of a number of mis-selling scandals amongst other things. Consumer protection issues are key topics considered by the EU in the European Consumer Agenda in 2012 and one of the priorities of the European Banking Authority. Combating unfair practices in the financial services sector, ensuring that retail investors are provided with key information to help them take informed investment decisions, the protection of vulnerable consumers and their access to loans or households' over-indebtedness are some of the main issues that remain at the centre of the debate.

Behavioural economics and finance focus on the belief that consumers and investors are not rational when taking decisions, and this therefore opens a new perspective about the effectiveness of current investor protection regulations which are based on consumer rational behaviour models.

This book, therefore, is an attempt to highlight the need for more theoretical and empirical research to be undertaken at both national and international levels with the hope of making comparisons and conclusions about the best corporate governance and investor protection practices which befit the global financial sector.

In the light of the above-mentioned factors, this book provides a timely and comprehensive overview into the effectiveness of corporate governance in the financial sector as well as an assessment of investor protection issues in the financial services sector. The findings will be of immense benefit to academics, practitioners and policymakers.

It is hoped that the book significantly contributes to our knowledge of the financial services sector in the global village in which we all exist.

Cantabria, Spain — Belén Díaz Díaz
London, UK — Samuel O. Idowu
Sharjah, UAE — Philip Molyneux
Summer 2017

Acknowledgements

We are eternally grateful to a number of people who have made the publication of this book on *Corporate Governance in Banking and Investor Protection* a reality. We express our thanks to all our contributors who have worked tirelessly despite their heavy professional commitments to put together their chapters. We also thank the anonymous peer reviewers of the chapters. Thank you to everyone. We are also grateful to Santander Financial Institute (SANFI), formed by the University of Cantabria and Santander Bank Plc, for supporting this publication in a number of ways, and Mr. Jaime Pérez Renovales, General Secretary and Secretary of the Board of Directors of Santander Bank, for writing a befitting foreword to our text.

We would also like to thank our publishing team at Springer headed by the Executive Editor, Christian Rauscher, Barbara Bethke and other members who have supported this project and all our other projects.

We are also grateful to our respective families for bearing with us during periods when we should have been with them but chose to spend the time meeting our obligations to completing the book.

Finally, we apologise for any errors or omissions that may appear anywhere in this text; please be assured that no harm was intended to anybody. Causing harm or discomfort to others is simply not the spirit of corporate social responsibility.

Corporate Governance in Banking and Investor Protection: An Introduction

This book provides an insight into corporate governance in banking and investor protection. The book has been fortunate in the sense that contributors to its 15 chapters are from 19 different universities from 10 different countries that belong to the five continents. The views many of them have expressed in their chapters are the results of their research studies on corporate governance at an international level or in their own countries. The book has been divided into three parts. Part I addresses international studies on corporate governance and investor protection, Part II contains studies focused on specific countries (Indonesia, Ghana, Nigeria, Spain and Italy) and Part III focuses on responsible investment.

Chapter 1 "Does regulating banks' corporate governance help? A review of the empirical evidence" written by Miguel Duro and Gaizka Ormazabal discusses whether and how regulating banks' corporate governance results in a better-functioning economy. In this chapter, they summarise the theoretical arguments for regulation and survey the empirical evidence on the role of corporate governance in the financial industry. The focus of their review is the post-crisis reform of banks' corporate governance, as seen from a historical perspective. The discussion is structured around the main corporate governance mechanisms, namely (i) internal governance mechanisms (i.e. managerial compensation, board monitoring and internal control systems), (ii) market discipline (i.e. the role of competition, the takeover market and shareholder activism) and (iii) regulatory intervention (i.e. capital requirements and regulatory supervision). Their analysis reviews corporate governance developments in important economies around the globe.

Chapter 2 entitled "Banks' interactions with listed non-financial firms as a determinant of corporate governance in banking: An agency theory analysis" written by Cicek Gurkan argues that banking regulation, including corporate governance, needs to strike a balance between the costs and benefits of regulatory intervention. This chapter aims at extending the theoretical base for the cost–benefit trade-off in bank governance regulation by providing a law and economics framework of how banks interact with listed non-financial firms in view of the modern financial intermediation literature. To this end, the chapter first takes up a qualitative analysis of the tension underlying governance regulation of banks by referring to the post-crisis regulatory measures in the European Union as an example. Subsequently, the chapter uses agency theory to investigate banks' roles for corporate governance of listed non-financial firms. Three qualitative case studies are presented, revealing that banks' influence over non-financial firms appears to be more multidimensional than commonly considered in the literature. Specifically, the author shows that bank monitoring and control can present opportunities as well as challenges for listed non-financial firms by affecting their governance arrangements with implications ranging from day-to-day business operations to fundamental capital market transactions in addition to the distress context. He also discusses the implications of differences in ownership structures and identifies influences in both concentrated and dispersed ownership contexts. Overall, the findings of this chapter contribute to the debate on the effectiveness of corporate governance in banking by bringing in a largely neglected dimension into the picture and establishing a theoretical basis for an improved balancing act in policymaking.

Chapter 3 entitled "Is Corporate Governance different in financial firms than in nonfinancial firms? Evidence for the pre- and post-crisis period in Europe" is written by Belén Díaz Díaz, Rebeca García-Ramos and Elisa Baraibar Díez, who in their contribution empirically analyse the following questions: Are governance structure the same in financial and non-financial firms? Are the same CG recommendations applicable to both sectors? Has the crisis changed the way financial and non-financial firms are governed? Without a deep knowledge of these issues, governance policies cannot be well developed. This chapter considers 33 variables that measure policies related to corporate governance, including the areas of board structure and functioning, committees, compensation policy, anti-takeover devices, shareholder rights and corporate social responsibility. The analysis focuses on a sample of 206 enterprises that belong to the main Stock Indexes of Spain (IBEX 35), France (DAX), Germany (CAC-40) and the UK (FTSE-100), dividing the sample into financial and non-financial firms and considering the pre-and post-crisis period. The results show sector-based differences in CG in six variables in 2007 and in eight variables in 2013 for the full sample. Therefore, financial firms were not worse governed than non-financial firms before the crisis, and after the crisis, financial firms are also governed similarly to non-financial firms. The crisis has affected almost half of the CG variables analysed in financial firms. There are also country-based differences in CG in 19 variables in financial firms. These differences amongst countries show the difficulty to develop common governance recommendations for all European countries without considering their own peculiarities.

Sabrina Leo and Ida Claudia Panetta in Chap. 4 entitled "IT governance: who cares more? First evidence from EU banks and supervisors" analyse IT governance disclosure on a sample of 12 EU banks (from Italy, Germany, France and Spain) to observe if, how and where banks report on their IT governance issues and to verify if after the crises, banks have started to pay more attention to IT governance. Since IT governance (like other aspect of banking business) can be influenced by regulatory environment, they examine whether any differences in Supervisors' attitude to the IT topic will induce differences in IT governance across countries. The analysis can be considered as a pilot study (with a limited sample size), but some key points arise from it: (i) banks denote an increasing level of disclosure, more evident starting from 2012; (ii) banks, within the IT Governance Framework, seem to pay more attention to IT Risk Management; and (iii) they prefer the Annual Reports as a place to release information on IT governance topics; (iv) there is a positive relationship between Supervisors' and banks' attention to IT, whilst (v) there is no evidence of Supervisors' influence on the banks' level in IT investments.

In Chap. 5 "Are there differences in boards of directors between banks and non-financial firms? Some evidence from EU listed companies", Vittorio Boscia, Valeria Stefanelli and Andrea Ventura use data from EU Board Index and from Corporate Governance Reports published by major EU banks and non-financial firms. This chapter extends the current literature by comparing characteristics of board of directors identified as relevant by academics and practitioners (like board size, diversity, independents, organisations, *etc.*) and describes their differences and similarities in the sample. The results show that the structure of the bank board is similar to that of non-financial firms; diversity's profile emerges in the board organisation and functioning in terms of a larger number of meetings and of board committees. These board's characteristics aim at a better protection of interests of a wide array of stakeholders and promote business integrity through the emphasis on supervisory and monitoring function of executives. Moreover, in some EU countries it has emerged that there is diversity in board profiles for non-financial firms. However, bank boards are more similar across countries due to the substantial harmonisation of European banking regulation.

The last two chapters of Part 1 discuss investor protection from an international perspective. Chapter 6, written by Begoña Torre Olmo, Sergio Sanfilippo Azofra and María Cantero Sáiz "Creditor rights and the bank lending channel of monetary policy", analyses how creditor rights influence the loan supply reaction of banks to monetary policy through the bank lending channel. Additionally, it tests whether the influence of creditor rights on lending is different before and after the crisis. Using a sample of 1096 listed banks from 36 countries between 2003 and 2015, the authors find that creditor rights do not directly influence loan supply, neither before nor after the crisis, but they play an important role during monetary shocks. In this regard, the bank lending channel of monetary policy is less effective in countries with stronger creditor rights.

Part I is completed by Chap. 7 "Economies of scope in the EU banking industry" by Ludovico Rossi and Elena Beccalli, who discuss the relationship between economies of scope and investor protection. This chapter documents the presence on average of cost economies of scope in the European banking industry, that is, banks minimise total costs, given a certain level of outputs, producing a differentiated mix of outputs. The results are particularly important in the light of the 2014 structural reform proposal on the EU banking industry, which aims to separate traditional commercial banking from investment activity. The loss of efficiency for banks might have consequences for customers who could suffer an increase in the costs of financial services to try to compensate banks for their loss of efficiency. Bank regulations would be myopic if they emphasise investor protections whilst neglecting bank efficiency.

Part II explores individual country studies about corporate governance in banking and investor protection. Chapter 8 by Tony Tony on "Corporate governance of financial conglomerates in Indonesia: Legal issues and gaps" aims to examine recent regulatory reform on corporate governance of financial conglomerates in Indonesia. These conglomerates give rise to intricate corporate governance issues due to their complexities. To minimise the issues and to endorse good corporate governance practices of financial conglomerates, the Indonesian Financial Service Authority enacted a regulation on the implementation of integrated corporate governance for financial conglomerates in November 2014. This is the first regulation that specifically addresses financial conglomerates in its entirety as a group in Indonesia. It sets out minimum requirements to be followed by financial conglomerates in establishing group-wide corporate governance arrangements. This is dissimilar to many other countries that adopted the financial holding company concept, which requires financial conglomerates to appoint lead entities, either a parent or sister company, to be held responsible for implementing integrated corporate governance across the group. This chapter critically evaluates the regulatory requirements on corporate governance of financial conglomerates, especially related to the lead entity, in this regulation. It finds that many requirements specified in this regulations conflict with the requirement stipulated in other prevailing laws. These conflicting regulatory requirements might raise legal issues for the parties within the financial conglomerate. Furthermore, this chapter argues that this new regulation has not fully addressed the corporate governance issues in financial conglomerates. It suggests that further legal reform is needed to enhance regulation of Indonesian financial conglomerates.

Also, with regard to Indonesia, Chap. 9 "Does diversity of bank board members affect performance and risk? Evidence from an emerging market", written by Bowo Setiyono and Amine Tarazi, investigates the influence of background diversity of bank board members on performance and risk. Using data from Indonesian banks from 2001 to 2011 covering 4200 individual year observations and 21 ethnic groups, they estimate the degree of diversity by considering various aspects (gender, citizenship, age, experience, tenure, ethnicity, nationality, education level and type) and find significant impacts on bank performance. On the whole, diversity is in general positively associated with performance except when it relates to ethnicity. It not only reduces performance per se but also increases risk. Female presence and professional diversity reduce risk, but nationality and ethnicity diversities are associated with higher risk. Education diversity generally leads to higher income volatility and leverage risk. Their results are generally robust to various alternative performance measures, including risk-adjusted returns, and estimation methods.

The following three chapters are focused on two main European economies: Spain and Italy. Chapters 10 and 11 focus on Spain. The first is on "Insider trading and corporate governance in the banking sector. New lessons on the entrenchment effect", written by Esther B. del Brio, Javier Perote, Alberto de Miguel and Gerardo Gómez, identifies the factors enhancing bank insider trading. The authors conclude that the more entrenched the directors, the less prestigious the bank, the bigger the firm and the lower the charter values for high levels of ownership, the higher the intensity of insider trading activity. Thus, the emerging picture is of a scenario where insider trading activity is triggered by the absence of efficient control mechanisms, either external (regulators control the level of bank capitalisation, but it is not easy for them to also control other opportunistic behaviours) or internal (shareholders fail to control managers when managers' stakes are very low or very high). Chapter 11, "Inside the board of Spanish saving banks", written by Pablo de Andrés-Alonso, Iñigo García-Rodríguez, M. Elena Romero-Merino and Marcos Santamaría-Mariscal, presents an in-depth descriptive analysis of Spanish saving banks' boards in terms of size, independence and quality (knowledge, experience and diversity). The authors build an original handmade database with the biographical profile of 1525 different directors for the entire population of Spanish savings banks during the period of 2004–2010. Their results show that on average, savings banks boards were larger with less knowledge in business and less professional experience in banking (but more gender diverse) than the private banks analysed in other studies. These board characteristics barely changed during the period of crisis. They also find that 52% of board members are designated by governments or affiliated with political parties. This figure seems to confirm that although the Spanish savings banks had the status of private entities, the real fact is that they were primarily controlled by politicians. Finally, they show several important differences in the board composition, depending on the savings banks' financial characteristics.

Focusing on Italy, Chap. 12 "Italian banks' ownership, governance and performance: the evolving role of foundations", written by Giuliana Birindelli and Paola Ferretti, aims at analysing the trend of the foundations' share in the capital of the Italian banks whilst also considering the evolution of the regulatory framework. Their principal goal is to highlight whether foundation shareholdings contribute to an improvement of the stability, governance and profitability of Italian banks. Banking foundations supported Italian banks in the process of consolidation and more recently in the process of recapitalisation. Furthermore, the loosening of the foundation-bank bond may have positive consequences. The authors conclude that it is very likely that this will improve the banks' governance, determine a broader opening to the markets for their shareholdings, favour opening to new investors and will make the Italian financial system more sound as well as better fitting the needs of the real economy. Foundations will loosen their ties to investee banks and be able to allocate their resources to projects and initiatives in favour of the community, strengthening their grant-making activities.

Chapter 13 by Franklin Nakpodia on "Corporate governance in the Nigerian banking sector: A bounded rationality conundrum" focuses on Africa's largest economy, Nigeria. This chapter explores corporate governance in the Nigerian banking system from a bounded rationality perspective. In doing this, this chapter undertakes a review of corporate governance in the Nigerian banking system, examines the rationality concerns influencing corporate governance practices amongst Nigerian banks and shows that attempts at addressing corporate governance issues must acknowledge that corporate governance is an information-based mechanism.

The final contribution of Part II is provided with Chap. 14 by Sam Sarpong on "Ensuring sanity in Ghana's financial sector: A focus on Ghana's microfinance institutions" drawing attention to consumer protection issues. The performance of Microfinance Institutions (MFIs) in Ghana has not created the much-touted messianic role it was meant to play. The scale of the malfeasance in the sector in the last 5 years has been quite steep. Loose regulations, massive failure of governance, both within the sector itself and at the level of the regulators and supervisors, poor supervision, inadequate enforcement, perverse incentives and other practices bordering on sheer criminality have constituted the main problems slashing away the gains of this sector. The author argues that what was supposed to help reduce poverty amongst the poor in society is fleecing them from the little that they lay claim to. Some MFIs have now fraudulently folded after collecting huge deposits from customers; others, meanwhile, have diverted their funds into unrelated activities with some directors facing legal action from aggrieved customers. The chapter examines the drawbacks within the MFI sector in particular and the financial sector in general. It also presents the gamut of issues at play and the doggedness of the central bank to put the sector on a sound footing.

Part III relates to investor protection and focuses on responsible investment. The whole book is completed with Chap. 15 by Anna Doś and Monika Foltyn-Zarychta entitled "Socially responsible investment and fiduciary duties of mutual funds". In this chapter, the authors aim at building a rationale for an individual investor's extended utility function that depends on return, risk and—additionally—non-financial characteristics of the investment (mainly environmental and social outcomes). The authors also aim at establishing a stronger link between institutional and individual investment decisions through identifying the best practices adopted by mutual funds with respect to incorporating environmental, social and governance criteria in their investment decisions.

These 15 chapters provide a comprehensive overview into the effectiveness of corporate governance in banking as well as an assessment of investor protection issues in the financial services sector. They illustrate drawbacks in recent regulations about corporate governance and differences in banking governance across countries. Therefore, the debate is still open and the conclusions achieved in these chapters contribute to the ongoing debate on appropriate corporate governance approaches and the related policy implications.

University of Cantabria, Santander, Spain — Belén Díaz Díaz
SANFI, Santander, Spain
London Metropolitan University — Samuel O. Idowu
London, UK
University of Sharjah, Sharjah, UAE — Philip Molyneux

Contents

Editor and Contributors

About the Editors

Belén Díaz Díaz is Associate Professor of Financial Economics at the University of Cantabria and Academic Director of Santander Financial Institute (SANFI). Previously, she has been Vice-Dean of the Faculty of Business and Economics at the UC, ERASMUS Coordinator of the Faculty of Business and Economics in the UC and the Director of the Area of Campus and Social Development of the UC reporting to the Vice-Chancellor of Campus and Social Development responsible for the social responsibility policies at the UC. She has served as a visiting scholar/researcher at universities in the USA (University of Berkeley), Australia (University of Technology of Sydney), England (London School of Economics and Political Science and Staffordshire University), Argentina (Universidad Nacional de Jujuy) and Chile (Universidad Internacional SEK). Her research focuses on corporate finance, mergers and acquisitions, corporate governance and corporate social responsibility. She has published scientific articles in relevant journals and books and has participated in several conferences showing the results of her research. The quality of her research was recognised with the "Sanchis Alcover Award", awarded by the Scientific Association of Economy and Management in 2006. She is member of the editorial board of different publications. Her teaching focuses on stock markets, corporate finance and business valuation to undergraduates, postgraduates and Ph.D. students. She is Director and professor of the "International Master in Banking and Financial Markets" (organised jointly by UC and Santander Bank through SANFI), in Spain, Morocco, Mexico, Chile and Brazil. She is also professor of other postgraduate courses such as the "Official Master in Business Administration (MBA)" in the UC and the "Master in Accounting and Auditing" in the UC, amongst others. She has written several reports and developed more than 20 R+D projects about different financial and economic issues commissioned by different public and private entities.

Samuel O. Idowu is a Senior Lecturer in Accounting and Corporate Social Responsibility at London Guildhall Faculty of Business & Law, London Metropolitan University, UK. He researches in the fields of corporate social responsibility (CSR), corporate governance, business ethics and accounting and has published in both professional and academic journals since 1989. He is a freeman of the City of London and a Liveryman of the Worshipful Company of Chartered Secretaries and Administrators. Samuel is the Deputy CEO and First Vice President of the Global Corporate Governance Institute. He has led several edited books in CSR and is the Editor-in-Chief of two Springer's reference books—the Encyclopedia of Corporate Social Responsibility and the Dictionary of Corporate Social Responsibility, an Editor-in-Chief of the International Journal of Corporate Social Responsibility (IJCSR), the Editor-in-Chief of the American Journal of Economics and Business Administration (AJEBA) and an Associate Editor of the International Journal of Responsible Management in Emerging Economies (IJRMEE). He is also a Series Editor for Springer's books on CSR, Sustainability, Ethics and Governance. One of his edited books won the most Outstanding Business Reference Book Award of the American Library Association (ALA) in 2016 and another was ranked 18th in the 2010 Top 40 Sustainability Books by *Cambridge University Sustainability Leadership Programme*. Samuel is also an Editor of the International Journal of Responsible Management in Emerging Economies. He is a member of the Committee of the Corporate Governance Special Interest Group of the British Academy of Management (BAM). He is on the Editorial Boards of the International Journal of Business Administration, Canada, and Amfiteatru Economic Journal, Romania. Samuel has delivered a number of Keynote Speeches at national and international conferences and workshops on CSR and has on two occasions 2008 and 2014 won Emerald's Highly Commended Literati Network Awards for Excellence. To date, Samuel has edited several books in the field of CSR, Sustainability and Governance and has written six forewords to CSR books. Samuel has served as an external examiner to the following UK Universities—Sunderland, Ulster, Anglia Ruskin, Plymouth, Robert Gordon University, Aberdeen, Teesside University, Middlesbrough, Sheffield Hallam University and Leicester De Montfort University.

Philip Molyneux is Dean of the College of Business Administration at the University of Sharjah (United Arab Emirates) and was previously Dean of the College of Law, Education and Social Sciences at Bangor University (UK). His main area of research is on the structure and efficiency of banking markets, and he has published widely in this area with recent papers in the Journal of Financial Intermediation, Review of Finance, Journal of Banking and Finance, Journal of Money, Credit and Banking, the European Central Bank and Bank for International Settlements working paper series. His most recent texts include An Introduction to Banking (with Barbara Casu and Claudia Girardone) Wiley 2015, Introduction to Global Financial Markets 8th edition (with Stephen Valdez) Palgrave Macmillan 2015 and The Oxford Handbook of Banking 2nd edition (edited with Allen N Berger and John Wilson) Oxford University Press 2014. In the past, he has acted as a consultant to

New York Federal Reserve Bank, European Commission, UK Treasury, Citibank Private Bank, Barclays Wealth, McKinsey & Company and various other international banks and consulting firms.

Notes on Contributors

Elisa Baraibar Díez holds a Ph.D. in Business Administration from the University of Cantabria with *cum laude* and international mention. In 2008, she became a teaching assistant at the University of Cantabria (UC) and was appointed a Lecturer in Business Administration at the same university in 2013. She works at the Faculty of Economics and Business at the UC, teaching subjects such as introduction to business administration, entrepreneurship and control management to undergraduates and postgraduates. She is also a lecturer at the "International Master in Banking and Financial Markets" (organised jointly by UC and Santander Bank) taught in Spain and the "Official Master in Business Administration (MBA)" at the UC. She has been visiting researcher to a number of universities in Germany (Institut für Management, Humboldt-Universität zu Berlin) and Guangzhou, China (Sun Yat-sen University). Her research focuses on corporate transparency, corporate social responsibility (CSR) and corporate reputation. She has published a number of scientific articles in Spanish and international journals (Revista Europea de Dirección y Economía de la Empresa, Regional and Sectoral Economic Studies, Universia Business Review, Corporate Social and Environmental Management and Corporate Reputation Review). She has also participated in more than ten national and international conferences. Since 2006, she has collaborated with the research group Economic Management for Sustainable Development of the Primary Sector at the UC and has contributed to 15 projects related to primary sector (fleet viability or social and environmental certification) and management systems, financed by several public institutions.

Elena Beccalli is full professor of Banking at the Faculty of Banking, Finance and Insurance (Università Cattolica del Sacro Cuore), where she is the Dean of the Faculty. She is visiting professor at the Department of Accounting (London School of Economics). She is research associate at the Centre for Analysis of Risk and Regulation (London School of Economics) and academic fellow at the Centre for Responsible Banking and Finance (University of St. Andrews). She is department editor (financial institutions) of the Journal of Financial Management, Markets and Institutions. She is the author of numerous academic articles and books in the field of banking.

Giuliana Birindelli, Ph.D., is a Full Professor in Financial Markets and Institutions at the "G. d'Annunzio" University of Chieti-Pescara, Italy. Her research focuses on Basel II and Basel III, internal rating systems, banking internationalisation, business models, corporate governance, operational risk, compliance risk and corporate social responsibility.

Vittorio Boscia (M.A., 1997, and Ph.D., 2001, in Banking and Finance, University of Wales, UK) is Full Professor in Financial Markets and Institutions at the University of Salento (Lecce, Italy). At the University of Salento, he has been Vice-Rector, Coordinator of internal evaluation auditing committee and Member of the Research Observatory, and Visiting Researcher at the School for Business and Regional Development, University of Wales (Bangor, UK). His academic fellowships are in The Wolpertinger Club (European Association of University Teachers of Banking and Finance), ADEIMF (Italian Association of Professors in Financial Markets and Institutions) and AIDEA (Italian Academy of Business Administration and Management). He is author of a number of articles on the following research topics: corporate governance, internal governance and compliance; corporate banking; lending and credit risk; financial planning; corporate bankruptcy and reorganisation; and digital innovation. He is a speaker at several workshops and seminars on issues related to his research interests. As a chartered public accountant, he has professional experience as an advisor in various areas covering governance and compliance, corporate strategy and financial planning. He has a long experience as member of the Board of Statutory Auditors of Italian firms. At present, he is member of the Board of Statutory Auditors of Banca Popolare di Puglia e Basilicata (Bari, Italy) and Chair of the board of directors of Apulia "High Tech" District (Lecce, Italy) and Chair of the Commission for "Research enhancement & development", University of Salento (Lecce, Italy).

María Cantero Sáiz is assistant professor at the University of Cantabria (Spain) where she teaches in the areas of corporate finance and financial markets, in both undergraduate and postgraduate programmes. She is also the director of the Debate League in this institution, through which she promotes and develops communication skills and public speaking abilities amongst students. Her research interests focus on banking, monetary policy, sovereign risk and credit restrictions. She has published several scientific articles in journals of national and international impact and book chapters related to teaching in prestigious edited volumes. She has participated in congresses and in several research, business consulting and innovation teaching projects. She held a research stay at Norwich Business School, University of East Anglia, UK (2013–2014). She has obtained several scholarships and awards, such as the Santander Financial Institute Award (2016) for the best doctoral thesis of Spain and Latin America related to the financial sector; the first prize in the Business Simulator "Beertual Challenge" (2013), organised by the company Grupo Modelo; and a scholarship to participate in the international scientific event "Cantabria Campus Nobel" (2012), supported by recognised Nobel Prizes in several fields.

Pablo de Andrés-Alonso (Ph.D. in Business Administration, University of Valladolid, 1995) is Professor of Finance at the Autónoma University of Madrid.

Previously, he had a position at the University of Valladolid, Spain. He was awarded the European Investment Bank Prize for young researcher (1997) for his work "Financial system models, corporate governance and capital investment in OECD countries: Some stylized facts" (with Prof. López-Iturriaga). His research interests range between corporate governance, corporate finance and real options. He has published his research in journals including the Journal of Corporate Finance, Journal Banking and Finance, Journal of Business Finance and Accounting, Corporate Governance: An International Review, Financial Review, Universia Business Review or Investigaciones Económicas. He has been editor of the Spanish Journal of Finance and Accounting (2009–2016) and head of R&D&I National Program for economic research (2012–2015). He has been Visiting Researcher at Harvard University in 2009 and Visiting Scholar in the Cass Business School (City University London) in Autumn 2012 and Spring 2014. He has taken part in several research projects granted by private and public institutions. He is the head of Carlos V International Center at the Autónoma University of Madrid.

Alberto de Miguel is Professor at Finance in the University of Salamanca (since 1995). His areas of research are corporate governance, financial markets and firm valuation. He has published in top journals such as the Strategic Management Journal, Journal of Business Finance & Accounting and European Financial Management.

Esther B. del Brio is Associate Professor of Finance at the University of Salamanca (Spain). She obtained an M.Phil. in Finance at the University of Cambridge (UK) and a Ph.D. in Financial Economics at the University of Salamanca in 1999. Her research is mainly focused on stock market efficiency, board behaviour and other topics of corporate governance. Her research has been published in several top journals, such as the Journal of Management Studies, Journal of Business Ethics, Journal of Business Finance & Accounting, European Financial Management, International Journal of Forecasting, Journal of Business Research and Quantitative Finance, amongst others. She has been a visiting scholar at several prestigious institutions such as the Saïd Business School (Oxford, 2012), Judge Business School (Cambridge, UK; 2004) and Universidad Carlos III (Madrid, Spain; 2008) and has given seminars in the University of Bristol, Birmingham, Luxembourg, Bologna, Milano and elsewhere.

Anna Doś is assistant professor in the Department of Corporate Finance and Insurance, Faculty of Finance and Insurance of the University of Economics in Katowice, Poland, since 2010. Fields of research interest and expertise cover the problems of corporate finance and financial management in the context of sustainability. She is passionate investigating if and how sound financial management can fight under-provisioning of public goods (including natural environment protection, equality, safety, etc.). Her doctoral dissertation—covering the topic of corporate ecological risk in the insurance market—was awarded second prize in a national competition for doctoral dissertations in the field of insurance, under the auspices of the Insurance Ombudsman, Financial Supervisor and the Polish Ministry of Science and Higher Education, as well as the Rector's Individual Award. She is member of a number of collaborative research projects covering risk management, financial innovation, corporate social responsibility and socially responsible investment. Didactic activities and experience include courses to bachelor's and master's students, in both Polish and English (for Erasmus students and English-language programmes). The main courses relate to corporate finance, financial management, operational risk for banks and public finance. She acted as Chairperson of International Week "Sustainable Banking and Finance 2017" held at the University of Economics in Katowice.

Miguel Duro received a Ph.D. and an M.Phil. in Business (Accounting) from Columbia Business School, an Executive M.B.A. from IESE Business School and a Bachelor's Degree in Business Administration from the University of Seville. He is a Certified International Investor Analyst (CIIA®) with 10 years of experience. He worked in senior management positions for Sybari Software (Microsoft), Pepsi Bottling Group and Metrovacesa, one of the biggest listed European real estate companies. His research focuses on the impact of corporate governance, corporate disclosure and public enforcement in capital markets, earnings management and other accounting attributes. Professor Duro has published in the Journal of Accounting and Economics and has co-authored several papers at different stages of review at top-tier finance and accounting journals (one is second round at The Accounting Review, and another is first round at Journal of Accounting and Economics). His dissertation on the role of institutional investors in enforcement has been recently submitted to the Journal of Accounting Research and has received several awards, such as the Nasdaq Educational Foundation Doctoral Dissertation Fellowship and the Jerome A. Chazen Institute Doctoral Research Grant.

Paola Ferretti Ph.D., is an Assistant Professor in Financial Markets and Institutions at the University of Pisa, Italy. Her research focuses on Basel II and Basel III, credit risk management, business models, profitability, operational risk management, compliance risk, corporate social responsibility, social media and corporate governance.

Monika Foltyn-Zarychta is a researcher in the Department of Investment and Real Estate in the Faculty of Finance and Insurance at the University of Economics in Katowice, Poland. Since 2008, her main fields of research interest and expertise cover issues surrounding capital investment budgeting and appraisal. Special attention in the research is given to intergenerational investment evaluation, intergenerational justice and its incorporation into investment appraisal, cost–benefit analysis, non-market goods valuation and environmental economics. Her Ph.D. on cost–benefit analysis in environmental investment appraisals was awarded the Rector's Individual Award. She has been the main investigator and member of several collaborative research projects on risk in project appraisal, sources of financing of investing activities, long-term investment evaluation and socially responsible investing. She has held a visiting research fellow at Erasmus Institute for Philosophy and Economics (EIPE), University of Rotterdam, The Netherlands, in 2016 under the 2015/16 European Fellowship Programme of the European Philosophy of Science Association. She was Chairperson of International Week "New Frontiers in Finance and Accounting" held at the University of Economics in Katowice since 2013. She has acted as an expert in the evaluation of project proposals for the Cohesion Fund (Infrastructure and Environment Programme) for the Polish Ministry of the Environment (2009–2013). Her teaching covers a number of B.A., M.A. and postgraduate courses relating to financial management, including Basics of Investments, Financial Investments Evaluation, Capital Budgeting and Capital Investment Appraisal, Methods of Financial Market Analysis, Environmental Investments Appraisal and Financial Management (for the ACCA F9 exam).

Rebeca García Ramos graduated in Economics and holds a Doctor of Business Administration from the University of Cantabria (UC), Spain. Since 2007, she has been a Professor of Financial Economics and Accounting at the University of Cantabria. Previously, during the period 2005–2007, she was a researcher in the field of Economics at the Research Team for Sustainable Development of the Primary Sector at UC, where she developed and coordinated R+D reports and projects about different economic issues requested by both public and private companies. She lectures at the Faculty of Economics and Business at the UC, teaching subjects such as Analysis of Stock Markets, Analysis and Evaluation of Investments, Financial Systems and Theory of Finance, in various degrees in Business and Economics. She also teaches in other areas of Higher Education: she is a Professor of the Official Master's Degree in Businesses Administration (M.B.A.) and of the Official Master's Degree in Businesses and Information Technology (IT) of the UC. She was also a visiting researcher at the *Business School* at the University of Essex (UK) and the University of Oviedo (Spain). Her research activities focus on the field of Finance and the Business Administration, being the author of several chapters in edited books and national and international prestigious scientific journals in her field. The results of her research papers have been presented at numerous national and international conferences. She also acts as a referee to a number of scientific journals in her field and has been a member of the organising committees of many international conferences.

Many of her research papers have won "Special Prizes"; for instance in 2009, she was awarded the Spanish Association of Accounting and Business Administration prize (Valladolid, Spain, 2009); she was a winner of the "Quality in Research Conferences on Small and Medium-sized Enterprises Businesses and Entrepreneurship", awarded by the Chairmen of the Bureau and members of the Editorial Board of the International Journal of the Small and Medium-sized Enterprise (Madrid, Spain, 2009); research award "Jeff Rothstein Award for the Most Creative Paper", granted by the Family Firm Institute (FFI) and Hubler Family Business Consultants (Chicago, USA, 2010); and "Research Award of the Section of Family Business" granted by the Scientific Association of Economics and Business Management

(Granada, Spain, 2010); she was a finalist at the research award "University of Alberta Best Research Paper Award" of the International Family Enterprise Research Academy (Lancaster, UK, 2010).

Iñigo García-Rodríguez is a Research Personnel in Training at the Autónoma University of Madrid (Spain). He is a Ph.D. Candidate in Business Economics from the University of Burgos. His research focuses on corporate governance and financial vulnerability of non-profit organisations. He has published articles in leading journals such as Voluntas: International Journal of Voluntary and Nonprofit Organizations and Nonprofit Management & Leadership.

Gerardo Gómez is Associate Professor in Accounting and Finance at the National University of Piura. He has previously been visiting scholar at the University of Salamanca, Carlos III, University of Oviedo and University of Alcalá. His research interests are mainly capital and ownership structure, business growth and financial analysis and markets.

Cicek Gurkan is a Ph.D. candidate at Hamburg University Faculty of Law in Germany within the framework of the international European Doctorate in Law and Economics Program. She holds an LL.M. degree from Harvard Law School and has obtained another master's degree in European studies as well as a bachelor's in law from Ankara University in Turkey. She is a qualified lawyer admitted to the New York State Bar and is also licensed to practice law in Turkey. Her research interests encompass issues of corporate governance, capital markets law and financial regulation from an interdisciplinary and comparative perspective.

Franklin Nakpodia (Ph.D.) is a lecturer at the Newcastle Business School, Faculty of Law and Business, Northumbria University, UK. He teaches on a number of modules within the Accounting and Finance undergraduate and postgraduate programmes. His areas of research are corporate governance and corporate social responsibility, focusing on the influence of institutional frameworks in emerging and developing economies. He actively engages with academics examining a variety of corporate governance issues in sub-Saharan Africa. His research has been published by the globally renowned Journal of Business Ethics (JBE) and the International Journal of Business Governance and Ethics (IJBGE).

Sabrina Leo is Ph.D. in Banking and Finance and Lecturer in Financial Intermediaries at "Sapienza" University of Rome. Her main research interests are lending, credit contraction, microcredit, microfinance, social impact investment, non-banking financial institutions/operators, corporate governance, risk management and audiovisual finance.

She is assistant of the university course on "Microfinance and Ethical finance" and "Financial intermediaries". She participates as a "Scientific member" in the Italian Advisory Board established by the G8 Taskforce on Social Impact Investment, and she focuses on asset management in the impact finance industry. She contributed to the report on "Impact investment" promoted by the Italian Advisory Board.

Gaizka Ormazabal received a Ph.D. in Business from Stanford University, a Ph. D. in Construction Engineering from Universitat Politecnica de Catalunya and a Bachelor's Degree in Civil Engineering (Ingeniería de Caminos, Canals y Puertos) from Universitat Politécnica de Catalunya. Professor Ormazabal's research focuses on executive compensation and corporate governance. His work examines the choice and valuation implications of corporate governance mechanisms. His current research projects analyse managerial risk-taking incentives, corporate risk oversight, financial regulation, asset securitisation and the role of corporate governance intermediaries. His research appears in leading academic journals including the Journal of Accounting and Economics, Journal of Financial Economics, Journal of Law and Economics and The Accounting Review. His research has been featured in the popular media, including outlets such as the Wall Street Journal and the New York Times, and has been cited in final rulings by the U.S. Securities and Exchange Commission. He is a Research Affiliate in the Financial Economics program of the Center for Economic Policy Research (CEPR). He has received several fellowships, honours and awards. He has received, amongst many others, the Research Fellowship "Ayudas a Investigadores y Creadores Culturales" (BBVA Foundation, 2016), the Best Discussion Award by the Review of Accounting Studies (RAST 2015 Conference), the IESE Alumni Association Research Excellence Award (2015), the Grant SGR 1496 by Agència de Gestió d'Ajuts Universitaris i de Recerca (AGAUR) (research fellowship granted by the Catalan Government, 2014), the Marie Curie Fellowship (European Commission research fellowship, 2012) and the Ramon y Cajal Fellowship (Spanish Government research fellowship, 2011). Finally, he has participated in several government-funded research and development projects coordinated by Xavier Vives (ECO2015-63711-P and ECON2011-29533). Professor Ormazabal is also an ad hoc reviewer at the American Accounting Association Annual Meeting (subliaison), Accounting and Business Research, Contemporary Accounting Research, European Accounting Review, European Journal of Finance, Journal of Accounting Research, Journal of Accounting and Economics, Journal of Accounting and Public Policy, Journal of Business, Finance, and Accounting, Journal of Business Ethics, Journal of Financial Intermediation, Management Science, North American Journal of Economics and Finance, Review of Accounting Studies and The Accounting Review. He sits on the Advisory Board of the Governance Committee of the American Accounting Association (2014–2015) and at the Editorial Boards of the Revista Española de Contabilidad y Financiación (Spanish Journal of Finance and Accounting) and the Journal of Financial Reporting.

Ida Claudia Panetta (Ph.D.) is associate professor at Sapienza University of Rome, where she teaches International Financial Institutions and Capital Markets. She is economic sciences working group coordinator at Sapienza Research Center for Cyber Intelligence and Information Security. Her main research interests are liquidity risk management, banking regulation and supervision and corporate governance and cyber security in the financial system. She has acted as a consultant and trainer for various banks and mutual credit guarantee institutions.

Javier Perote is Associate Professor in quantitative economics at the University of Salamanca. He has previously been Associate Professor at the Rey Juan Carlos University (Madrid), teaching assistant at the University of Alicante, visiting scholar at the University of Vienna and visiting researcher at the London School of Economics (LSE), University of Westminster and University of Luxembourg and Oxford University. His research interests cover different areas: macroeconomics, financial econometrics, semi-nonparametric distributions, risk management and experimental and behavioural economics. In these areas, he has published articles in top journals such as Journal of Banking and Finance, Experimental Economics, Scientometrics, International Journal of Forecasting, Oxford Bulletin of Economics and Statistics, Journal of Economic Psychology, Physica A, Emerging Markets Review, Insurance: Mathematics and Economics, Theory and Decision, Economics Letters, Quantitative Finance, Journal of Business Finance and Accounting, Mathematical Social Sciences and European Journal of Finance.

M. Elena Romero-Merino studied Economics and Business Administration in Valladolid (Spain). She is assistant professor of Finance at the University of Burgos. She received her Ph.D. in Economics and Business Administration at the University of Valladolid. She is director of the Degree in Business Administration at the University of Burgos. Her main research focuses on the corporate governance, ownership structure, non-profit organisations, knowledge, growth and R&D. Her research is published in international journals of business, management and social issues such as Research Policy, British Journal of Management, Nonprofit and Voluntary Sector Quarterly and Managerial and Decision Economics, amongst others.

Ludovico Rossi is a Ph.D. candidate in finance at the ICMA Centre—Henley Business School. He holds a Bachelor's in Financial Markets and Institutions (cum laude) and a Master of Science in Banking and Finance (cum laude), both from the Università Cattolica of Milan, Italy.

Sergio Sanfilippo Azofra is assistant professor of Finance at the University of Cantabria, teaching on both undergraduate and postgraduate programmes. After taking his B.S. in Economics, he completed his Ph.D. in finance at the University of Cantabria. His research interests focus on banking, monetary policy, mergers and acquisitions and corporate finance. He has published more than 30 articles in prestigious scientific journals and has collaborated in several books. He has also presented numerous papers at national and international conferences and has received three awards for best papers. He has supervised two doctoral theses and taken part in numerous national and international research projects. He was visiting researcher at Cass Business School (City University of London) and was in charge of the University of Cantabria Summer School in Laredo.

Marcos Santamaría-Mariscal is assistant professor of Finance at the University of Burgos. He studied Economics and Business Studies at UNED, and he received his Ph.D. in the interuniversity programme (Universities of Valladolid, Salamanca, Burgos and Leon) "New Trends in Business Management". He obtained the Special Ph.D. Award at the University of Burgos, and he was also awarded by the Center of Financial Studies in 2008 for his research about corporate governance in banks. His research focuses on corporate governance and banking. His works are published in journals such as the Corporate Governance: An International Review, Journal of Banking and Finance or Managerial and Decision Economics, amongst others. He is member of the Editorial Board of Universia Business Review. He has been Secretary of the Faculty of Economic and Business Sciences at the University of Burgos.

Sam Sarpong completed his Ph.D. at Cardiff University and his M.B.A. at the University of South Wales. He is currently an Associate Professor of Management at Narxoz University. Prior to taking up his current role, he taught at University of Mines and Technology, Ghana. He has also taught at Cardiff University, Swansea Metropolitan University and Birkbeck College, University of London. His research interests lie in the relationship between society, economy, institutions and markets. He tends to explore the nature and ethical implications of social-economic problems. He has published in leading journals and recently received Society and Business Review's (Emerald) Best Paper Award for 2016.

Bowo Setiyono is a lecturer and consultant and was born and raised in Purworejo before moving to Yogyakarta, a vibrant and culturally rich city in Indonesia. He is currently the Deputy Director for the Master of Management Program, following his appointment as the Director for International Undergraduate Program (IUP) and Banking Corner/Dashboard at the Faculty of Economics and Business, Universitas Gadjah Mada (www.feb.ugm.ac.id). His research focuses on bank governance, ownership, disclosure, risk and performance particularly in Asia and emerging markets. Despite his teaching duties, he was a research fellow at Central Bank of Indonesia in 2013 and joined the Wharton Global Faculty Development at the University of Pennsylvania in 2016. He was a visiting professor at Saxion University, Enschede, the Netherlands, and actively participates in the Indonesian Finance Association, International Finance and Banking Society and Indonesian Banker Institute programmes. His co-authored paper on "Disclosure, ownership structure and bank risk: Evidence from Asia" won best paper in banking at 8th APBRC conference in Kuala Lumpur. He also serves as a consultant/trainer for numerous corporations and government agencies including Bank Mandiri, Bank BTN, Bank BNI, Indonesia Ministry of Finance, Indonesian Financial Transaction Reports and Analysis Center/INTRAC. He also holds CFP® and QFE professional certificates. Bowo did his Master of Commerce from the School of Banking and Finance,

UNSW, Sydney, Australia, and earned his Ph.D. in 2015 from Laboratoire d'Analyse et de Prospective Economiques (LAPE), University of Limoges, thanks to the generous Bourse de la région du Limousin, France. He was an awardee for Sumitomo, DIKTI, ADS/AusAid and Fulbright-AMINEF. He has been the reviewer for the Journal of Economics, Business and Accountancy Ventura, Journal of Indonesia Economics and Business and Gadjah Mada International Journal of Business.

Valeria Stefanelli is Lecturer in Financial Markets and Institutions at the University of Salento (Lecce, Italy). She holds a Ph.D. in Banking and Finance at the University of Rome Tor Vergata, and she is Visiting Fellow at the University of Wales (Bangor, UK). She is Delegate of Rector at shareholdings and spin-off at the University of Salento and member of the Department of Economic Sciences Council. She is member of the Nedcommunity, the Italian Association of non-executive and independent directors (Milan, Italy), and member of the Board of Statutory Auditors of ADEIMF, the Italian Association of Professors in Financial Markets and Institutions (Parma, Italy). She is Associate Editor at the Business and Management Research Journal. She has been a speaker at several conference and seminars on issues related to her research interests. She is author of a number of articles on several topics in the banking field covering corporate governance and internal controls in commercial and cooperative banks; M&A's and value creation, banking regulation, credit quality and lending technologies, transparency and compliance, digital banking and fintech. At present, she is also member of Banking and Finance Arbitrator at the Bank of Italy (Bari, Italy).

Amine Tarazi is a professor of Economics and Finance at the University of Limoges (France) where he is currently the Director of a research center, LAPE, and Head of Master and Ph.D. programmes in Banking and Finance. He served as a Vice-President in charge of Research and President of the Scientific Board of the University and as head of the Economics Department and head of international affairs. He earned his Ph.D. in Economics from the University of Limoges in 1992 and holds an M.Sc. in Money, Banking and Finance from the University of Birmingham (UK). He also served as a research consultant for ACPR (French Prudential Supervisory Authority), where he is currently a member of the Scientific Committee, and has visited universities in many countries. He has coordinated several European Commission-backed research projects and other international research programmes and grants. In particular, he has acted as the global coordinator of a European Commission Program (ASIALINK/B7-301/2005/105-139) involving various universities in Europe and Asia. He serves as an associate editor of the Journal of Banking and Finance, the European Journal of Finance and other Finance and Economics Journals. His current research interests relate to financial institutions, bank risk and prudential regulation. His work has appeared in journals such as the Journal of Financial Economics, Review of Finance, Journal of Banking and Finance, Journal of International Money and Finance, Journal of Economic

Behavior and Organization, Journal of Economic Surveys, Journal of Comparative Economics, Applied Economics, Journal of Financial Services Research and others.

Tony Tony is a Ph.D. Candidate at Griffith Law School, Griffith University, Australia. Prior to his PhD study, he was part of team responsible for developing an integrated regulation and supervision framework for financial conglomerates at the Indonesian Financial Service Authority. He has Master of Law in banking and financial law from Boston University and bachelor of law and bachelor of accounting from the University of Indonesia. His research interests include prudential regulation and supervision, financial conglomeration, corporate governance, risk management and capital adequacy.

Begoña Torre Olmo is associate professor in Banking and Finance at the University of Cantabria. She is professor at the "International Master in Banking and Financial Markets" (linked to Bank of Santander) and taught in Santander, Mexico and Brazil. She is also the Director of Summer Programs in Banking and Corporate Finance run jointly between the University of Cantabria and UNCC Charlotte (USA). Her research interests focus on banking, microfinance and corporate finance. She has published in scientific journals and also various book chapters. Begoña has supervised several doctoral theses and collaborated in national and international projects. She is also the Subdirector of the Santander Financial Institute (SANFI), the Center that the UCEIF Foundation between The University of Cantabria and Bank of Santander set up 11 years ago to promote the development of research and teaching in banking and finance. Previously, she has held several management positions at the University of Cantabria, as Dean of the School of Business and Economics (2010–2014), Manager of Human Resources (2004–2010) and Head of Department of Business Administration (2003–2004). She has professional experience in Venture Capital and Private Equity and currently is Member of the Boards (as an independent director) of various public and private companies.

Andrea Ventura (Ph.D. in Physics, University of Lecce, 2003) is a Researcher of Experimental Physics of Fundamental Interactions at the University of Salento (Lecce, Italy). In 2012, he received the Excellence Award, funded by Banca Popolare Pugliese, as best researcher of the scientific area of the University of Salento. Previously, he has had a permanent position as a High School Teacher and then spent a postdoc period at CERN, Geneva. His main research field is in high energy experimental physics, and his interests range from software development and maintenance for monitoring systems to physics data analysis for precision measurements and discovery searches. He has taken part in two international collaborations: KLOE (at LNF, Frascati) from 2000 to 2007 and ATLAS (at CERN, Geneva) since 2004. His latest research work concerns the search for new scenarios beyond the Standard Model of particle physics, predicted by supersymmetric theories. Presently, he coordinates the subnuclear research group in the Lecce division of INFN (National Institute for Nuclear Physics), and he is member of the National Scientific Committee of particle physics research in INFN. He has published more than 700 papers on national and international scientific reviews, both as main author or in collaboration. He is a reviewer for a few journals, such as "Nuclear Physics A" and "Journal of Physics: Conference Series". He is very active in outreach activities and has co-organised several workshops and conferences in High Energy Physics, such as the annual Nuclear and Subnuclear Ph.D. School "F. Romano" in Otranto, Italy.

Part I
International Studies About Corporate Governance in Banking and Investor Protection

Chapter 1
Does Regulating Banks' Corporate Governance Help? A Review of the Empirical Evidence

Miguel Duro and Gaizka Ormazabal

1.1 Introduction

The 2007–2008 financial crisis is considered the most serious and disruptive economic downturn since 1929. The debate about the causes of the breakdown often starts with the perception that financial institutions suffered from severe corporate governance problems. In particular, the managers of these institutions are believed to have taken excessive risks to enrich themselves, in the process destroying the long-term value of their companies and generating systemic risk (ACCA 2008).

In response to the crisis, national and international authorities examined the case for stronger regulatory frameworks and introduced new regulatory requirements. The debate about these responses is ongoing. For example, a few months ago, the Financial Stability Board (FSB) launched a peer review of, and invited feedback from stakeholders about, the G20/OECD Principles of Corporate Governance. Also, the forthcoming UK departure from the EU ("Brexit") may bring about a reassessment of all the EU corporate governance regulation that has been adopted or is pending adoption into UK legislation.

This article analyzes the reforms of banks' corporate governance since the 2007–2008 financial crises. We start by summarizing the theoretical arguments for regulation of corporate governance, but in the context of the financial industry.

M. Duro
IESE Business School, Barcelona, Spain
e-mail: mduro@iese.edu

G. Ormazabal (✉)
IESE Business School, Barcelona, Spain

C.E.P.R., London, UK
e-mail: gormazabal@iese.edu

B. Díaz Díaz et al. (eds.), *Corporate Governance in Banking and Investor Protection*, CSR, Sustainability, Ethics & Governance,
https://doi.org/10.1007/978-3-319-70007-6_1

In light of these arguments and of the available empirical evidence, we discuss recent reforms in the main corporate governance mechanisms, namely (i) internal governance mechanisms (i.e., executive compensation, board monitoring, and internal control systems), (ii) market discipline (i.e., the roles of competition, the takeover market, and the shareholder activism), and (iii) regulatory intervention (i.e., capital requirements and regulatory supervision). Although much of the evidence we analyze uses US data, our analysis has an international perspective and examines corporate governance developments in important economies around the globe.

1.2 The Case for Regulating Banks' Corporate Governance

The debate over imposing regulation when parties can freely contract with each other is not trivial. As explained by Hart (2009), the difficulty is that it is not clear why the parties cannot design their own penalties to control bad behavior. Nor is it clear why regulation that introduces a restriction in the feasible set of contracts available to the parties would make the parties better off.

While the previous arguments have intellectual appeal, one might wonder why, then, is regulation so ubiquitous around the world. This question hints at a missing piece in the argument. This piece is that, in the real world, there are imperfections in the contracting process. For example, one of the contracting parties may have an informational advantage over the other(s), or the contracting parties may be unable to enforce the agreed-upon penalties. These contracting imperfections (also called "frictions" in the economics literature) justify the intervention of a third party (i.e., the regulator) in the contracting process. An efficient regulation should identify and address these imperfections without interfering unnecessarily in the contracting process.

As corporate securities are contracts between capital providers and the firm, knowledge of the previous contracting framework is crucial if one is to understand the need for corporate governance. The need for corporate governance stems from a specific imperfection of the contracting process: managers who profit at the expense of shareholders. The costs of managerial opportunism are usually referred to as "agency costs." Corporate governance arises as a set of mechanisms designed to protect shareholders' interests by incenting and monitoring managerial behavior.

When the financial industry is studied from this perspective, the question is whether its agency costs are different from those of other industries. In other words, should the corporate governance system be designed differently in the financial industry? Two key features distinguish banks from nonfinancial firms. First, banks have more stakeholders than nonfinancial firms do (Mehran et al. 2012). In addition to shareholders, the list of stakeholders includes depositors, debt-holders, and the government. (The government acts both as an insurer of deposits and a residual claimant on systemic externalities.) The economic interests of these stakeholders are large—over 90% of the balance sheet of banks is debt—and differ in many dimensions. For example, shareholders are more likely to favor risk-taking than are stakeholders whose claims have a limited upside (depositors and debt-holders, for example). Second, the financial sector plays a central role in the economy and thus can exert important externalities in other industries. These externalities are difficult to understand, given the complexity of the risks to which financial institutions are subject (Levine 2004). As a consequence, banks are heavily regulated and closely supervised.

These two features of the financial industry make corporate governance in this sector substantially more complex than in other industries. Designing a socially efficient governance of financial institutions would entail not only preventing self-interested managerial behavior, but also aligning a multiplicity of heterogeneous interests in the bank. This is a daunting task, given the complex and far-reaching spillovers of banking activity. In fact, even regulators face a difficult tradeoff when supervising financial institutions. To supervise banks efficiently, they must balance microprudential-financial stability (i.e., protecting investors and depositors from the cost of distress by preventing excessive risk taking) against macroprudential-regulatory forbearance (i.e., delaying regulatory intervention in troubled banks to limit system-wide distress that may reduce GDP).

The difficulties in governing financial institutions highlight the challenges in designing socially efficient corporate governance regulation for this industry. In the next sections we individually analyze the main corporate governance mechanisms we observe in practice. For each mechanism, we describe the reforms introduced after the 2007–2008 financial crises in the United States and Europe and analyze the empirical evidence on the effect of these reforms in light of economic theory.

1.3 Internal Corporate Governance Mechanisms

1.3.1 Executive Compensation

Because compensation contracts can make managerial payoffs dependent on shareholders' wealth creation, they are powerful instruments by which to align shareholders' and managers' economic interests. However, the fairness of executive compensation practices is a subject of considerable debate among both practitioners and scholars. Indeed, academic papers on this topic can be classified as those supporting the "efficient contracting hypothesis" (i.e., on average, managerial contracts are designed in the best interest of shareholders) and those supporting the "managerial power hypothesis" (i.e., on average managerial contracts are *not* designed in the best interest of shareholders) (Bebchuck and Fried 2004; Core et al. 2003; Hitz and Müller-Bloch 2015).

In the financial industry, compensation practices are often viewed as a key contributor to the financial crisis (e.g., Bebchuck et al. 2010). Many observers have argued that the executive pay structure generated excessive risk-taking incentives for bankers. This concern added fuel to a longstanding controversy—one that predated the crisis—around the size and growth of executive pay levels (especially in the financial industry). The available empirical evidence suggests that banks whose incentives for CEOs more closely aligned with the interests of shareholders performed worse during the crisis (e.g., Fahlenbrach and Stulz 2011; Mehran et al. 2012). Moreover, prior literature shows that higher risk-taking incentives led to higher volatility that was not associated with higher performance (e.g., DeYoung et al. 2010; Ellul and Yerramilli 2013).

Not surprisingly, the end result of the crisis was that substantial regulation was introduced. Shortly after the crisis, the 2010 Dodd-Frank Act brought important reforms in US compensation practices. The most hotly debated of these reforms may have been the introduction of an advisory vote on executive compensation (called "Say-On-Pay" or just SOP). Another reform, which was more specific to banking, stipulated that bank holding companies and certain other financial institutions be prohibited from providing executive officers, employees, directors, or principal shareholders with compensation that is excessive or that could lead to material financial loss to the financial institution. The evidence on the wealth effects of these regulatory developments is mixed. Cuñat et al. (2012) show that, before SOP became mandatory, shareholder approval of SOP proposals was associated with positive stock returns. However, Larcker et al. (2015) suggest that firms made suboptimal compensation changes in anticipation of the first SOP mandatory vote in 2011.

In 2009, the UK introduced the Remuneration Code, a regulation focused on executive bonuses. The stated objective of the code was to decrease short-termism among executives by requiring them to defer a larger portion of their bonus compensation. According to the new rules, at least 50% of bonuses must be deferred for at least 3 years. To increase pay-for-performance sensitivity, the Remuneration Code also required performance vesting conditions. These rules applied not only to top executives but also to second-tier executives who receive more than 33% of total remuneration in variable pay and whose total remuneration exceeds £500,000. Kleymenova and Tuna (2016) document a positive market reaction to the announcement of this regulation. Consistent with the intended purpose of the regulation, the authors also find that UK banks became less risky and exhibited higher pay-performance sensitivity after the regulation was implemented. However, their results suggest a higher CEO turnover among UK bank firms post-2010 compared to other EU and US banks.

In Europe, the European Directive CRD IV, which was introduced in 2013, mandates that the variable component of the total remuneration not exceed 100% of the fixed component of the total remuneration.[1] Kleymenova and Tuna (2016) find that the introduction of bonus caps by the new set of EU rules was perceived negatively by equity investors, which suggests that the regulation had some unintended costs. This evidence is in-line with Díaz et al. (2017), who find that

[1]Exceptionally, and under certain conditions, shareholders could increase this maximum ratio to 200%.

the introduction of European Directive CRD III in 2010 was perceived negatively by investors in a sample of European banks.

Other regulatory proposals suggest tying compensation at least in part to a measure of the default risk of the bank. Supporting the efficacy of these proposals, Bolton et al. (2010) show that increased CEO pay at risk is associated with lower credit default swap spreads. By showing that the CDS spread decreases with the percentage of CEO pay revealed to be in the form of higher ratios of inside debt (deferred compensation and pensions), the authors demonstrate theoretically and empirically that linking compensation to CDS spreads can reduce risk-taking. They interpret this to mean that the market believes that CEOs who stand to lose more financially if their bank fails take lower risks. Along the same lines, Tung and Wang (2012) show that higher inside debt incentives for CEOs are negatively associated with numerous measures of risk-taking by banks during the financial crisis (Mehran et al. 2012).

1.3.2 Board Monitoring

The board of directors is elected by shareholders to monitor and advise management. In terms of regulation, the debate over board monitoring focuses on whether there are desirable characteristics that should be imposed on the boards of public firms, and specifically on the boards of banks. Corporate governance rules are usually articulated through legal or regulatory requirements, listing standards of stock exchanges, or "codes of good governance" (usually developed under the "comply or explain" principle).[2] Sarbanes Oxley (SOX) and the New York Stock Exchange listing rules impose specific requirements in terms of director independence. Similarly, most of the codes of good governance advocate that independent directors be well represented on the board.

Imposing rules on the composition of corporate boards is controversial. Opponents of regulating board characteristics argue that such characteristics should be adaptable to each firm's specific needs. This alternative view is supported by a substantial body of empirical evidence suggesting that the efficacy of mandates such as SOX is unclear (e.g., Duchin et al. 2010).

Academic research has studied three main factors that influence board effectiveness in the banking industry: board size, the fraction of independent directors, and board experience. We will assess each of these factors in succession.

Regarding board size, it is well known that banks have larger boards than non-financial firms do (Adams and Mehran 2003). This would seem to make economic

[2]The codes of good governance gather corporate governance best practices suggested by professional organizations and investor activists. Unlike legal, regulatory, and listing requirements, the adoption of these best practices is voluntary. However, investors may penalize companies if firms' governance practices do not follow the codes of good governance.

sense since banks are usually larger than non-financial firms (e.g., Yermack 1996) and tend to be more complex organizations.[3] Moreover, while banks often engage in M&A activity, their acquisitions are rarely hostile. As a consequence, most board members of the target company remain on the board of the consolidated entity until their term expires.

A more controversial issue is whether banks' boards are *too* big. Indeed, some research finds that non-financial firms with larger boards exhibit lower valuations (Yermack 1996), suggesting that board size could introduce inefficiencies. While possible, recent research suggests that this is not a prevalent effect among banks. In fact, there is evidence that, in the banking industry, board size is positively related to performance (e.g., Andres and Vallelado 2008; Adams and Mehran 2012). Moreover, Adams and Mehran (2012) provide evidence suggesting that it makes sense to increase board size by adding directors with subsidiary directorships.[4]

Regarding board independence, empirical evidence is not conclusive about the effect of independent directors on firm performance. International evidence shows that the percentage of independent directors is positively related to bank performance (Andres and Vallelado 2008). However, US evidence indicates that the percentage of independent directors is unrelated to bank performance (Adams and Mehran 2012) and is negatively related to risk (Pathan 2009). Other papers show that banks with more independent directors on their boards suffered larger losses during the crisis (Adams 2012; Erkens et al. 2012). One plausible explanation for this result is that independent directors were less likely to have the financial expertise to understand the complexity and risks taken by the securitization business.

Regarding boards' financial expertise, Minton et al. (2014) find no evidence that US banks whose boards had more financial expertise fared better during the crisis. In the case of European banks, however, the evidence points in the opposite direction. Using a sample of large German banks, Hau and Thum (2009) find that board members' financial expertise was negatively related to losses during the financial crisis. Similarly, Garicano and Cuñat (2010) show that, in the case of Spanish "cajas," chairmen who had no previous banking experience (or postgraduate education) had significantly worse performance at the peak of the financial crisis.[5] That said, the nonprofit nature of the "cajas" and the political

---

[3]For example, banks often own or control many subsidiary banks, each of which has its own board. Coordination among these different boards may affect the structure of the board of the bank because of the need to include directors from the subsidiary Adams and Mehran (2003).

[4]In the United States, most publicly traded banks are organized as a bank holding company (BHC) in which each subsidiary is chartered and has its own board. Often, directors of the parent BHC will sit on the board of the subsidiaries. This differs from most non-financial firms, which are organized along divisional lines and whose subsidiaries often do not have separate legal identities Adams (2012).

[5]The "cajas de ahorro" are nonprofit institutions in the Spanish financial system governed by representatives of their depositors, employees, and the local authorities. With the liberalization of the Spanish financial system in the 1980s, the cajas evolved into full-service financial institutions and started to expand beyond their geographic regions.

links of Spanish and German banks make this result difficult to generalize to international banks (Mehran et al. 2012).

The post-crisis period induced significant changes in board composition. The Dodd-Frank Act required new stock exchange listing standards, mandated resolutions for public company proxy statements, and expanded disclosures for all public companies soliciting proxies or consents. As a result of these provisions, companies changed the composition and operation of their compensation committees, and adopted new policies surrounding governance, compensation, and disclosure. For instance, Ormazabal (2016) shows that the post-crisis institutional emphasis on risk oversight has heightened the costs of serving on risky boards, and that this, in turn, has induced director turnover and reshaped board composition. Specifically, he documents that directors at riskier boards are younger, have less board experience, hold fewer directorships, and have less academic qualifications and a smaller network than directors in less risky boards, and that this gap has widened after the crisis.

1.3.3 Internal Control Systems

Alignment of incentives and monitoring at the top management level might not be enough to prevent excessive risk taking. Bank governance requires an effective internal control system that (i) provides relevant information, and (ii) curbs misbehavior at the lower levels of the organization. In fact, a common criticism of financial institutions during the crisis was that they lacked effective risk-management controls—that they were unaware of the risks they were facing and did not appropriately monitor their employees' risk-taking behavior.

Probably as a consequence of this concern, bank risk management has been subject to substantial regulation after the crisis. Notably, in the United States, the Dodd-Frank Act mandated, among other requirements, that bank holding companies with total consolidated assets greater than $50bn establish a risk-management framework, designate a Chief Risk Officer (CRO), and establish a board-level risk committee with at least one independent member and one risk management expert.

Ellul and Yerramilli (2013) examine empirically the effect of risk-management controls in US banks and find that banks with stronger controls experienced less volatility during the crisis. Similarly, Keys et al. (2009) document that loans issued by banks with more powerful CROs exhibited lower default rates. When Barakat and Hussainey (2013) study the effect of the audit committee in banks from 20 EU countries from 2008 to 2010 (risk management is usually included among the responsibilities of the audit committee), they find that banks whose audit committees met more frequently provided higher-quality operational risk disclosures.

1.4 Market Discipline

The previous sections have analyzed governance mechanisms that are internal to the organization. However, there are also powerful external mechanisms to discipline managerial behavior. In what follows, we analyze three of these mechanisms that relate to the disciplining effect of market participants: product market competition, the market for corporate control, and shareholder monitoring.

1.4.1 Competition

Competition in the product market is a powerful force for disciplining managers. If managers of a firm waste or consume large amounts of resources, the firm will lose its competitive edge and could even go bankrupt (Allen and Gale 2000). Consistent with this notion, Giroud and Mueller (2010, 2011) find that corporate governance issues are more frequent in less competitive industries.

In the banking industry, however, the effect of competition is not obvious, because the rivalry among banks could lead to financial instability (Matutes and Vives 1996). First, competition could exacerbate coordination problems between depositors or investors. A prominent example of this is bank runs. Second, competition could induce risk-taking, which in turn could lead to systemic risk. For example, the period after the liberalization of the banking industry in the 1970s fostered innovation (Carletti and Vives 2009) but was also associated with a number of problems (e.g., the US savings and loan crisis in the 1980s, and crises in Japan, Scandinavia, Mexico, and East Asia in the 1990s).

Historically, two important regulatory developments in the United States have affected bank competition. The Glass-Steagall Act of 1933 prohibited financial institutions from conducting both commercial banking and investment banking businesses. This regulation was overturned in 1999 by the Gramm-Leach-Bliley Act, which lifted the barriers to universal banking. Opponents of Gramm-Leach-Bliley argued that its passage was driven by pressure from industry lobbyists. From an empirical perspective, the act's efficacy is also controversial (e.g., Morrison and Wilhelm 2007).

After the crisis, the Dodd-Frank Act in the United States incorporated a version of the Volcker Rule, which limits banks from engaging in certain activities that are generally viewed as risky (i.e., proprietary investments and relationships with hedge funds and private equity funds). In the UK, restrictions that separate commercial and investment banking by ring-fencing retail activities have been added. Similar restrictions have been proposed in the EU, based on recommendations by Erkki Liikanen, the governor of Finland's central bank.

1.4.2 The Takeover Market

The threat of an unfriendly takeover can curtail managerial opportunism and incentivize managers to pursue shareholder value maximization. This is because a change in control often involves replacing the top management of the company. Thus, the takeover market is often seen as a powerful corporate governance mechanism (Martin and McConnell 1991). However, an alternative view is that corporate governance mechanisms that control agency problems can substitute for the absence of a market for corporate control (Huson et al. 2001).

While the banking sector has experienced substantial consolidation in recent years, few acquisitions have been hostile. Adams and Mehran (2003) offer several reasons why hostile takeover bids have been scarce in the US banking industry. First, state laws and federal banking regulations limit takeovers by non-banks, and impose substantial delays on hostile or large bids by banks. For example, state banking regulators and the Federal Reserve took over 3 years to approve the M&T/Hudson City transaction. Second, the medium of exchange in hostile offers is typically cash (Fishman 1989), but banks cannot borrow additional debt easily since they are already highly indebted. Third, many banks hold a significant share of their ultimate parent company as pension trustee or as fund manager (Adams and Mehran 2003). This large stake decreases the probability of success of a hostile offer. In short, these considerations raise doubts about the efficacy of the takeover threat as a governance mechanism in the financial industry.

1.4.3 Shareholder Monitoring

As explained by Larcker and Tayan (2011), institutional shareholders can be powerful monitors: They can communicate their opinions directly to management and the board. If the response they receive is not satisfactory, they can seek to have directors removed, vote against proxy proposals sponsored by management, put forth their own proxy measures, or express their dissatisfaction by selling their shares ("voting with their feet").

However, shareholder activism in the banking industry faces several challenges. To begin with, the stake of equity ownership that is needed for effective monitoring and intervention is often too large for most investors to acquire. This is true even for large institutions and hedge funds (a typical hedge fund activist considers an ownership of 5–15% of equity appropriate for launching activism). Also, regulation imposes limits on the percentage of bank capital that can be owned by a single non-bank entity. And the intricate nature of the financial products and the positions on derivatives and other instruments makes it difficult for outsiders to monitor banks effectively.

In addition, shareholder monitoring incentives are controversial for at least two reasons. First, it is not clear why most shareholders would engage in costly monitoring, especially if other shareholders will do it for them (Grossman and Hart 1980). Shareholders who do engage in monitoring would only reap a small portion of the benefits created through their efforts. Second, some authors have conjectured that the US government's implicit guarantee of "too-big-to-fail" institutions generated incentives for certain shareholders to encourage risk-taking by banks (e.g., Armour and Gordon 2014). There is some empirical evidence consistent with this conjecture. For example, Laeven and Levine (2009) find that higher institutional ownership is associated with higher risk-taking by banks. Beltratti and Stulz (2012) and Erkens et al. (2012) also find that, during the recent US crisis, risk-taking was higher in banks with more concentrated ownership. In Europe, Bouvatier et al. (2014) find that European commercial banks with highly concentrated ownership use discretionary loan-loss provisions to smooth their income and conceal risk-taking.

1.5 Regulatory Intervention

1.5.1 Capital Requirements

As previously explained, the banking industry is unique in its multiplicity and heterogeneity of stakeholders and in the important externalities of its economic activity. In particular, the interests of shareholders can conflict with those of other stakeholders and of the society as a whole. A prominent example of this problem is the preference toward risk. Given that banks are highly leveraged, their risk-taking increases the value of equity claims on them, but decreases the value of debt claims. More importantly, an implicit bailout guarantee (i.e., being "too-big-to-fail") exacerbates shareholders' risk-taking incentives, potentially at the expense of taxpayers. This suggests that the classical corporate governance mechanisms, which aim at aligning managers' and shareholders' interests, could result in significant costs to society.

To be effective, the corporate governance mechanisms analyzed in the prior sections may need to be complemented by monitoring mechanisms that protect societal interests. One such mechanism is to impose limitations on the amount of leverage a bank can take and thus rein in the risk-taking incentives of banks' equity holders. These restrictions are commonly referred to as "capital requirements" or "Basel rules" ("Basel" being short for "Basel Committee on Banking Supervision," the group that recommended these reforms).[6]

---

[6]The Basel Committee on Banking Supervision ("Basel Committee") issued Basel I and Basel II, a global voluntary regulatory framework focused primarily on the level of bank loss reserves that banks are required to hold. Moreover, the Basel Committee issued Basel III, which focuses primarily on the risk of a run on the bank and requires differing levels of reserves for different forms of bank deposits and other borrowings.

After the financial crisis, the efficacy of the regulatory capital requirements for banks was called into question and, not surprisingly, reforms quickly ensued. The U.S. Federal Reserve announced in December 2011 that it would implement virtually all of the Basel III rules. In July 2013, US regulatory authorities adopted a sweeping overhaul (the "Revised Capital Framework") of their regulations, implementing both the Basel III Accord and the requirements set forth in the Dodd-Frank Act. The Revised Capital Framework took effect on January 1, 2015, for all institutions subject to the rules (generally those with more than $1bn in total consolidated assets). Similarly, Europe has also implemented the Basel III agreements through a new legislative package approved in May 2013: the Directive 2013/36/EU (CRD IV) and Regulation 575/2013 (CRR).

The evidence suggests that bank capital requirements can curb risk-taking incentives (Kim and Santomero 1988; Morrison and White 2005; Mehran et al. 2012). However, there is also evidence that meeting these requirements does not necessarily reduce bank risk. For example, Acharya et al. (2011) find that a large part of the newly raised capital during the financial crisis came from debt-like hybrid claims such as preferred equity and subordinated debt, and that banks continued to pay dividends in the first part of the crisis. As a result, the exposure to future potential crises could have increased (Berger and Bouwman 2013).

1.5.2 Regulatory Supervision

While some view capital requirements as a powerful regulatory mechanism, these requirements are probably not enough to keep banks' risk-taking incentives at the optimal societal level. The common criticism is that these requirements are based on accounting rules and measurement procedures that are subject to estimation error and perhaps even to manipulation (Boyson et al. 2016). As a consequence, there is need for regulatory supervision.

There have been a number of developments in banks' regulatory supervision during the post-crisis period. In 2009, the European System of Financial Supervision (ESFS) was created as a system of micro- and macro-prudential supervision by European and national supervisors. The micro-prudential supervision is performed by the European Banking Authority (EBA), the European Securities and Markets Authority (ESMA), and the European Insurance and Occupational Pensions Authority (EIOPA), which work together in the Joint Committee of the European Supervisory Authorities (ESAs). The micro-prudential supervision is performed by the European Systemic Risk Board (ESRB). In 2012, the EU members agreed to create a version of a banking union through the Single Supervisory Mechanism (SSM), with the European Central Bank (ECB) as the centralized supervisor, a Single Resolution Mechanism (SRM) to coordinate bank resolution, and a common European Deposit Insurance Scheme (EDIS). Through the SSM, banks deemed "significant" are supervised directly by the ECB, while smaller banks continue to be directly monitored by their national authorities.

In the US, Dodd-Frank created the interagency Financial Stability Oversight Council (FSOC) to monitor systemic risk, and consolidated bank regulation from five agencies to four by eliminating the Office of Thrift Supervision (OTS).[7] For banks and non-banks designated by the FSOC as creating systemic risk, the Federal Reserve has oversight authority, and the Federal Deposit Insurance Corporation (FDIC) has resolution authority.

Regulatory banking supervision is subject to significant debate (Barth et al. 2004). At the heart of the problem is that the interests of the supervisor could deviate from those of the taxpayers, or in general the society (Schuler 2004). This incentive problem is exacerbated by incomplete information and accountability issues. In particular, there is debate about whether there should be one or multiple (competing) supervisors, about the supervisory role of the central bank, and about the scope of the supervisory activity. The evidence in Agarwal et al. (2014) illustrates these concerns by suggesting a lack of coordination between the supervisory agencies in the United States. They report that state and federal banking regulators implement identical rules inconsistently due to differences in their institutional design and incentives.

1.6 Emerging Economies

If corporate governance is a problem in developed economies, it could be a more acute problem in emerging countries, which constitute a large and increasingly important part of global GDP. Thus, we cannot end without a brief analysis of the banking industry in emerging economies.

To analyze corporate governance in the banking industry of emerging economies (EEs), one must be aware of three important considerations. First, compared to the developed economies of the United States and Europe, EEs have less developed financial markets. In EEs, banks are the main capital providers, so economic development more closely depends on the performance of the banking industry. The crises in Mexico and East Asia during the 1990s are powerful examples of the risks generated by this type of dependence (Vives 2016). Second, EEs have weaker institutions and lower enforcement intensity. This limits the ability of regulation to solve market imperfections. Third, ownership is significantly concentrated in those countries. This exacerbates the conflicts of interest between major shareholders and other stakeholders. Consistent with this concern, there is ample evidence of rent extraction from minority shareholders in these countries (Bebchuk and Weisbach

[7]Banks in the U.S. can choose between a national and a state charter. Only federal regulators, in particular the Office of the Comptroller of the Currency (OCC), supervise nationally chartered commercial banks. State-chartered banks are supervised both by state banking departments and federal regulators. The primary federal regulator of state banks is determined by their membership in the Federal Reserve System. The Federal Reserve supervises state member banks, while the Federal Deposit Insurance Corporation (FDIC) supervises nonmember banks.

2010). The problem may be compounded by the fact that, in EEs, it is relatively easy to hide the actual owner of a firm through the use of pyramidal structures and indirect holdings (Ard and Berg 2010).[8]

With these considerations in mind, and in keeping with our previous analysis, we assess the extent to which managerial compensation contracts alleviates the bank-governance problems in emerging economies. The answer appears to be "not much." To begin with, the pay-for-performance sensitivity is relatively low in important developing economies like China (Luo 2015). In addition, the significant ownership concentration in emerging countries may render agency issues between managers and shareholders (and thus managerial incentives) less relevant than in economies with dispersed ownership (like the United States). In EEs, the relevant issue is not necessarily how to influence managerial behavior, but how to curb potential self-serving behavior among the banks' block-holders.

For similar reasons, boards of directors do not seem very effective in EEs. There is evidence that board monitoring reduces the likelihood of fraud (Chen et al. 2006) and expropriation through related-party transactions (Lo et al. 2010; Claessens and Yurtoglu 2013). However, the boards of banks are often dominated by a controlling shareholder (Gandy et al. 2007); independent directors often have personal links with management; and top executives and directors tend to have less expertise than their peers in developed economies (Berger et al. 2010).

Can shareholder monitoring help the governance of banks in EEs? A significant proportion of banks' assets are public debt. With little possibility of diversifying their portfolios, banks are vulnerable to inflationary policies, which are common in EEs (Vives 2016). This issue is even more concerning for state-owned banks, for whom the government is controller and debtor alike (Gandy et al. 2007). This conflict of interest may be one reason why government ownership of banks is associated with slower financial development, lower economic growth, and a higher likelihood of banking crises (Ard and Berg 2010).

Many EEs have carried out processes of bank privatization in recent decades (Beck et al., 2005 (Brazil); Williams and Nguyen 2005 (Asia); Zhao et al. 2010 (India); Love and Rachinsky 2015 (Russia and Ukraine)), but private ownership, like public ownership, is problematic in these nations. Private banks are often controlled by an individual or family that also owns a substantial stake in other firms. This common ownership opens the possibility that minority shareholders can be expropriated through party-lending or other mechanisms. Although increasingly limited by regulation, these practices do still exist (Bebchuk and Weisbach 2010). In any case, a substantial part of the banking industry in EEs is still state-owned; for

[8]That said, concentrated ownership can also have significant advantages Shleifer and Vishny (1997). In fact, some authors argue that, in developing corporate governance regulation for European countries, policy makers should recognize that the separation of ownership and control is a lesser issue in the Southern European countries than in countries whose economies are dominated by widely held firms (e.g., Aguilera and Cuervo-Cazurra 2004). Following this logic, García-Ramos and García-Olalla (2014) question whether all governance practices that are common in the US should be applied to Southern European firms.

example, the four largest Chinese banks are controlled by the Chinese government (Whatley 2014).

Although regulation could be a powerful mechanism to improve bank governance in EEs, it faces at least two significant challenges. First, the supervisory structures in EEs are often somewhat weak and not fully independent of the political process (Vives 2016). Second, the supply of reputable monitors may be lower than in developed economies (Gandy et al. 2007). Despite these problems, however, a number of countries are moving towards more stringent regulation by adopting of International Financial Reporting Standards (IFRS) and/or introducing higher disclosure requirements (Covrig et al. 2007; Claessens and Yurtoglu 2013).

The governance improvements in EEs could be driven, in part, by the need to raise capital from international investors. By implementing improvements, the EEs can avoid having foreign investors impose a higher cost of capital in order to protect themselves against governance risk (Claessens and Yurtoglu 2013). Moreover, firms listed in foreign stock exchanges are subject to higher disclosure and governance standards. While there is evidence that firms select capital markets with softer requirements (Licht 2001, 2003; Siegel 2005), this evidence can also be interpreted as supportive, in that the governance changes imposed by other markets are costly and therefore meaningful. In fact, there is evidence that the firms in EEs with the highest corporate governance standards are subsidiaries of foreign banks and firms with a wide shareholder base (Gandy et al. 2007). In this regard, at least, globalization has brought an improvement in the corporate governance of banks in EEs.

1.7 Conclusions

In this article, we analyze the role of corporate governance—notably the regulatory reforms introduced after the 2007–2008 Financial Crisis—on bank performance. In doing so, we rely on a large body of scholarly research on corporate governance and the banking industry. Due to space limitations, our analysis is by no means exhaustive, neither in terms of regulatory developments nor of the surveyed academic literature. For example, we have excluded from our analysis potentially important alternative mechanisms to discipline managerial behavior, such as the legal system or the media (among others).

Our analysis does not offer specific recommendations. We believe that, given the complexity and relevance of bank governance as well as the space limitations of this article, such recommendations are beyond the scope of this analysis. Instead, this article aims to assist the reader in drawing her own conclusions about corporate governance in the financial industry. An informed reader should be cognizant of the significant tradeoffs underlying regulatory choices, as well as the difficulty in understanding the effect of corporate governance in banks—organizations that cater to a very diverse set of stakeholders and whose decisions impose significant and complex externalities in the economy. We hope these lines are helpful in this regard.

Acknowledgments We thank Eloy Lanau and Vicent Peris for their excellent research assistance. Gaizka Ormazabal thanks the Marie Curie and Ramon y Cajal Fellowships and the Spanish Ministry of Science and Innovation, grants ECO2010-19314 and ECO2011-29533.

References

Acharya, V. V., Gujral, I., Kulkarni, N., & Shin, H.S. (2011). *Dividends and bank capital in the financial crisis of 2007–2009*. National Bureau of Economic Research. No. w16896.

Adams, R. (2012). Governance and the financial crisis. *International Review of Finance, 12*, 7–38.

Adams, R., & Mehran, H. (2003). Is corporate governance different for bank holding companies? *FRBNY Economic Policy Review, 9*, 123–142.

Adams, R., & Mehran, H. (2012). Bank board structure and performance: Evidence for large bank holding companies. *Journal of Financial Intermediation, 21*, 243–267.

Agarwal, S., Lucca, D., Seru, A., & Trebbi, F. (2014). Inconsistent regulators: Evidence from banking. *Quarterly Journal of Economics, 129*, 889–938.

Aguilera, R. V., & Cuervo-Cazurra, A. (2004). Codes of good governance worldwide: What is the trigger? *Organization Studies, 25*(3), 415–443.

Allen, F., & Gale, D. (2000). Financial contagion. *The Journal of Political Econnomy, 108*, 1–33.

Andrés, P., & Vallelado, E. (2008). Corporate governance in banking: The role of the board of directors. *Journal of Banking & Finance, 32*(12), 2570–2580.

Ard, L., & Berg, A. (2010). The financial crisis: What are the corporate governance lessons for emerging market countries? In: Corporate governance in the wake of the financial crisis. (UNCTAD/DIAE/ED/2010/2), pp. 79–88.

Armour, J., & Gordon, J. (2014). Systemic harms and shareholder value. *Journal of Legal Analysis, 6*, 35–85.

Association of Chartered Certified Accountants (ACCA). (2008). *Climbing out of the credit crunch*.

Barakat, A., & Hussainey, K. (2013). Bank governance, regulation, supervision, and risk reporting: Evidence from operational risk disclosures in European banks. *International Review of Financial Analysis, 30*, 254–273.

Barth, J., Gan, J., & Nolle, D. (2004). *Global banking regulation and supervision: What are the issues and what are the practices? Focus on Financial Institutions and Services*. New York: Nova Science Publisher.

Bebchuk, L. A., & Fried, J. (2004). *Pay without performance: The unfufilled promise of executive compensation*. Cambridge, MA: Harvard University Press.

Bebchuk, L. A., & Weisbach, M. S. (2010). The state of corporate governance research. *Review of Financial Studies, 23*, 939–961.

Bebchuk, L. A., Cohen, A., & Spamann, H. (2010). The wages of failure: Executive compensation at Bear Stearns and Lehman 2000-2008. *Yale Journal on Regulation, 27*, 257–282.

Beck, T., Crivelli, J. M., & Summerhill, W. (2005). State bank transformation in Brazil – choices and consequences. *Journal of Banking & Finance, 29*, 2223–2257.

Beltratti, A., & Stulz, R. M. (2012). The credit crisis around the globe: Why did some banks perform better? *Journal of Financial Economics, 105*, 1–17.

Berger, A. N., & Bouwman, C. H. (2013). How does capital affect bank performance during financial crises? *Journal of Financial Economics, 109*, 146–176.

Berger, A. N., Hasan, I., & Zhou, M. (2010). The effects of focus versus diversification on bank performance: Evidence from Chinese banks. *Journal of Banking & Finance, 34*, 1417–1435.

Bolton, P., Mehran, H., & Shapiro, J. (2010). *Executive compensation and risk taking*. No 456, Staff Reports, Federal Reserve Bank of New York.

Bouvatier, V., Lepetit, L., & Strobel, F. (2014). Bank income smoothing, ownership concentration and the regulatory environment. *Journal of Banking & Finance, 41*, 253–270.

Boyson, N. M., Fahlenbrach, R., & Stulz, R. M. (2016). Why don't all banks practice regulatory arbitrage? Evidence from usage of trust-preferred Securities. *The Review of Financial Studies, 29*, 1821–1859.

Carletti, E., & Vives, X. (2009). Regulation and competition policy in banking. In E. Carletti & X. Vives (Eds.), *Competition policy in Europe fifty years after the treaty*. New York: Oxford University Press.

Chen, G., Firth, M., Gao, D. N., & Rui, O. M. (2006). Ownership structure, corporate governance, and fraud: Evidence from China. *Journal of Corporate Finance, 12*, 424–448.

Claessens, S., & Yurtoglu, B. B. (2013). Corporate governance in emerging markets: A survey. *Emerging Markets Review, 15*, 1–33.

Core, J., Guay, W., & Larcker, D. (2003). Executive equity compensation and incentives: A survey. *FRBNY Economic Policy Review, 9*, 27–50.

Covrig, V., Defond, M. L., & Hung, M. (2007). Home bias, foreign mutual fund holdings, and the voluntary adoption of international accounting standards. *Journal of Accounting Research, 45*, 41–70.

Cuñat, V., Giné, M., & Guadalupe, M. (2012). The vote is cast: The effect of corporate governance on shareholder value. *Journal of Finance, 67*, 1943–1977.

DeYoung, R., Peng, E. Y., & Yan, M. (2010). Executive compensation and business policy choices at U.S. commercial banks. *Research Working Paper*, 10–12.

Díaz Díaz, B., García-Ramos, R., & García Olalla, M. (2017). Shareholder wealth responses to European legislation on bank executive compensation. *Journal of Economic Policy Reform*, 1–21.

Duchin, R., Matsusaka, J. G., & Ozbas, O. (2010). When are outside directors effective? *Journal of Financial Economics, 96*, 195–214.

Ellul, A., & Yerramilli, V. (2013). Stronger risk controls, lower risk: Evidence from US bank holding companies. *The Journal of Finance, 68*, 1575–1803.

Erkens, D. H., Hunga, M., & Matos, P. (2012). Corporate governance in the 2007–2008 financial crisis: Evidence from financial institutions worldwide. *Journal of Corporate Finance, 18*, 389–411.

Fahlenbrach, R., & Stulz, R. M. (2011). Bank CEO incentives and the credit crisis. *Journal of Financial Economics, 99*, 11–26.

Fishman, M. J. (1989). Preemptive bidding and the role of the medium of exchange in acquisitions. *The Journal of Finance, 44*, 41–57.

Gandy, B., Shaw, P., Tebbutt, P., & Young, M. (2007). Corporate governance in emerging market banks. In: Corporate governance in financial institutions. *SUERF Studies, 2007*(3), 93–143.

García-Ramos, R., & García-Olalla, M. (2014). Board independence and firm performance in Southern Europe: A contextual and contingency approach. *Journal of Management & Organization, 20*(03), 313–332.

Garicano, L., & Cuñat, V. (2010). Did good Cajas extend bad loans? Governance, human capital, and loan portfolios. In S. Bentolila, M. Boldrin, J. Diaz-Gimenez, & J. J. Dolado (Eds.), *The crisis of the Spanish economy: Economic analysis of the great recession*. Madrid: Fedea.

Giroud, X., & Mueller, H. M. (2010). Does corporate governance matter in competitive industries? *Journal of Financial Economics, 95*, 312–331.

Giroud, X., & Mueller, H. M. (2011). Corporate governance, product market competition, and equity prices. *Journal of Finance, 66*, 563–600.

Grossman, S., & Hart, O. (1980). Takeover bids, the free rider problem, and the theory of the corporation. *The Bell Journal of Economics, 11*, 42–64.

Hart, O. (2009). Regulation and Sarbanes-Oxley. *Journal of Accounting Research, 47*(2), 437–445.

Hau, H., & Thum, M. P. (2009). Subprime crisis and board (in-) competence: Private vs. public banks in Germany. *Economic Policy, 24*, 701–751.

Hitz, J. M., & Müller-Bloch, S. (2015). Market reactions to the regulation of executive compensation. *European Accounting Review, 24*(4), 659–684.

Huson, M. R., Parrino, R., & Starks, L. T. (2001). Internal monitoring mechanisms and CEO turnover: A long term perspective. *Journal of Finance, 56*, 2265–2297.

Keys, B. J., Mukherjee, T., Seru, A., & Vig, V. (2009). Financial regulation and securitization: Evidence from subprime loans. *Journal of Monetary Economics, 56*, 700–720.

Kim, D., & Santomero, A. (1988). Risk in banking and capital regulation. *The Journal of Finance, 43*, 1219–1233.

Kleymenova, A., & Tuna, I. (2016). *Regulation of compensation*. Chicago Booth Research Paper 16-07.

Laeven, L., & Levine, R. (2009). Bank governance, regulation and risk taking. *Journal of Financial Economics, 93*, 259–275.

Larcker, D., & Tayan, B. (2011). *Corporate governance matters*. Pearson FT Press.

Larcker, D., McCall, L., & Ormazabal, G. (2015). Outsourcing shareholder voting to proxy advisory firms. *Journal of Law and Economics, 58*, 173–204.

Levine, R. (2004). *The corporate governance of banks: A concise discussion of concepts and evidence*. Working paper 3404, World Bank Research, Washington, DC.

Licht, A. N. (2001). Managerial opportunism and foreign listing: Some direct evidence. *University of Pennsylvania Journal of International Economic Law, 22*, 325–347.

Licht, A. N. (2003). Cross-listing and corporate governance: Bonding or avoiding? *Chicago Journal of International Law, 4*, 141–163.

Lo, A. W. Y., Wong, R., & Firth, M. (2010). Can corporate governance deter management from manipulation earnings? Evidence from related-party sales transactions in China. *Journal of Corporate Finance, 16*, 225–235.

Love, I., & Rachinsky, A. (2015). Corporate governance and bank performance in emerging markets: Evidence from Russia and Ukraine. *Emerging Markets Finance & Trade, 51*, S101–S121.

Luo, Y. (2015). CEO power, ownership structure and pay performance in Chinese banking. *Journal of Economics and Business, 82*, 3–16.

Martin, K. J., & McConnell, J. J. (1991). Corporate performance, corporate takeovers, and management turnover. *The Journal of Finance, 46*, 671–687.

Matutes, C., & Vives, X. (1996). Competition for deposits, fragility, and insurance. *Journal of Financial Intermediation, 5*, 184–216.

Mehran, H., Morrison, A., & Shapiro, J. (2012). Corporate governance and banks: What have we learned from the financial crisis? In M. Dewatripont & X. Freixas (Eds.), *The crisis aftermath: New regulatory paradigms*. London: Centre for Economic Policy Research.

Minton, B. A., Taillard, J. P., & Williamson, R. (2014). Financial expertise of the board, risk taking, and performance: Evidence from bank holding companies. *Journal of Financial and Quantitative Analysis, 49*, 351–380.

Morrison, A. D., & White, L. (2005). Crises and capital requirements in banking. *American Economic Review, 95*, 1548–1572.

Morrison, A. D., & Wilhelm, W. J., Jr. (2007). *Investment banking: Institutions, politics, and law*. Oxford: Oxford University Press.

Ormazabal, G. (2016). Are directors more likely to relinquish their riskier directorships after the crisis? Working paper.

Pathan, S. (2009). Strong boards, CEO power and bank risk-taking. *Journal of Banking & Finance, 33*, 1340–1350.

Schuler, M. (2004). Incentive problems in banking supervision: The European case. Center for European Economic Research working paper.

Shleifer, A., & Vishny, R. W. (1997). A Survey of Corporate Governance. *The Journal of Finance, 52*, 737–783.

Siegel, J. (2005). Can foreign firms bond themselves effectively by renting U.S. securities laws? *Journal of Financial Economics, 75*, 319–359.

Tung, F., & Wang, X. (2012). Bank CEOs, inside debt compensation, and the global financial crisis. Boston University School of Law Working Paper, pp. 11–49.

Vives, X. (2016). *Competition and stability in banking: The role of regulation and competition policy*. Princeton, NJ: Princeton University Press.

Whatley, H. D. (2014). Corporate governance in China's banking system. *Studies of Organisational Management & Sustainability, 2*, 1–14.

Williams, J., & Nguyen, N. (2005). Financial liberalisation, crisis, and restructuring: a comparative study of bank performance and bank governance in South East Asia. *Journal of Banking & Finance, 29*, 2119–2154.

Yermack, D. (1996). Higher market valuation of companies with a small board of directors. *Journal of Financial Economics, 40*, 185–211.

Zhao, T., Casu, B., & Ferrari, A. (2010). The impact of regulatory reforms on cost structure, ownership and competition in Indian banking. *Journal of Banking & Finance, 34*, 246–254.

Chapter 2
Banks' Interactions with Listed Non-Financial Firms as a Determinant of Corporate Governance in Banking: An Agency Theory Analysis

Cicek Gurkan

2.1 Introduction

Banks are considered vital to economic development since they act as an intermediary between surplus units and entrepreneurs through their maturity and liquidity transformation functions (Diamond and Dybvig 1983). In fulfilling this role, it is essential that they ensure their borrowers are capable of utilizing the financial resources they receive efficiently and indeed do so throughout the lifetime of financing (Tirole 2006). The screening and monitoring functions of a bank (Diamond 1984) derived from this economic concern form the basis for understanding the complex interactions between banks and non-financial listed firms.

In the academic literature, banks' relationships with non-financial large firms have been subject to extensive debates as regards the comparison between the two well-known types of financial systems, the bank-based financial system and the market-based financial system (e.g., Porter 1992; Aoki and Patrick 1995). Diverging from the dichotomous view presented in most of the earlier works, modern understanding of financial intermediation suggests that banks can exert control over industrial companies' governance regardless of the underlying financial system (Allen and Gale 2000; Boot 2000). It is important to realize that this influence will evidently differ depending on the underlying institutional factors, an idea which will be explored further in this chapter.

Despite the move towards a market-based system in many countries in the last decades, the global financial crisis of 2007 has made it evident that the linkages between banks as financial intermediaries and the real economic sector remain

C. Gurkan (✉)
European Doctorate in Law and Economics (EDLE) Program, Institute of Law and Economics, University of Hamburg, Hamburg, Germany
e-mail: cicek.gurkan@edle-phd.eu

B. Díaz Díaz et al. (eds.), *Corporate Governance in Banking and Investor Protection*, CSR, Sustainability, Ethics & Governance,
https://doi.org/10.1007/978-3-319-70007-6_2

extremely important. The regulatory aftermath of the financial crisis has brought in sweeping changes on both sides of the Atlantic, and especially in Europe corporate governance of banks has become one of the key areas of focus (Hopt 2013). Currently, regulatory measures specific to bank governance in the European Union ("EU") cover, particularly, remuneration, internal controls, and risk management aspects (Armour et al. 2016; Hopt 2013). Furthermore, while not exclusive to banks, certain other measures within the realm of the general corporate governance framework, such as disclosure of non-financial and diversity information (Directive 2014/95/EU) and enhancement of shareholder rights (Directive (EU) 2017/828) also affect the playing field for banks (Sum 2016).

The underlying challenge when it comes to policymaking in bank governance is to devise the optimum set of incentive mechanisms that minimize the agency costs arising out of a bank's operations. This challenge involves looking beyond the considerations already applicable to governance of non-financial firms because the complexity of banks' business and the diversity of principal-agent conflicts arising out of a banking organization call for a differentiated approach (Hopt 2012; Mehran et al. 2011). In this regard, a rich debate has emerged addressing whether specific banking governance measures and initiatives introduced or under consideration in the post-crisis era are fit to remedy the control and risk management failures seen as contributing factors to the global financial crisis (e.g., Bebchuk and Spamann 2010; Adams 2012; Hopt 2012, 2013; Armour et al. 2016).

This chapter takes these discussions a step further by looking at the subject of corporate governance in banking from the perspective of the larger ecosystem banks operate in. More precisely, it explores banks' relationships with non-financial firms across different settings as a dimension affecting the trade-offs involved in regulating the governance of banks. As a form of financial regulation, corporate governance in banking needs to be developed further on the basis of a cost-benefit analysis. Accordingly, the next section briefly presents the trade-offs involved in regulating banks' corporate governance, highlighting the link between these regulations and their potential impact on banks' financial intermediation costs. Subsequently, Sect. 2.3 undertakes an analysis of banks' corporate governance roles as the main independent variable in this study. Through the lens of agency theory and by way of selected examples, this section shows that interactions between banks and listed non-financial firms in modern financial markets are multidimensional in nature and can bring about costs as well as benefits for the latter. Section 2.4 concludes by stating the policy implications of these findings for corporate governance of banks.

2.2 Corporate Governance in Banking as a Subset of Financial Regulation

Market failures constitute the starting point for design and assessment of the limits of financial regulation (Stiglitz 2008; Dodd 2002; Heremans and Pacces 2012). In the aftermath of the financial crisis of 2007, an intense debate has erupted over how best to address systemic risk in an increasingly interconnected and complex world while sustaining market efficiency (e.g., Schooner and Taylor 2010; Brunnermeier et al. 2009; Armour et al. 2016). As the goals of financial regulation are not always in alignment with each other (Spong 2000; Armour et al. 2016), it is necessary to think in terms of trade-offs and strike a balance taking into account the underlying institutional dynamics.

Corporate governance in banking represents one of the most controversial topics in financial regulation. Issues tackled by earlier contributions differentiating banks' governance from that of non-financial firms include optimal bank board size and composition (e.g., Adams and Mehran 2003, 2008; Andres and Vallelado 2008), fiduciary duties of bank directors (e.g., Macey and O'Hara 2003), the link between internal control mechanisms and the market for corporate control in banking industry (e.g., Brickley and James 1987), and the role of insider ownership in banks (e.g., Saunders et al. 1990; Lee 2002). As policymaking efforts towards achieving sound corporate governance practices in banking organisations around the world proliferated in recent decades (e.g., Basel Committee 2006), researchers have also directed their attention to understanding how the regulatory setting and banks' governance arrangements interact (e.g., Laeven and Levine 2009; Hagendorff et al. 2010). The global financial crisis in 2007 has led to a surge in interest in bank governance topics, with contributors engaging in a vivid debate as to the prevalence and possible remedies of control failures in banking organisations (e.g., Adams 2012; Mehran et al. 2011; Bebchuk and Spamann 2010). As research currently stands, it is generally accepted that governance failures in banks contributed to the global financial crisis (Hopt 2013), however, the question of how to effectively address the shortcomings of control and risk management processes in these institutions is not yet settled. As a result, regulations in this area are expected to evolve further. In this context, the following paragraphs sketch the costs and benefits of regulation pertaining to banks' corporate governance by reference to the relevant measures taken in the EU legal framework. Concretizing the trade-offs of regulatory intervention with specific attention to bank governance as a subset of financial regulation is essential to lay the groundwork for the analyses in Sect. 2.3.

2.2.1 Controlling Market Failures

As with other elements of financial regulation, market failures that the bank governance regulation seeks to target are information asymmetries and systemic risk as a form of negative externality. By their nature, financial markets are highly complex and intertwined systems and as key financial intermediaries operating therein, banks exhibit a much higher degree of opacity than non-financial firms (Caprio and Levine 2002; Mehran et al. 2011). Moral hazard and adverse selection problems underlie banks' relationships with both their depositors and borrowers and are crucial in shaping party incentives (Heremans and Pacces 2012; Schooner and Taylor 2010). Furthermore, systemic risk element means that through the interconnectedness of the modern financial system, the insolvency and illiquidity risks inherent in banks' business models can transform one bank's failure to a large scale contagion (Freixas et al. 2000; Schooner and Taylor 2010).

Banks' special attributes not only drive the economic rationale for regulation, but they also help explain why corporate governance of banks is treated differently than that of non-financial firms (Caprio and Levine 2002; Mehran et al. 2011; Hopt 2012). As banks are highly leveraged institutions, their shareholder-creditor agency conflicts are particularly pronounced and cannot be fixed through market solutions given the presence of a large depositor base subject to collective action and incentive problems (Levine 2004). In addition, as it became evident during the global financial crisis, the complexity and opaqueness of banks' business bears implications for regulatory strategies used to counter the agency problems between shareholders and managers in non-financial firms (Armour et al. 2016; Mehran et al. 2011).

Given these market failures surrounding banks, a brief look at the bank-relevant major regulatory measures taken in the EU in the aftermath of the financial crisis is helpful to gain an understanding of how the legal system can seek to shape party incentives towards achieving financial market stability. In this regard, especially the Capital Requirements Directive (Directive 2013/36/EU; hereinafter "CRD IV") and the Capital Requirements Regulation (Regulation (EU) No 575/2013), cumulatively referred to as the CRD IV package, deserve mentioning. With an emphasis on board structure and risk management among other aspects of banking regulation, these legal acts reflect the insight that strengthening internal controls is instrumental to having banks internalize the costs of their activities. Stipulations regarding the oversight function of the management bodies, their duties and composition, as well as the procedural and substantive requirements concerning risk management are all measures that the CRD IV has chosen to address the problem of excessive risk-taking by financial institutions. Remuneration provisions of CRD IV similarly reflect the concern of achieving a better alignment between compensation of executives and material risk-takers, and the risk appetite, values and long-term interests and performance of the firm. In addition to these bank-specific measures, general corporate governance provisions also bear implications for agency problems surrounding banks. A relevant development concerns the recent amendments to the Shareholder Rights Directive, whereby the new regime envisages a framework for addressing short-termism in capital markets and to this end provides for certain obligations to banks in their capacity as intermediaries, notably concerning information transmission and facilitation of exercise of shareholder rights (Directive (EU) 2017/828).

2.2.2 *Impact on the Costs of Financial Intermediation*

While corporate governance regulation of banks entails certain benefits, as any other type of regulatory intervention, it also comes with costs. From a general corporate governance perspective, it is well established that a delicate balance exists between managerial accountability and delegation of wide discretionary authority necessary for running a modern business entity (Fama and Jensen 1983; Klein et al. 2010). In the case of banks, the fact that their core business is financial intermediation (Diamond and Dybvig 1983; Diamond and Rajan 2001) adds another dimension to the picture as regards the cost-benefit analysis. In this respect, it is worth noting that the presence of market failures is a necessary but not a sufficient condition for regulation (Armour et al. 2016), which brings out the need to look at the subject of banks' corporate governance also from the perspective of the costs they may impose on these firms and consequently on the larger economy.

Effects of regulation on banks' activities have lately been a topical issue particularly as regards capital requirements, with researchers investigating the link between these norms and bank lending (e.g., Kashyap et al. 2010; Bridges et al. 2014; Dermine 2013). The operation of liquidity creation is essential to bear in mind to understand how various measures aimed to regulate corporate governance in banking might overshoot. Banks earn money through the provision of illiquid loans to borrowers while giving the depositors the ability to withdraw their funds on demand (Diamond and Dybvig 1983). In fulfilling this function, banks incur certain production costs which need to be incorporated in the price of their products or services for a market to exist. In this context, regulations inevitably constrain financial intermediaries because these measures increase their transaction costs (Benston and Smith 1976). Accordingly, regulatory intervention needs to rely on a balance between benefits achieved through fixing market failures, on the one hand, and costs on the market players, on the other. These considerations are at play also as regards the EU regulations mentioned in the previous subsection. For instance, in the context of remuneration provisions of CRD IV, a recent EU Commission Report has called for a need to reassess the application of certain norms to small and non-complex institutions to ensure proportionality (European Commission 2016). In a similar vein, CRD IV's imposition of a cap on the ratio of variable pay to fixed pay has been subject to criticism, most notably on the grounds that this approach could lead to unintended consequences on risk-taking by bank executives and reduce incentives to create value (Murphy 2013), as well as for its likely employment selection effects (Armour et al. 2016). More generally, measures concerning risk management and internal control elements inevitably also impose substantial implementation and compliance costs on banks. The same goes for many of the measures not specifically intended for banks, but which apply to them by virtue of being corporate governance norms targeting a broader set of firms such as the recent legislation on disclosure of non-financial and diversity information (Directive 2014/95/EU).

Overall, the net effect of a given banking governance measure is an empirical question which goes beyond the focus of this study. The aim of this section has instead been to put the insights that have been developed in the literature for financial regulation into perspective as regards the particular topic of corporate governance in banking. The tension underlying the design of corporate governance in banking as shown through the above analyses suggests the need to look deeper into the variables that can have an impact on the cost-benefit analysis. Drawing from this insight, the next section explores selected aspects of banks' interactions with listed non-financial firms with a view to contributing to an improved balance in regulation.

2.3 Banks' Corporate Governance Roles as a New Determinant

Banks do not operate in a vacuum; indeed, their interactions with other economic actors constitute the basis for their existence, which is inline with previous research emphasizing their fundamental role in the real economic activity (Cetorelli 2015). The link between banks and the non-financial sector has for a long time been analyzed from a dichotomous perspective which attributes a corporate governance role to banks as a particularity of bank-based systems (Albert 1993; Hall and Soskice 2001). In this view, strong complementarities exist between banks' roles as financial intermediaries linking surplus units and entrepreneurs, and their close control over industrial firms exercised through organic and financial ties such as equity participations and bank representation on corporate boards (Baums 1992; Schmidt and Tyrell 2005). This is in contrast to the market-based systems where capital markets are considered the key mechanism for allocating external finance to firms. As opposed to a bank-based financial system, in a market-based system control over firms' management is viewed as an external force that operates through the takeover mechanism (Schmidt and Tyrell 2005). While this approach to the operation of financial intermediation provides a useful starting point for evaluating their differences, recent research provides a more complete and realistic picture of the relationships between markets and intermediaries by seeing them as complementary rather than two distinct alternatives (Allen and Gale 2000; Levine 2002). This view stands in alignment with the insights of the rich modern financial intermediation literature that explores how banks and other intermediaries help overcome frictions and make markets work (Greenbaum and Thakor 2007; Tirole 2006).

Parallel to these developments in the understanding of banks' place in modern financial markets, corporate governance theory has also recently evolved to incorporate the complexities in the way listed firms around the world are owned and controlled into its framework. Comparative studies have come to acknowledge that the move towards the U.S. outsider model of corporate governance does not imply full convergence and that jurisdictional differences might still exist in the way they address similar problems (Kraakman et al. 2017). Based on the current understanding, Germany, earlier a paradigmatic example of a bank-based insider control system, has recently moved towards an outsider system, whereby ownership concentration started diffusing and banks have moved away from their traditional roles (Ringe 2015). On the other side of the Atlantic, commentators have noted the emergence of a new set of agency costs in the U.S. firms driven by the reconcentration of ownership in the hands of investment intermediaries (Gilson and Gordon 2013). Last but not least, the trend of divergence despite convergence is even more emphasized in the case of developing and emerging countries' corporate ownership and control dynamics (Pargendler 2015). As another related point, the modern corporate governance literature deals with a much broader palette of issues than its original central focus on the conflicts of interest between managers and shareholders. Indeed, topical issues extend from investor protection under different ownership structures (Gilson 2006) to stakeholder interests (Jensen 2001), as well as the role of gatekeepers such as auditors and financial analysts (Coffee 2006; Leyens 2011).

Taken together, these developments in the understanding of corporate governance and financial intermediation open up a new avenue of looking into banks' interactions with non-financial listed firms. This new approach would evidently differ from the traditional narrative of banks' corporate governance roles while also taking account of the fact that banks still remain in the picture and can shape the agency costs of listed non-financial firms through other channels and to different degrees. Based on this insight, this section aims at providing a basis, by way of selected examples, for the modern understanding of banks' interactions with listed firms as a determinant of corporate governance in banking.

2.3.1 *Setting the Stage: Agency Theory in Corporate Governance*

Information advantages of banks vis-à-vis other economic actors provide the rationale for using agency theory as a yardstick for assessing the economic implications of their interactions with listed non-financial firms. Complex regulatory issues surrounding modern listed firms have led to an expansion of the earlier focus on the Berle and Means type of separation of ownership and control (Berle and Means 1933), with current corporate governance scholarship applying the agency framework to a wider range of relationships. As such, instances of opportunism covered in the debate deal not only with the tension between managers and shareholders, but the intra-shareholder principal-agent problems and conflicts between shareholders and other stakeholders are also increasingly present in the analyses (Schleifer and Vishny 1997; Kraakman et al. 2017). Incorporation of diverse interests in the corporate agency cost framework allows for capturing the differences in ownership structures, and also for effectively accommodating the possible divergences in seemingly similar systems. From this perspective, the recent tendency of diffusion of ownership in Continental European firms parallels the regulatory developments seeking to address managerial agency costs, whereas path dependent divergences (e.g., Bebchuk and Roe 1999; Claessens and Yurtoglu 2013) justify the continued need to take a broad perspective to governance issues surrounding modern corporations.

Inline with the stand of the debate, multiple sources of opportunism and differences in ownership structures of listed firms across the world are relevant variables also when approaching the issue of banks' corporate governance roles. From this perspective, examining banks' interactions with listed non-financial firms in modern financial markets by reference to the principal-agent framework is essential to a systematic understanding of the benefits and costs of bank influence over firms. Accordingly, in analyzing banks' interactions with firms across different dimensions, the following paragraphs will take account of agency issues in both dispersed and concentrated ownership contexts. Furthermore, reflecting yet another learning point from the recent expansion of corporate governance themes in scholarship (e.g., Kraakman et al. 2017), this section considers banks' interactions with non-financial firms by reference to different stages in their life cycle, specifically the ordinary course of business, fundamental transactions, and bankruptcy.

2.3.2 Selected Cases of Banks' Corporate Governance Roles

2.3.2.1 Lender Governance in the Ordinary Course of Business

The relevance of bank credit for non-financial firms is particularly evident for companies operating in environments with a low level of stock market development. In addition, recent studies have underscored the importance of bank lending as an external financing source also for listed firms in dispersed ownership contexts (e.g., Shepherd et al. 2008; Nini et al. 2009). Keeping in mind this variety in institutional settings is essential to an understanding of the explanatory power of the relatively young lender governance literature with respect to banks' corporate governance roles.

A large body of literature has addressed the conflict between equity and debt claims from a corporate finance perspective and its impact on contractual arrangements (e.g., Jensen and Meckling 1976; Smith and Warner 1979). Furthermore, the free cash flow hypothesis already attributes a corporate governance role to banks through the disciplinary impact of debt on managers, thereby helping alleviate the manager-shareholder agency conflicts (Jensen 1986). Banks, along with other creditors, also enter the equation when a firm enters the vicinity of insolvency; many jurisdictions indeed envisage a regime for shift in directors' duties as well as surrender of control rights in some cases (Skeel 2004).

Differently from these earlier approaches to understanding the balance of powers within a corporation with regard to the creditors' role, recent studies, with their focus on the concept of lender governance (Shepherd et al. 2008; Tung 2009; Triantis and Daniels 1995), provide a more enriched way of assessing the agency cost implications of banks' interactions with non-financial firms. At the core of this narrative lies the empirical finding that monitoring by banks as creditors improves firm value, especially in the presence of high agency costs (Shepherd et al. 2008). This is explained by reference to the mechanics of bank monitoring which involves intense information exchange and control over financial and operational aspects of the borrower firm's affairs through covenants (Shepherd et al. 2008; Tung 2009). In this context, representation of bankers on non-financial firms' boards is viewed as another avenue for lender monitoring, which has the potential to mitigate agency costs of borrower firms' shareholders (Tung 2009; Sisli-Ciamarra 2012). A complementary explanation for banks' potential benefits to borrower firms' shareholders is found in the information asymmetry theory, which implies an impact on agency costs through the market mechanism. This theory lies at the basis of a number of earlier empirical studies showing positive abnormal stock returns for borrower firms triggered by bank loan announcements (Billett et al. 1995; Best and Zhang 1993).

Monitoring and information intermediation functions of banks in their capacity as lenders as envisaged by the lender governance literature has applications for both dispersed and concentrated ownership settings. For firms with dispersed ownership, empirical findings suggest a divergence from the standard account of pervasive conflicts of interest between debt and equity (Jensen and Meckling 1976), suggesting the existence of a shared interest, at least to a certain degree, between shareholders and creditors in controlling managerial shirking (Shepherd et al. 2008). For concentrated ownership jurisdictions, one can adapt this narrative to envisage a value enhancement due to creditor bank's disciplining function over controlling shareholders (Perera 2011). These propositions, however, have to be taken with caution, for there is also a possibility that banks might exhibit conflicts of interest, thereby reducing the value for shareholders of the firms they interact with. A major challenge in this regard for concentrated ownership jurisdictions appears to be ensuring the independence of creditor banks from the controlling owners as a first condition for the bank to act as an agent to minority shareholders. Similarly, in dispersed ownership jurisdictions, the value from creditor banks' monitoring and information intermediation function is conditioned on their being independent of the borrower firms' management. Overall, as these examples reveal, banks' lender governance role promises positive effects for borrower firms and their investors through its impact on corporate agency costs on an ongoing basis, but these benefits have to be evaluated against the risk of conflicts of interest. The latter consideration, in turn, points to the close linkage between legal norms, including financial regulation pertaining to banks, and the role of banks for corporate governance of non-financial firms.

2.3.2.2 Fairness Opinions in Control Transactions

Control transactions such as corporate mergers or takeovers present particular challenges for corporate governance as they fundamentally alter the balance of power among corporate actors (Kraakman et al. 2017). In order to mitigate the risk that managers might pursue entrenchment objectives or benefit themselves at the expense of shareholders, obtaining fairness opinions from investment bankers is a settled practice reinforced also through the legal system in many countries (Bebchuk and Kahan 1989). From an agency theory perspective, this strategy brings in the banks as trustees vis-à-vis the shareholders of the merging or target firms, providing these actors with valuable information as to the merits of the offer (Kraakman et al. 2017). The concrete value from this improvement in information situation of principals is then expected to be materialized in their voting outcomes as to the transaction in question.

Given the apparent association between takeover mechanism and dispersed ownership, banks' impact on corporate governance as suppliers of fairness opinions operates largely through the market mechanism. At this point, incorporating the opposite side of the coin into the analysis and considering the potential for conflicted advice on the part of the banks reveals further implications for agency costs of shareholders. Despite its potential benefits, banks' advisory role in providing fairness opinions is also a matter of high controversy. Criticisms in this regard relate particularly to the concern that the repeated game setting underlying banks' interactions with senior management might alter bankers' incentives. The discretionary element inherent in the definition and estimation of a fair price is also thought to aggravate this problem (Bebchuk and Kahan 1989).

In addition to the importance of bankers' fairness opinions for an informed shareholder voting process, another important channel through which this mechanism can influence corporate agency costs can be contemplated by reference to the value of information for the capital markets in general. Given the explained controversy around fairness opinions, banks' reputation in this regard is crucial to the shareholders' beliefs about the credibility of their advice. If the shareholders are to discount an honest fairness opinion based on their wrongful belief that it is biased, this would cause distortions in stock market efficiency, possibly leading to a partial market failure as in Akerlof's framework of market for used cars (Akerlof 1970).

While not being as common as in dispersed ownership, takeovers can take place also in concentrated ownership settings. Accordingly, corporate governance implications of banks' interactions with non-financial firms' shareholders in the context of fairness opinions could materialize on a wider scale than they appear at the first sight. An additional consideration in this respect stems from the insight that control transactions in concentrated ownership jurisdictions might be serving a side function of helping ownership diffusion. From this perspective, through their explained role in control transactions, banks have the potential to shape agency costs in non-financial firms in internal as well as in external governance sense.

2.3.2.3 Bank Intervention in the Distress Context

A third example of how banks can shape agency costs in non-financial firms in a way relevant for banking governance pertains to the distress context. As previously mentioned, bank involvement when a borrower approaches insolvency has long been recognized in the literature as a conventional case of bank control over firms (Skeel 2004). The rationale for this intervention stems from the divergences of risk preferences between equity holders as residual claimants and debtholders which intensify as the firm's financial situation deteriorates (Jensen and Meckling 1976).

In addition to triggering a control change from the managers to the creditors or their representatives (Skeel 2004), financial distress is considered to ex ante shape the incentives of borrower firms in another more subtle way. This channel of influence takes its basis from the disciplinary effect of sophisticated loan covenants which give banks the power to effectuate changes in the business organization of debtors, amounting even to a change of senior management, in the event of a default (Baird and Rasmussen 2006). Default does albeit not necessitate distress; however, bank control already at this early stage of financial difficulties can strongly predetermine the dynamics of bank intervention that might follow in a later distress situation.

As in previous case studies, the virtues of bank control in the distress context have to be weighed against the particular challenges it bears for agency costs of non-financial firms in different settings. From this perspective, benefits are more readily visible for concentrated ownership settings where bank control in case of distress could provide a shield for minority shareholders from the controlling owner's opportunism, possibly helping reorganize the business in a more efficient way. Parallel insights apply to the situation of other smaller creditors, who could benefit from the bank's negotiation power, thereby resulting in an alleviation of the agency conflicts between themselves and the controlling owner. The countervailing challenge in both of these cases is ensuring control over possible opportunism on the part of the intervening bank. In contrast, in a dispersed ownership setting, any possible positive effects are largely a function of the degree of incentive alignment between managers and shareholders (Kraakman et al. 2017). As the shareholders usually have more effective mechanisms at their disposal, it might be that banks' possible conflicts in intervening with a distressed borrower might outweigh any benefits. However, this proposition needs in turn to be assessed against the risk that too many restrictions on bank intervention in distress context might have a chilling effect on bank lending, thereby implying reduced benefits from lender governance analysed above as the first case study.

2.4 Conclusion

From a welfare economics standpoint, banking regulation, including corporate governance in banking, involves a delicate balance between addressing market failures arising out of banks' operations while avoiding inefficient restraints on the operation of market forces. This chapter has analyzed selected aspects of banks' interactions with non-financial listed firms as a variable affecting the trade-off of banking governance regulation. As the analysis shows, banks can come into play as corporate governance actors across different scenarios comprising of variations in ownership structures and firm life cycles. Inline with the modern understanding of financial intermediation which sees banks and markets as complementary institutions (Allen and Gale 2000), the findings of this chapter indicate that interactions between banks and non-financial listed firms can have agency cost implications for the latter also through the market mechanism. The approach pursued in this chapter allows for placing banks' influence on non-financial firms in a broader context than the prior research which assigns corporate governance roles to banks as an attribute of bank-based systems (e.g., Baums 1992; Schmidt and Tyrell 2005). Accordingly, the linkages taken as examples in the previous section can find application along a spectrum of institutional settings and are relevant in thinking about regulatory reform also in market-based contexts.

Within the vast interdisciplinary banking regulation literature, consideration of factors influencing the regulatory framework represents a relatively recent trend (Tung 2009; Sum 2016; Konoe 2014). Furthermore, in the debates on the impact of regulations on banks' liquidity provision function (e.g., Kashyap et al. 2010; Bridges et al. 2014; Dermine 2013; Sum 2016), elements of banking governance have so far not been treated separately. Against this background, the contributions of this study are twofold. As regards the latter point, this chapter provides insights into the trade-offs involving corporate governance regulation in banking as a subset of the larger banking regulation framework. Another novelty of the present study concerns its detailed treatment of banks' interactions with non-financial listed firms as a determinant of corporate governance regulation in banking. As shown through selected examples, banks can benefit or harm the corporate governance of non-financial firms they interact with, and because their overall net impact is a function of particular institutional factors, banks will inevitably vary in terms of their utility as corporate governance actors. From a policy perspective, it would be worthwhile to consider this dimension when the regulators are trying to strike a balance between the trade-offs underlying corporate governance regulation in banking. To this end, the current chapter has provided a theoretical basis which can hopefully inspire future empirical research seeking to better understand the incentive effects of banking regulation given the constraints of banks' interactions with other market actors.

Acknowledgments I would like to thank Prof. Dr. Patrick C. Leyens for initial discussions. I also thank the anonymous referee for helpful comments on an earlier version of this chapter.

References

Adams, R. B. (2012). Governance and the financial crisis. *International Review of Finance, 12*(1), 7–38.

Adams, R., & Mehran, H. (2003). Is corporate governance different for bank holding companies? *Federal Reserve Bank of New York Economic Policy Review, 9*(1), 123–142.

Adams, R. B. & Mehran, H. (2008). *Corporate performance, board structure and its determinants in the banking industry*, Staff Report No. 330, Federal Reserve Bank of New York Staff Reports.

Akerlof, G. A. (1970). The market for "Lemons": Quality uncertainty and the market mechanism. *The Quarterly Journal of Economics, 84*(3), 488–500.

Albert, M. (1993). *Capitalism against capitalism*. London: Whurr.

Allen, F., & Gale, D. (2000). *Comparing financial systems*. Cambridge, MA: MIT Press.

Andres, A., & Vallelado, P. (2008). Corporate governance in banking: The role of the board of directors. *Journal of Banking & Finance, 32*(12), 2570–2580.

Aoki, M., & Patrick, H. (1995). *The Japanese main bank system: Its relevance for developing and transforming economies*. Oxford: Oxford University Press.

Armour, J., Awrey, D., Davies, P. L., Enriques, L., Gordon, J. N., Mayer, C. P., & Payne, J. (2016). *Principles of financial regulation*. Oxford: Oxford University Press.

Baird, D. G., & Rasmussen, R. K. (2006). Private debt and the missing lever of corporate governance. *University of Pennsylvania Law Review, 154*(5), 1209–1252.

Basel Committee on Banking Supervision. (2006). *Enhancing corporate governance for banking organisations*.

Baums, T. (1992). Corporate governance in Germany: The role of the banks. *The American Journal of Comparative Law, 40*(2), 503–526.

Bebchuk, L. A., & Kahan, M. (1989). Fairness opinions: How fair are they and what can be done about it? *Duke Law Journal, 27*(1), 27–53.

Bebchuk, L. A., & Roe, M. J. (1999). A theory of path dependence in corporate ownership and governance. *Stanford Law Review, 52*(1), 127–170.

Bebchuk, L. A., & Spamann, H. (2010). Regulating bankers' pay. *Georgetown Law Journal, 98*(2), 247–287.

Benston, G., & Smith, C. (1976). A transactions cost approach to the theory of financial intermediation. *The Journal of Finance, 31*(2), 215–231.

Berle, A. A., & Means, G. C. (1933). *The modern corporation and private property*. New York: Macmillan.

Best, R., & Zhang, H. (1993). Alternative information sources and the information content of bank loans. *The Journal of Finance, 48*(4), 1507–1522.

Billett, M. T., Flannery, M. J., & Garfinkel, J. A. (1995). The effect of lender identity on a borrowing firm's equity return. *The Journal of Finance, 50*(2), 699–718.

Boot, A. W. A. (2000). Relationship banking: What do we know? *Journal of Financial Intermediation, 9*(1), 7–25.

Brickley, J., & James, C. (1987). The takeover market, corporate board composition, and ownership structure: The case of banking. *The Journal of Law & Economics, 30*(1), 161–180.

Bridges, J., Gregory, D., Nielsen, M., Pezzini, S., Radia, A., & Spaltro, M. (2014). *The impact of capital requirements on bank lending*. London: Bank of England.

Brunnermeier, M. K., Crockett, A., Goodhart, C., Persaud, A. & Shin, H. S. (2009). *The fundamental principles of financial regulation*. Centre for Economic Policy Research.

Caprio, G., & Levine, R. (2002). Corporate governance in finance: Concepts and international observations. In R. E. Litan et al. (Eds.), *Financial sector governance: The roles of the public and private sectors*. Washington, DC: Brookings Institution Press.

Cetorelli, N. (2015). Banking and real economic activity. In A. N. Berger et al. (Eds.), *Oxford handbook of banking*. Oxford: Oxford University Press.

Claessens, S., & Yurtoglu, B. B. (2013). Corporate governance in emerging markets: A survey. *Emerging Markets Review, 15*, 1–33.

Coffee, J. C. (2006). *Gatekeepers: The professions and corporate governance*. New York: Oxford University Press.

Dermine, J. (2013). Bank regulations after the global financial crisis: Good intentions and unintended evil. *European Financial Management, 19*(4), 658–674.

Diamond, D. W. (1984). Financial intermediation and delegated monitoring. *The Review of Economic Studies, 51*(3), 393–414.

Diamond, D. W., & Dybvig, P. H. (1983). Bank runs, deposit insurance, and liquidity. *Journal of Political Economy, 91*(3), 401–419.

Diamond, D. W., & Rajan, R. G. (2001). Liquidity risk, liquidity creation, and financial fragility: A theory of banking. *Journal of Political Economy, 109*(2), 287–327.

Directive 2013/36/EU of the European Parliament and of the Council of 26 June 2013 on access to the activity of credit institutions and the prudential supervision of credit institutions and

investment firms, amending Directive 2002/87/EC and repealing Directives 2006/48/EC and 2006/49/EC.
Directive 2014/95/EU of the European Parliament and of the Council of 22 October 2014 amending Directive 2013/34/EU as regards disclosure of non-financial and diversity information by certain large undertakings and groups.
Directive (EU) 2017/828 of the European Parliament and of the Council of 17 May 2017 amending Directive 2007/36/EC as regards the encouragement of long-term shareholder engagement.
Dodd, R. (2002). *The economic rationale for financial market regulation*, Special Policy Report 12. Washington, DC: Financial Policy Forum, Derivatives Study Center.
European Commission. (2016). *Assessment of the remuneration rules under Directive 2013/36/EU and Regulation (EU) No 575/2013*. Luxembourg: Publications Office of the European Union.
Fama, E. F., & Jensen, M. C. (1983). Separation of ownership and control. *The Journal of Law and Economics, 26*(2), 301–325.
Freixas, X., Parigi, B. M., & Rochet, J. C. (2000). Systemic risk, interbank relations, and liquidity provision by the central bank. *Journal of Money, Credit and Banking, 32*(3), 611–638.
Gilson, R. J. (2006). Controlling shareholders and corporate governance: Complicating the comparative taxonomy. *Harvard Law Review, 119*(6), 1641–1679.
Gilson, R. J., & Gordon, J. N. (2013). The agency costs of agency capitalism: Activist investors and the revaluation of governance rights. *Columbia Law Review, 113*(4), 863–928.
Greenbaum, S. I., & Thakor, A. V. (2007). *Contemporary financial intermediation*. Amsterdam: Elsevier Academic Press.
Hall, P. A., & Soskice, D. W. (2001). *Varieties of capitalism: The institutional foundations of comparative advantage*. Oxford: Oxford University Press.
Hagendorff, J., Collins, M., & Keasey, K. (2010). Board monitoring, regulation, and performance in the banking industry: Evidence from the market for corporate control. *Corporate Governance: An International Review, 18*, 381–395.
Heremans, D., & Pacces, A. M. (2012). Regulation of banking and financial markets. In R. J. van den Beergh & A. M. Pacces (Eds.), *Regulation and economics*. Cheltenham: Edward Elgar.
Hopt, K. J. (2012). Corporate governance of banks after the financial crisis. In E. Wymeersch et al. (Eds.), *Financial regulation and supervision: A post-crisis analysis*. Oxford, UK: Oxford University Press.
Hopt, K. J. (2013). Corporate governance of banks and other financial institutions after the financial crisis. *Journal of Corporate Law Studies, 13*(2), 219–253.
Jensen, M. C. (1986). Agency costs of free cash flow, corporate finance, and takeovers. *The American Economic Review, 76*(2), 323–329.
Jensen, M. C. (2001). Value maximization, stakeholder theory, and the corporate objective function. *Journal of Applied Corporate Finance, 14*(3), 8–21.
Jensen, M. C., & Meckling, W. H. (1976). Theory of the firm: Managerial behavior, agency costs and ownership structure. *Journal of Financial Economics, 3*(4), 305–360.
Kashyap, A. K., Stein J. C., & Hanson, S. (2010). An analysis of the impact of "substantially heightened" capital requirements on large financial institutions, Mimeo.
Klein, W. A., Coffee, J. C., & Partnoy, F. (2010). *Business organization and finance: Legal and economic principles*. New York: Thomson Reuters/Foundation Press.
Konoe, S. (2014). *The politics of financial markets and regulation: The United States, Japan, and Germany*. Basingstoke: Palgrave Macmillan.
Kraakman, R., Armour, J., Davies, P., Enriques, L., Hansmann, H. B., Hertig, G., et al. (2017). *The anatomy of corporate law: A comparative and functional approach*. Oxford: Oxford University Press.
Laeven, L., & Levine, R. (2009). Bank governance, regulation and risk taking. *Journal of Financial Economics, 93*(2), 259–275.
Lee, S. W. (2002). Insider ownership and risk–taking behaviour at bank holding companies. *Journal of Business Finance & Accounting, 29*(7), 989–1005.

Levine, R. (2002). *Bank-based or market-based financial systems: Which is better?* Cambridge, MA: National Bureau of Economic Research.
Levine, R. (2004). *The corporate governance of banks: A concise discussion of concepts and evidence*, World Bank Policy Research Working Paper.
Leyens, P. C. (2011). Intermediary independence: Auditors, financial analysts and rating agencies. *Journal of Corporate Law Studies, 11*, 33–66.
Macey, J. R., & O'Hara, M. (2003). The corporate governance of banks. *Federal Reserve Bank of New York Economic Policy Review, 9*(1), 91–107.
Mehran, H., Morrison, A., & Shapiro, J. (2011). *Corporate governance and banks: What have we learned from the financial crisis?* New York, NY: Federal Reserve Bank of New York.
Murphy, K. J. (2013). Regulating banking bonuses in the European Union: A case study in unintended consequences. *European Financial Management, 19*(4), 631–657.
Nini, G., Smith, D. C., & Sufi, A. (2009). Creditor control rights and firm investment policy. *Journal of Financial Economics, 92*(3), 400–420.
Pargendler, M. (2015). Corporate governance in emerging markets. In J. Gordon et al. (Eds.), *The Oxford handbook of corporate law and governance*. Oxford: Oxford University Press.
Perera, S. (2011). *Corporate ownership and control: Corporate governance and economic development in Sri Lanka*. Hackensack, NJ: World Scientific Publication.
Porter, M. E. (1992). Capital disadvantage: America's failing capital investment system. *Harvard Business Review, 70*(5), 65–82.
Regulation (EU) No 575/2013 of the European Parliament and of the Council of 26 June 2013 on prudential requirements for credit institutions and investment firms and amending Regulation (EU) No 648/2012.
Ringe, W.-G. (2015). Changing law and ownership patterns in Germany: Corporate governance and the erosion of Deutschland AG. *American Journal of Comparative Law, 63*(2), 493–538.
Saunders, A., Strock, E., & Travlos, N. G. (1990). Ownership structure, deregulation, and bank risk taking. *Journal of Finance, 45*(2), 643–654.
Schmidt, R. H., & Tyrell, M. (2005). Information theory and the role of intermediaries in corporate governance. In K. J. Hopt et al. (Eds.), *Corporate governance in context: Corporations, states and markets in Europe, Japan and the US*. Oxford: Oxford University Press.
Schooner, H. M., & Taylor, M. (2010). *Global bank regulation: Principles and policies*. London: Academic.
Shepherd, J. M., Tung, F., & Yoon, A. H. (2008). What else matters for corporate governance? The case of bank monitoring. *Boston University Law Review, 88*(4), 991–1042.
Shleifer, A., & Vishny, R. W. (1997). A survey of corporate governance. *The Journal of Finance, 52*(2), 737–783.
Sisli-Ciamarra, E. (2012). Monitoring by affiliated bankers on board of directors: Evidence from corporate financing outcomes. *Financial Management, 41*(3), 665–702.
Skeel, D. A. (2004). Corporate anatomy lessons. *Yale Law Journal, 113*(7), 1519–1578.
Smith, C. W., & Warner, J. B. (1979). On financial contracting: An analysis of bond covenants. *Journal of Financial Economics, 7*(2), 117–161.
Spong, K. (2000). *Banking regulation: Its purposes, implementation, and effects*. Federal Reserve Bank of Kansas City.
Stiglitz, J. (2008). *Government failure vs. market failure: Principles of regulation*. New York: Columbia University Academic Commons.
Sum, K. (2016). *Post-crisis banking regulation in the European Union: Opportunities and threats*. Cham: Springer International Publishing.
Tirole, J. (2006). *The theory of corporate finance*. Princeton, NJ: Princeton University Press.
Triantis, G. G., & Daniels, R. J. (1995). The role of debt in interactive corporate governance. *California Law Review, 83*(4), 1073–1114.
Tung, F. (2009). Leverage in the board room: The unsung influence of private lenders in corporate governance. *UCLA Law Review, 57*(1), 115–182.

[illegible]

[illegible] National Bureau of Economic Research.

[illegible] World Bank Policy Research Working Paper.

[illegible] Journal of [illegible]

[illegible]

[illegible] New York [illegible]

[illegible] Journal of Management [illegible]

[illegible]

[illegible]

[illegible]

[illegible] Harvard Business Review [illegible]

[illegible]

[illegible]

[illegible]

[illegible] Oxford University Press.

[illegible]

[illegible]

[illegible]

[illegible]

[illegible]

[illegible] Journal of Financial Economics [illegible]

[illegible]

[illegible] University Press [illegible]

[illegible]

[illegible]

[illegible]

[illegible]

Chapter 3
Is Corporate Governance Different in Financial Firms than in Non-Financial Firms? Evidence for the Pre- and Post-Crisis Period in Europe

Belén Díaz Díaz, Rebeca García-Ramos, and Elisa Baraibar Díez

3.1 Introduction

Banks' corporate governance has been severely criticised for its role in the last financial crisis (De Haan and Vlahu 2016). The weak governance of banks did not serve its purpose of safeguarding against excessive risk taking by a number of financial services companies and the failure of boards, mainly in large financial institutions, to manage risks properly has been viewed as contributing to the crisis (Mongiardino and Plath 2010). Moreover, regulatory requirements proved insufficient in some areas (Kirkpatrick 2009) and consequently, since 2008 several legal reforms have enacted new corporate governance codes to strengthen governance (Tihanyi et al. 2014).

Until the financial crisis, national governance systems in Europe were dominated by informal institutions, in which voluntary compliance with codes of conduct dominated governance activities (Díaz Díaz et al. 2017). Most of the recommendations in governance codes placed great emphasis on formal board structures and board characteristics, such as size, the number of independent directors, the number of board meetings, board committees, etc. The disclosure of these structural elements enabled market participants to evaluate whether boards of directors were complying with the corporate governance recommendations. However, as recent

B. Díaz Díaz (✉) • R. García-Ramos
Departamento de Administración de Empresas, Universidad de Cantabria, Santander, Spain

Santander Financial Institute (SANFI), Santander, Spain
e-mail: belen.diaz@unican.es; garciarr@unican.es

E. Baraibar Díez
Departamento de Administración de Empresas, Universidad de Cantabria, Santander, Spain
e-mail: elisa.baraibar@unican.es

B. Díaz Díaz et al. (eds.), *Corporate Governance in Banking and Investor Protection*, CSR, Sustainability, Ethics & Governance,
https://doi.org/10.1007/978-3-319-70007-6_3

corporate failures have shown, complying with "formal" standards is not enough (Van den Berghe and Levrau 2004).

Corporate scandals during the crisis period raised serious doubts about the effectiveness of such corporate governance policies, and therefore, codes of conduct for banks were introduced in several countries as well as hard law regulation of corporate governance.

In this economic environment, this paper will analyse the differences in corporate governance practices in financial and non-financial firms, pre- and post-crisis, as well as the differences in these practices between European countries. This research focuses on four of the largest economies in Europe (Germany, the United Kingdom, France and Spain) in order to draw conclusions about significant differences in corporate governance practices between them. Our research will be valuable for policy makers, practitioners and researchers in the field of corporate governance, because it will help to answer the following relevant questions: are there systematic differences in the governance structures between financial and non-financial firms? Is the governance structure of financial firms prior to the crisis a reason to justify why banks' governance has been blamed for the crisis? Is it necessary for governance reforms to take into account industry or country differences? In order to evaluate reforms of the governance structure of financial firms, it is important to understand current governance practices, as well as how governance differs between financial and non-financial firms.

This paper is structured as follows: Sect. 3.2 reviews governance codes and governance regulation for banks. Section 3.3 describes the sample, corporate governance variables, and the methodology for the empirical analysis. Section 3.4 shows the main results obtained when comparing financial and non- financial firms' governance policies during the pre- and post-crisis periods in different countries. Finally, Sect. 3.5 summarises our main conclusions.

3.2 Literature Review: Governance Codes and Governance Regulation for Banks

The crisis showed the need to reform some aspects in governance codes and illustrated the need for reforms concerning governance codes specifically aimed at banks. Although in 1999 there was already an international code for banks, "Enhancing Corporate Governance for Banking Organisations" proposed by the Basel Committee on Banking Supervision, it was not until the crisis that governance codes for banks appeared in different countries, both in Europe and in non-European countries (Table 3.1).

The European Commission also developed specific regulations to guarantee banks' governance quality, focusing on two main issues: remuneration and shareholder rights. With regards to remuneration, *Directive 2010/76/EU* requires credit institution and investment firm remuneration policies to consider present and future

Table 3.1 Corporate governance codes for banks

Country	Governance code for banks
International	Enhancing Corporate Governance for Banking Organisations (1999)
EUROPE	
Ireland	Corporate Governance Code for Credit Institutions and Insurance Undertakings (2013, 2010)
Italy	New Regulation on Banks' Organisation and Corporate Governance (2008)
The Netherlands	Banking Code (2009)
United Kingdom	A review of corporate governance in UK banks and other financial industry entities: Final recommendations (The Walker Review) (2009)
NON-EUROPEAN COUNTRIES	
Jordan	Corporate Governance Code for Banks in Jordan (2007)
Nigeria	Code of Corporate Governance for Banks and Discount Houses in Nigeria, and Guidelines for Whistle Blowing in the Nigerian Banking Industry (2014) Code of Corporate Governance for Banks in Nigeria Post Consolidation (2006)
Qatar	Corporate Governance Guidelines for Banks and Financial Institutions (2008)
Singapore	Guidelines on Corporate Governance for Banks, Financial Holding Companies and Direct Insurers which are incorporated in Singapore (2010)
Yemen	Corporate Governance Code for the Banking Sector (2013)

Source: ECGI

risks and to define categories of staff whose professional activities have a material impact on their risk profile (Ben Shlomo et al. 2013). Not only focusing on banks but on listed companies, *Directive 2007/36/EC* aims to strengthen shareholder rights, in particular through the extension of rules on transparency, proxy voting rights, the possibility of participating in general meetings electronically, and ensuring that cross-border voting rights can be exercised.

Moreover, at a national level, European countries also developed regulations with the aim of improving the governance of banks. For example, the Spanish Government approved a Code of Good Practices (Royal Decree-Law 6/2012)[1] which credit institutions and other entities that, professionally, perform the activity of granting loans or mortgage loans can voluntarily comply with.

However, do financial firms deserve specific treatment in governance codes and in governance regulation?

As De Haan and Vlahu (2016, p. 230) pointed out, financial firms are different from non-financial firms for two main reasons: "First, the failure of financial firms may have more serious consequences because of their unique position in financial intermediation and the payment system. Thus, excessive risk taking by banks can create significant negative externalities and systemic risk, which is one of the reasons that the financial sector is more heavily regulated than non-financial sectors (Flannery 1998). Second, banks rely on depositors for their funding, but they do not

[1]After the passing of this Royal Decree-Law, it has been modified several times: Law 1/2013 of 14 May 2013, Law 8/2013 of 26 de June and Royal Decree-Law 1/2015 of 27 February.

have incentives enough to monitor bank managers, due to high information asymmetry and coordination costs (Demirgüç-Kunt and Detragiache 2002). Depositors are therefore generally protected by some deposit–insurance system, but this provides the intermediary with an even stronger incentive for risky behavior (Merton 1977)".

These differences mean that the governance of banking firms becomes especially important for the economy as a whole and that the banking governance structure may be different from that of unregulated, non-financial firms. For instance, constraints on hostile acquisitions in the banking industry can potentially increase the size of their boards, because the resulting board after the success of a hostile takeover would be a combination of both entities (Adams and Mehran 2003). With regards to executive compensation, stock-based compensation motivates managers to undertake value-enhancing decisions but also affects risk taking. To protect non-shareholding stakeholders in banking, such as depositors, banks are expected to have less stock-based compensation packages.

However, the finding of such differences becomes an empirical issue. Adams (2012) documents that the governance of U.S. financial firms is not obviously worse than in non-financial firms, based on a large sample of data of non-financial and financial firms for the period 1996–2007. The author uses simple governance scores and governance indices that focus on eight characteristics (board size, independence, number of directorships, fraction of directors with attendance problems at board meetings, fraction of female directors, total CEO compensation, fraction equity-based pay for the CEO, and director compensation) to conclude that banks and non-bank financial firms generally appear to be better governed than non-financial firms. Similarly, Beltratti and Stultz (2012) and Erkens et al. (2012) found no evidence that better governance of financial firms led to improved performance during the crisis.

3.3 Sample, Variables and Methodology

3.3.1 Sample

The empirical analysis considers a sample of 204 firms that belong to Europe's three largest economies, plus Spain (which is in fifth place, based on its GDP). The firms belong to the stock market indexes of Spain (IBEX 35), France (DAX), Germany (CAC-40) and the United Kingdom (FTSE-100).

Table 3.2 presents the number of financial and non-financial firms in the sample in each country.

Table 3.2 Number of firms in the sample

	Full sample	Spain	France	Germany	UK
Non-financial firms	160	25	35	25	75
Financial firms	44	9	5	5	25
Total	204	34	40	30	100

3.3.2 *Variables*

Corporate governance variables were obtained from the *Datastream* database. After the analysis of the 287 variables provided by *Datastream*, 33 governance variables were selected. They were divided in 6 main groups according to the main governance policy they represent.

Following Díaz Díaz et al. (2017), the following categories were established: (1) Board structure/Functioning, (2) Committees, (3) Compensation Policy, (4) Anti-takeover devices, (5) Shareholder rights, (6) Corporate Social Responsibility.

Appendix describes all the variables used.

3.3.3 *Methodology*

Different tests were performed to gauge differences in governance variables between financial and non-financial firms, between countries and between periods of time (pre- and post-crisis). Based on Aizenman et al. (2016) and Taylor and Williams (2009) we define the beginning of the global crisis as in mid-2007. Therefore, 2007 will be considered the pre-crisis year, and 2013 the post-crisis period.

The Mann Whitney U test is performed to statistically analyse the difference in corporate governance variables between financial and non-financial firms and the Kruskal-Wallis test is used to analyse differences across countries. Both tests are used when governance variables are continuous. These tests are appropriate when the variable in one of the groups is not normally distributed. The Kolmogorov-Smirnov test and Shapiro-Wilk test (appropriate for small sample sizes: the sample of financial firms in all countries is below 50) were conducted to test normality.

The ANOVA test will be used when the governance variables are continuous and normally distributed and there is homogeneity of variances (gauged by Levene's test).

When the governance variable is dichotomous (categorical), a chi-square test and the Fisher's Exact test are used for small samples.

In addition, a paired t-test is conducted to analyse the difference in continuous governance variables pre- and post-crisis (same sample in two different periods of time). In those cases where the governance variable is dichotomous, the McNemar test is conducted.

3.4 Corporate Governance Structure in Financial and Non-Financial Firms in Europe

3.4.1 *Board Structure/Functioning*

The board of directors' composition and structure remain at the centre of policy debates and different countries have developed legal and institutional frameworks to improve board efficiency in its role of monitoring management and therefore improving firms' performance (Kumar and Zattoni 2014).

3.4.1.1 Board Size

To guarantee optimal board performance, its size should be adequate to meet business requirements, but not so large as to be unwieldy. When considering the full sample, boards had a mean size of 13 members with very few differences before and after the crisis and between financial and non-financial firms (Table 3.3, panel A).

Financial firms had larger boards than non-financial firms, but this difference was only statistically significant in the UK in 2007 (12 members in financial firms and 11 members in non-financial firms). Therefore, our results for Europe do not support Adams and Mehran (2003), who expected larger boards for financial firms.

The crisis did not affect the number of board members in financial firms or in non-financial firms (with the exception of France where there was a slight increase in board members, from 14 to 15). However, there were country-based significant differences. The UK had the smallest boards, with a mean value of 11 directors in 2013, and Germany had the biggest ones, with a mean value of 16 directors. In Spain and France, the size of the board was around 14.

Most governance codes, and even the EBA (European Banking Association) Guidelines on Corporate Governance (GL44) of 27 September 2011, do not make a specific recommendation about board size, one of the exceptions being the Spanish Code that recommends between 5 and 15 members.

3.4.1.2 Independent Directors

The EBA Guidelines recommend financial firms to have a sufficient number of independent members on the management body, as an element of strong governance. Independent members of the management body are non-executive directors who are independent of the subsidiary and of its group, and of the controlling shareholder.

Most governance codes also recommend the presence of a significant proportion of independent directors in order to improve the quality of the board of directors in its role of monitoring managers (Fama and Jensen 1983) or in its role of providing advice or access to external resources (Adams and Ferreira 2007). In Spain, France

Table 3.3 Corporate governance variables in financial and non-financial firms in Europe: a comparison between Spain, Germany, France and the UK

Variables		Spain		France		Germany		United Kingdom		Sample (Spain + France + Germany + United Kingdom)		Country differences	Country differences
PANEL A		2007	2013	2007	2013	2007	2013	2007	2013	2007	2013	2007	2013
Board Structure/Functioning													
Board size (1)	Financial firms	15.50	15.88	15.20	16.00	18.40	16.80	11.88	11.80	13.74	13.63	*** (4)	*** (4)
	Non-Financial	14.20	13.72	13.62	14.53*	17.16	16.32	10.93	10.80	13.03	12.93	*** (4)	*** (4)
	Sector differences	N.S. (4)	N.S. (4)	N.S. (4)	N.S. (4)	N.S. (4)	N.S. (4)	* (4)	N.S. (4)	N.S. (4)	N.S. (4)		
Non-executive Directors (1)	Financial firms	78.59	78.47	85.48	93.38	100.00	100.00	62.30	70.43***	72.51	78.03**	*** (4)	*** (4)
	Non-Financial	80.79	84.00	90.04	90.80	99.55	100.00	67.83	72.28***	79.58	82.44***	*** (4)	*** (4)
	Sector differences	N.S. (4)	* (4)	N.S. (4)	N.S. (4)	N.S. (4)	N.S. (4)	* (4)	N.S. (4)	** (4)	** (4)		
CEO Duality (2)	Financial firms	50.00%	50.00%	20.00%	40.00%	0.00%	0.00%	0.00%	0.00%	11.90%	13.95%	*** (5)	*** (5)
	Non-Financial	55.00%	56.00%	44.12%	67.65% **	0.00%	0.00%	2.86%	2.67%	18.79%	24.53% **	*** (5)	*** (5)
	Sector differences	N.S. (5)	N.S. (5)	N.S. (5)	N.S. (5)	N.C. (5)	N.C. (5)	N.S. (5)	N.S. (5)	N.S. (5)	* (5)		
Chairperson Experience (2)	Financial firms	62.50%	50.00%	40.00%	60.00%	60.00%	40.00%	12.50%	0.00%	30.95%	20.93%	** (5)	*** (5)
	Non-Financial	55.00%	64.00%	61.76%	76.47%	20.00%	16.00%	10.00%	6.67%	29.53%	32.08%	*** (5)	*** (5)
	Sector differences	N.S. (5)	N.S. (5)	N.S. (5)	N.S. (5)	N.S. (5)	N.S. (5)	N.S. (5)	N.S. (5)	N.S. (5)	N.S (5)		
Director Tenure (1)	Financial firms	6.52	8.4688**	5.80	5.48	5.40	5.91	5.92	5.23	5.97	5.96	N.S. (4)	* (4)
	Non-Financial	5.90	7.82***	6.32	7.435**	5.64	7.09	5.26	5.54*	5.65	6.49***	N.S. (4)	*** (4)
	Sector differences	N.S. (4)	N.S. (4)	N.S. (4)	* (4)	N.S. (4)	N.S. (4)	N.S. (4)	N.S. (4)	N.S. (4)	N.S. (4)		

(continued)

Table 3.3 (continued)

Variables		Spain		France		Germany		United Kingdom		Sample (Spain + France + Germany + United Kingdom)		Country differences	Country differences
Meetings per year (1)	Financial firms	11.63	13.00	8.00	8.00	5.60	7.00*	8.40	9.00	8.63	9.45*	*** (4)	*** (4)
	Non-Financial	11.50	10.32	8.15	8.50	5.67	5.54	9.20	8.59	8.64	8.38	*** (4)	*** (4)
	Sector differences	N.S. (4)	** (4)	N.S. (4)	N.S. (4)	N.S. (4)	* (4)	N.S. (4)	N.S. (4)	N.S. (4)	** (4)		
Meetings attendance (1)	Financial firms	93.00	95.00	89.40	94.00**	98.00	95.50	95.05	97.32*	93.97	96.46***	** (4)	N.S. (4)
	Non-Financial	96.20	97.50	87.91	91.20***	62.86	85.83	93.00	96.42***	89.48	94.00***	*** (4)	*** (4)
	Sector differences	N.S. (4)	N.S. (4)	N.S. (4)	N.S. (4)	* (4)	N.S. (4)	* (4)	N.S. (4)	** (4)	* (4)		
PANEL B		2007	2013	2007	2013	2007	2013	2007	2013	2007	2013	2007	2013
Committees													
Corporate Governance Committee (2)	Financial firms	37.50%	62.50%	80.00%	100.00%	60.00%	60.00%	8.00%	28.00%*	27.91%	46.51% **	*** (5)	** (5)
	Non-Financial	25.00%	28.00%	35.29%	61.76% ***	24.00%	20.00%	17.65%	24.32% **	23.81%	32.28% ***	N.S (5)	*** (5)
	Sector differences	N.S. (5)	* (5)	* (5)	N.S. (5)	N.S. (5)	N.S. (5)	N.S. (5)	N.S. (5)	N.S. (5)	* (5)		
Audit Committee (2)	Financial firms	25.00%	62.50%	80.00%	80.00%	60.00%	60.00%	100.00%	100.00%	79.07%	86.05%	*** (5)	** (5)
	Non-Financial	55.00%	84%**	73.53%	91.18% **	52.00%	72.00%	86.76%	95.95%	73.47%	89.24% ***	*** (5)	*** (5)
	Sector differences	N.S. (5)	N.S. (5)	N.S. (5)	N.S. (5)	N.S. (5)	N.S. (5)	* (5)	N.S. (5)	N.S. (5)	N.S (5)		
Compensation Committee (2)	Financial firms	100.00%	100.00%	100.00%	100.00%	100.00%	100.00%	100.00%	100.00%	100.00%	100.00%	N.C. (5)	N.C. (5)
	Non-Financial	95.00%	100.00%	100.00%	100.00%	88.00%	84.00%	98.57%	100.00%	96.64%	97.48%	** (5)	*** (5)
	Sector differences	N.S. (5)	N.C. (5)	N.C. (5)	N.C. (5)	N.S. (5)	N.S. (5)	N.S. (5)	N.C. (5)	N.S. (5)	N.S (5)		

PANEL C		2007	2013	2007	2013	2007	2013	2007	2013	2007	2013	2007	2013
Compensation Policy													
Equity-based pay CEO (2)	Financial firms	25.00%	37.50%	20.00%	40.00%	20.00%	80%*	87.50%	92.00%	59.52%	74.42% **	*** (5)	*** (5)
	Non-Financial	5.00%	16.00%	14.71%	17.65%	20.00%	20.00%	90.00%	84.00%	49.66%	49.06%	*** (5)	*** (5)
	Sector differences	N.S. (5)	N.S. (5)	N.S. (5)	N.S. (5)	N.S. (5)	** (5)	N.S. (5)	N.S. (5)	N.S (5)	*** (5)		
Performance-based compensation policy (2)	Financial firms	87.50%	100.00%	100.00%	100.00%	100.00%	100.00%	100.00%	100.00%	97.62%	100.00%	N.S. (5)	N.C. (5)
	Non-Financial	50.00%	88%***	70.59%	94.12% ***	92.00%	100.00%	100.00%	100.00%	85.23%	96.86% ***	*** (5)	** (5)
	Sector differences	* (5)	N.S. (5)	N.S. (5)	N.S. (5)	N.S. (5)	N.C. (5)	N.C. (5)	N.C. (5)	** (5)	N.S. (5)		
ESG related compensation policy (2)	Financial firms	12.50%	0.00%	0.00%	80.00%	0.00%	40.00%	33.33%	72%***	21.43%	55.81% ***	N.S. (5)	*** (5)
	Non-Financial	5.00%	24.00%	5.88%	35.29% ***	0.00%	40%***	24.29%	69.33%	13.42%	50.31% ***	*** (5)	*** (5)
	Sector differences	N.S. (5)	N.S. (5)	N.S. (5)	* (5)	N.C. (5)	N.S. (5)	N.S. (5)	N.S. (5)	N.S (5)	N.S. (5)		
Compensation Policy attract/retain executives (2)	Financial firms	0.00%	12.50%	40.00%	60.00%	20.00%	20.00%	100.00%	96.00%	64.29%	67.44%	*** (5)	*** (5)
	Non-Financial	25.00%	44.00%	23.53%	41.18%*	4.00%	16.00%	94.29%	97.33%	53.69%	64.15% ***	*** (5)	*** (5)
	Sector differences	N.S. (5)	N.S. (5)	N.S. (5)	N.S. (5)	N.S. (5)	N.S. (5)	N.S. (5)	N.S. (5)	N.S (5)	N.S. (5)		
Say on pay (executive compensation) (2)	Financial firms	25.00%	100%*	0.00%	0.00%	0.00%	80.00%	37.50%	100% ***	26.19%	86.05% ***	N.S (5)	*** (5)
	Non-Financial	30.00%	56.00% **	2.94%	8.82%	4.00%	60%***	12.86%	89.33%	11.41%	62.26% ***	** (5)	*** (5)
	Sector differences	N.S. (5)	** (5)	N.S. (5)	N.S. (5)	N.S. (5)	N.S. (5)	** (5)	* (5)	** (5)	*** (5)		
Say on pay (stock-based compensation) (2)	Financial firms	25.00%	75.00%	40.00%	80.00%	0.00%	20.00%	4.17%	56.00% ***	11.90%	58.14% ***	* (5)	N.S. (5)
	Non-Financial	30.00%	60%*	11.76%	50.00% ***	8.00%	28%*	0.00%	61.33%	8.05%	53.46% ***	*** (5)	** (5)
	Sector differences	N.S. (5)	N.S. (5)	N.S. (5)	N.S. (5)	N.S. (5)	N.S. (5)	N.S. (5)	N.S. (5)	N.S (5)	N.S. (5)		

(continued)

Table 3.3 (continued)

Variables		Spain		France		Germany		United Kingdom		Sample (Spain + France + Germany + United Kingdom)		Country differences	Country differences
PANEL D		2007	2013	2007	2013	2007	2013	2007	2013	2007	2013	2007	2013
Anti-takeover devices													
Policy limiting anti-takeover devices (2)	Financial firms	25.00%	25.00%	0.00%	20.00%	0.00%	0.00%	4.17%	4.00%	7.14%	9.30%	N.S. (5)	N.S. (5)
	Non-Financial	10.00%	8.00%	2.94%	11.76%	4.00%	4.00%	5.71%	6.67%	5.37%	7.55%	N.S. (5)	N.S. (5)
	Sector differences	N.S. (5)	N.S. (5)	N.S. (5)	N.S. (5)	N.S. (5)	N.S. (5)	N.S. (5)	N.S. (5)	N.S. (5)	N.S. (5)		
Golden parachutes (2)	Financial firms	20.00%	28.57%	0.00%	0.00%	100.00%	100.00%	40.91%	40.91%	42.86%	44.44%	** (5)	** (5)
	Non-Financial	62.50%	38.10%	26.92%	55.56%	37.50%	54.17%	34.92%	37.88%	37.21%	43.41%	N.S. (5)	N.S. (5)
	Sector differences	N.S. (5)	N.S. (5)	N.S. (5)	N.S. (5)	** (5)	* (5)	N.S. (5)	N.S. (5)	N.S. (5)	N.S. (5)		
Staggered Board (2)	Financial firms	57.14%	75.00%	100.00%	100.00%	20.00%	25.00%	95.83%	4%***	80.49%	26.32% ***	*** (5)	*** (5)
	Non-Financial	35.00%	88.89% ***	72.73%	97.06% ***	45.83%	15.79%*	88.57%	6.67%	70.75%	39.04% ***	*** (5)	*** (5)
	Sector differences	N.S. (5)	N.S. (5)	N.S. (5)	N.S. (5)	N.S. (5)	N.S. (5)	N.S. (5)	N.S. (5)	N.S. (5)	N.S. (5)		
Supermajority vote requirement (2)	Financial firms	40.00%	83.33%	66.67%	100.00%	66.67%	40.00%	19.05%	100% ***	31.25%	89.19% ***	N.S. (5)	*** (5)
	Non-Financial	41.67%	84.21%	34.78%	93.33%	57.14%	69.57%	21.57%	98.63%	33.64%	90.77% ***	** (5)	*** (5)
	Sector differences	N.S. (5)	N.S. (5)	N.S. (5)	N.S. (5)	N.S. (5)	N.S. (5)	N.S. (5)	N.S. (5)	N.S. (5)	N.S. (5)		
Veto power (2)	Financial firms	0.00%	37.50%	25.00%	20.00%	0.00%	0.00%	0.00%	4.00%	3.13%	11.63%	* (5)	* (5)
	Non-Financial	33.33%	20.00%	13.04%	12.50%	10.00%	16.67%	0.00%	5.41%	7.37%	10.97%	** (5)	N.S. (5)
	Sector differences	N.S. (5)	N.S. (5)	N.S. (5)	N.S. (5)	N.S. (5)	N.S. (5)	N.C. (5)	N.S. (5)	N.S. (5)	N.S. (5)		

PANEL E		2007	2013	2007	2013	2007	2013	2007	2013	2007	2013	2007	2013
Shareholders Rights													
Limited rights to call special meetings (2)	Financial firms	83.33%	25%*	0.00%	100.00%	0.00%	75.00%	20.00%	41.67%	29.03%	44.00%	** (5)	N.S. (5)
	Non-Financial	93.33%	16.67% ***	25.00%	75.00%	23.53%	81.25%	11.36%	64.44% ***	29.00%	56.70%	*** (5)	*** (5)
	Sector differences	N.S. (5)	N.S. (5)	N.S. (5)	N.S. (5)	N.S. (5)	N.S. (5)	N.S. (5)	N.S. (5)	N.S. (5)	N.S. (5)		
Majority vote for board members election (2)	Financial firms	50.00%	87.50%	40.00%	80.00%	40.00%	60.00%	20.83%	84%***	30.95%	81.40% ***	N.S. (5)	N.S. (5)
	Non-Financial	25.00%	84.00% ***	20.59%	76.47% ***	52.00%	96%***	25.71%	96.00%	28.86%	89.94% ***	** (5)	*** (5)
	Sector differences	N.S. (5)	N.S. (5)	N.S. (5)	N.S. (5)	N.S. (5)	* (5)	N.S. (5)	* (5)	N.S. (5)	N.S. (5)		
Minimum shares to vote (2)	Financial firms	0.00%	0.00%	0.00%	0.00%	0.00%	0.00%	0.00%	4.00%	0.00%	2.33%	N.C. (5)	N.S. (5)
	Non-Financial	5.00%	8.00%	0.00%	0.00%	0.00%	0.00%	0.00%	0.00%	0.67%	1.26%	* (5)	** (5)
	Sector differences	N.S. (5)	N.S. (5)	N.C. (5)	N.C. (5)	N.C. (5)	N.C. (5)	N.C. (5)	N.S. (5)	N.S. (5)	N.S. (5)		
Director liability limitation (2)	Financial firms	25.00%	100.00%	50.00%	100.00%	33.33%	100.00%	61.90%	100% ***	53.13%	100.00% ***	N.S. (5)	N.C. (5)
	Non-Financial	33.33%	88.24%	24.00%	100%**	17.65%	100% ***	4.55%	98.67%	14.13%	97.60% ***	* (5)	* (5)
	Sector differences	N.S. (5)	N.S. (5)	N.S. (5)	N.C. (5)	N.S. (5)	N.C. (5)	*** (5)	N.S. (5)	*** (5)	N.S. (5)		
Shares with different rights (2)	Financial firms	0.00%	0.00%	0.00%	0.00%	20.00%	0.00%	4.17%	16.00%	4.76%	9.30%	N.S. (5)	N.S. (5)
	Non-Financial	0.00%	8.00%	0.00%	5.88%	4.00%	20.00%	7.14%	12.00%	4.03%	11.32% **	N.S. (5)	N.S. (5)
	Sector differences	N.C. (5)	N.S. (5)	N.C. (5)	N.S. (5)	N.S. (5)	N.S. (5)	N.S. (5)	N.S. (5)	N.S. (5)	N.S. (5)		
Shareholder engagement/ activism (2)	Financial firms	62.50%	87.50%	20.00%	20.00%	80.00%	80.00%	54.17%	92%**	54.76%	81.40% ***	N.S. (5)	*** (5)
	Non-Financial	70.00%	96.00% **	14.71%	61.76% ***	44.00%	68%*	42.86%	86.67%	40.27%	79.87% ***	*** (5)	*** (5)
	Sector differences	N.S. (5)	N.S. (5)	N.S. (5)	N.S. (5)	N.S. (5)	N.S. (5)	N.S. (5)	N.S. (5)	* (5)	N.S. (5)		

(continued)

Table 3.3 (continued)

Variables		Spain		France		Germany		United Kingdom		Sample (Spain + France + Germany + United Kingdom)		Country differences	Country differences
PANEL F		2007	2013	2007	2013	2007	2013	2007	2013	2007	2013	2007	2013
CSR													
CSR Committee (2)	Financial firms	12.50%	87.5%**	60.00%	100.00%	40.00%	100.00%	75.00%	96%*	57.14%	95.35% ***	** (5)	N.S. (5)
	Non-Financial	35.00%	88.00% ***	38.24%	97.06% ***	32.00%	88%***	64.29%	96%***	48.99%	93.71% ***	*** (5)	N.S. (5)
	Sector differences	N.S. (5)	N.S. (5)	N.S. (5)	N.S. (5)	N.S. (5)	N.S. (5)	N.S. (5)	N.S. (5)	N.S. (5)	N.S. (5)		
Sustainability Report (2)	Financial firms	75.00%	100.00%	100.00%	100.00%	80.00%	100.00%	75.00%	100%*	78.57%	100.00% ***	N.S. (5)	N.C. (Constant)
	Non-Financial	95.00%	100.00%	85.29%	100%*	76.00%	100%**	75.71%	100% ***	80.54%	100.00% ***	N.S. (5)	N.C. (Constant)
	Sector differences	N.S. (5)	N.C. (5)	N.S. (5)	N.C. (5)	N.S. (5)	N.C. (5)	N.S. (5)	N.C. (5)	N.S. (5)	N.C. (5)		
External auditor for sustainability report (2)	Financial firms	100.00%	87.50%	100.00%	100.00%	33.33%	100.00%	50.00%	87.50%	61.29%	90.91%	* (5)	N.S. (5)
	Non-Financial	94.12%	100.00%	64.29%	100% ***	31.82%	85.71% ***	67.86%	92.45%	64.23%	94.57% ***	*** (5)	* (5)
	Sector differences	N.S. (5)	N.S. (5)	N.S. (5)	N.C. (5)	N.S. (5)	N.S. (5)	N.S. (5)	N.S. (5)	N.S. (5)	N.S. (5)		
Sustainability index (2)	Financial firms	62.50%	87.50%	100.00%	100.00%	100.00%	100.00%	75.00%	84.00%	78.57%	88.37%*	N.S. (5)	N.S. (5)
	Non-Financial	80.00%	80.00%	76.47%	88.24%	72.00%	76.00%	65.71%	72.00%	71.14%	77.36% **	N.S. (5)	N.S. (5)
	Sector differences	N.S. (5)	N.S. (5)	N.S. (5)	N.S. (5)	N.S. (5)	N.S. (5)	N.S. (5)	N.S. (5)	N.S. (5)	* (5)		
GRI Guidelines (2)	Financial firms	85.71%	100.00%	100.00%	100.00%	100.00%	100.00%	100.00%	92.31%	94.44%	96.55%	N.S. (5)	N.S. (5)
	Non-Financial	93.75%	100.00%	94.44%	100.00%	90.00%	100.00%	80.65%	95.35%	88.24%	98.33% **	N.S. (5)	N.S. (5)
	Sector differences	N.S. (5)	N.C. (5)	N.S. (5)	N.C. (5)	N.S. (5)	N.C. (5)	N.S. (5)	N.S. (5)	N.S. (5)	N.S. (5)		

UN Global Compact (2)	Financial firms	62.50%	87.50%	100.00%	100.00%	80.00%	80.00%	25.00%	36.00%	47.62%	58.14%	*** (5)	*** (5)
	Non-Financial	95.00%	80.00%	79.41%	88.24%	64.00%	80.00%	25.71%	38.67% ***	53.69%	62.26% ***	*** (5)	*** (5)
	Sector differences	* (5)	N.S. (5)	N.S. (5)	N.S. (5)	N.S. (5)	N.S. (5)	N.S. (5)	N.S. (5)	N.S. (5)	N.S. (5)		
Stakeholder engagement (2)	Financial firms	62.50%	87.50%	80.00%	100.00%	80.00%	100.00%	58.33%	60.00%	64.29%	74.42%	N.S. (5)	* (5)
	Non-Financial	65.00%	80.00%	52.94%	70.59%*	68.00%	76.00%	61.43%	77.33% ***	61.07%	76.10% ***	N.S. (5)	N.S. (5)
	Sector differences	N.S. (5)	N.S. (5)	N.S. (5)	N.S. (5)	N.S. (5)	N.S. (5)	N.S. (5)	* (5)	N.S. (5)	N.S. (5)		

1. Paired t-test. Differences between different periods of time (pre and post crisis). Continuous variable
2. McNemar Test. Differences between different periods of time (pre and post crisis). Dichotomous variable
3. One-way ANOVA. Differences between financial and non-financial firms and among countries (2007 and 2013). Normal continuous variable
4. Mann-Whitney U Test. Differences between financial and non-financial firms. Kruskal-Wallis Test. Differences among countries (2007 and 2013). No normal continuous variable
5. Fisher's Exact Test. Differences between financial and non-financial firms. Chi-square test. Differences among countries (2007 and 2013). Dichotomous variable

Statistically significant at 1% (***), 5% (**) and 10% (*). N.S.: Not significant. N.C.: Not conducted

and the UK it is recommended that at least half the board be comprised of non-executive directors. In companies with controlling shareholders, independent directors should account for at least one third in Spain and France. The two-tier board structure in Germany distinguishes between the management board, where by definition all members are executives, and the supervisory board, where employees represent one-third or one-half in companies with more than 500 or 2000 employees, respectively (Díaz Díaz et al. 2017).

Table 3.3 panel A shows significant differences in the mean proportion of independent directors in financial and non-financial firms, before and after the crisis and across countries. For the full sample, financial firms had a lower proportion of independent directors (78.03% in 2013) than non-financial firms (82.44%). This result does not support Adams and Mehran (2003) who found a larger percentage of outside directors in financial firms (68.7%) than in non-financial firms (60.6%) for the USA.

After the crisis, the proportion of independent directors increased in financial firms (from 72.51% to 78.03%) and in non-financial firms (from 79.58% to 82.44%). This result shows how firms adapted their governance structure to the recommendation of having a higher proportion of independent directors.

However, there were also significant differences across countries. The mean value of independent directors in financial firms varies from 70.43%, for the UK, to 100% for Germany. When analysing countries individually, the UK was the one that presented a significant increase in the proportion of independent directors after the crisis and also presents a significant difference in the proportion of independent directors between financial and non-financial firms before the crisis which becomes non-significant after the crisis. This result shows how in the UK financial firms reacted to the crisis, by increasing the proportion of independent directors by 8% points (from 62.30% to 70.43%) as compared to non-financial firms which increased this proportion by 5% points (from 67.83% to 72.28%).

3.4.1.3 Separation of Chairperson of the Board and CEO (No CEO Duality)

The EBA Guidelines recommend that in a one-tier system, the chair of the management body and the chief executive officer of an institution should not be the same person. They recommend division of responsibilities at the head of the company between the running of the board and the executive responsibility for the administration of the company's business, as do most corporate governance codes. However, where the chair of the management body is also the chief executive officer of the institution, EBA Guidelines recommend that the institution have measures to minimise the potential detriment on its checks and balances, such as having a lead senior independent member of the management body in its supervisory function or a similar position.

The results show significant differences in the proportion of firms with CEO duality between financial and non-financial firms in 2013 for the full sample, with financial firms showing a lower percentage (13.95% in financial firms and 24.53% in non-financial firms). An increase in CEO duality was also observed in non-financial firms after the crisis in France (from 44.12% to 67.65%) and for the full sample (from 18.79% to 24.53%). It is worth highlighting the significant country-based differences. For financial firms, while CEO duality was 0% for Germany and the UK, it was 40% for France and 50% for Spain. For non-financial firms, CEO duality was 0% for Germany, 2.67% for the UK, 56% for Spain and 67.65% for France (Table 3.3, Panel A). Differences between pre- and post-crisis values are observed for the full sample and for France only for non-financial firms, where CEO duality increased after the crisis. Therefore, financial firms seem to follow the recommendation about CEO duality to a greater extent than non-financial firms, but the crisis has not improved the way firms are following the recommendation about the elimination of CEO duality.

3.4.1.4 Chairperson Experience, Director Tenure, Number of Board Meetings and Meetings Attendance

There are also significant country-based differences in other variables related to board structure and functioning. First, for financial firms chairperson/CEO experience rate in companies was 0% for the UK, 40% for Germany, 50% for Spain and 60% for France in 2013. For non-financial firms, chairperson/CEO experience rate was 6.67% for the UK, 16% for Germany, 64% for Spain and 76.47% for France. However, the difference between financial and non-financial firms was not significant, nor was the difference between pre- and post-crisis values.

Second, the average number of years each board member has been on the board (director tenure) was between 5.23 for the UK and 8.47 for Spain for financial firms and between 5.54 for the UK and 7.82 for Spain for non-financial firms. The difference between financial and non-financial firms was statistically significant for the full sample, for the UK and for France, showing financial firms with a lower director tenure. For Spain, the difference was also significant, but financial firms show longer director tenure, which has even increased after the crisis (from 6.52 to 8.47).

EBA Guidelines recommend that membership and chairmanship of a committee might be rotated occasionally. The rotation of membership and chairmanship helps to avoid undue concentration of power and to promote fresh perspectives. However, in Spain financial firms not only had the worst compliance record with this recommendation, their compliance level has worsened after the crisis.

Third, the mean number of board meetings during the year was higher in financial firms. It ranges from 7, for Germany to 13 for Spain. For non-financial firms, it ranges from 5.54 for Germany to 10.32 for Spain. The result supports Adams and Mehran (2003) who also found a higher meeting frequency for financial firms. Also, financial firms have increased the number of board meetings after the crisis, with significant results for Germany (from 5.6 to 7) and for the full sample (from 8.63 to 9.45). Despite the significant country-based differences, the results suggest that financial firms are complying with the recommendation of governance codes of meeting often enough to discharge board duties effectively, to a greater extent than non-financial firms.

Fourth, the average overall attendance percentage of board meetings was higher for financial firms than non-financial firms during both the pre- and post-crisis period for the full sample and it has increased after the crisis (from 93.97% to 96.46% for financial firms and from 89.48% to 94% in non-financial firms). This increase was also observed to be significant in a country-based analysis of France and the UK. Spain was the only country in the sample where financial firms had lower meeting attendance than non-financial firms, but the difference was not statistically significant.

According to the seven corporate governance variables analysed related to board structure and functioning, we can conclude that financial firms were not worse governed than non-financial firms before de crisis. Only two variables show statistically significant differences in 2007: the percentage of independent directors (lower for financial firms) and meeting attendance (higher for financial firms). After the crisis, these two variables improved for financial firms, with the percentage of independent directors and meeting attendance rising.

3.4.2 Committees

Three main committees have been considered in this section: the audit committee, the compensation committee, and the corporate governance committee. The results show significant differences between countries. An audit committee was found in 100% of financial firms in the UK in 2013, while only 62.5% of Spanish financial firms had one in 2013. There was also a significant difference between financial and non-financial firms, with financial firms showing a lower presence of audit committees (except in the UK). Moreover, an increase was observed in the percentage of non-financial firms with an audit committee after the crisis in the full sample, in Spain and in France, while financial firms did not experience a significant change.

According to EBA Guidelines, an audit committee (or equivalent) should monitor the effectiveness of the company's internal control, internal audit, and risk management systems, oversee the institution's external auditors, recommend for approval by the management body the appointment, compensation and dismissal of the external auditors, review and approve the audit scope and frequency, review audit reports, and check that the management body in its management function takes necessary corrective actions in a timely manner to address and control weaknesses, non-compliance with laws, regulations and policies, and other problems identified by the auditors. In addition, the audit committee should oversee the establishment of accounting policies by the company. Therefore, audit committees are important from a corporate governance perspective, but their presence was still low in 2013 in financial firms in countries such as Spain (62.5%) or Germany (60%).

A compensation committee was found in 100% of financial firms in all the countries analysed pre- and post-crisis. Only Germany presented a percentage for compensation committee lower than 100% for non-financial firms after the crisis. Corporate Governance committees were less frequent in non-financial European firms than in financial firms. Their presence in financial firms varied, from 28%, in the UK, to 100% in France in 2013 (Table 3.3, Panel B) showing a statistically significant increase after the crisis for the full sample.

3.4.3 Compensation Policy

According to Adams (2012), in order to align the incentives of CEOs and directors with those of shareholders, CEOs and directors should receive a certain amount of performance-based pay in the form of equity. However, equity incentives may induce managers to take excessive risks. Therefore, it is not always clear whether a certain compensation contract is effective or not.

Equity-based pay increased after the crisis in financial firms for the full sample and for Germany. There was also a significant difference between financial and non-financial firms, with the presence of equity-based pay being higher in financial firms (Table 3.3, panel C). Moreover, the results indicate statistically significant differences in compensation policies between the countries considered. While in the UK 92% of financial firms in 2013 had equity-based pay, in Spain this percentage was 37.5%. Also, in the UK the percentage of firms with a compensation policy related to ESG (Economic Social Governance principles) was higher (72%), than in Spain (0%) or Germany (40%) for financial firms. However financial and non-financial firms did not present significant differences in this compensation policy (with the exception of France in 2013 where financial firms had higher values for their ESG-related compensation policy).

The crisis has increased performance-based pay in Spain, France and the full sample for non-financial firms. However, almost 100% of financial firms already had this policy in place before the crisis in all countries. The top country in terms of a compensation policy to attract and retain executives was the UK, with 96% of financial firms having such a policy. This percentage lowers to 60% for France, 20% for Germany and 12.5% for Spain. There was no significant difference between financial and non-financial firms, and only France experienced an increase after the crisis for non-financial firms.

Shareholder voting on executive pay, commonly known as say on pay, provides an additional tool for shareholder governance via the "voice" channel (Stathopoulos and Voulgaris 2015). Say on pay was initially introduced in the UK in 2002, and mandates an advisory shareholder vote on executive remuneration proposed by the board of directors (Díaz Díaz et al. 2017). A number of countries have followed the UK's lead, with the introduction of similar legislation (Germany in 2010, Spain in 2011 and France in 2014).

In 2013, 100% of financial firms from the UK and Spain required shareholder approval for executives' compensation (say on pay). This percentage dropped to 80% and 0% for German and French financial firms, respectively. Financial firms had higher values than non-financial firms and all the countries experienced an increase in say on pay when comparing 2007 with 2013. However, the requirement of shareholder approval prior to the adoption of any stock-based compensation plan in financial firms was frequently used in France (80%) as well as in Spain (75%) and the UK (56%), but less common in Germany (20%). There was no significant difference between financial and non-financial firms.

3.4.4 Anti-Takeover Devices

Governance Codes include recommendations to avoid board entrenchment (Millstein 2014) and from the governance perspective, anti-takeover devices should be reduced to allow a free market for corporate control.

Financial and non-financial firms did not present significant differences in the anti-takeover devices variables (with the exception of Germany where 100% of financial firms had golden parachutes in 2013 as compared to 54.17% of non-financial firms). The existence of golden parachutes varies from 100% in Germany to 0% in France for financial firms (Table 3.3, panel D).

We can observe a significant change in takeover devices after the crisis in two variables. First, there was an increase in the supermajority vote requirement in the full sample after the crisis, although there were differences across countries. While 100% of financial firms in France and Germany had it in 2013, only 40% of financial firms required a supermajority vote in the UK. The UK was the only country where the supermajority vote requirement decreased after the crisis in financial firms, while in all other countries this value increased, as well as for non-financial firms. Second, staggered boards were found in 100% of French financial firms after the crisis while in only 4% of financial firms in the UK. The crisis reduced the presence of staggered boards in financial and non-financial firms in the full sample, although there were differences across countries.

According to our results, in Europe very few companies had a policy limiting the use of anti-takeover devices. Spain and France had the highest values in 2013, with 25% and 20% of the financial companies having such a policy, respectively. In Germany and the UK this percentage lowered to 0%. However, this difference between countries was not statistically significant, and neither are the pre- and post-crisis values. Moreover, very few financial companies had veto power or golden shares held by the biggest shareholder in Germany (0%) and the UK (4%). Veto power was more common in financial firms in Spain (37.5%) and France (20%).

3.4.5 Shareholder Rights

European companies are making an effort to establish policies to facilitate shareholder engagement because of the benefits they can provide in terms of corporate governance, and after the crisis the percentage of firms with shareholder engagement increased, mainly in the UK and Spain. However, there are significant country-based differences. 87.5% of Spanish financial companies had such a policy, as compared to 20% of French firms (Table 3.3, Panel E).

Country-based differences are also found in the percentage of companies that have limited the rights of shareholders to call special meetings, which was lower in Spain (25%) than in other countries (41.67% in the UK, 100% in France, and 75% in Germany) in 2013 for financial firms. However, there are no country-based differences regarding other variables. In most European financial firms, company board members are elected by a majority vote, but very few set requirements for a minimum number of shares to vote, and very few have shares with different rights.

It is worth noting the increase in director liability limitation in companies from all countries after the crisis, with values of 100% in financial firms and without a significant difference with non-financial firms (where the value was 97.6% in the full sample).

3.4.6 Corporate Social Responsibility

Nowadays, boards have a mayor responsibility for achieving CSR objectives and sustainability. The empirical evidence found in our research for this category of variables showed a statistically significant increase in most of the items related to CSR after the crisis in all the countries analysed (Table 3.3, Panel F). Most of the companies in the sample had CSR committees in 2013, 100% of companies published a separate sustainability report or a section in their annual reports on sustainability, most of the companies had an external auditor for their sustainability reports, and almost 100% published the report in accordance with the Global Reporting Initiative (GRI) guidelines. More than 84% of financial companies and 72% of non-financial firms reported belonging to a specific sustainability index, and between 60% and 100% explained how they engage with their stakeholders. There were no significant differences between financial and non-financial firms (with the exception of firms belonging to the UN Global Compact in Spain in 2007 and stakeholder engagement in the UK in 2013).

Therefore, the crisis increased the commitment to CSR policies in all countries, but above all in the UK, where 4 out of 7 of the variables for non-financial firms and 2 variables for financial firms presented a significant difference when comparing them before and after the crisis. Before the crisis there were country differences in financial firms in three variables: CSR committees, with the highest level in the UK (75%) and the lowest in Spain (12.5%), external auditors, with the highest level in

Spain and France (100%) and the lowest in Germany (33.3%), and belonging to the UN Global Compact, with values between 25% and 100% for the UK and France, respectively.

However, after the crisis there were no significant differences in CSR variables between the countries, except for membership of the UN Global Compact. It is worth mentioning the small percentage of UK firms that subscribed to the UN Global compact (36% of financial firms and 38.67% of non-financial firms as compared to more than 80% in other countries).

3.5 Conclusions

This paper analyses CG policies in financial and non-financial firms in four European countries. It considers 33 variables that measure policies related to corporate governance, including the areas of board structure and functioning, committees, compensation policy, anti-takeover-devices, shareholder rights, and corporate social responsibility. The results show sector-based differences in CG in 6 variables in 2007 and in 8 variables in 2013 for the full sample. Differences between financial and non- financial firms were found in the percentage of non-executive directors and CEO duality (lower for financial firms) and in the number of board meetings, attendance at meetings, corporate governance committee, CEO equity-based pay, say on pay for executive compensation and using a sustainability index (higher for financial firms). In 2007, the difference between financial and non-financial firms was only found in 6 variables in the UK, in 2 variables in Spain and Germany and in 1 variable in France. In 2013, the difference between financial and non-financial firms was similar and was only found in 4 variables for Spain and Germany, in 3 variables in the UK and in 2 variables in France. Therefore, we can conclude that financial firms were not worse governed than non-financial firms before the crisis, and that after the crisis financial firms have been similarly governed to non-financial firms.

We found pre- and post- crisis differences for financial firms in 16 CG variables for the full sample (13 variables in the UK, 5 variables in Spain and 2 variables in France and Germany). Therefore, we can conclude that the crisis has affected almost half of the corporate governance variables analysed. The legal initiatives and governance recommendations developed since 2008 and the need to improve governance to restore confidence in financial firms can explain the change in CG variables. However, the crisis affected corporate governance in common law countries (UK) to a greater extent than in civil law ones.

There are also country-based differences in CG in 19 variables in financial firms in 2007 and in 2013. The difference between countries was higher in non-financial firms, where 26 variables showed differences in 2007 and 27 in 2013. These differences between countries show the difficulty in developing common governance recommendations for all European countries without considering their own specific characteristics.

Acknowledgments This paper is part of the research project entitled "Governance, incentives, and risk management in global banks" (APIE Num. 2/2015-2017), funded by the Santander Financial Institute (SANFI) with the sponsorship of Banco Santander, awarded by public call of the University of Cantabria (Official Bulletin of Cantabria. BOC Number 236, 9 December 2014).

Appendix: Description of the Variables

Name	Description	Type of variable
Board structure/functioning		
Board size	Size of board (The total number of board members at the end of the fiscal year)	C
Non-executive Directors (%)	Percentage of non-executive board members	C
CEO Duality	Does the CEO simultaneously chair the board?	D
Chairperson Experience as CEO	Has the chairperson of the board been the CEO of the company?	D
Director Tenure	Average number of years each board member has been on the board	C
Meetings per year	The number of board meetings during the year	C
Meetings attendance	The average overall attendance percentage of board meetings as reported by the company	C
Committees		
Corporate Governance Committee	Does the company have a corporate governance committee?	D
Audit Committee	Does the company have an audit committee with at least three members and at least one "financial expert" within the meaning of Sarbanes-Oxley?	D
Compensation Committee	Does the company have a compensation committee?	D
Compensation policy		
CEO equity-based pay	Is the CEO's compensation linked to total shareholder return (TSR)?	D
Performance-based compensation policy	Does the company have a performance oriented compensation policy?	D
ESG related compensation policy	Does the company have an ESG related compensation policy?	D
Compensation Policy attract/retain executives	Does the company have a compensation policy to attract and retain executives?	D
Say on pay (executive compensation)	Do the company's shareholders have the right to vote on executive compensation?	D
Say on pay (stock-based compensation)	Does the company require that shareholder approval is obtained prior to the adoption of any stock-based compensation plans?	D
Anti-takeover devices		
Policy limiting anti-takeover devices	Does the company have a policy limiting the use of anti-takeover devices?	D

(continued)

Name	Description	Type of variable
Golden parachutes	Does the company have a golden parachute or other restrictive clauses related to changes of control (compensation plan for accelerated pay-out)?	D
Staggered Board	Does the company have a staggered board structure?	D
Supermajority vote requirement	Does the company have a supermajority vote requirement or qualified majority (for amendments of charters and bylaws or lock-in provisions)?	D
Veto power	Does the biggest owner (by voting power) hold the veto power or own golden shares?	D
Shareholders rights		
Limited rights to call special meetings	Has the company limited the rights of shareholders to call special meetings?	D
Majority vote for board members' election	Are the company's board members elected by a majority vote?	D
Minimum shares to vote	Has the company set requirements for a minimum number of shares to vote?	D
Director liability limitation	Does the company have a limitation of director liability?	D
Shares with different rights	Does the company have shares with different rights like priority shares or transfer limitations?	D
Shareholder engagement/ activism	Does the company have a policy to facilitate shareholder engagement, resolutions or proposals?	D
CSR		
CSR Committee	Does the company have a CSR committee or team?	D
Sustainability Report	Does the company publish a separate sustainability report or publish a section in its annual report on sustainability?	D
External auditor for sustainability report	Does the company have an external auditor of its sustainability report?	D
Sustainability index	Does the company report on belonging to a specific sustainability index?	D
GRI Guidelines	Is the company's sustainability report published in accordance with the GRI guidelines?	D
UN Global Compact	Has the company signed the UN Global Compact?	D
Stakeholder engagement	Does the company explain how it engages with its stakeholders?	D

D Dichotomous, *C* Continuous

References

Adams, R., & Mehran, H. (2003). Is corporate governance different for bank holding companies? *Economic Policy Review, 9*(1), 123–142.

Adams, R. B. (2012). Governance and the financial crisis. *International Review of Finance, 12*(1), 7–38.

Adams, R. B., & Ferreira, D. (2007). A theory of friendly boards. *Journal of Finance, 62*, 217–250.

Aizenman, J., Jinjarak, Y., Lee, M., & Park, D. (2016). Developing countries' financial vulnerability to the eurozone crisis: An event study of equity and bond markets. *Journal of Economic Policy Reform, 19*(1), 1–19.

Beltratti, A., & Stulz, R. M. (2012). The credit crisis around the globe: Why did some banks perform better during the credit crisis? *Journal of Financial Economics, 105*(1), 1–17.

Ben Shlomo, J., Eggert, W., & Nguyen, T. (2013). Regulation of remuneration policy in the financial sector: Evaluation of recent reforms in Europe. *Qualitative Research in Financial Markets, 5*(3), 256–269.

COM (Commission of the European Communities). (2010, June 2). *Green paper: Corporate governance in financial institutions and remuneration policies* COM (2010) 284. Brussels.

De Haan, J., & Vlahu, R. (2016). Corporate governance of banks: A survey. *Journal of Economic Surveys, 30*(2), 228–277.

Demirgüc-Kunt, A., & Detragiache, E. (2002). Does deposit insurance increase banking system stability? An empirical investigation. *Journal of Monetary Economics, 49*(7), 1373–1406.

Díaz Díaz, B., García Ramos, R., & Baraibar Díez, E. (2017). Corporate governance in Europe: Has the crisis affected corporate governance policies? In M. Aluchna & S. O. Idowu (Eds.), *Responsible Corporate Governance. Towards Sustainable and Effective Governance Structures*. Berlin: Springer.

Erkens, D. H., Hung, M., & Matos, P. (2012). Corporate governance in the 2007–2008 financial crisis: Evidence from financial institutions worldwide. *Journal of Corporate Finance, 18*(2), 389–411.

Fama, E. F., & Jensen, M. C. (1983). Separation of ownership and control. *Journal of Law and Economics, 26*, 301–325.

Flannery, M. J. (1998). Using market information in prudential bank supervision: A review of the U.S. empirical evidence. *Journal of Money, Credit and Banking, 30*(3), 273–305.

Kirkpatrick, G. (2009). The corporate governance lessons from the financial crisis. *OECD Journal: Financial Market Trends, 2009*(1), 61–87.

Kumar, P., & Zattoni, A. (2014). Corporate governance, board of directors, and the firm: A maturing field. *Corporate Governance: An international Review, 22*(5), 365–366.

Merton, R. (1977). An analytic derivation of the cost of deposit insurance and loan guarantees: An application of modern option pricing theory. *Journal of Banking and Finance, 1*, 3–11.

Millstein, M. I. (2014). *International comparison of selected corporate governance guidelines and codes of best practice*. United States, United Kingdom, France, Germany, OECD, Netherlands, Norway, Switzerland, Australia, Brazil, China, Hong Kong, India, Russia, United Arab Emirates. New York: Weil, Gotshal & Manges LLP, 1-149.

Mongiardino, A., & Plath, C. (2010). Risk governance at large banks: Have any lessons been learned? *Journal of Risk Management in Financial Institutions, 3*(2), 116–123.

Stathopoulos, K., & Voulgaris, G. (2015). The importance of shareholder activism: The case of say-on-pay. *Corporate Governance: An International Review*. https://doi.org/10.1111/corg.12147.

Taylor, J. B., & Williams, J. C. (2009). A black swan in the money market. *American Economic Journal: Macroeconomics, 1*(1), 58–83.

Tihanyi, L., Graffin, S., & George, G. (2014). Rethinking governance in management research. *Academy of Management Journal, 57*(6), 1535–1543.

Van den Berghe, L. A. A., & Levrau, A. (2004). Evaluating boards of directors: What constitutes a good corporate board? *Corporate Governance: An International Review, 12*(4), 461–478.

Chapter 4
IT Governance: Who Cares More? First Evidence from EU Banks and Supervisors

Sabrina Leo and Ida Claudia Panetta

4.1 Introduction

Even if first scientific research regarding the concept of IT governance was developed in the 1960s, only in the late 1990s did this topic obtain systematic attention from scholars. From then on, the concept of IT governance has become an object of greater attention and has been analysed in the broader context of corporate governance mechanisms. The literature provides various definitions and a range of constructs to describe the concept of IT governance (see Table 4.1) in the form of different structures, processes, domains, facets, and elements, analogous to the study of corporate governance in general.

It is important to note however that IT governance merits distinct attention within other corporate governance mechanisms for two reasons:

- most organizations in today's complex and competitive business environment rely heavily on IT to improve operating efficiency and sustain competitive advantage (Mata et al. 1995);
- IT governance can help firms to arrange and specify an efficient IT decision-making structure for a range of IT-related topics, such as IT investment, IT principles, and IT infrastructure management (Sambamurthy and Zmud 1999; Weill and Ross 2004; Xue et al. 2008, 2011).

Therefore, the effective governance of IT can support organizations in generating value-added objectives on top of IT, thereby contributing to the broader objectives of corporate governance (Weill and Ross 2004).

S. Leo (✉) • I.C. Panetta
Sapienza University of Rome, Rome, Italy
e-mail: sabrina.leo@uniroma1.it; ida.panetta@uniroma1.it

B. Díaz Díaz et al. (eds.), *Corporate Governance in Banking and Investor Protection*, CSR, Sustainability, Ethics & Governance,
https://doi.org/10.1007/978-3-319-70007-6_4

Table 4.1 IT governance: most cited definitions

Authors (year)	Definitions of IT governance
ITGI (2003, p. 10)	[it ensured that] the organization's IT sustains and extends the organization's strategy and objectives
IT Governance Institute (2003, p. 11)	[. . .] consists of the leadership and organizational structures and processes that ensure that the organization's IT sustains and extends the organization's strategies and objectives
Weill and Ross (2004, p. 8)	[. . .] is decision rights and accountability framework to encourage desirable behaviour in using IT
ISO/IEC 17799 (2005)	[. . .] is integral part of organizational management and responsibility of managing and supervising boards and it consists of leadership, organizational structure and processes that ensure IT is used as enhancer of organizational strategy and goals
Webb et al. (2006, p. 7)	[. . .] is the strategic alignment of IT with business such that maximum business value is achieved through the development and maintenance of effective IT control and accountability, performance management and risk management
Spremić (2009, p. 906)	[. . .] implies that IT processes are fully integrated into life cycle of business process and it influences on quality of service and business agility

IT, as for other industries, is an intrinsic component of banks' operational functioning too; and has become the backbone of almost all banking processes considering the growing role assumed in: a) supporting management in strategic decisions; b) facilitating the automated control environment on which core banking data are based; c) developing new products and services to compete in the financial markets; and d) the improvement of distribution channels.

While IT has emerged as a strategic resource in today's banking business environment, it can also raise critical issues, such as effective IT decision making and management control, IT investment priorities, and IT risk management. Regarding the latter, one lesson learned from the financial crisis that began in 2008 was that banks' IT and data architectures were, on the one hand, necessary to improve banks' efficiency and risk management process, and, on the other, deeply inadequate to support the broad management of financial risks.

Banks' capacity to capture robust data for timely and automated risk identification increasingly relies on data and technology infrastructures. Two are the relationships between risk management and IT that are most relevant:

- risk management in banks is increasingly supported by IT: for instance, databases allow the recording and analysis of risk events, systems support models for risk quantification, internal rating models, etc.;
- the more that IT penetrates the banking processes, the greater the dependence of business activities on IT, which, in turn, increases the relevance of IT risk management.

The lack of the ability of many banks to efficiently and effectively provide Senior Management with a true picture of the risks the organization faces—more evident during the global financial crisis—has led to a renewed attention on IT management from regulators.

For instance, at the international level BCBS and EBA have intervened defining a set of new rules (e.g. Basel III framework) and guidelines (e.g. Principles for effective risk data aggregation and risk reporting) which affect—albeit indirectly—IT governance. However, regulators do not specifically address banks requisites for effective IT governance and risk management systems, even so these changes likely result in strategy overhaul, process review and IT systems impact on the banking industry.

Given the awareness that risk management systems have failed in many cases due to inadequate corporate governance mechanism rather than the failure of IT systems *strictu sensu*, in this chapter we wish to highlight if banks have begun to ascribe greater importance to the coordinated management of all IT resources, in other words to IT governance.

We explore the attention payed to IT governance in four EU countries by a sample of banks and national Supervisors, to point out if, after the crisis, the interest on this topic as well as the level of investments in IT has increased.

In contrast to previous studies which use case studies and/or questionnaires to investigate IT governance practices, we base our analysis on banks' public disclosure. We root our research on the largely shared assumptions that firms with good IT governance tend to disclose more on related mechanisms (e.g. Clarkson et al. 2004).

To observe if the attention to IT governance has increased in the last few years, we develop an original descriptive framework of IT governance (ITGF) disclosure tailored to the banking sector.

Using the ITGF we perform a content analysis to measure the level of attention on IT governance through the years (2008–2015) and cross countries from both banks and Supervisors.

This study, to the extent that constitutes a pilot study, provides several insights into the academic debate within the macro strand of literature on corporate governance mechanisms, and more specifically on the less analysed topic of IT governance focusing on the banking sector.

The chapter is organized as follows: Sect. 4.2 provides the background of the research, including the existing literature and development of research questions, Sect. 4.3 describes the research methodology and the sample and data collection, the main results are presented in Sect. 4.4; finally, Sect. 4.5, presents the conclusions and outlines areas for future research.

4.2 Background and Development of Research Questions

4.2.1 IT Governance and Transparency

Traditionally, the literature has deepened our understanding of the role of Information Technology issues in the banking sector and typically analyses linkages with efficiency: the results demonstrate that on the one hand IT is considered a key resource in improving banks' operating efficiency (Banker et al. 2009; Berger 2003; Chiasson and Davidson 2005; Chowdhury 2003; Fuβ et al. 2007; Zhu et al. 2004); and, on the other , the presence of a weak or non-existent relationship between IT and bank productivity (CEA 2001; McKinsey Global Institute 2001; Beccalli 2007).

More recently a limited part of literature has started to look at IT in the banking sector from another perspective: IT governance (e.g. Pardo et al. 2011).

Broadly speaking, IT governance provides structures, processes, and relational mechanisms to control and monitor the effectiveness of IT (Peterson 2004; De Haes and Van Grembergen 2009; Willson and Pollard 2009). IT governance and its mechanisms are conceptualized in the literature following corporate governance principles (Korac-Kakabadse and Kakabadse 2001; ITGI 2003; Weill and Ross 2004; Peterson 2004; Jordan and Musson 2004; Mähring 2006; Raghupathi 2007; Van Grembergen and De Haes 2009; Heart et al. 2010); and decision rights, accountability, and risk management are some linked mechanisms included in more recent research (Brown 1997; Sambamurthy and Zmud 1999; Weill and Ross 2004; Brown and Grant 2005; Parent and Reich 2009; Huang et al. 2010).

In trying to identify effective IT governance arrangements, scholars have extended their analysis to different areas of IT governance (Sambamurthy and Zmud 1999; Kambil and Lucas 2002; Trites 2004; Weill and Ross 2004; Andriole 2009; Huang et al. 2010; Xue et al. 2011), covering areas such as the role of the Board of Directors, the effectiveness of the IT steering committee, IT control and firm performance, IT investment performance, and IT audit issues (Trites 2004; Huff et al. 2006; Mähring 2006; Boritz and Lim 2008; Gu et al. 2008; Merhout and Havelka 2008; Prasad et al. 2009).

While most of the principles of corporate governance are integrated into the major IT governance literature, scholars seem to have paid less attention to IT governance transparency. The latter is defined as the ability of firms to provide adequate and relevant IT governance information in a timely and effective manner to stakeholders (investors, policy makers, and regulatory bodies), to enable them to assess management's behaviour in using IT (Millar et al. 2005; Eldomiaty and Choi 2006; Raghupathi 2007; Joshi et al. 2013).

As demonstrated in the existing literature, firms provide information on IT governance—voluntarily—if they obtain benefits such as a reduced cost of capital (Barry and Brown 1985, 1986; Vanstraelen et al. 2003; Easley and O'Hara 2004), an improvement in liquidity (Diamond and Verrecchia 1991; Kim and Verrecchia 1994), and better information intermediation (Bhushan 1989; Lang and Lundholm 1996).

Based on the study of Lang and Lundholm (1996) and Clarkson et al. (2004), we infer that the more firms have good IT governance in place, the more they are incentivised to disclose.

Based on this theoretical premise, the first two research questions that we try to answer are:

Q1 Has the level of IT governance disclosure changed after financial turmoil?
Q2 What topics of IT governance are publicly disclosed and where (in which public document) the information on IT governance topics can be found?

In our knowledge, there is no specific study on IT governance disclosure in the banking sector, except the contribution from Joshi et al. (2013) that demonstrate differences in level of disclosure are related to varying institutional settings.

4.2.2 Changes in the IT Risk Management Regulation Framework

Since IT governance (like other aspect of banking business) can be influenced by the regulatory environment, it is important to understand in which direction Supervisors and Regulators have moved. As mentioned above, the recent financial turmoil has catalysed attention, among others, on risk management and in particular on the processes, data management and the new emerging risks such as IT risk (Taplin 2016).

IT risk is differently defined across time and countries as shown in the Table 4.2. In the banking sector, it is generally considered as a key type of operational risk; subject to very specific challenges given that the financial system has become more complex and interconnected (EBA 2015a).

More specifically, from an IT governance perspective, Parent and Reich (2009) identify several types of IT risks such as IT project risk, IT competence risk, IT infrastructure risk, business continuity, and information risk, which can have adverse impacts on business.

Generally, for the assessment of IT risks all banks have mechanisms and measures in placein certain forms depending on regulation at the local level (Johnson 2015).

Table 4.2 IT-related-risk: main definition

Authors (year)	Definitions
Loch et al. (1992)	[. . .] IT operational risk could result in the disclosure, modification, destruction, or denial of use of IT resources
Straub and Welke (1998, p. 442)	[. . .] define "systems risk" as uncertainty related to using computer-based systems and interpret this risk to be "broadly construed to mean modification, destruction, theft, or lack of availability of computer assets such as hardware, software, data, and services"
Jordan and Silcock (2005)	An IT risk is something that can go wrong with IT and cause a negative impact on the business
ITGI (2008)	[. . .] IT risk is business risk – specifically, the business risk associated with the use, ownership, operation, involvement, influence and adoption of IT within an enterprise
Goldstein et al. (2011, p. 610)	[. . .] IT operational risk is any threat that may lead to the improper modification, destruction, theft, or lack of availability of IT assets
EBA (2015b)	[. . .] operational risk related to information and communication technologies

The renewed interest in risk management has culminated in the necessity to review the regulatory framework. In fact, at the international level the BCBS has:

- started a comprehensive review of Basel II, culminating in the release of a reform package known as the Basel III Framework (corresponding to Capital Requirements Regulation (CRR) and Capital Requirements Directive (CRD IV) in EU countries) which has affected—albeit indirectly—IT governance, emphasizing that risk management systems should have appropriate Management Information Systems (MIS);
- rolled out a new set of Principles with the aim to develop banks' Risk Data Aggregation and Risk Reporting, requesting banks to comply starting from 2016.

In the renewed Basel framework, there is no specific reference to IT related risk and IT risk management process, (nor in other international regulatory intervention); IT risk is considered as a sub-type of operational risk (art 85 CRD IV).

Articles 4 and 321 to 325 of the CRR set out the measures that financial institutions should take to manage operational risk (and the related capital they need to hold to cover such risks), including risks related to cyber-attacks (CRR, CRD IV). Banks also need to have contingency lens that ensure continuity of their business and limit losses in case of severe disruptions.

The CRD IV requires banks to perform a major update to their IT risk management in terms of:

- process: the implementation of rules and standards in their business, leading to new opportunities and adapted business processes;
- data: under the new rules, banks will need to demonstrate data quality and traceability;
- technology: one of the biggest impacts from a technological standpoint is the ability to produce integrated reports, with consistent reporting across the company.

Furthermore, in Europe, to reinforce the importance of adequate IT risk management for banks, the EBA Guidelines provide direction to the Supervisors for assessing banks' IT risk (EBA 2016): one more time, regulators don't address banks specific requests for an effective IT risk management system, but set a framework for Supervisors to monitor this topic at an institutional level.

Considering that all these changes in the regulatory environment may result in strategy overhaul, process review and IT systems impact, we want to examine whether any differences in Supervisors' attitude to IT concerns at the national level, will induce differences in banks' IT governance, and level of investments in IT projects. So, the last research questions are:

Q3 To what extent—if any-has Supervisors' behaviour beens affected by the attention paid by banks to this theme?

Q4 Have Supervisors' indications influenced the banks' level of IT systems investment?

4.3 Research Methodology

Our analysis is devoted to evaluate IT governance practices for a sample of EU banks and to observe if the attention to this issue has increased over time (2008–2015) and/or varies across countries (Italy, Germany, France and Spain). Geographical differences can be surely influenced by different regulatory approaches used by Supervisors at the national level.

The first two research questions are oriented towards analysing the level (Q1) and the content (Q2) of disclosure of IT governance performed by each institution; to investigate IT governance transparency, we use content analysis to build-up the dataset to be employed in the empirical analysis (Weber 1985). Information is obtained from public disclosure documents of banks included in the sample (see Sect. 4.3.2).

To carry out the content analysis, we identify a set of items related to IT governance grouped into four focus areas/categories (IT Role & Responsibility, IT Resources & Plans, IT Risk Management, IT Investment); the resulting original IT governance framework (ITGF) is elaborated by adapting and enriching the Joshi et al. (2013) approach to fit our purpose (see Sect. 4.3.1).

For each focus area under ITGF, the items were selected on the basis of current literature (see Tables 4.3, 4.4, 4.5 and 4.6), including terms that have emerged from the regulatory environment and practitioner debate as well as on a pilot study we conducted on bank annual reports.

Using the selected set of items within the ITGF, we inspect the institutions' documents using the program MAXQDA to verify whether each item is present (1 = present; 0 = not present) and how many times it is enumerated. We then build up a unique dataset to be used to measure the level of IT governance disclosure. In particular for each institution (bank and Supervisor) it was possible to compute:

- a *total IT governance score*, which represents the number of times that each item is disclosed in the reports analysed; for example, if we find evidence of Internal Audit position five times in the Annual report, then it is assigned an item score of 5. As it is difficult to discriminate if institutions write a short sentence or an entire section regarding IT governance in their reports, we decided to consider not only the presence of each item (0,1), but also the total number of times they are enumerated (item score). The underlying assumption is that the more banks and Supervisors mention ITGF items, the higher the level of disclosure. The total IT governance score (or focus area score) is obtained by simply adding the scores related to items within ITGF (or within focus areas).
- a *total IT governance disclosure index* (ITGF_Index) and four IT governance indices, one for each focus area within ITGF (ITRR_Index, ITRP_Index, ITRM_Index, ITINV_Index) are constructed. The indices are obtained by simply adding the score of each focus area divided by the number of items in each category (Bollen et al. 2006; Joshi et al. 2013):

Table 4.3 ITRR Index: description of items and literature references

N°	Items	Description	Relevant literature
1	IT audit/EDP audit	Presence of IT and information assets related risk are on the agenda of the Audit or Risk committee	Hadden and Hermanson (2003), De Haes and Van Grembergen (2008), Joshi et al. (2013)
2	Information security control function	Presence of control function related to information security	Pilot study
3	Business continuity management	Presence of responsible for business continuity	
4	CERT/SOC	Presence of Computer Emergency Response Team/Security Operations Centre	
5	Data management office/centre	Presence of organizational position related to Data management	
6	IT service/function	Presence of specific organizational position	
7	CIO	Presence of CIO or an equivalent position with respect to IT and information assets at an executive level	Peterson (2004), De Haes and Van Grembergen (2008), Joshi et al. (2013)
8	CISO	Presence of CISO with respect to IT security at an executive level	Pilot study
9	IT management	Presence of senior management dedicated to IT asset	
10	Technology committee	Presence of a special committee which looks after IT and related technology architecture, projects, and governance issue at an executive level	Premuroso and Bhattacharya (2007), Joshi et al. (2013)
11	Other IT committee	Presence of: i) a committee looking after IT and information assets at the board level; ii) a committee which monitors IT management, IT spending, and related cost allocations (IT steering committee); iii) a committee which looks after strategic planning and investment decisions on IT and information assets (IT planning committee)	Sambamurthy, et al. (1993), Karimi et al. (2000), Peterson (2004), Trites (2004), Van Grembergen and De Haes (2004), Nolan and McFarlan (2005), De Haes and Van Grembergen (2008), Joshi et al. (2013)

$$\text{IT Y\_Index} = \frac{1}{Ny} \sum\nolimits_{i=1}^{Ny} (x_i)$$

Where IT $Y_{\_Index}$ = IT governance Index related to the focus area/categories Y (namely GF: entire Governance Framework; RR: Role and Responsibility; RP: Resources and Plans; RM: Risk Management; INV: Investment); x_i = Sum of

Table 4.4 ITRP Index: description of items and literature references

N°	Items	Description	Relevant literature
1	Information security policy	Presence of a clear information and security policy	Trites (2004), Jordan and Silcock (2005), Joshi et al. (2013)
2	IT plan/s		
3	IT strategy	Presence of any kind of reference to IT strategies	Pilot study
4	EDP	Presence of explicit reference to Electronic Data Processing	
5	IT resources governance	Presence of specific IT process and procedures in place	
6	IT processes/ procedures		
7	IT/Data infrastructure/ Architecture	Terms related to the relevance assumed by data governance after 2008 financial crisis, as a key resource to support strategic planning and tactical decision making	SSG (2010), BCBS (2013)
8	IT resources/ solution	Presence of explicit reference to IT resources and solutions	Pilot study
9	ITIL/COBIT/ NIST	Presence of explicit reference to the adoption of any IT governance framework/ standard	ITGI (2003), De Haes and Van Grembergen (2008), Joshi et al. (2013)
10	ISO 27001-5		
11	Other IT governance Standards		

the item scores within each focus area/categories, and N_y number of items included in Y focus area/categories.

These indices are used to compare the level of IT governance disclosure across time and countries (Q1). From the dataset, it is also possible to have a look at how and where banks disclose details on IT governance (Q2).

To measure changes in attention paid by different Authorities to IT governance, we perform content analysis on a selected group of Supervisors' documents. We consider items included in the first three focus areas (ITRR, ITRP, ITRM), verifying whether each item is present (1 = present; 0 = not present) in the Authorities' Annual reports or national law. The underlying hypothesis is that in these kinds of documents it is possible to find signals of a greater level of attention to IT governance paid by Supervisors. Starting from the resulting original dataset we build a comprehensive ITGF_Index for each Authority.

To evaluate the influence of Supervisors' attitude on banks' IT governance behaviour we investigate the relationship between ITGF_Index_Banks and ITGF_Index_Supervisors (Q3) using an OLS regression model estimates.

Finally, we calculate the banks' level of investments in IT systems (ITEXP), as a proxy of banks' efforts to maintain IT systems and security at adequate levels and infer that related internal controls remain "robust". We measure the level of investments in IT considering all expenditure (registered both in the Balance

Table 4.5 ITRM Index: description of items and literature references

N°	Items	Description	Relevant literature
1	Cyber risk/ Attack IS breach	Presence of reference to identification of IT risk	Jordan and Silcock (2005), Joshi et al. (2013), Regulatory environment & practitioners debate
2	IT fraud		
3	IT Incident/ failure		
4	IT risk		
5	IT risk/Business continuity/Cyber security model	Presence of elements related to the evaluation of IT risk	Pilot study
6	IT risk appetite		
7	IT risk assessment		
8	IT risk report		
9	Business continuity plan	Presence of IT and related technology continuity plans; these plans, in case of disaster, are also expressed required by regulatory framework	Jordan and Silcock (2005), Joshi et al. (2013)
10	Contingency plan		
11	Disaster recovery plan		
12	Information/ Cyber security plan	Presence of special program to mitigate IT risk	Jordan and Silcock (2005), De Haes and Van Grembergen (2008), Merhout and Havelka (2008), Joshi et al. (2013)
13	IT risk management		
14	IT risk regulation/compliance	Presence of explicit reference to regulations and compliance requirements	Trites (2004), Jordan and Silcock (2005), Li et al. (2007)

Table 4.6 ITINV Index: description of items and literature references

N°	Items	Description	Relevant literature
1	Expenses in income statement	Presence of IT related expenses, mentioned under the administrative cost	Joshi et al. (2013)
2	Investment in balance sheet	Presence of IT related investment, mentioned as intangible assets	
3	IT budget	Presence of information regarded budget on IT and information assets	Takemura et al. (2005), De Haes and Van Grembergen (2008)
4	IT Expenses	Presence of information on the overall IT expenditure	Takemura et al. (2005), De Haes and Van Grembergen (2008)
5	IT hardware/ software	Presence of information on IT hardware/ software cost mentioned under the IT expenditure	Takemura et al. (2005)

Sheet and Income Statement) made by banks to maintain an adequate level of the efficiency of the system. The level of investments in IT over time is normalised by Total Assets to obtain the ITEXP_Index. We use this index to verify if there is an influence of Supervisors' indications on the banks' level of IT investments (Q4).

The analysis, at this stage, can be considered as a pilot study (with a limited sample size) to test banks' and supervisors' behaviour on IT governance issues.

4.3.1 IT Governance Framework: Development of Categories

The existing IT governance literature does not propose any single standard framework to assess IT governance using disclosure practices: all empirical analysis, except Joshi et al. (2013), are based on surveys and/or single case studies, in other words are based on internal information. Analysing banks' from 'outside' we are aware that banks do not disclose all aspects of their IT governance, also because they are not forced to describe specific procedures relating to their IT strategy and so on. Following Lang and Lundholm (1996) and Clarkson et al. (2004), we assume that the more banks have good IT governance in place, the more they are incentivized to disclose.

Considering this premise, we expect to find some clues of specific structural IT governance mechanisms in place in each institution analysed. For example, a bank might disclose the presence of a Technology Committee to implement IT strategy, or of CIO to support business goals with IT management at the top level. The underlying assumption is that the dissemination of this kind of information makes clear to stakeholders that the bank has an IT governance structure and that—probably–IT policies and procedures are in place.

To develop content categories, we construct a so-called IT Governance Framework according to previous scholars contributions in assessing IT governance and base this on our pilot study conducted on the Annual Reports of banks/Supervisors and on key international regulations; Tables 4.3, 4.4, 4.5 and 4.6 provide a brief description and highlight the supporting literature for each item included in each of the four focus areas/categories.

According to the prevalent literature (Table 4.3) we suggest that the level of transparency on IT roles and responsibilities (IT Role & Responsibility, ITRR) can be used as a proxy of good IT governance practices. In our view it is possible to summarise previous scholars' contribution on the relevance of IT roles assigned among firms, focusing on the following:

- IT strategic roles;
- IT senior management;
- IT operational roles;
- IT control roles.

The definitions of corporate governance (OECD 1999, 2004), of which IT governance can be considered a sub-set, presents a need for leadership (strategic roles), direction (Senior Management) and control (roles). Therefore, IT governance must be driven from the highest levels within the organisation not only from the IT department or business unit levels (operational roles) across the organisation (Webb et al. 2006). In order for IT to be effectively governed the presence of a variety of roles can be considered a necessary premise (Table 4.3).

Compared with previous studies, we extend the number of items related to control functions: starting from the main three obligatory control functions in banks defined by Basel documents (risk control, compliance and internal audit), we consider IT risk control, IT compliance, and IT audit; the underlying assumption is that with a growing level of complexity and interdependencies of banks' technology and operating structures, IT control roles should be reinforced.

With the second focus area (IT Resources & Plans, ITRP) we aim to investigate the relevance attributed to IT resources/process and infrastructures, in the belief that, due to both competitive and regulatory pressures, the relevance of IT management elements would increase, and consequently, the related information in public documents (Table 4.4).

To capture IT risk management practices (IT Risk Management, ITRM) we construct an index that considers the main phases of risk management processes: identification, evaluation, treatment and monitoring. The basic assumption is that the main constituent of IT risk management should be communicated to all relevant stakeholders. With this indicator, we try to determine if banks disclose IT-related risk management policies/processes in place, and if IT risk is treated jointly or independently with respect to the operational risk management framework (Table 4.5).

The last focus area ITINV, concentrates on IT budget/investments. In the past two decades, practitioners and scholars (ITGI 2003; Weill and Ross 2004) have paid great attention to this topic, but the major part of these studies typically focus on the relationship between the disclosure on IT financial matters and economic benefits for firms. In our research, we analyse IT investments as an attribute of IT governance disclosure, since budgeting and investments are the responsibilities of Top Management (ITGI 2003); and better IT governance practices are based on clear information on IT investments useful to assess the business value of IT (Table 4.6).

4.3.2 The Sample and the Data Collection

Countries selected for our analysis are France, Germany, Italy and Spain due to the dimension of the national banking system in term of total assets, representing together around 73% of total assets of the EU banking sector (ECB 2016). For each country, we consider the three major banks, being sure to include in the sample at least one G-SIB for each country: the final sample consists of 12 international banking groups (Table 4.7). As mentioned in the previous pages, to perform the content analysis, we record data from different sources of public disclosure of banks included in the sample (281 documents), namely:

- Annual Reports;
- Corporate Governance reports;
- Pillar III reports;
- CSR/Sustainability reports, if any.

To calculate the ITGF_Index for Supervisors we perform the content analysis on the following sources:

- Supervisors' Annual Reports (30 documents in total, Table 4.8);
- Regulations which, during the period 2008–2015:
  - put in place the Basel III framework;

Table 4.7 Banks' sample composition and documents collected (2015)

Country	Total assets (bln €)[a]	Share of Euro area total assets[a]	Bank	G-SIB (2015)[b]	Total assets (mln €)	Share of total assets of countries banking system	N° of documents analysed
France	6940	25%	Crédit Agricole	×	1,529,294	20%	8[(1)(2)]
			BNP Paribas	×	1,292,206	17%	16[(1)(2)]
			Société Générale	×	1,334,391	17%	15[(1)(3)]
Germany	6955	25%	Deutsche Bank	×	1,629,130	21%	32
			CommerzBank		532,641	7%	23[(1)]
			Landesbank Baden-Württemberg		234,015	3%	23[(1)]
Italy	2724	10%	Unicredit	×	860,433	22%	32
			Intesa San Paolo		676,496	17%	32
			Monte dei Paschi di Siena		169,012	4%	24[(4)]
Spain	3664	13%	Banco Santander	×	1,340,260	48%	32
			BBVA		397,303	14%	24[(3)]
			Banco Sabadell		208,628	7%	20[(5)]

Note: [(1)] no separated CG Report; [(2)] no separated Pillar III; [(3)] no separated CSR Report; [(4)] CSR n.a.; [(5)] Separated CG Report for 2009; Pillar III n.a. In English, for the period 2011–2015; CSR n.a. for the period 2013–2014

Source: [a]ECB (2016), p. 69; [b]FSB (2015), p. 2; bank's website

Table 4.8 Supervisors' sample composition and documents collected

Supervisor (acronym)	Country	N° of annual report analysed (time span)
Supervisory and Resolution Authority—Autorité de Contrôle prudentiel et de résolution (ACPR)	France	6 (2010–2015)
Federal Financial Supervisory Authority—Bundesanstal für Finanzdienstleistungsaufsicht (BaFin)	Germany	8 (2008–2015)
Bank of Italy—Banca d'Italia (BoI)	Italy	8 (2008–2015)
Bank of Spain—Banco de España (BoS)	Spain	8 (2008–2015)

- apply EBA Guidelines on internal Governance (GL44);
- specifically refer to the BCBS (2013) Principles of effective Risk Data aggregation and Risk Reporting (PRDARR);

and any other specific regulation on IT governance, if available in English (see Table 4.9).

Even if we find other important regulatory provisions in the analysed countries, it was difficult to perform further content analysis because of the absence of English translations.

4.4 Results and Discussion

Table 4.10 provides descriptive statistics for the variables employed in this study. The mean for the overall IT disclosure index (ITGF_Index) is 2.85, representing that on average, during the period considered, banks mentioned around 117 times items within ITGF (consisting of 41 items); however, the range of the index is broad among the sample (from 0.3 to 17). Similar considerations can be done for Supervisors' ITGF index (from 0.03 to 1.8) even if the mean value and the range of variation are smaller than for banks.

Table 4.11 provides the evolution of IT Governance Indices calculated for the banks' sample and grouped by country (Q1). Looking at the results it is evident that there is a generalized increase of IT governance disclosure through the years with more intensity starting from 2013 and for Risk Management issues. ITINV_Index doesn't indicate any particular evidence since it shows depressed values across the year and across country.

It is also possible to highlight differences across countries. For instance, Spanish banks in the sample have started to pay greater attention to ITRM categories in 2012 and give more importance to all items related to ITRR and ITRP focus areas in 2015. Spain differs from other countries, also because of the presence of a larger number of roles and responsibilities related to IT governance.

Table 4.9 Regulations considered in ITGF_Index for supervisors

References	Italian implementation	French implementation	German implementation	Spanish implementation
EBA Guidelines on Internal Governance EBA/CEBS (2011)	• Circular 288/2015 • 15th update (2013) of Circular no 263/2006 • 15th up date (2015) of Circular no 285/2015	• Article 511.41 French Monetary and Financial Code(Code Monétaire et Financier), update in 2014	• German Banking Act, 2012 (Kreditwesengesetz–KWG) • Circular 10/2012 MaRisk	Adoption of the Guidelines as their own on 27 June 2012
BCBS Principles for effective Risk Data Aggregation and Risk Reporting (2013)	• 15th update (2015) of Circular no 285/2015	Not found	• German Banking Act (Kreditwesengesetz-KWG) • Circular 10/2012 MaRisk	Not found
CRD IV—Directive 2013/36/EU of the European Parliament (2013)	• 15th update (2013) of Circular no 263/2006 • 15th update (2015) of Circular no 285/2015	• French Monetary and Financial Code (Code Monétaire et Financier), update in 2014	• German Banking Act (Kreditwesengesetz–KWG) • Circular 5/2014 (BA)	• Ley 10/2014 • Royal Decree 84/2015 • Circular 2/2016 • Law 14/2013 of 29 November 2013
Other		• Regulation 97-02 of 21 February 1997, relating to internal control in credit institutions and investment firms (revised in 2010)		

Table 4.10 Descriptive statistics

Variable	Obs	Mean	Std. dev.	Min	Max
ITGF_Index_Banks	96	2.847257	2.082997	0.2909091	16.95844
ITRR_Index	96	0.4554924	0.7064599	0	6.090909
ITINV_Index	96	0.4666667	0.3802123	0	2
ITRM_Index	96	1.329454	1.114778	0	7.285714
ITRP_Index	96	0.5956439	0.7446337	0	3.181818
ITEXP_Index	96	0.0012736	0.0010066	0	0.0056655
ITGF_Index_Supervisors	90	0.660019	0.5650148	0.02849	1.823362

Table 4.11 Evolution of banks' IT governance indices[a]: distribution by country[b]

	2008	2009	2010	2011	2012	2013	2014	2015
ITGF_Index								
France	6.91	7.42	5.22	6.13	7.15	5.77	7.93	10.07
Germany	3.93	3.88	4.64	5.5	6.97	8.11	10.47	9.79
Italy	8.67	10.56	8.3	9.91	8.28	9.04	10.03	12.92
Spain	5.27	6.62	5.83	7.09	6.38	8.46	13.85	23.72
Total	24.77	28.48	23.99	28.62	28.79	31.38	42.29	56.5
ITRR_Index								
France	0.18	0.55	0.55	0.55	0.64	0.55	0.64	2.55
Germany	0.55	0.45	0.64	0.55	0.73	1.36	1.91	1.82
Italy	1.27	1.27	1.09	1	1	1.27	1.27	2.36
Spain	1.73	1.45	1.27	1	1.36	1.82	2.73	7.64
Total	3.73	3.73	3.55	3.09	3.73	5	6.55	14.36
ITRP_Index								
Germany	0.18	0.36	0	0.82	0.91	1.55	1.91	1.64
Spain	0.27	0.36	0.09	0.09	0.82	0.91	1.73	4.82
France	0.73	0.55	0.55	1.18	1.18	1.09	1.36	1.45
Italy	2.73	4.82	3.55	4.91	3.82	3.64	4.09	5.09
Total	3.91	6.09	4.18	7	6.73	7.18	9.09	13
ITRM_Index								
France	4.8	5.13	3.73	4	4.33	3.53	5.33	5.67
Germany	1	0.67	0.6	0.93	1.93	1.60	3.85	4.13
Italy	3.67	3.27	2.87	3.2	2.87	3.33	3.47	4.47
Spain	2.47	3.60	3.47	5	3.20	4.73	8.20	10.07
Total	11.93	12.67	10.67	13.13	12.33	13.2	20.85	24.33
ITINV_Index								
France	1.20	1.20	0.40	0.40	1.00	0.60	0.60	0.40
Germany	2.20	2.40	3.40	3.20	3.40	3.60	2.80	2.20
Italy	1	1.20	0.80	0.80	0.60	0.80	1.20	1
Spain	0.80	1.20	1	1	1	1	1.20	1.20
Total	5.20	6.00	5.60	5.40	6.00	6.00	5.80	4.80

Note: [a]ITGF_Index is the sum of the indices related to the four focus areas (ITRR_Index, ITRP_Index, ITRM_Index, ITINV_Index)

[b]The value of indices for each country is calculated as the sum of banks' indices included in the sub-sample

Italian banks recorded a slight upward trend over time for all indices particularly for the ITRP_Index.

To answer to Q2 we analysed the percentage of IT governance items disclosed by banks in the sample (Table 4.12) and the documents in which they are disclosed (Table 4.13). Considering data reported in the following Tables we notice a lack of disclosure of organizational positions (see category ITRR); more attention is paid instead to IT services/functions and to Operational roles relating to business continuity.

ITRP exhibits an increasing attention to IT resources and to Electronic Data Processing starting from 2013. While few banks refer to IT policy and IT plans.

Within ITGF, ITRM is the most reported focus area; an increasing number of banks in the sample refer directly to IT risk, starting to consider it as a specific category instead of being included under operational risk. Business continuity plans and Information security are critically important.

Finally, ITINV, indicates that in the most part banks report IT expenditures, but this seems mainly related to accounting policies instead of disclosure about investment plans. Maybe this attitude is due to the strategic and competitive relevance of IT investments and the need for banks to preserve the related programs' details.

Table 4.13 represents the banks' preferences regarding the documents used to disclose about IT governance (Q2). Considering the general content of the four types of documents we would expect to find more evidence regarding items grouped as follows:

- ITRR and ITRP in the CG Report;
- ITRM in the Pillar III Report;
- ITINV in the Annual Report.

Looking at the results it is evident that banks included in the sample use the Annual Report as the most important document to disseminate information on IT governance issues. It is true for ITRR and ITRP categories as well as ITRM. Surprisingly, banks do not refer to RM practices in the Pillar III Report but—again—prefer the Annual Report.

As expected information related to the ITINV focus area is described in the Annual Report, even if we note that some banks often include IT expenses in the CSR Report, suggesting that banks assign to IT investment a specific role in value creation for all stakeholders.

Before analysing the results of the Supervisors' behaviour, we would like to point out that it was not possible to find out the English version of dispositions which transposed CRD IV and EBA Guidelines into national regulation (Table 4.9), namely:

- the Code monétaire et financier, updated in 2014, for France;
- 15th update to Circular 263/2006 and 285/2015, for Italy.

Nevertheless, we performed the content analysis using the available version of the three documents: while in Italy we have some findings due to the use of English terms in national legislation, for France we have no results. Considering these

Table 4.12 Percentage[a] of banks disclosing IT governance items

Categories	Items	2008	2009	2010	2011	2012	2013	2014	2015
ITRR	IT audit/EDP audit	–	–	–	–	8%	8%	17%	25%
	Information security control function	–	–	–	–	–	–	–	8%
	Business continuity management	17%	25%	25%	33%	25%	50%	33%	33%
	CERT/SOC	25%	25%	42%	25%	25%	25%	42%	42%
	Data management Office/centre	8%	–	17%	25%	25%	8%	8%	25%
	IT service/Function	58%	50%	25%	33%	50%	42%	58%	67%
	CIO	25%	17%	8%	–	8%	17%	25%	25%
	CISO	–	–	–	–	–	–	17%	42%
	IT management	25%	25%	8%	25%	17%	8%	17%	25%
	Technology committee	–	8%	8%	8%	8%	8%	17%	25%
	IT committee	–	–	8%	–	–	–	–	–
ITRP	Information security policy	–	–	–	–	–	–	–	–
	IT plan	17%	17%	–	8%	17%	17%	25%	42%
	IT strategy	–	–	–	17%	–	25%	42%	33%
	EDP	17%	25%	25%	25%	33%	50%	50%	42%
	IT resources governance	17%	17%	8%	8%	8%	8%	17%	33%
	IT processes/procedures	17%	17%	17%	33%	33%	33%	33%	50%
	IT/Data Infrastructure/Architecture	42%	58%	42%	67%	67%	67%	92%	75%
	IT resources/solutions	25%	17%	8%	25%	33%	33%	25%	50%
	ISO 27001-5	8%	8%	8%	8%	8%	17%	17%	25%
	ITIL/COBIT/NIST	25%	25%	17%	33%	25%	17%	42%	33%
	Generic standards	–	–	–	–	–	–	–	–
ITRM	Cyber risk/Attack IS breach	–	–	8%	25%	25%	25%	33%	67%
	IT fraud	–	–	–	–	8%	8%	8%	17%
	IT incident/failure	58%	67%	42%	67%	50%	50%	67%	75%
	IT risk	33%	42%	25%	33%	58%	67%	83%	83%
	IT risk/Business continuity/Cyber security model	–	8%	–	–	–	–	–	17%
	IT risk appetite	–	–	–	–	–	–	–	8%
	IT risk assessment	–	–	–	–	–	–	–	17%
	IT risk report	–	–	–	–	–	–	8%	8%
	Business continuity plan	67%	67%	67%	83%	75%	75%	75%	75%

(continued)

Table 4.12 (continued)

Categories	Items	2008	2009	2010	2011	2012	2013	2014	2015
	Contingency plan	67%	58%	67%	58%	58%	58%	58%	58%
	Disaster recovery plan	25%	17%	17%	17%	17%	17%	8%	25%
	Information/Cyber security plan	50%	25%	33%	33%	42%	42%	75%	75%
	IT risk management	8%	8%	8%	8%	8%	–	33%	17%
	IT risk regulation/ compliance	–	–	–	–	–	–	8%	–
ITINV	Expenses in income statement	58%	67%	67%	67%	67%	67%	67%	67%
	Investment in balance sheet	58%	58%	58%	58%	58%	58%	67%	67%
	IT budget	–	8%	–	–	–	–	–	–
	IT expenses	67%	58%	33%	33%	42%	33%	50%	42%
	IT hardware/ software	8%	17%	25%	17%	8%	25%	17%	8%

[a]Number of banks that disclose the Items of each category within ITGF divided by the number of banks included in the sample

limitations, we analyse the percentage of Supervisors that enumerate the items included into three focus areas (Table 4.14): ITRR, ITRP, ITRM. Comparing results between banks and Supervisors we notice a homogeneous behaviour between the two groups regarding the items enumerated.

This evidence allows us to deepen our understanding of the existence of a relationship between Supervisors' attitude and banks' behaviours (Q3).

We estimate the relationship between the ITGF_Index for banks and Supervisors using OLS regression with control variables equal to Country (dummies 1–4), the banks' size effect expressed by the natural logarithm of Total Asset (LogTa) and annual GDP growth: given the impossibility to control for bank and/or time fixed effect—due to the limited sample size-, we decided to control for geographical differences (Country and GDP) and banks' size. We use the 0 constant model to avoid the dummy variable trap. The model estimates, reported in Table 4.15, provide the following results:

- the coefficient of ITGF_Index_Supervisors is significantly positive as expected (1.75) and its magnitude suggests that changes in banks' behaviour are positively related to Supervisors' attention to IT;
- the selected control variables, with the exception of GDP, have a strong high influence on the dependent variable; in particular, it seems that larger banks pay more attention to IT issues (LogTa 3.54).

The model demonstrates good explanatory power expressed by the R-squared (0.81) and F test (although the F test for zero slopes in the absence of a constant is not easily interpretable).

Table 4.13 Distribution IT governance items by type of documents

		2008		2009		2010		2011		2012		2013		2014		2015	
CAT	DOC	n.	%	n.	%	n.	%	n.	%	n.	%	n.	%	n.	%	n.	%
ITRR	AR	28	68	26	63	26	67	24	71	30	73	33	60	40	56	97	61
	CG	–	–	1	2	1	3	–	–	1	2	4	7	11	15	21	13
	PIII	3	7	3	7	5	13	4	12	5	12	10	18	13	18	15	9
	CSR	10	24	11	27	7	18	6	18	5	12	8	15	8	11	25	16
	Total	41	100	41	100	39	100	34	100	41	100	55	100	72	100	158	100
ITRP	AR	23	53	27	40	29	63	39	51	39	53	42	53	63	63	80	56
	CG	6	14	9	13	1	2	13	17	8	11	10	13	12	12	20	14
	PIII	3	7	16	24	11	24	13	17	20	27	20	25	19	19	30	21
	CSR	11	26	15	22	5	11	12	16	7	9	7	9	6	6	13	9
	Total	43	100	67	100	46	100	77	100	74	100	79	100	100	100	143	100
ITRM	AR	104	58	111	58	104	65	125	63	115	62	123	62	187	60	189	52
	CG	12	7	18	9	15	9	16	8	12	6	19	10	33	11	56	15
	PIII	31	17	40	21	40	25	52	26	55	30	53	27	73	23	89	24
	CSR	32	18	21	11	1	1	4	2	3	2	3	2	19	6	31	8
	Total	179	100	190	100	160	100	197	100	185	100	198	100	312	100	365	100
ITINV	AR	10	83	12	80	9	69	8	67	9	60	7	47	8	62	5	63
	CG	–	–	–	–	–	–	–	–	–	–	–	–	–	–	1	13
	PIII	–	–	1	7	1	8	1	8	5	33	5	33	4	31	–	–
	CSR	2	17	2	13	3	23	3	25	1	7	3	20	1	8	2	25
	Total	12	100	15	100	13	100	12	100	15	100	15	100	13	100	8	100

CAT = ITGF categories; DOC = type of documents [AR = Annual Report; CG = Corporate Governance Report; PIII = Pillar III report; CSR = CSR report]; n. = number of items found in each type of documents under each ITGF category; % = n. divided by Total Items of each ITGF category

Table 4.14 Percentage[a] of supervisors enumerating IT governance keywords

Categories	Items	2008	2009	2010	2011	2012	2013	2014	2015
ITRR	IT audit/EDP audit	–	–	–	25%	–	25%	25%	25%
	Information security control function	–	–	–	–	–	–	–	–
	Business continuity management	–	–	–	–	25%	25%	25%	25%
	CERT/SOC	25%	–	–	–	–	–	–	–
	Data management Office/centre	–	–	–	–	–	–	–	–
	IT service/ Function	50%	25%	50%	25%	50%	75%	75%	75%
	CIO	25%	–	–	–	–	–	–	–
	CISO	–	–	–	–	25%	–	–	–
	IT management	–	–	–	25%	50%	25%	25%	25%
	Technology committee	–	–	–	–	–	–	–	–
	IT committee	–	–	–	–	–	–	–	–
ITRP	Information security policy	–	–	–	–	–	25%	25%	25%
	IT plan	–	–	25%	25%	–	75%	100%	75%
	IT Strategy	–	–	–	25%	–	50%	25%	50%
	EDP	–	–	–	25%	50%	50%	50%	50%
	IT resources governance	–	–	–	–	–	50%	50%	50%
	IT processes/ procedures	–	–	25%	25%	50%	50%	75%	50%
	IT/Data infrastructure/Architecture	–	–	50%	75%	50%	75%	50%	75%
	IT resources/ solutions	25%	25%	25%	25%	50%	50%	50%	50%
	ISO 27001-5	–	–	–	–	–	–	–	–
	ITIL/COBIT/ NIST	–	–	–	–	–	–	–	–
	Generic standards	–	–	–	–	–	–	–	–
ITRM	Cyber Risk/Attack IS Breach	–	–	–	–	–	–	–	75%
	IT fraud	–	–	–	–	–	–	–	–
	IT incident/failure	25%	–	–	–	–	25%	25%	25%
	IT risk	25%	25%	25%	25%	25%	50%	50%	75%
	IT risk/Business continuity/Cyber security model	–	–	–	–	–	25%	25%	25%
	IT risk appetite	–	–	–	–	–	–	–	–
	IT risk assessment	–	–	–	–	–	25%	25%	50%
	IT risk report	–	–	–	–	–	–	–	–

(continued)

Table 4.14 (continued)

Categories	Items	2008	2009	2010	2011	2012	2013	2014	2015
	Business continuity plan	–	–	–	–	50%	75%	75%	75%
	Contingency plan	–	25%	25%	–	75%	100%	75%	75%
	Disaster recovery plan	25%	–	25%	25%	25%	50%	50%	50%
	Information/Cyber security plan	–	–	–	–	25%	25%	25%	75%
	IT risk management	–	–	–	–	–	50%	25%	25%
	IT risk regulation/ compliance	–	–	–	–	–	25%	25%	25%

[a]Number of supervisors which refer about the Items of each category within ITGF divided by the number of authorities considered in the study. We remind that—at this stage of the analysis—four supervisors are included in the sample

Regarding the last research question (Q4), we measure the level of investments in IT systems (IT Expenditure, ITEXP_Index) considering all expenditures made by banks; we expect an increasing level of investments, considering, on one hand, the growing level of business complexity expressed by banks' dimension, and, on the other, the increase in Supervisors' attention to IT concerns. Furthermore, we control for Country dummies and we considered the influence of the annual GDP growth rate.

Looking at the level of ITEXP_Index, it seems that banks in the sample have invested adequately in the maintenance of existing IT infrastructure, instead of commissioning large-scale and expensive IT change programmes. In fact, the Index remains substantially steady over the time within each country (Table 4.10). To assess if there is a relationship between the level of investment made by banks and the increasing level of attention paid to IT governance concerns by Supervisors we perform an OLS regression; the results are summarised in Table 4.16 and show the absence of influence of increased Supervisors' attention to IT on bank IT investment policy (the coefficient is not significant). There is a more significant link between banks size and the level of IT investment made, even if the intensity of this relation is not so high.

In addition, the level of investment does not depend on the state of the economy (GDP); this suggests that IT investments are not pro-cyclical.

Table 4.15 Model OLS estimates of ITGF_Index_Banks

Source	SS	df	MS		Number of obs = 90	
					F(6, 84) = 51.23	
Model	928.674208	7	132.667744		Prob > F = 0.0000	
Residual	214.941063	83	2.58965136		R-squared = 0.8121	
Total	1143.61527	90	12.7068363		Adj R-squared = 0.7962	
					Root MSE = 1.6092	
ITGF_Index_Banks	**Coef.**	**Std. Err.**	**t**	**P > |t|**	**[95% Conf. Interval]**	
ITGF_Index_Supervisors	1.753872	0.4240605	4.14	0.000	0.9104329	2.597312
GDP	15.37453	8.117	1.89	0.062	−0.7698561	31.51892
LogTa	3.542551	0.5545266	6.39	0.000	2.43962	4.645482
dummy1	−19.80093	3.28289	−6.03	0.000	−26.33047	−13.27139
dummy2	−17.30702	3.127079	−5.53	0.000	−23.52665	−11.08738
dummy3	−22.25799	3.510357	−6.34	0.000	−29.23995	−15.27603
dummy4	−17.59086	3.183921	−5.52	0.000	−23.92335	−11.25817

Note: Dependent variable = ITGF_Index_Banks, the level of IT governance disclosure recorded by banks. Independent variable = ITGF_Index_Supervisors, level of IT governance disclosure of Supervisors. Control variables = LogTa, logarithm of banks' Total Asset; Countries dummy variables (dummy1 = Germany, dummy2 = Spain, dummy3 = France, dummy4 = Italy); and GDP, the annual GDP growth rate
We estimate OLS regression with dummy variables and no constant

Table 4.16 Model 2 OLS estimates of ITEXP_Index

Source	SS	df	MS		Number of obs = 90	
					F(7, 83) = 28.01	
Model	0.00017228	7	0.000024611		Prob > F = 0.0000	
Residual	0.00007294	83	0.0087879		R-squared = 0.7026	
Total	0.000245219	90	0.027247		Adj R-squared = 0.6775	
					Root MSE = 0.00094	
ITEXP_Index	**Coef.**	**Std. Err.**	**t**	**P > |t|**	**[95% Conf. Interval]**	
ITGF_Index_Supervisors	0.0005165	0.000247	2.09	0.040	0.0000252	0.0010079
LogTa	0.0012927	0.000323	4.00	0.000	0.0006502	0.0019352
GDP	−.0003268	0.0047284	−0.07	0.945	−0.0097315	0.0090779
dummy1	−0.0065061	0.0019124	−3.40	0.001	−0.0103098	0.0027024
dummy2	−0.0061942	0.0018216	−3.40	0.001	−0.0098174	0.0025711
dummy3	−0.0073953	0.0020449	−3.62	0.001	−0.0114625	0.0033281
dummy4	−0.0062605	0.0018547	−3.38	0.001	−0.0099495	0.0025715

Note: Dependent variable = ITEXP, level of investment in IT disclosed by banks. Independent variables = ITGF_Index_Supervisors, the level of IT governance disclosure of Supervisors; LogTa, logarithm of banks' Total Asset. Control variables = Countries dummy variables (dummy1 = Germany, dummy 2 = Spain, dummy 3 = France, dummy 4 = Italy); GDP, the annual GDP growth rate
We estimate OLS regression with dummy variables and no constant

4.5 Concluding Remarks: Key Findings, Limitation and Future Research

IT governance represents an important aspect to monitor for both supervisors and banks as the reach and complexity of IT continues to increase across the financial sector. IT sits in a critical part of banks as it is the backbone of all banking processing. In fact, while IT plays a key role in supporting banking business, it has also revealed its dark side during the recent financial turmoil: banks have shown an inadequate ability to exploit the potential that IT can ensure to provide Senior Management with a true picture of the risks the bank faces. Therefore, IT governance, ensuring that IT processes are fully integrated into all business processes—risk management included—can be considered a strategic asset for banks and a new challenge for Supervisors.

One of the questions to which this study sought to answer is whether this awareness has been reached before by banks or by Supervisors.

As far as the scope of this study is concerned, we have analysed public corporate disclosure of IT governance practices across major EU banks. Adopting a revised descriptive framework of IT governance disclosure developed by Joshi et al. (2013), we conduct a content analysis to examine the level of attention paid to IT governance issues across time (2008–2015) and countries (Germany, Spain, France, Italy). It is important to underline that corporate disclosure of IT governance does not adhere to any standardised or mandatory reporting format which could be used by banks. This is an important premise to develop our research: as reported in the literature, the fact that banks' IT governance disclosure is voluntary and linked to the benefits that it can ensure, leaves space for further research to investigate if IT governance practices are in place.

Similar considerations can be made on the Supervisors' side. There are no provisions at the international level regulating directly IT governance: some of the more recent interventions concerning this issue (EBA, BCBS, EC) only indirectly affect IT Governance, allowing regulators large degrees of autonomy to regulate the issue at a national level. This permits us to use the same methodology developed for banks to analyse the differences in Supervisors' behaviour.

Even if at this stage the analysis can be considered as a pilot study (with a limited sample size), we can summarize some key findings: i) banks have an increasing level of IT disclosure, more evident starting from 2012; ii) banks, within the IT Governance Framework, seem to pay more attention to IT Risk Management; and iii) prefer Annual Reports to release information on IT governance topics; iv) there is a positive relationship between Supervisors' and banks' attention to IT; while v) there is no evidence of Supervisors' influence on bank IT investments. At this stage of the study, these results can't be considered statistically strong, because: i) the sample includes a limited number of both banks and Supervisors; ii) the unavailability of all the national regulatory provisions in English. Consequently, we cannot exclude alternative explanations, such as the presence of causality bias.

Despite this, the study contributes to the existing literature in several ways. It is intended to enrich the current understanding of IT governance in banks, focusing on the level and on the content of IT governance disclosure. Secondly, it highlights the regulatory environment that favours IT governance practices in banks and tries to measure the intensity of this relationship. In so doing, our anlaysis adds to the IT governance disclosure literature providing an original methodological framework based on a solid theoretical background.

The theoretical approach used in this study may well serve as a basis for further analysis. The study may be replicated across the rest of EU countries using a larger dataset and this would allow the findings to be statistically more robust.

References

Andriole, S. J. (2009). Boards of directors and technology governance: The surprising state of the practice. *Communications of AIS, 24*(Article 22), 373–394.

Banker, R., Chen, P. Y., Liu, F. C., & Ou, C. S. (2009). Business value of IT in commercial banks. *ICIS 2009 Proceedings*, 76.

Barry, C. B., & Brown, S. J. (1985). Differential information and security market equilibrium. *Journal of Financial and Quantitative Analysis, 20*(4), 407–422.

Barry, C. B., & Brown, S. J. (1986). Limited information as a source of risk. *Journal of Portfolio Management, 12*(2), 66–72.

BCBS. (2013). *Principles for effective risk data aggregation and risk reporting*. BIS: Basilea.

Beccalli, E. (2007). Does IT investment improve bank performance? Evidence from Europe. *Journal of Banking & Finance, 31*(7), 2205–2230.

Berger, A. N. (2003). The economic effects of technological progress: Evidence from the banking industry. *Journal of Money, Credit, and Banking, 35*(2), 141–175.

Bhushan, R. (1989). Collection of information about publicly traded firms: Theory and evidence. *Journal of Accounting and Economics, 11*(2–3), 183–206.

Bollen, L., Hassink, H., & Bozic, G. (2006). Measuring and explaining the quality of investor relations activities: A multinational empirical analysis. *International Journal of Accounting Information Systems, 7*(4), 273–298.

Boritz, E., & Lim, J.-H. (2008, August). *IT control weaknesses, IT governance and firm performance*. Paper presented at the American Accounting Association's Annual Meeting, Anaheim, California.

Brown, C. V. (1997). Examining the emergence of hybrid IS governance solutions: Evidence from a single case site. *Information Systems Research, 8*(1), 69–94.

Brown, A., & Grant, G. G. (2005). Framing the frameworks: A review of IT governance research. *Communications of AIS, 15*, 696–712.

CEA. (2001). *The annual report of the council of economic advisors*. Washington, DC: The Economics of the President, U.S. Government Printing Office.

Chiasson, M. W., & Davidson, E. (2005). Taking industry seriously in information systems research. *MIS Quarterly, 29*(4), 591–605.

Chowdhury, A. (2003). Information technology and productivity payoff in the banking industry: Evidence from the emerging markets. *Journal of International Development, 15*(6), 693–708.

Clarkson, P., Li, Y., & Richardson, G. (2004). The market valuation of environmental expenditures by pulp and paper companies. *Accounting Review, 79*(2), 329–353.

De Haes, S., & Van Grembergen, W. (2008). An exploratory study into the design of an IT governance minimum baseline through Delphi Research. *Communications of AIS, 22*(Article 24), 443–458.

De Haes, S., & Van Grembergen, W. (2009). An exploratory study into IT governance implementations and its impact on business/IT alignment. *Information Systems Management, 26*(2), 123–137.

Diamond, D. W., & Verrecchia, R. E. (1991). Disclosure, liquidity, and the cost of capital. *The Journal of Finance, 46*(4), 1325–1359.

DTCC (2014). *Cyber risk – A global system IT great.* A white paper to the industry of systemic risk, October.

Easley, D., & O'Hara, M. (2004). Information and the cost of capital. *The Journal of Finance, LIX* (4), 1553–1582.

EBA. (2015a). *Risks and vulnerabilities in the EU financial system.* London: EBA.

EBA. (2015b). *Risk assessment of the European banking system.* London: EBA.

EBA. (2016). *Guidelines on ICT risk assessment under the supervisory review and evaluation process (SREP).* London: EBA.

ECB. (2016). Report on financial structures, October.

Eldomiaty, T. I., & Choi, C. J. (2006). Corporate governance and strategic transparency: East Asia in the international business systems. *Corporate Governance, 6*(3), 281–295.

FSB-Financial Stability Board. (2015). 2015 update of list of global systemically important banks (G-SIBs), 3 November.

Fuβ, C., Gmeiner, R., Schiereck, D., & Strahringer, S. (2007). ERP usage in banking: An exploratory survey of the world's largest banks. *Information Systems Management, 24*(2), 155–171.

Goldstein, J., Chernobai, A., & Benaroch, M. (2011). An event study analysis of the economic impact of IT operational risk and its subcategories. *Journal of the Association for Information Systems, 12*(9), 606–631.

Gu, B., Xue, L., & Ray, R. (2008, December). *IT governance and IT investment performance: An empirical analysis.* Paper presented at the International Conference on Information Systems, Paris, France.

Hadden, L. B., & Hermanson, D. R. (2003, July/August). Is your audit committee watching IT risks? *The Journal of Corporate Accounting & Finance, 14*(5), 35–39.

Heart, T., Maoz, H., & Pliskin, N. (2010). From governance to adaptability: The mediating effect of IT executives' managerial capabilities. *Information Systems Management, 27*(1), 42–60.

Huang, R., Zmud, R. W., & Price, L. R. (2010). Influencing the effectiveness of IT governance practices through steering committees and communication policies. *European Journal of Information Systems, 19*(3), 288–302.

Huff, S. L., Maher, P. M., & Munro, M. C. (2006). Information technology and the board of directors: Is there an IT attention deficit? *MIS Quarterly Executive, 5*(2), 55–68.

ISO/IEC 17999:2005 Information technology – Security techniques – Code of practice for information security management

IT Governance Institute [ITGI]. (2003). Board briefing on IT governance (2nd ed.). Rolling Meadows, IL: IT Governance Institute. Retrieved from http://www.itgi.org

IT Governance Institute [ITGI]. (2008). IT governance global status report, ISBN: 978-1-60420-064-5. Rolling Meadows, IL: IT Governance Institute.

Johnson, K. N. (2015). Cyber risks: Emerging risk management concerns for financial institutions. *Georgia Law Review, 50*(1), 131.

Jordan, P. E., & Musson, D. (2004). *Corporate governance and IT governance: Exploring the board's perspective.* Retrieved from http://ssrn.com/abstract=787346

Jordan, E., & Silcock, L. (2005). *Beating IT risks.* West Sussex, UK: Wiley.

Joshi, A., Bollen, L., & Hassink, H. (2013). An empirical assessment of IT governance transparency: Evidence from commercial banking. *Information Systems Management, 30*(2), 116–136.

Kambil, A., & Lucas, H. (2002). The board of directors and the management of information technology. *Communications of AIS, 8*(Article 26), 380–391.

Karimi, J., Bhattacherjee, A., Gupta, Y. P., & Somers, T. M. (2000). The effects of MIS steering committees on information technology management sophistication. *Journal of Management Information Systems, 17*(2), 207–230.

Kim, O., & Verrecchia, R. (1994). Market liquidity and volume around earnings announcements. *Journal of Accounting and Economics, 17*(1–2), 41–67.

Korac-Kakabadse, N., & Kakabadse, A. (2001). IS/IT governance: Need for an integrated model. *Corporate Governance, 1*(4), 9–11.

Lang, M. H., & Lundholm, R. J. (1996). Corporate disclosure policy and analyst behaviour. *Accounting Review, 71*, 467–492.

Li, C., Lim, J.-H., & Wang, Q. (2007). Internal and external influences on IT control governance. *International Journal of Accounting Information Systems, 8*(4), 225–239.

Loch, K. D., Carr, H. H., & Warkentin, M. E. (1992). Threats to information systems: Today's reality, yesterday's understanding. *MIS Quarterly, 16*(2), 173–186.

Mähring, M. (2006, August). *The role of the board of directors in IT governance: A review and agenda for research*. Paper presented at the Twelfth Americas Conference on Information Systems, Acapulco, Mexico.

Mata, F. J., Fuerst, W. L., & Barney, J. B. (1995). Information technology and sustained competitive advantage: A resource-based analysis. *MIS Quarterly, 19*(4), 487–505.

McKinsey Global Institute. (2001). *U.S. productivity growth 1995-2000: Understanding the contribution of information technology relative to other factors*. Washington, D.C.: McKinsey Global Institute.

Merhout, J. W., & Havelka, D. (2008). Information technology auditing: A value-added IT governance partnership between IT management and audit. *Communications of AIS, 23*(Article 26), 463–482.

Millar, C., Eldomiaty, T., Choi, C., & Hilton, B. (2005). Corporate governance and institutional transparency in emerging markets. *Journal of Business Ethics, 59*(1), 163–174.

Nolan, R., & McFarlan, F. W. (2005). Information technology and board of directors. *Harvard Business Review, 83*(October), 96–106.

OECD. (1999). *OECD principles of corporate governance*. Paris: OECD.

OECD. (2004). *OECD principles of corporate governance*. Paris: OECD.

Pardo, C., Pino, F. J., García, F., Piattini, M., Baldassarre, M. T., & Lemus, S. (2011, June). Homogenization, comparison and integration: a harmonizing strategy for the unification of multi-models in the banking sector. In *International Conference on Product Focused Software Process Improvement* (pp. 59–72). Berlin: Springer .

Parent, M., & Reich, B. H. (2009). Governing information technology risk. *California Management Review, 51*(3), 134–152.

Peterson, R. (2004). Crafting information technology governance. *Information Systems Management, 21*(4), 7–22.

Prasad, A., Heales, J., & Green, P. (2009). *Towards a deeper understanding of information technology governance effectiveness: A capabilities-based approach*. Paper presented at the International Conference on Information Systems, Phoenix, Arizona, USA.

Premuroso, R. F., & Bhattacharya, S. (2007). Is there a relationship between firm performance, corporate governance, and a firm's decision to form a technology committee? *Corporate Governance: An International Review, 15*(6), 1260–1276.

Raghupathi, W. R. (2007). Corporate governance of IT: A framework for development. *Communications of the ACM, 50*(8), 94–99.

Sambamurthy, V., & Zmud, R. W. (1999). Arrangements for information technology governance: A theory of multiple contingencies. *MIS Quarterly, 23*(2), 261–291.

Sambamurthy, V., Venkataraman, S., & Desanctis, G. (1993). The design of information technology planning systems for varying organizational contexts. *European Journal of Information Systems, 2*(1), 23–35.

Spremić, M. (2009). IT governance mechanisms in managing IT business value. *WSEAS Transactions on Information Science and Applications, 6*(6), 906–915.

SSG. (2010). *Observations on developments in risk. Appetite frameworks and IT infrastructure*, SSG.

Straub, D. W., & Welke, R. J. (1998). Coping with systems risk: security planning models for management decision making. *MIS Quarterly, 22*(4), 441–469.

Takemura, T., Ukai, Y., & Nagaoka, H. (2005). Disclosure and circumstances concerning information system assets. In Y. Ukai (Ed.), *Economic analysis of information system investment in banking industry* (pp. 107–125). Tokyo: Springer.

Taplin, R. (2016). *Managing cyber risk in the financial sector: Lessons from Asia, Europe and the USA*. Routledge, London.

Trites, G. (2004). Director responsibility for IT governance. *International Journal of Accounting Information Systems, 5*(2), 88–99.

Van Grembergen, W., & De Haes, S. (2004). IT governance and its mechanisms. *Information Systems Control Journal, 1*, 1–7.

Van Grembergen, W., & De Haes, S. (2009). *Enterprise governance of information technology: Achieving strategic alignment and value*. New York: Springer.

Vanstraelen, A., Zarzeski, M. T., & Robb, S. (2003). Corporate nonfinancial disclosure practices and financial analyst forecast ability across three European countries. *Journal of International Financial Management & Accounting, 14*(3), 249–279.

Webb, P., Pollard, C., & Ridley, G. (2006, January). *Attempting to define IT governance wisdom or folly?* Paper presented at the 39th Hawaii International Conference on System Sciences, Kauai, Hawaii.

Weber, S. (1985). *Basic content analysis*. Beverly Hills, CA: Sage Publications.

Weill, P., & Ross, J. (2004). *IT governance, how top performers manage IT decision rights for superior results*. Boston, MA: Harvard Business School Press.

Willson, P., & Pollard, C. (2009). Exploring IT governance in theory and practice in a large multinational organisation in Australia. *Information Systems Management, 26*(2), 98–109.

Xue, Y., Liang, H., & Boulton, W. R. (2008). Information technology governance in information technology investment decision processes: The impact of investment characteristics, external environment, and internal context. *MIS Quarterly, 32*(1), 67–96.

Xue, L., Ray, G., & Gu, B. (2011). Environmental uncertainty and IT infrastructure governance: A curvilinear relationship. *Information Systems Research, 22*(2), 389–399.

Zhu, K., Kraemer, K. L., Xu, S., & Dedrick, J. (2004). Information technology payoff in e-business environments: An international perspective on value creation in the financial services industry. *Journal of Management Information Systems, 21*(1), 17–54.

Chapter 5
Are There Differences in Boards of Directors Between Banks and Non-financial Firms? Some Evidence from EU Listed Companies

Vittorio Boscia, Valeria Stefanelli, and Andrea Ventura

5.1 Introduction[1]

Corporate governance (CG) mechanisms play a central role in all economic sectors (OECD 2009, 2015). In recent years, with regard to the financial industry, the growing importance of corporate governance is due to more risky financial activities and to some recent financial firms' crises (BIS 2010, 2015; EBA and ESMA 2016). Besides the importance of good governance in banks, several studies remark that bank corporate governance is different and requires more radical departures from governance of non-financial firms (Booth et al. 2002; Macey and O'Hara 2003; Adams and Mehran 2003; Berger et al. 2012; Becht et al. 2011). The board of directors (BoD) of a bank is placed in a crucial role in the governance structure (Macey and O'Hara 2003; Levine 2004). In fact, banking supervisors and regulators (BIS 2010, 2015; ECB 2011, 2016) encourage and promote much more responsible, authoritative and independent boards: they maintain that the directors of banking institutions are responsible to a broader set of stakeholders than just shareholders and they enforce boards to be compliant and aware of this more risky business. From this introduction we derive the following main research question of this chapter: Considering the wide and extensive regulation on corporate governance, are bank boards really different from boards of non-financial firms? Due to the special nature of financial services, most previous studies on corporate governance

[1]The chapter is a result of a joint effort between the authors. In particular, Vittorio Boscia wrote Sects. 5.2 and 5.8; Valeria Stefanelli wrote Sects. 5.1, 5.3, 5.5 and 5.7; Andrea Ventura wrote Sects. 5.4 and 5.6.

V. Boscia • V. Stefanelli (✉) • A. Ventura
Department of Economic Sciences, University of Salento, Lecce, Italy
e-mail: vittorio.boscia@unisalento.it; valeria.stefanelli@unisalento.it; Andrea.Ventura@le.infn.it

B. Díaz Díaz et al. (eds.), *Corporate Governance in Banking and Investor Protection*, CSR, Sustainability, Ethics & Governance,
https://doi.org/10.1007/978-3-319-70007-6_5

exclude banks from their data and focus on non-financial firms (Adams et al. 2010; De Haan and Vlahu 2013). So, using data from EU Board Index and from Annual Corporate Governance Reports published by major EU banks and non-financial firms, this chapter extends the current literature by comparing the characteristics of bank and non-financial company boards covering areas such as board size, diversity, the number of independent directors and so on. We structure the chapter in 8 sections, including this first part by way of introduction. The second part deals with the theoretical framework and the research question that will be examined in the empirical analysis. The third section describes the variables used; the fourth section describes the methodology used and the following section presents the sample and data; the sixth and seventh parts discuss the main results, and finally we present the conclusions as well as limitations and policy and managerial implications.

5.2 Background and Research Hypothesis

Nowadays, there is agreement among academics, practitioners and supervisors around the theory of corporate governance and about its crucial role for the business integrity of a company. As "*the system by which companies are directed and controlled*" (EU Commission 2011), CG is necessary to reduce and balance the potential conflicts between executives and shareholders (according to the "*shareholder perspective*"), or the potential conflicts between executives and a wider array of stakeholders (according to the more recent "*stakeholder perspective*," see Freemann 1984).

A company with a sound CG ensures market confidence for the growth, stability and long term investments and, consequently, the potential availability of the most active companies to raise resources for their growth and competitive plans. On the other hand, a weak CG, with inefficiencies and faults leads to malfunctioning of a company and to potential crisis.

CG became more relevant for banks in the period post-crisis when it was important to strengthen confidence in the market and financial system by reducing short-termism and the excessive risk taking by managers.

EBA and ESMA (2016) point out that "*weaknesses in corporate governance, including inadequate oversight by and challenge from the supervisory function of the management body in a number of credit institutions and investment firms, have contributed to excessive and imprudent risk-taking in the financial sector which has led in turn to the failure of individual institutions and systemic problems.*"

In managing the CG of a company, the board of directors (BoD) plays a central role, as many studies on the recent crisis have emphasised (OECD 2009): it guarantees the proper functioning of a company and its business integrity by supervising executives and, consequently, by reducing agency problems, information asymmetries, moral hazard and potential conflicts of interest at the expense of shareholders and several other kinds of stakeholders. For their part, BoD should ensure the maximum accountability of their activity, in order to signal to market participants their full commitment in this aim.

BoD should design sound CG given their understanding of the company activities and strategy, the related risk-return profile, and this should seek to effectively control managers.

In particular, BoD meetings are the most significant occasion where directors, on a regular and periodic base: are informed about a specific topic; discuss a proposal made by executives on the topic; exchange their opinions and, make decisions after having reached a certain level of consensus.

A sound CG is important and vital especially for listed companies as issuers: indeed, in these companies, some of the traditional agency problems between principals (shareholders-stakeholders) and agents (managers) are more critical for the dimension of the company and for the composition of shareholders. Therefore, shareholders and stakeholders of 'issuers' should feel 'fully' confident in order to be convinced as market participants to invest their money. In order to persuade listed companies to implement sound CG, and in the absence of a specific CG Directive or domestic regulation, many EU stock market organisations promote domestic '*codes of conduct*': this is a form of soft-law, that is a set of self-regulations to which listed companies decide to be compliant on a voluntary basis. This signals to third parties that the company is governed according to principles on several aspects: the composition, appointment and remuneration of the BoD; the presence and functioning of internal committees of the BoD; the design of internal controls and risk management of the company; and relationships with shareholders.

For example, these codes state that factors like the number of board members, diversity in professional competences, gender, time to dedicate to the BoD, and so on, are parameters of a sound CG: for example, the more the diversity among board members is, the better board decisions are believed to be. Moreover, codes suggest—*inter alia*—that members of committees shall be composed of independent directors, since it allows an "independence of opinions" that make decisions more close to company interests. Independence is ensured by personal, ethical, professional, property relationships between the director and the company and its board. For listed and non-listed companies, financial and non-financial companies, single statutory clauses may often state different definitions of independent directors (see for example, UK Corporate governance Code or French Corporate Governance Code, etc.); the Germany Companies Act states, in fact, that all members of supervisory boards are considered independent; with reference to the Italian case, there are differences in the definition of independent director (see D.Lgs. n.58/98 and Italian Code of conduct).[2] For banking, see EU banking regulation on corporate governance (lately, EBA 2016).

In order to have a more effective BoD, code of conducts state that they should establish internal committees with exploratory, consultative or proposing functions,

[2]Nedcommunity (2015), Il punto sugli amministratori indipendenti, EGO. n. 3, January (available at: http://www.nedcommunity.com/Contents/Documents/EGO%20n%203%20gennaio%202015.pdf)

allowing BoD to increase the efficiency and effectiveness of its workings thanks to a more informed and aware decision-making process. The performance of BoD should be self-evaluated annually in order to assess whether they and their committees work properly taking into account "*its membership, organisation and operation as a group, the competence and effectiveness of each board member and of the board committees, and how well the board has performed against any performance objectives set.*" (EU Commission 2011). Finally, codes suggest that companies shall publish on a yearly basis a CG statement[3] in which it describes how the relative code of conduct is operationally adopted by the company, applying the principle "*comply or explain.*"[4] The CG statement allows shareholders and stakeholders to be aware about the organisation of company CG in order to make more conscious investment decisions.

CG should also be designed on the basis of the business of the company in order to ensure effective business integrity. Thus, for example, it could be inferred that the differences between financial and non-financial companies should lead to variation in their approach to CG. This view is based on several factors that highlight the differences between banks and non-financial firms:

- financial intermediaries play a crucial role in the development of the economy, for their fundamental activities in payment services, savings and financing, and transferring risks;
- so that, the range of third parties interested in the soundness of the company—the stakeholders—is wider for banks than other non-financial firms: bank's depositors and bond holders, often also shareholders, encompass a different kind of stakeholder. Depositors (who are the main debtors) are generally less financial informed and need stronger protection;
- the failure of banks has much greater economic and social externalities compared to the failure of non-financial firms;
- moreover, financial activity is intangible, dynamic, volatile and technical; so that, managing a financial firm is deemed to be more complex and more risky than for other kinds of non-financial activities. Banks and other financial firms are subject to a host of regulations especially in terms of ensuring minimum requirements for capital, liquidity and asset quality;
- finally, financial intermediaries, often, are very large (in asset terms) and complex: thus, they need to be managed, governed, regulated and supervised

[3]Directive 2013/34/EU on the annual financial statements requires companies to include the CG statement

[4]EU Commission Recommendation of 9 April 2014 on the quality of corporate governance reporting ('comply or explain'). In particular, n. 4 of the "whereas" states: The corporate governance statement should provide essential information on the corporate governance arrangements of the company, such as information relating to the relevant corporate governance code (s) applied by that company, the internal control and risk management systems, the shareholder meeting and its powers, shareholders' rights, administrative, management and supervisory bodies and their committees.

differently from other non-financial firms, especially as the biggest firms pose potential systemic risks.

These specificities involve the need for particular regulation on the financial system and its components. The prevention of crises or panic is fundamental for the activities of the financial system.

In order to be more effective and influence the behaviour of directors and managers it is also necessary to have an effective implementation of CG principles since financial and non-financial companies are also different in terms of the dynamics of CG. For example, in banks the interest of creditors (and especially for depositors and bondholders) conflicts with those of shareholders: while the former prefer bank investments in safe projects, shareholders prefer banks to finance more risky and then theoretically more profitable projects.[5] But the former stakeholders, namely, creditors and debtors, do not have the right to decide about strategies, directors or executive, while shareholders do.

Therefore, in order to balance bank internal relationships, according to the "*stakeholder view*," CG principles for financial intermediaries are *regulated* at the international and European level. In particular, the BIS and EU (EBA and EU Commission) have on CG for banks from nearly 20 years (BIS 1999, 2006, 2010, 2015; EBA 2011, 2016; EU Commission 2010).

Moreover, in the case of banks, there are also some principles and rules for *internal governance*. In particular, the EU Commission (2010) states: "*Internal governance is a limited but crucial component of corporate governance, focusing on the internal structure and organisation of an institution.*" The BoD shall ensure both, a suitable and transparent corporate governance and internal governance of the bank. In practice, internal governance is "*a clear organisational structure with well defined, transparent and consistent lines of responsibility, effective processes to identify, manage, monitor and report the risks it is or might be exposed to, adequate internal control mechanisms, including sound administrative and accounting procedures, and remuneration policies and practices that are consistent with and promote sound and effective risk management*" (EU Commission 2010).

Weak internal governance issues have been identified as "*a crucial underlying factor*" of the financial crisis. Indeed, many studies and researchers have attributed among the causes of the crisis of 2007–2008 to limitations in CG practices including:

- executives taking on too much risk and underestimating the complexity and the risks tolerance/appetite levels of business, and over influenced by short-term remuneration;
- directors incapable of planning strategies and products, to set the appropriate risk-return of banking business, to understand risk management frameworks and supervise executive decision-making;

[5]EU Commission Green Paper (2010), corporate governance in financial institutions and remuneration policies of 2 June 2010.

- shareholders too focused on short-term value creation neglecting ethical issues and corporate social responsibility;
- stakeholders, such as workers, bondholders and depositors, too confident about "too big too fail" and the "bail-out" policy of governments.

All these causes have resulted in a lack of confidence "on" and "in" the financial market (Arsalidou 2016).

Actually, after the crisis of 2008, regulation tried to reform this scenario: first of all, tougher regulation on the structure of banks, like Basel III has been introduced;; new rules on bank bailouts aimed at improved recovery and resolution plans for banks have been put in place, and a range of other regulations have been implemented in order to ensure the safety of the financial system and make sure taxpayers are not on the hook if banks fail in the future. Finally, according to article 88 of the Capital Requirements Directive (CRD) 2013/36/EU, among the duties and responsibilities of the BoD, it "*must have the ultimate and overall responsibility for the institution and defines, oversees and is accountable for the implementation of the governance arrangements within the institution that ensure effective and prudent management of the institution.*" And regarding internal governance, "*The management body's responsibilities should include setting, approving and overseeing the implementation of an adequate, effective and independent internal control framework.*"

In this scenario, the role of the BoD has become even more important, at the centre of the relationship between parts of CG. Most recently the EBA (2016) published a consultation on draft guidelines on internal governance in order to update and redesign CG arrangement toward "*the sound management of risk.*" The new set of rules designs BoD so that supervisory and management functions interact effectively.

Finally, another set of new rules are also under consultation by ESMA and EBA who published Joint Guidelines on "the assessment of the suitability of members of the management body and key function holders under Directive 2013/36/EU and Directive 2014/65/EU," in order to ensure diversity practices within bank's BoD. Thus, regulation and supervision principles on financial firms actually provide a clear and practical set of rules about the structure and the functions of BoD directed to ensure a strong CG and internal governance. In contrast to banks, non-financial firms, although listed, have more independence to organise their BoD.

From the above discussion arises the main research question tested in this chapter: are banks' BoD different from those of non-financial companies? If this is confirmed CG should be designed according to the specific nature, scale and complexity of the businesses in questions and there should be different rules for banks compared to non-financial firms. Specifically, CG should be designed according to firm "*size, shareholders structure or sectorial specificities*" (EU Commission 2014).

5.3 Selection and Description of the Variables Used

The chapter focuses on the BoD as the main corporate governance mechanism. Previous studies on corporate governance is particularly rich in analysis about corporate governance and performance particularly focusing on the role of board characteristics—relating to the structural and organizational features of the board—in order to test the existence of significant relationships with the internal processes of strategy and control and, consequently, with performance for the overall business. Often starting from different theoretical perspectives, the analysis aims to decide the best configuration of the board for efficacy and overall company performance. As part of the aforementioned studies the main variables under investigation relate to the structural profiles, organization and functioning of the board (see, among others, the study of Carretta et al. 2007; Adams et al. 2010). Table 5.1 reports variables' definition of board's characteristics used in our empirical analysis

Such variables have enabled our empirical study to capture dimensions of board diversity. The diversity of a board's profile is distinct at three levels:

(a) *industry-specific board diversity*: aims to capture diversity in board arrangements between banks and non-financial firms, regardless of nationality;
(b) *country-specific board diversity*: aims to capture the diversity in the board arrangements between banks and non-financial firms due to the nationality, compared to the European context;
(c) *domestic-specific board diversity*: aims to capture board diversity between banks and non-financial firms belonging to the same European country.

To complete the analysis, our results allow, by differences, to capture similarity aspects of the sample compared to the structural, organization and functioning of the board of directors.

Table 5.1 Variables' definition of board's characteristics

Board's characteristics	Abrev.	Measures
Country	C	Italy, UK, France, Germany, Spain
Industry sector	IS	Bank board or non-financial board
Board size	BS	No. of executive and non-executive directors in the board
Board age	BA	Average of age of directors
Foreigners	FO	Percentage of foreigner directors in the board
Board gender	BG	Percentage of female directors in the board
Independents	IND	Percentage of independent directors in the boards per year
Board committees	BC	No. of board committees
Meeting activity	MA	No. of board meetings in the year

5.4 Empirical Analysis and Methodology

In order to study diversities between banks' and non-financial firms' boards, for each of the three analysis levels described above, specific starting hypotheses on variables must be enunciated. The statistical accuracy of the analysis strongly depends on how large the sample and time period covered: the most accurate analysis level is that which focuses on the industry-specific board diversity across countries (where no distinction is made between countries). Less robust statements are possible when numerically reducing the sample size where we focus on *country-specific* and *domestic-specific board diversity* analyses.

For every considered sample of firms, the above-mentioned numerical variables (i.e. the seven listed: BS, BC, IND, FO, BG, MA, BA) are treated in terms of the mean value μ and of the corresponding standard deviation σ_μ. This is done according to the assumption of a normally distributed population with Gaussian behaviour in the case of the absolute variables (BS, BC, MA, BD), and with binomial behaviour for computed percentages (IND, FO, BG).

For each variable, the comparison of two samples, banks' boards ("1") and non-financial firms' boards ("2") is considered regardless of the multiplicities (n_1 and n_2) of the samples themselves (to be kept homogeneous whenever possible, to avoid any bias) thanks to the use of a Student's *t*-distribution two-sided test, comparing the means μ_1 and μ_2 by using the corresponding standard deviations $\sigma_{\mu 1}$ and $\sigma_{\mu 2}$ with the adequate numbers of degrees of freedom (i.e. n_1-1 and n_2-1, respectively). In the present work we decide *a priori* to set a 90% confidence level in order to quantity how confident we are in accepting (or discarding) a given hypothesis on the computed *t*-value regarding diversities between potentially different firms. As will be discussed in Sect. 5.6, the extent of every possible discrepancy between two samples of firms will be quantified in terms of *t*, and compared to the maximum expected *t*-value for the given multiplicities n_1 and n_2.

5.5 Sample and Data

Our sample consists of listed European banks and industry firms (measured at 14th January 2017 by Sole 24 Ore Journal); and we consider industry sectors (pharmaceutical, power, luxury, automotive, etc.) comparing to banking sector With reference to these major banks and firms, we weselectthe top three in different industrial sectors for each European country. The European countries of concern are: Italy, Great Britain, France, Germany and Spain. Overall, the sample consists of 30 companies, equally divided between banks and non-financial firms.

Data used in our empirical analysis relating to the BoD from the Corporate Governance Annual Report and further documents published on websites of banks and industrial firms in year 2015. In the case of two-tier corporate governance, the board characteristics refer only to the supervisory board. Further information about

Table 5.2 Descriptive statistics of variables used in the empirical analysis

Board's characteristics	Obs.	Mean	Min	Max	St. dev.	Med.
Board size	30	15.40	8.00	21.00	3.35	15.00
– Banks	15	16.20	11.00	21.00	3.19	17.00
– Non financial firms	15	14.60	8.00	20.00	3.42	14.00
Board age	30	59.29	55.15	66.00	2.76	59.05
– Banks	15	59.80	56.47	66.00	3.14	59.05
– Non financial firms	15	58.70	55.15	62.90	2.29	58.50
Foreigners	30	3.60	0.00	9.00	2.63	3.50
– Banks	15	3.40	0.00	9.00	2.59	2.00
–Non financial firms	15	3.80	0.00	9.00	2.76	4.00
Board gender (%)	30	33.00	5.56	75.00	12.07	33.00
– Banks	15	32.60	20.00	50.00	8.52	33.00
– Non financial firms	15	33.50	5.56	75.00	15.12	30.00
Independents (%)	30	67.86	25.00	100.00	25.04	71.00
– Banks	15	69.30	28.57	100.00	23.16	72.73
– Non financial firms	15	66.40	25.00	100.00	28.00	64.00
Board committees	30	4.70	2.00	8.00	1.45	4.50
– Banks	15	5.40	4.00	8.00	1.06	5.00
– Non financial firms	15	3.90	2.00	7.00	1.44	4.00
Meeting activity	30	9.67	4.00	21.00	3.99	9.50
– Banks	15	11.20	6.00	21.00	3.97	10.00
– Non financial firms	15	8.10	4.00	15.00	3.48	7.00

banks' and industrial firms' boards can be extracted from the Board Index 2015 (see Spencer Stuart 2015) referring to countries under investigation.

Table 5.2 shows the descriptive statistics of our sample (in whole), and also distinguishes between sub-samples, banks and non-financial firms (excluding dummies variables). As can be seen, at the European level, BoDs have an average size of 15.40 directors; this value ranges from a minimum of 8 directors to a maximum of 21 directors. Banks show a size, on average, higher than non-financial firms (16.20 vs. 14.60 members).

In our sample, directors have an average age of over 59.29 and bank board have older directors than non-bank boards. The presence of foreigners is relatively small with on average fewer than four foreign directors; in some cases, this value is equal to zero both for banks and non-financial firms. Women on average account for one third of directors and is slightly higher for non-financial firms compared to banks (33.50% vs. 32.60%). The presence of independent directors is, on average, higher in our sample: it is equal to 67.86% and reaches 100%, in the German case; in banks, this value is higher than for non-financial firms (69.30% vs. 66.40%). On average, board committees are equal to 4.70, with a minimum value equal to 2 and a maximum of 8 committees; in banks, this value is higher than for non-financial firms (5.40% vs. 3.90%). Meeting activity variable is, on average, equal to 9.67, with a minimum value of 4 and a maximum of 21 board meetings per year; this last case is related to the bank sub-sample.

Focusing on our bank sub-sample, these are generally similar to that of Adams and Mehran's (2003).

5.6 Results

For each of the board characteristics described previously, the analysis involving the entire sample of 30 banks and non-financial firms in Europe brings us to a comparison which can be summarized in terms of *t*-values as reported in Table 5.3.

Taking properly into account the sample size of both bank and non-financial firms in this case ($n_1 = n_2 = 15$), the two-sided Student's *t* test is such that the *t*-value needs to be outside the range from -1.75 to 1.75, in order to claim a significant difference. This happens for only two of the seven considered variables: BC and MA (reported in bold font in the table). In both cases, a negative value indicates a larger mean value for bank boards with respect to non-financial boards: in other words, banks are organized with a larger number of committees and are characterized by a more frequent meeting activity per year.

Results on *country-specific board diversity* can be first summarized by means of the radar diagrams (shown in Fig. 5.1) separately for non-financial boards and for bank boards: for each of the seven considered variables (put at the vertices of the diagrams along suitably scaled axes) the average value at the European level is computed and set to 1 for an adequate comparison to the mean values related to each of the five countries, C variable (Italy, Great Britain, France, Germany and Spain), represented with different symbols and line types.

A more detailed and quantitative comparison for the *country-specific* analysis for each industrial sector (IS) is based on a Student's *t*-distribution two-sided test comparing the means μ_C and μ_{Eur} of the country (C) and of the total European sample, by using the corresponding standard deviations $\sigma_{\mu C}$ and $\sigma_{\mu Eur}$ and setting the needed sample multiplicities ($n_C = 3$, $n_{Eur} = 15$). In Table 5.4 the *t*-values obtained for each of the board's characteristics are reported in each cell separately

Table 5.3 Industry-specific comparison between non-financial boards and bank boards in EU

Board's characteristics	Abrev.	*t*-value	*t* outside the 90% C.L. range
Board size	BS	−1.33	No
Board age	BA	−1.09	No
Foreigners	FO	0.41	No
Board gender	BG	0.21	No
Independents	IND	−0.64	No
Board committees	BC	**−3.18**	Yes
Meeting activity	MA	**−2.25**	Yes

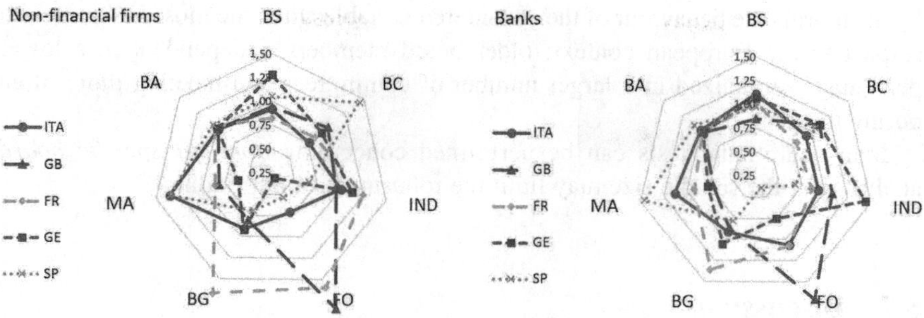

Fig. 5.1 Radar diagrams showing for each country the variables' mean value normalized to the European mean value, concerning non-financial boards (left) and bank boards (right)

Table 5.4 Country-specific comparison with respect to the European average for non-financial boards (value above in each cell) and bank boards (value reported below)

Board's characteristics	Abrev.	*t*-value Italy	*t*-value Great Britain	*t*-value France	*t*-value Germany	*t*-value Spain
Board size	BS	−0.70 −1.16	−0.56 −1.50	−1.46 0.08	**2.39** 0.65	0.43 −0.34
Board age	BA	−1.47 0.19	−1.15 −1.36	1.13 −0.99	−0.80 −1.17	**2.33** **3.33**
Foreigners	FO	−0.76 0.19	**2.20** **1.99**	1.56 0.21	**−1.81** −0.70	−1.21 −1.72
Board gender	BG	−0.42 −0.67	−0.87 −0.98	**3.02** **2.83**	−0.37 0.46	−1.38 −1.67
Independents	IND	0.04 −0.42	−0.23 −0.52	1.20 −0.86	0.72 **2.74**	−1.68 **−1.96**
Board committees	BC	1.30 −0.74	−0.87 −1.66	−0.85 **−2.05**	−0.36 1.11	**2.19** 0.48
Meeting activity	MA	1.60 0.71	−0.87 −1.66	−0.63 −0.45	**−1.85** −1.29	1.59 **2.49**

for non-financial boards (above) and for bank boards (below), in each of the considered countries C: positive (or negative) *t*-values higher (or lower) than the critical value +1.75 (or −1.75) show a significantly larger (or smaller) value with respect to the corresponding European mean value, as also reported in bolded font.

As already qualitatively evident from Fig. 5.1, the data reported in Table 5.4 are that Italian firms are in the average of the European context for what concerns all the considered board's characteristics. The same holds for Great Britain, except for a higher percentage of foreigners on the boards, regardless of the industrial sector. French firms also follow the average, but they have an evidently higher percentage of female board members on both banks and non financial firms. In Germany a larger size of non-financial boards is observed with respect to Europe, with a lower proportion of foreigner members and reduced meeting activity per year, while a higher proportion of independent board members can be reported. Finally, in

Spanish firms the behaviour of the considered variables look the most different with respect to the European context: older board members, independent in a lower percentage, organized in a larger number of committees and meeting more often during the year.

Many additional tests can be performed concerning *domestic-specific board* analysis but the sample size may limit the robustness of our findings.

5.7 Discussion

Our results lead to interesting considerations on the three diversity's profile check in the analysis. With reference to *industry-specific board diversity*, the results demonstrate how, in a European contest, banks and non-financial BoDs are similar in terms of size and composition. Therefore, although we detect differences in terms of a greater presence of independents on bank boards [similarly as to what was detected by the Italian Board Index by Spencer Stuart (2016)] and the greater presence of foreigners on non-financial BoDs, although these differences do not appear statistically significant.

Similarly, although the banks' BoDs are more numerous, despite the efforts of regulators, the differences are not statistically significant. This result contrasts with the study of Adams and Mehran (2003), who highlight that governance structures are *industry-specific*. In our study, however, board diversity is also analysed with respect to the number of board meetings and the presence of board committees highlighting how board organizations are *industry-specific*. Indeed, the specificity of the banking sector connected to the greater business complexity and the risk of the market as well as to the related regulatory compliance leads to a diversity of the BoD organization and functioning.

In our sample, banks have, on average, more than five committees, while committees in non-financial firms are less than four. The most common committees are the Nomination Committee, the Audit and Control and Risk Committee and the Remuneration Committee: the first is present in 27 cases out of 30, the second and third, respectively, in 25 cases and 23 cases. Other board committees most popular are the Related Party Transactions Committee and the Strategic Committee. The presence of committees is related to the needs to investigate issues connected with the business and supervisory purposes. In the case of non-financial firms, the board committees focus on the commercial, communications and corporate reputation of the business. The presence of internal committees allows the board to take advantage of specific directors' skills (related to crucial business areas) enabling better internal control on mangers; also, it may reduce the need to recognize the economic incentives to management. Some studies show that the presence of a large and independent Audit Committee improves internal monitoring and financial reporting processes in firms (among others, Bronson et al. 2009). The meeting activity in bank board is related to improving the effectiveness of internal controls since it facilitates the exchange of reporting and information about the company and its performance which can boost business integrity (Conger et al. 1998).

With reference to *country-specific board diversity*, the results demonstrate, in some cases, greater board diversity between banks and non-financial firms, arising from the nationality of companies. In general, we note that the bank board present similarity between different countries due to the substantial harmonization process in banking regulations, with some exceptions.[6]

In the Italian case, the BoDs of banks and non-financial firms are no different from the European sample. In the British case, the board of banks and non-financial firms have a higher share of foreigners compared to our European sample; in particular, in British non-financial firms registering the largest number of foreign directors. In the French case, it is noted that banks have a smaller number of committees as compared to the European sample; furthermore, bank boards are characterized by the increased presence of women. About gender diversity, our European sample has a higher percenathe of female directors compared with that found in other studies (EU Commission 2016). Compared to 2010, when the same data was equal to 11.9%, the increase in female representation is significant. Our study shows that the highest gender diversity is in France, and where like Italy, has introduced ad hoc legislative measures (respectively, Loi relative à l'égalité wage entre les femmes et les hommes, Loin. 2006-340 and L. n.120/2011, called Golfo-Mosca Law). By contrast, in Spain, the Ley de Igualdad (2007) introduced only a recommendation to increase the number of women on boards. In the German case, as expected, bank boards have the largest share of independents[7]; furthermore, German non-financial firms have larger board size, alongside a greater share of foreigners and a higher meetings activity.

Finally, in the Spanish case, bank board structures differ from the European average: it is characterized by the presence of older directors, a lower number of independents and foreigners and a higher meeting activity. With respect to board diversity, overall we agree with Adams and Mehran (2003), who find that differences between board structures of banks and non-financial firms may not be a cause for concern. In the case of non-financial boards, the differences relate to the higher age of the directors and the greater presence of committees. With reference to *domestic-specific board diversity*, as already explained, the results show no statistical significance.

---

[6]This result appears to be consistent with EBA (2016): *"These draft Guidelines aim at further harmonising institutions' internal governance arrangements, processes and mechanisms across the EU, in line with the new requirements in this area introduced in the Capital Requirements Directive (CRD) and also taking into account the proportionality principle."*

[7]In fact, Germany Code of Conduct states that all members of supervisory boards, taking into account in this study, are considered independent.

5.8 Conclusions, Limits and Implications

Many studies point to the importance of corporate governance for listed companies. In particular, several studies on governance-performance confirm how the BoD structure and organisation may affect the (intermediate) performance of the company, although empirical evidence about the relationship (positive or negative) is mixed. While many studies focus on the BoD of companies in non-regulated industries, there has been less research on BoD operated in regulated industries and even less focusing between unregulated and regulated businesses.

Our study examines whether there is a difference between the BoD of banks and those of non-financial firms at European level, for a sample of listed companies. Indeed, under the "stakeholder view," banks' CG should be different from non-financial firms as they have a wider stakeholder group—shareholders, depositors, government—to meet their needs.

Firstly, looking at *industry-specific board diversity*, the structure of bank boards are similar to that of non-financial firms; diversity emerges in terms of board organization and functioning relating to the larger number of meetings and of board committees. In principle, taking into account the limitations of our study, these aspects support the BoD behavior in the internal governance framework; in fact, these bank board characteristics aim at a better protection of interests of a wide array of stakeholders and to promote business integrity through the emphasis on supervisory and monitoring function of executives.

Second, when we consider *country-specific board diversity*, bank' board are similar apart from where we find substantial difference in Spain.

Finally, when we look at *domestic-specific board diversity*, our results find no statistically significant differences.

These results have some limitations. Further investigation might use an extended sample of companies and time series on board's characteristics; other analysis could also consider data on the skills and experiences of BoDs that could be *industry-specific* or some measures of performance, effectiveness and efficiency, of the related company or BoD. In conclusion, the results of this study might have some supervisory implications, confirming the validity of some revised recent financial regulations. For example, about the same CG aspects, guidelines published by EBA and ESMA (2016) point out: *"a sufficient number of independent directors within the supervisory function of the management body helps to ensure a discussion that looks at all different aspects in the absence of conflicts of interests and other biases. The guidelines provided in this regard are based on the Commission Recommendation of 15 February 2005 on the role of non-executive or supervisory directors of listed companies and on the committees of the (supervisory) board."* To increase the effectiveness of CG in banks, board diversity seems also strengthened within the CG Guidelines on internal governance and also the role of supervision and monitoring is emphasised; *"these draft Guidelines put more emphasis on the duties and responsibilities of the management body in its supervisory function in risk oversight, including the role of their committees."* (EBA 2016).

References

Adams, R., & Mehran, H. (2003). Is corporate governance different for bank holding companies? *Economic Policy Review, 9*(1), 123–144.

Adams, R. B. & Mehran, H. (2008a). *Board structure, performance and organizational structure: The case of bank holding companies*. Federal Reserve Bank of New York paper.

Adams, R. B. & Mehran, H. (2008b). *Corporate performance, board structure, and their determinants in the banking industry*. FRB of New York Staff Report.

Adams, R. B., Hermalin, B. E., & Weisbach, M. S. (2010). The role of boards of directors in corporate governance: A conceptual framework and survey. *Journal of Economic Literature, 48*(1), 58–107.

Arsalidou, D. (2016). *Rethinking corporate governance in financial institutions*. New York: Routledge.

Bank for International Settlements (BIS). (1999). *Enhancing corporate governance for banking organisations*. Available at www.bis.org

Bank for International Settlements (BIS). (2006). *Enhancing corporate governance for banking organisations*. Available at www.bis.org

Bank for International Settlements (BIS). (2010). *Enhancing corporate governance for banking organisations*. Available at www.bis.org

Bank for International Settlements (BIS). (2015). *Enhancing corporate governance for banking organisations*. Available at www.bis.org

Becht, M., Patrick Bolton, P., & Ailsa Roell, A. (2011). Why bank governance is different. *Oxford Review of Economic Policy, 27*(3), 437–463.

Berger, A. N., Kick, T., & Schaeck, K. (2012). *Executive board composition and bank risk taking*. Deutsche Bundesbank working paper, No. 3.

Booth, J. R., Cornett, M. M., & Tehranian, H. (2002). Boards of directors, ownership, and regulation. *Journal of Banking and Finance, 26*(10), 1973–1996.

Bronson, S. N., Carcello, J. V., & Hollingsworth, C. W. (2009). Are fully independent audit committees really necessary? *Journal of Accounting and Public Policy, 28*(4), 265–280.

Carretta, A., Farina, V., & Schwizer, P. (2007). Organizzazione e funzionamento dei Consigli di amministrazione negli intermediari finanziari. Condizioni di efficacia, competenze e performance. In L. Munari (Ed.), *Attualità e prospettive negli studi di economia dei mercati e degli intermediari finanziari* (pp. 73–98). Parma: Mup.

Conger, J. A., Finegold, D., & Lawler, E. (1998). Appraising boardroom performance. *Harvard Business Review, 76*(1), 136–148.

de Haan J., Vlahu R. (2013, July). *Corporate governance of banks: A survey*. De Nederlandsche Bank working paper no. 386.

Directive 2013/34/EU on the annual financial statements.

Directive 2013/36/EU of the European Parliament and of the Concil of 26 June 2013 on access to the activity of credit institutions and the prudential supervision of credit institutions and investment firms, amending Directive 2002/87/EC and repealing Directives 2006/48/EC and 2006/49/EC.

EBA. (2011, September 27). *Guidelines on internal governance* (GL 44), London.

EBA. (2016). Consultation paper on the draft guidelines on internal governance EBA/CP/2016/16–28/10/2016.

EBA and ESMA. (2016). Joint ESMA and EBA guidelines on the assessment of the suitability of members of the management body and key function holders under Directive 2013/36/EU and Directive 2014/65/EU.

ESMA and EBA. (2016). Joint guidelines on the assessment of the suitability of members of the management body and key function holders under Directive 2013/36/EU and Directive 2014/65/EU, Consultation paper.

EU Commission. (2010). Green paper, Corporate governance in financial institutions and remuneration policies of 2 June 2010.

EU Commission. (2011, April). Green paper, The EU corporate governance framework.

EU Commission. (2014, October). Recommendation of 9 April 2014, on the quality of corporate governance reporting European Banking Authority (2016), Consultation paper on internal governance.

European Central Bank (ECB). (2011, March). *Banking supervision and corporate governance in the European architecture*.

European Central Bank (ECB). (2016, July). *SSM supervisory statement on governance and risk appetite*.

European Commission. (2016). *Report on equality between women and men*, 64.

Freeman, R. E. (1984). *Strategic management: A stakeholder approach*. Marshfield: Pitman.

Levine, R. (2004). *The corporate governance of banks: A concise discussion of concepts and evidence*. Policy Research working paper, No.3404, Washington: World Bank.

Macey, J. & O'Hara, M. (2003, April). *The corporate governance of banks*. FRBNY Economic Policy Review.

Nedcommunity. (2015, January). *Il punto sugli amministratori indipendenti*, EGO. n. 3. Available at: http://www.nedcommunity.com/Contents/Documents/EGO%20n%203%20gennaio%202015.pdf

OECD. (2009, June). *Corporate governance and the financial crisis: Key findings and main messages*, Paper.

OECD. (2015, November). Principles of corporate governance.

Spencer Stuart. (2015). *Board index (related to Italy, UK, France, Germany, Spain)*. Available at www.spencerstuart.com/

Spencer Stuart. (2016). *Board index (related to Italy, UK, France, Germany, Spain)*. Available at www.spencerstuart.com/

Chapter 6
Creditor Rights and the Bank Lending Channel of Monetary Policy

Begoña Torre Olmo, Sergio Sanfilippo Azofra, and María Cantero Sáiz

6.1 Introduction

The role played by banks as loan suppliers is essential to understanding how monetary policy influences the economy, as they are a key element in this process. In recent years, there has been a renewed interest in analyzing the bank lending channel as a monetary policy transmission mechanism.[1] This channel asserts that a restrictive monetary policy deteriorates banks' access to loanable funds, giving rise to a reduction in lending (Bernanke and Blinder 1988).

Most studies reveal that banks' reaction to monetary restrictions depends on their financial strength or ability to access alternative sources of funding. In this regard, smaller, less liquid and more poorly capitalized banks are less able to insulate their lending from monetary shocks, so they extend fewer loans during monetary contractions (Kashyap and Stein 1995a, b, 2000; Kishan and Opiela 2000, 2006; Altunbas et al. 2002, 2010).

Apart from banks' financial strength, the different impact of the bank lending channel across banks might well be explained by legal factors in each country. One possible explanation, which has scarcely been explored, is the existence of creditor legal rights. Monetary restrictions will be less effective in countries with stronger creditor rights, since banks in these countries will be more able to access deposits and debt securities to finance their loans (Houston et al. 2010). Besides, these banks will be more likely to control firms in case of bankruptcy, seize collateral and force

[1]See, for example, Gambacorta and Marques-Ibanez (2011), Said (2013), Cantero-Saiz et al. (2014), Apergis and Christou (2015), Halvorsen and Jacobsen (2016), Salachas et al. (2017), Borio and Gambacorta (2017).

B. Torre Olmo (✉) • S. Sanfilippo Azofra • M. Cantero Sáiz
University of Cantabria, Santander, Spain
e-mail: torreb@unican.es; sanfilis@unican.es; maria.cantero@unican.es

B. Díaz Díaz et al. (eds.), *Corporate Governance in Banking and Investor Protection*, CSR, Sustainability, Ethics & Governance,
https://doi.org/10.1007/978-3-319-70007-6_6

repayments, so they will provide more lending (Djankov et al. 2007). Although several articles have analyzed the influence of creditor rights on bank lending (Desai et al. 2004; Djankov et al. 2007; Qian and Strahan 2007; Houston et al. 2010; Acharya et al. 2011), none of these have examined how creditor rights influence monetary policy transmission through the bank lending channel.

As far as we are aware, this is the first study that analyzes how creditor rights affect the bank lending channel of monetary policy. In this regard, our article provides two contributions to the existing literature. Firstly, we analyze how creditor rights influence banks' loan supply reaction to monetary policy through the bank lending channel. Secondly, we test whether the effects of creditor rights on lending are different prior to and following the crisis. The global financial crisis led to strong credit restrictions and funding problems, which may have weakened the positive effects of creditor rights on loan supply.

Our empirical analysis comprises a sample of 1096 listed banks from 36 countries between 2003 and 2015. The analysis is performed using the System-GMM methodology for panel data. This methodology allows for controlling both unobservable heterogeneity and the problems of endogeneity through the use of instruments (Arellano and Bond 1991). We find that creditor rights do not directly influence loan supply, neither before nor after the crisis, but they play an important role during monetary shocks. In this regard, the bank lending channel is only present in countries with weak legal creditor protection, while it is weakened or even neutralized in countries with stronger creditor rights. These results are of great interest to central banks because they suggest that they should consider the degree of creditor legal protection when implementing monetary policy decisions.

The remainder of the article is structured as follows: Sect. 6.2 reviews the previous literature. Section 6.3 focuses on empirical analysis and discussion of the results. Section 6.4 presents the conclusions.

6.2 Literature Review

6.2.1 The Bank Lending Channel

Monetary policy exerts its influence through several channels: effects via interest rates, exchange rates, asset prices and the credit channel (Mishkin 1995). The credit channel includes two sub-channels that arise through financial frictions in credit markets (Bernanke and Blinder 1988): the balance sheet channel and the bank lending channel. The first sub-channel, the balance sheet channel, operates through the net worth of firms. Monetary restrictions deteriorate the balance sheets of borrowers, which increases their debt service and reduces the collateral value of their assets (Bernanke and Gertler 1995). Lower net worth of firms implies having less collateral on which to secure loans, causing lenders to require higher compensation. If borrowers are not able to pay higher credit costs, their access to loans will be reduced.

The second sub-channel, the bank lending channel, which is the main focus of this paper, highlights the special role played by banks in the financial systems (Bernanke and Blinder 1988). According to the bank lending channel, monetary policy variations lead to a shift in the credit provided by banks. In this regard, a restrictive monetary policy increases the level of required reserves that banks must maintain at the central bank, which reduces the availability of deposits due to the greater volume of reserves required (Kashyap and Stein 1995a; Walsh 2003). Besides, an increase in interest rates, caused by monetary tightening, reduces deposit yields in relation to other assets, which makes households more reluctant to hold these deposits (Kishan and Opiela 2000; Ehrmann et al. 2003). Since deposits are an important source of funding for banks, the reduction in the deposit base caused by monetary restrictions will force banks to curtail lending.

Three conditions are necessary for the bank lending channel to be effective (Bernanke and Blinder 1988). First, firms must be dependent on bank credit, and not able to deal with the reduction in bank loans caused by monetary restrictions by switching to alternative funding sources. Second, central banks must be able to affect loan supply, which implies that during monetary restrictions banks cannot offset the decline in deposits by funds from other sources. Third, there must be imperfections in the aggregate price level adjustment to prevent any monetary policy shock from being neutral.

These conditions have been criticized by other authors, especially the second relating to the limited funding alternatives to deposits for banks. In this regard, Romer and Romer (1990) report that banks can easily overcome the drain on deposits by simply raising non-deposit funds through the issue of CDS or bonds. The existence of alternative funding sources to deposits has led other authors to propose a new mechanism that supports the bank lending channel. This new mechanism focuses on market-based funding for banks (Bernanke 2007; Disyatat 2011). In this regard, a restrictive monetary policy increases banks' external finance premium, subjecting them to a higher cost of funds, which are then passed on to borrowers.

To sum up, the underlying mechanism of the bank lending channel is one in which a restrictive monetary policy is followed by a decline in funding via deposits and/or an increase in banks' external finance premium. As a result, this leads to a reduction in credit supply.

A large number of studies have analyzed the reaction of loan supply to shifts in monetary policy, depending on bank-specific characteristics. This is because monetary restrictions cause a drop in deposits, which forces banks to substitute through uninsured sources of funds. Raising uninsured funds is more difficult for banks with weaker balance sheets, so they are more sensitive to monetary shocks (Kishan and Opiela 2006). Moreover, the external finance premium of banks is sensitive to their financial health. Consequently, during monetary contractions, banks with weaker balance sheets experience a greater variability in their external finance premium and, consequently, their lending is more adversely affected (Disyatat 2011).

In this context, the balance sheet strength of banks has been measured in terms of size, liquidity, and capitalization. Smaller banks are more affected by a monetary restriction, since they normally have simpler capital structures, higher information asymmetries and, hence, they cannot access alternative sources of funds (Kashyap and Stein 1995a, b, 2000; Kishan and Opiela 2000, 2006). Less liquid banks have less cash to compensate the loss of deposits during monetary contractions, so they are more responsive to monetary contractions (Kashyap and Stein 2000; De Bondt 1999; Gambacorta 2005; Matousek and Sarantis 2009). Poorly capitalized banks are perceived also to be more risky by market participants, so it is more difficult for them to access external finance. Besides, low capitalized banks are more exposed to information asymmetries and moral hazard problems, so they have greater difficulties in obtaining finance in the capital markets to protect their loan portfolios. Thus, they suffer a greater reduction in loan supply after a monetary tightening (Peek and Rosengren 1995; Kishan and Opiela 2000, 2006; Altunbas et al. 2002).

6.2.2 Creditor Protection and the Bank Lending Channel

The relationship between creditors and shareholders is often conditioned by agency problems. They have conflicting interests because managers emphasise decisions that promote shareholder value and this may conflict with creditors' interests. Creditors lend funds to the firm and claim part of the firm's earnings in return. In contrast, shareholders control the firm's managers, whose decisions affect the profitability and risk of the firm. Shareholders have greater incentives for risk than creditors. The former are more prone to highly risky projects because if a project becomes successful they will receive all the profits, whereas the creditors will get a fixed rate of return. However, if a project fails creditors might have to bear the losses.

In every country, this agency problem between creditors and shareholders is conditioned by creditor's legal rights. The strength of creditor rights has a crucial influence on creditors' incentive to lend funds (Djankov et al. 2007). In countries with stronger creditor rights, creditors are more powerful when firms file for bankruptcy and their recovery rates in such an event are higher. When creditor rights are strong, banks will bear less risk because they are more likely to seize collateral, force repayments and take control of bankrupt firms (Houston et al. 2010). Thus, they will be more willing to grant more loans. In this regard, in an analysis of 129 countries over 25 years, Djankov et al. (2007) find that the creditor rights are associated with higher levels of private sector credit in developed countries but not in poor ones. Qian and Strahan (2007) show that interest rates are lower and maturities longer in countries with stronger creditor protection. Moreover, strong creditor rights might well encourage banks to grant credit to riskier borrowers because they have greater protection in the event of a default. Actually, creditor rights might well be related with creditor monitoring activity. As the recovery rates are higher when creditor protection is stronger, the incentive to monitor borrowers decreases. In this regard, in an analysis of 2400 banks in

69 countries, Houston et al. (2010) find a positive relationship between creditor rights and bank risk.

Contrary to creditors, which are more willing to take more risk in countries with strong creditor rights, firms in these countries often choose more secure projects, which can reduce the agency problem and facilitate their access to bank financing. In this regard, in an analysis of a sample of mergers and acquisitions in 38 countries between 1994 and 2004, Acharya et al. (2011) find that in countries with better protected rights firms are less willing to take high risk. Moreover, Desai et al. (2004) show that foreign affiliates of U.S. multinational firms in countries with weak creditor rights borrow less externally.

Creditor right might also affect the willingness of creditors to provide funds to banks themselves (Houston et al. 2010). Banks in countries with strong creditor protection will have easier access to financing and lower financing costs, as creditors will be more willing to deposit funds and buy securities because they are more protected in the event of bankruptcy. In contrast, banks in countries with weaker creditor rights will tend to face greater funding costs and lower funding availability.

Regarding the impact that creditor protection has on the bank lending channel, a monetary policy restriction is highly likely to lead to a higher credit reduction in countries with weaker creditor protection. On the one hand, banks in these countries will have higher funding costs and restrictions, which is an essential part of the bank lending channel and, on the other hand, they will be less willing to grant credit to firms as these banks are less protected in the event of bankruptcy. Banks in countries with strong creditor rights will be more able to insure the loan supply from monetary shocks as depositors or debt holders will be more willing to finance them. Moreover, banks in these countries will grant more credit as they are more likely to take control of bankrupt firms, seize collateral and force repayments. In conclusion, we propose that: creditor rights will reduce the effectiveness of the bank lending channel, so the loan supply of banks in countries with stronger creditor protection will be less negatively affected by monetary policy restrictions.

6.3 Empirical Analysis

6.3.1 Selection of the Sample

We use a sample of listed banks from 36 countries[2] between 2003 and 2015. Table 6.1 shows the number of banks and observations for each country and the distribution of the sample. We use a panel of banks with data available for a

[2]Argentina, Australia, Austria, Belgium, Brazil, Canada, Chile, Colombia, Denmark, Egypt, Finland, France, Germany, Greece, India, Indonesia, Ireland, Italy, Japan, Malaysia, Mexico, Norway, Pakistan, Peru, Philippines, Portugal, Republic of Korea, Singapore, South Africa, Spain, Sri Lanka, Sweden, Switzerland, Thailand, United Kingdom and United States.

Table 6.1 Sample

Panel A: Number of banks per country		
	Number of observations	Number of banks
Argentina	85	7
Australia	90	7
Austria	90	7
Belgium	35	3
Brazil	304	26
Canada	120	10
Chile	90	7
Colombia	69	7
Denmark	260	23
Egypt	124	12
Finland	26	2
France	233	19
Germany	124	11
Greece	83	8
India	279	40
Indonesia	358	37
Ireland	26	2
Italy	216	17
Japan	1095	88
Malaysia	130	10
Mexico	43	4
Norway	102	17
Pakistan	215	21
Peru	80	7
Philippines	179	16
Portugal	56	5
Republic of Korea	96	8
Singapore	39	3
South Africa	75	7
Spain	65	5
Sri Lanka	124	11
Sweden	52	4
Switzerland	281	25
Thailand	114	11
United Kingdom	95	9
United States	6345	600
Total	11,798	1096

Panel B: Yearly distribution of the sample

	2003	2004	2005	2006	2007	2008	2009	2010	2011	2012	2013	2014	2015	Total Obs.
N. of banks	733	802	839	877	905	937	965	951	969	997	970	945	908	11,798

minimum of four consecutive years between 2003 and 2015. This condition is essential in order to test for second-order serial correlation, which is performed to ensure the robustness of the estimates from System-GMM (Arellano and Bond 1991). The financial information on each institution comes from the Datastream database. The macroeconomic information is from the World Development Indicators database of the World Bank, the International Monetary Fund, and Datastream.

6.3.2 Econometric Model and Data

To test the hypotheses, we propose the following model based on the approach of Kashyap and Stein (1995a). However, we contribute by considering the importance of creditor rights and its interaction with monetary policy:

$$
\begin{aligned}
\Delta \ln(\text{loans})_{i,t} = \; & \rho_0 + \rho_1 \Delta \ln(\text{loans})_{i,t-1} + \rho_2 \text{CR1}_m \\
& + \rho_3 \text{CR2}_m + \rho_4 \text{CR3}_m + \rho_5 \text{CR4}_m + (\rho_6 + \rho_7 \text{CR1}_m) \Delta i_{m,t} \\
& + (\rho_6 + \rho_8 \text{CR2}_m) \Delta i_{m,t} + (\rho_6 + \rho_9 \text{CR3}_m) \Delta i_{m,t} \\
& + (\rho_6 + \rho_{10} \text{CR4}_m) \Delta i_{m,t} + \rho_{11} \text{SIZE}_{i,t-1} + \rho_{12} \text{LIQ}_{i,t-1} \\
& + \rho_{13} \text{CAP}_{i,t-1} + \rho_{14} \Delta i_{m,t} * \text{SIZE}_{i,t-1} + \rho_{15} \Delta i_{m,t} * \text{LIQ}_{i,t-1} \\
& + \rho_{16} \Delta i_{m,t} * \text{CAP}_{i,t-1} + \rho_{17} \Delta \ln(\text{GDP})_{m,t} + \textstyle\sum_{t=1}^{13} \pi_t \text{Year}_t \\
& + \textstyle\sum_{m=1}^{36} \vartheta_m \text{Country}_m + \varepsilon_{i,t}
\end{aligned}
\tag{6.1}
$$

The dependent variable, *$\Delta ln(Loans)_{i,t}$*, is the growth rate in the logarithm of loan supply from bank *i* in year *t* relative to year *t*−1. This variable has been widely used in the bank lending channel literature (Ehrmann et al. 2003; Gambacorta 2005; Jimborean 2009; Olivero et al. 2011; Gambacorta and Marques-Ibanez 2011). Following previous studies, we include loan growth lagged one year (*$\Delta ln(Loans)_{i,t-1}$*) as an independent variable to capture the persistence of the dependent variable.

Creditor rights are denoted by *CR*, which consist of four components. Following La Porta et al. (1998), each component is a dummy variable that takes the value 1 if creditor right exists in a country and 0 otherwise. The four rights are: *CR1*, which takes value of 1 in countries with no automatic stay on assets; *CR2*, which takes value of 1 in countries where secured creditors are paid first. *CR3* takes a value of 1 in countries that prevent managers from unilaterally seeking court protection from creditors by filing for reorganization without creditor consent. *CR4* takes a value of 1 in countries where managers are replaced in the event of reorganization procedures.

Δi is the change in the short-term money market rate, and represents the monetary policy indicator (De Bondt 1999; Ehrmann et al. 2003; Altunbas et al. 2010; Olivero et al. 2011). The bank lending channel contends that an increase in

short-term money market rate leads to a reduction in the growth of loan supply. Thus, we expect this variable to have a negative and significant coefficient.

We interact the four creditor rights variables with the monetary policy variable ($CR1{*}\Delta i_{m,t}$, $CR2{*}\Delta i_{m,t}$, $CR3{*}\Delta i_{m,t}$ and $CR4{*}\Delta i_{m,t}$). These interaction variables are used to demonstrate whether the existence of creditor rights determines the effects of monetary policy on loan supply growth. The effects of monetary policy on lending in countries with weak creditor protection[3] are measured by the coefficient ρ_6. On the other hand, the effects of monetary policy on lending in countries where the creditor right *CR1*, *CR2*, *CR3*, or *CR4* exists, are measured by the sum of the coefficients ($\rho_6 + \rho_7$), ($\rho_6 + \rho_8$), ($\rho_6 + \rho_9$), and ($\rho_6 + \rho_{10}$) respectively. Banks provide more loans when they enjoy superior credit protection (Cole and Turk-Ariss 2007), which is why they can be less affected by monetary restrictions.

We introduce in model (6.1) three bank-specific characteristics[4]:

SIZE is defined as the log of total assets. Large banks experience normally higher loan growth rates, so we expect this variable to have a positive and significant coefficient (Kashyap and Stein 1995a, b, 2000).

LIQ is the ratio of securities and cash due from banks to total assets. Liquid banks are more able to provide higher lending volumes, so we expect that this variable is significant with a positive sign (De Bondt 1999; Kashyap and Stein 2000).

CAP is the ratio of total equity to total assets. Usually, higher capitalized banks extend more credit, so we expect that this variable has a positive and significant coefficient (Kishan and Opiela 2000, 2006).

We include interaction terms between the monetary policy variable ($\Delta i_{m,t}$) and the bank-specific characteristics variables (*SIZE, LIQ,* and *CAP*) to capture the effect that these characteristics have on monetary policy changes.

First, we introduce the interaction term between *SIZE* and the monetary policy indicator ($\Delta i_{m,t}$). Smaller banks are less capable to access alternative sources of funding to deposits, so they are more sensitive to monetary policy restrictions (Kashyap and Stein 1995a, b, 2000; Kishan and Opiela 2000; Kakes and Sturm 2002). Consequently, we expect this variable to have a significant and positive coefficient.

Second, we introduce the interaction variable between *LIQ* and the monetary policy indicator ($\Delta i_{m,t}$). Liquid banks are less affected by monetary shocks, since they have more cash to overcome the reduction in deposits (Kashyap and Stein 2000; Ehrmann et al. 2003; Gambacorta 2005). As a result, a positive sign for this interaction variable is expected.

Third, we introduce the interaction term between *CAP* and the monetary policy indicator ($\Delta i_{m,t}$). Poorly capitalized banks are perceived as more risky and, hence, have greater difficulties to obtain non-deposit funds (Peek and Rosengren 1995;

[3]In these countries, $CR1 = 0$, $CR2 = 0$, $CR3 = 0$, and $CR4 = 0$.

[4]Following previous studies, we use these three bank-specific characteristics lagged one year to avoid endogeneity bias (Kashyap and Stein 1995a, b, 2000; Ehrmann et al. 2003).

Kishan and Opiela 2000, 2006; Altunbas et al. 2002). Therefore, we expect a positive coefficient for this variable.

We use continuous variables to create the previous interaction terms. To interpret these interaction terms properly, the three bank-specific variables (*SIZE, LIQ*, and *CAP*) are normalized with respect to their mean across all banks in the sample.[5]

$$SIZE_{it} = logA_{it} - \frac{\sum_{i=1}^{N} logA_{it}}{N_t}$$

$$LIQ_{it} = \frac{L_{it}}{A_{it}} - \frac{\sum_{t=1}^{T}\left(\sum_{i=1}^{N}(L_{it}/A_{it})/N_t\right)}{T}$$

$$CAP_{it} = \frac{E_{it}}{A_{it}} - \frac{\sum_{t=1}^{T}\left(\sum_{i=1}^{N}(E_{it}/A_{it})/N_t\right)}{T}$$

Here, A_{it} is total assets, L_{it} is securities and cash due from banks, E_{it} is total equity, and N_t is the number of banks.

The normalization implies that for the Eq. (6.1), the mean of the interaction terms is zero and the parameter ρ_6 is interpreted as the average effect of monetary policy on the growth of loans. The coefficients for the bank characteristics (ρ_j; j: 11,..,13) represent the effect of these characteristics on lending growth when the change in short-term money market rate ($\Delta i_{m,t}$) is zero. The coefficients for the interaction terms ($\rho_{14}, \rho_{15}, \rho_{16}$) indicates whether the considered bank characteristic affects the reaction of bank lending to monetary policy variations.

The variable *Δln(GDP)* is the nominal GDP growth rate (Altunbas et al. 2010). Better economic conditions increase the demand for credit (Kashyap et al. 1993; Jimborean 2009). Therefore, we expect a positive relationship between this variable and the growth in loan supply.

Country and year effect dummies are included to capture country and year-specific factors. The error term is $\varepsilon_{i,t}$; $i = 1,2,\ldots, N$ indicates a specific bank *i*; $m = 1,2,\ldots, M$ indicates a particular country *m*; $t = 1,2,\ldots, T$ indicates a particular year *t* and *j* denotes the number of lags.

Table 6.2 presents the descriptive statistics of the variables used in the analysis. Table 6.3 presents the correlations between variables to identify potential collinearity problems between variables.

The model in Eq. (6.1) is estimated using two step System-GMM (Generalized Method of Moments). The analysis of the relationship between bank lending and monetary policy can be affected by endogeneity problems. Monetary policy decisions affect credit supply, but the situation of the banking sector could affect monetary decisions as well (Gambacorta and Marques-Ibanez 2011). To control

[5]Other previous studies have followed the same approach (Ehrmann et al. 2003; Gambacorta 2005; Jimborean 2009).

Table 6.2 Sample statistics

Variable	Mean	Standard deviation	Minimum	Maximum
Δln(loans)	0.1125	0.2335	−5.2658	6.6304
Δln(GDP)	0.0218	0.0243	−0.0958	0.2333
Δi	−0.0018	0.0170	−0.3761	0.1052
SIZE	15.1277	2.2894	7.1033	24.2705
LIQ	0.0392	0.0414	0.0000	0.4884
CAP	0.0967	0.0549	−0.0551	0.9074

The statistics of the variables SIZE, LIQ, and CAP are calculated before the normalization to show more comprehensive information

Table 6.3 Correlations

	$\Delta\ln(\text{loans})_{t-1}$	Δln(GDP)	Δi	SIZE	LIQ	CAP
$\Delta\ln(\text{loans})_{t-1}$	1					
Δln(GDP)	0.1113	1				
Δi	0.0443	0.1913	1			
SIZE	_0.0211	_0.0507	0.0094	1		
LIQ	0.0491	0.2609	0.0286	_0.0068	1	
CAP	0.0876	0.0750	_0.0202	_0.3412	0.0729	1

for this problem, we use the System-GMM methodology with robust errors, which is consistent in the presence of any pattern of heteroscedasticity and autocorrelation. This method allows us to for control for the problems of endogeneity and allows us to obtain consistent and unbiased estimates by using lagged independent variables as instruments (Arellano and Bond 1991). Following Jimborean (2009), the monetary policy indicator and the macroeconomic variables are considered to be exogenous and the bank characteristics and their interactions endogenous.

For the endogenous variables, we use collapsed instruments from the second to the fourth lags.[6] The exogenous variables are instrumented by themselves.

6.3.3 *Empirical Results*

The results of our analysis are shown in Table 6.4. None of the coefficients associated with the dummy variables that capture different aspects of creditor rights (*CR1*, *CR2*, *CR3* and *CR4*) are significant. Thus, in our sample, creditor protection does not directly affect the growth of bank loans, which implies that banks are not willing to grant more credit in countries with strong creditor protection.

[6]Collapsed instruments, by constraining all of the annual moment conditions to be the same, effectively reduces the instrument count and the number of moment conditions used in the difference-in-Hansen test of exogeneity of instrument subsets, which makes this test more powerful (Wintoki et al. 2012).

Table 6.4 Results

	Coefficient	T-student	P-value
$\Delta\ln(\text{loans})_{t-1}$	0.5356	2.14	0.032**
CR1	−0.0020	−0.29	0.772
CR2	0.0035	0.62	0.538
CR3	−0.0114	−1.30	0.195
CR4	−0.0021	−0.41	0.683
Δi_t	−10.0190	−2.61	0.009***
$(\Delta i_t \times \text{CR1})$	−0.3168	−0.09	0.925
$(\Delta i_t \times \text{CR2})$	5.3992	1.83	0.068*
$(\Delta i_t \times \text{CR3})$	10.2383	1.77	0.077*
$(\Delta i_t \times \text{CR4})$	−0.7429	−0.53	0.596
SIZE_{t-1}	0.0159	1.23	0.218
LIQ_{t-1}	0.0823	0.17	0.865
CAP_{t-1}	1.9229	3.35	0.001***
$(\Delta i_t \times \text{SIZE}_{t-1})$	1.5713	3.00	0.003***
$(\Delta i_t \times \text{LIQ}_{t-1})$	−49.3123	−1.08	0.281
$(\Delta i_t \times \text{CAP}_{t-1})$	96.1339	3.17	0.002***
$\Delta\ln(\text{GDP})_t$	1.0594	2.07	0.038**
CONS	0.0567	1.76	0.078*
LR Test. CR1	−10.33578	−1.53	0.125
LR Test. CR2	−4.619765	−3.15	0.002***
LR Test. CR3	0.219261	0.08	0.938
LR Test. CR4	−10.76191	−2.81	0.005***
M2			0.130
Hansen			0.104

Coefficients, T-student, and p-values associated with each variable. M2 is the p-value of the second order serial correlation statistic. Hansen is the p-value of the over-identifying restriction test. LR Test. CR1 is the linear restriction tests associated with the variable sum of the coefficients associated to $\Delta i + (\Delta i_t \times \text{CR1})$. LR Test. CR2 is the linear restriction tests associated with the variable sum of the coefficients associated to $\Delta i + (\Delta i_t \times \text{CR2})$. LR Test. CR3 is the linear restriction tests associated with the variable sum of the coefficients associated to $\Delta i + (\Delta i_t \times \text{CR3})$. LR Test. CR4 is the linear restriction tests associated with the variable sum of the coefficients associated to $\Delta i + (\Delta i_t \times \text{CR4})$ *** indicates a level of significance of 0.01, ** indicates a level of significance of 0.05, * indicates a level of significance of 0.1

Despite the apparent irrelevance of creditor protection to the loan supply, our results also show that strong creditor rights are relevant to the loan growth after monetary shocks as they influence the way monetary restrictions affect loan supply. In this regard, the coefficient associated to the monetary policy indicator (Δi), which captures the effect of monetary policy changes on the loan supply of banks operating in countries with weak creditor protection,[7] is negative and significant. This result, which supports the presence of the bank lending channel in countries with weak creditor rights, implies that an increase in the short term interest rate gives rise to a reduction in the growth of bank loans. However, banks that operate in countries with no automatic stay on assets are not going to suffer this reduction because the linear restriction test of the coefficient associated to the variable *CR1*, which captures the effects of monetary policy on lending when the creditor right *CR1* exists, is not significant. Moreover, the linear restriction test of the coefficient associated to the variable *CR3* is not significant either. Thus, monetary policy restrictions do not affect the bank lending in countries that prevent managers from unilaterally seeking court protection from creditors by filing for reorganization without creditor consent. These results show that the bank lending channel is less effective in countries with strong creditor protection, as we proposed previously.

The linear restriction tests of the coefficient associated to the variable *CR2* and *CR4* are negative and significant. Thus, the loan supply of banks in countries where secured creditors are paid first (*CR2*) and where managers are replaced in the event of reorganization procedures (*CR4*) is affected by monetary policy restrictions. Although the bank lending channel is effective in countries with these types of creditor protection, the coefficient associated to the linear restriction test of *CR2* is much lower than the one associated to a country with weak creditor rights (with all the creditor right variables equal 0) represented in Table 6.4 by Δi. Thus, the protection of secured creditors reduces the effectiveness of the bank lending channel, which supports our hypothesis. In contrast, the coefficient associated to the linear restriction test of *CR4* is quite similar to the coefficient associated to a country with weak creditor rights. Thus, the effect of monetary policy restrictions on the growth of loans is similar in countries with and without manager replacement.

To sum up, creditor rights do not directly affect the growth of loans but they play an important role when there are monetary shocks. After monetary policy restrictions, banks in countries with strong creditor rights are more likely to suffer less financing restrictions, so they can insure themselves from such shocks. In this regard, the bank lending channel, which is present in countries with weak legal creditor protection, is weakened or even neutralized in countries with stronger creditor protection. Management replacement is the only creditor right variable out of the four used that does not seem to affect the negative relationship between monetary policy restrictions and loan supply.

With regard to the rest of the significant variables in Table 6.4, $\Delta ln(loans)$ has a significant positive coefficient which reflects the persistence effects of the growth of loans. $\Delta ln(GDP)$ has also a significant positive coefficient, so better economic conditions expand loans. The interaction term between *SIZE* and the monetary policy indicator (Δi) is negative and significant. Thus, bigger banks are less

[7]In these countries $CR1 = 0$, $CR2 = 0$, $CR3 = 0$, and $CR4 = 0$.

Table 6.5 Results—dummy crisis

	Coefficient	T-student	P-value
$\Delta \ln(\text{loans})_{t-1}$	0.0552	0.18	0.859
CR1	0.0440	1.23	0.219
CR2	−0.0222	−1.19	0.232
CR3	−0.0093	−0.73	0.465
CR4	−0.0497	−1.29	0.197
Δi_t	−12.3398	−2.88	0.004***
$(\Delta i_t \times \text{CR1})$	−53.7390	−1.30	0.194
$(\Delta i_t \times \text{CR2})$	8.9887	2.04	0.042**
$(\Delta i_t \times \text{CR3})$	15.4583	1.98	0.048**
$(\Delta i_t \times \text{CR4})$	53.0310	1.29	0.198
SIZE_{t-1}	0.0398	1.83	0.067*
LIQ_{t-1}	−0.4603	−0.51	0.614
CAP_{t-1}	1.6442	2.16	0.030**
$(\Delta i_t \times \text{SIZE}_{t-1})$	0.1544	0.13	0.893
$(\Delta i_t \times \text{LIQ}_{t-1})$	−83.8864	−1.10	0.272
$(\Delta i_t \times \text{CAP}_{t-1})$	32.2651	0.60	0.550
$\Delta \ln(\text{GDP})_t$	2.8453	2.42	0.016**
(CRISIS × CR1)	−0.0804	−1.42	0.155
(CRISIS × CR2)	0.0138	1.07	0.284
(CRISIS × CR3)	−0.0093	−1.39	0.163
(CRISIS × CR4)	0.0734	1.48	0.140
CONS	0.1054	2.33	0.020**
LR Test. (Δit − CR1)	−66.0787	−1.52	0.128
LR Test. (Δit − CR2)	−3.3511	−1.95	0.051*
LR Test. (Δit − CR3)	3.1186	0.65	0.516
LR Test. (Δit − CR4)	40.6912	1.02	0.306
LR Test. (CRISIS − CR1)	−0.0363	−1.55	0.121
LR Test. (CRISIS − CR2)	−0.0084	−1.11	0.269
LR Test. (CRISIS − CR3)	−0.0185	−1.58	0.113
LR Test. (CRISIS − CR4)	0.0237	1.39	0.165
M2			0.411
Hansen			0.146

Coefficients, T-student, and p-values associated with each variable. M2 is the p-value of the second order serial correlation statistic. Hansen is the p-value of the over-identifying restriction test. LR Test. Δi_t − CR1 is the linear restriction tests associated with the variable sum of the coefficients associated to Δi + (Δi_t × CR1). LR Test. Δi_t − CR2 is the linear restriction tests associated with the variable sum of the coefficients associated to Δi + (Δi_t × CR2). LR Test. Δi_t − CR3 is the linear restriction tests associated with the variable sum of the coefficients associated to Δi + (Δi_t × CR3). LR Test. Δi_t − CR4 is the linear restriction tests associated with the variable sum of the coefficients associated to Δi + (Δi_t × CR4). LR Test. CRISIS − CR1 is the linear restriction tests associated with the variable sum of the coefficients associated to CRISIS + (CRISIS × CR1). LR Test. CRISIS − CR2 is the linear restriction tests associated with the variable sum of the coefficients associated to CRISIS + (CRISIS × CR2). LR Test. CRISIS − CR3 is the linear restriction tests associated with the variable sum of the coefficients associated to CRISIS + (CRISIS × CR3). LR Test. CRISIS − CR4 is the linear restriction tests associated with the variable sum of the coefficients associated to CRISIS + (CRISIS × CR4)
*** indicates a level of significance of 0.01, ** indicates a level of significance of 0.05, * indicates a level of significance of 0.1

sensitive to monetary policy restrictions than smaller ones. Finally, the variable *CAP* and its interaction with the monetary policy indicator have significant and positive coefficients. This result indicates that well-capitalized banks are more likely to expand their supply of loans and have less difficulty in accessing non-deposit financing, which insulates their loan supply from monetary shocks.

The financial crisis has hampered the access of banks to funding and led most of them to hoard liquidity for reasons of precaution rather than to grant more credit. In order to evaluate if the financial crisis affects the relationship between creditor rights and loan supply, we estimate Eq. (6.1) adding the interaction terms between the creditor rights variables (*CR1*, *CR2*, *CR3* and *CR4*) and a dummy variable *CRISIS*, which takes the value of 1 for the years 2008–2015 and of 0 otherwise. The results, which are reported in Table 6.5, show that creditor protection does not affect the growth of loan before or after the crisis. In this regard, the variables *CR1*, *CR2*, *CR3* and *CR4*, which capture the effect before the crisis, are not significant. The linear restriction tests of these variables and the dummy variable *CRISIS*, which capture the effect of creditor rights after the crisis are not significant either.

Similar to the results in Tables 6.4 and 6.5 shows that creditor rights weaken or neutralize the bank lending channel. Thus, banks in countries with strong creditor protection tend to grant more loans after a monetary policy restriction than those ones in countries with weak creditor rights.[8] This result supports our assumptions again and adds robustness to our results.

6.4 Conclusions

A lot of studies have analyzed the effect of the bank lending channel on the transmission mechanism of monetary policy. However, little research has been done on the effect that creditor protection has on this channel, which is the aim of this study. Banks are more willing to grant credit in countries with strong creditor rights, as they are more protected in the event of bankruptcy. Moreover, depositors and debt holders are also more protected, so they are more willing to finance banks. Thus, when creditors are strongly protected, bank financing is likely to be less affected by monetary policy shocks and therefore the bank lending channel will be less effective.

Using a sample of 1096 listed banks from 36 countries over the period of 2003–2015, we find that creditor rights do not directly affect the loan supply of banks, but they affect the effectiveness of the bank lending channel. Our results show that banks in countries with weak creditor protection reduce their lending after monetary policy restrictions. However, in countries with strong creditor

[8] In this model, management replacement (CR4) is not significant, so monetary restrictions do not affect loan supply in countries where managers are replaced in the event of reorganization procedures.

protection, the loan supply is less likely to decrease after those restrictions, both before and after the onset of the financial crisis. Specifically, our findings support that the bank lending channel is not present in countries with no automatic stay on assets and in those that prevent managers from unilaterally seeking court protection from creditors by filing for reorganization without creditor consent. Protection of secured creditors does not eliminate the bank lending channel, but reduces its effectiveness. In contrast there is little evidence to suggest that the bank lending channel differs in countries with and without management replacement.

Our findings are significant for understanding the way monetary policy is conducted. They suggest that central banks should take into account creditor rights when they conduct monetary policy actions. This is a preliminary analysis and further research is needed to understand the effects of creditor rights on the transmission mechanism of monetary policy.

References

Acharya, V. V., Amihud, Y., & Litov, L. (2011). Creditor rights and corporate risk-taking. *Journal of Financial Economics, 102*(1), 150–166.

Altunbas, Y., Fazylov, O., & Molyneux, P. (2002). Evidence on the bank lending channel in Europe. *Journal of Banking and Finance, 26*(11), 2093–2110.

Altunbas, Y., Gambacorta, L., & Marques-Ibanez, D. (2010). Bank risk and monetary policy. *Journal of Financial Stability, 6*(3), 121–129.

Apergis, N., & Christou, C. (2015). The behaviour of the bank lending channel when interest rates approach zero lower bound: Evidence from quantile regressions. *Economic Modelling, 49*, 296–307.

Arellano, M., & Bond, S. (1991). Some tests of specification for panel data: Monte Carlo evidence and an application to employment equations. *Review of Economic Studies, 58*(2), 277–297.

Bernanke, B. S. (2007). *The financial accelerator and the credit channel*. In remarks at a Conference at the Federal Reserve Bank of Atlanta.

Bernanke, B. S., & Blinder, A. S. (1988). Credit, money and aggregate demand. *The American Economic Review, 78*(2), 435–439.

Bernanke, B. S., & Gertler, M. (1995). Inside the black box: The credit channel of monetary policy transmission. *Journal of Economic Perspectives, 9*(4), 27–48.

Borio, C., & Gambacorta, L. (2017). Monetary policy and bank lending in a low interest rate environment: Diminishing effectiveness? *Journal of Macroeconomics*, In Press.

Cantero-Saiz, M., Sanfilippo-Azofra, S., Torre-Olmo, B., & Lopez-Gutierrez, C. (2014). Sovereign risk and the bank lending channel in Europe. *Journal of International Money and Finance, 47*, 1–20.

Cole, R. A., & Turk-Ariss, R. (2007). *Legal origin, creditor protection and bank lending around the world*. MPRA papers.

De Bondt, G. J. (1999). Banks and monetary transmission in Europe: Empirical evidence. Banca Nazionale del Lavoro. *Quarterly Review, 52*(209), 149–168.

Desai, M. A., Foley, C. F., & Hines, J. R. (2004). A multinational perspective on capital structure choice and internal capital markets. *The Journal of Finance, 59*(6), 2451–2487.

Disyatat, P. (2011). The bank lending channel revisited. *Journal of Money, Credit and Banking, 43* (4), 711–734.

Djankov, S., McLiesh, C., & Shleifer, A. (2007). Private credit in 129 countries. *Journal of Financial Economics, 84*(2), 299–329.

Ehrmann, M., Gambacorta, L., Martínez-Pagés, J., Sevestre, P., & Worms, A. (2003). Financial systems and the role of banks in monetary policy transmission in the Euro Area. In I. Angeloni, A. Kashyap, & B. Mojon (Eds.), *Monetary policy transmission in the Euro area* (pp. 235–269). Cambridge: Cambridge University Press.

Gambacorta, L. (2005). Inside the bank lending channel. *European Economic Review, 49*(7), 1737–1759.

Gambacorta, L., & Marques-Ibanez, D. (2011). The bank lending channel: Lessons from the crisis. *Economic Policy, 26*(66), 135–182.

Halvorsen, J. I., & Jacobsen, D. H. (2016). The bank-lending channel empirically revisited. *Journal of Financial Stability, 27*, 95–105.

Houston, J. F., Lin, C., Lin, P., & Ma, Y. (2010). Creditor rights, information sharing, and bank risk taking. *Journal of Financial Economics, 96*(3), 485–512.

Jimborean, R. (2009). The role of banks in the monetary policy transmission in the new EU member states. *Economic Systems, 33*(4), 360–375.

Kakes, J., & Sturm, J. E. (2002). Monetary policy and bank lending: Evidence from German banking groups. *Journal of Banking and Finance, 26*(11), 2077–2092.

Kashyap, A. K., & Stein, J. C. (1995a). The impact of monetary policy on bank balance sheets. *Carnegie-Rochester Conference Series on Public Policy, 42*, 151–195.

Kashyap, A. K., & Stein, J. C. (1995b). *The role of banks in the transmission of monetary policy*. NBER Reporter, Fall, National Bureau of Economic Research.

Kashyap, A. K., & Stein, J. C. (2000). What do a million observations on banks say about the transmission of monetary policy? *The American Economic Review, 90*(3), 407–428.

Kashyap, A. K., Stein, J. C., & Wilcox, D. W. (1993). Monetary policy and credit conditions: Evidence from the composition of external finance. *American Economic Review, 83*, 78–98.

Kishan, R. P., & Opiela, T. P. (2000). Bank size, bank capital and the bank lending channel. *Journal of Money, Credit and Banking, 32*(1), 121–141.

Kishan, R. P., & Opiela, T. P. (2006). Bank capital and loan asymmetry in the transmission of monetary policy. *Journal of Banking and Finance, 30*(1), 259–285.

La Porta, R., Lopez-de-Silanes, F., Shleifer, A., & Vishny, R. W. (1998). Law and finance. *The Journal of Political Economy, 106*(6), 1113–1155.

Matousek, R., & Sarantis, N. (2009). The bank lending channel and monetary transmission in Central and Eastern European Countries. *Journal of Comparative Economics, 37*(2), 321–334.

Mishkin, F. S. (1995). Symposium on the monetary transmission mechanism. *The Journal of Economic Perspectives, 9*(4), 3–10.

Olivero, M. P., Li, Y., & Jeon, B. N. (2011). Consolidation in banking and the lending channel: Evidence from bank-level data in Asia and Latin America. *Journal of International Money and Finance, 30*(6), 1034–1054.

Peek, J., & Rosengren, E. S. (1995). *Bank lending and the transmission of monetary policy*. In Conference series-Federal Reserve Bank of Boston. Federal Reserve Bank of Boston, pp. 47–68.

Qian, J., & Strahan, P. E. (2007). How laws and institutions shape financial contracts: The case of bank loans. *The Journal of Finance, 62*(6), 2803–2834.

Romer, C. D., & Romer, D. H. (1990). New evidence on the monetary transmission mechanism. *Brookings Papers on Economic Activity, 1990*(1), 149–213.

Said, F. F. (2013). The dynamic of bank lending channel: Basel regulatory constraint. *Economic Modelling, 31*, 606–613.

Salachas, E. N., Laopodis, N. T., & Kouretas, G. P. (2017). The bank-lending channel and monetary policy during pre- and post-2007 crisis. *Journal of International Financial Markets, Institutions and Money, 47*, 176–187.

Walsh, C. E. (2003). *Monetary theory and policy* (2nd ed.). Cambridge: MIT Press.

Wintoki, M. B., Linck, J. S., & Netter, J. M. (2012). Endogeneity and the dynamics of internal corporate governance. *Journal of Financial Economics, 105*, 581–606.

Chapter 7
Economies of Scope in the EU Banking Industry

Ludovico Rossi and Elena Beccalli

7.1 Introduction

In presence of economies of scope, diversifying the output mix can decrease banks total costs and, therefore, induce an efficiency improvement in the economic system. On the other hand, if there are diseconomies of scope, total costs would increase if banks produce a more diversified output mix. The estimation of economies or diseconomies of scope is particularly relevant from a regulatory point of view, because regulations that prevent banks from producing a diversified output mix might introduce inefficiencies in the economic system, in presence of scope economies. Our contribution suggests that regulators should assess the cost of regulation in terms of loss of efficiency for banks, and therefore, this might have consequences for customers who could suffer an increase in the costs of financial services to try to compensate banks for their loss of efficiency.

Whilst the literature on economies of scale is large and growing (Vander Vennet 2002; Altunbas et al. 2001; Dijkstra 2013; DeYoung and Jiang 2013; Beccalli et al. 2015), to our knowledge no published empirical work investigates economies of scope for European banks in the crisis and post-crisis period. According to the banking literature (Berger et al. 1987), the four classical main drivers of economies of scope are: the opportunity of spreading fixed costs over different outputs, the possibility of re-employing clients' information, the risk reduction thanks to increasing diversification, and customer costs saving. A regulation that prevents

L. Rossi (✉)
ICMA Centre, Henley Business School, University of Reading, Reading, UK
e-mail: l.rossi@pgr.reading.ac.uk

E. Beccalli
School of Banking Finance and Insurance, Università Cattolica del Sacro Cuore, Milano, Italy
e-mail: elena.beccalli@unicatt.it

B. Díaz Díaz et al. (eds.), *Corporate Governance in Banking and Investor Protection*, CSR, Sustainability, Ethics & Governance,
https://doi.org/10.1007/978-3-319-70007-6_7

banks to exploit one of these four channels may give room to inefficiencies. Regulators in the US (under the Dodd Frank Act of 2010) and in the EU (as in recommendations by the Liikanen Report 2012 being implemented into EC law as well as by the Vickers Report 2011 implemented into UK law) have sought to impose limitations on banks by restricting riskier areas of activity. Specifically, the European Commission established a high-level expert group (chaired by Erkki Liikanen) to examine possible reforms to the structure of the EU's banking sector and to determine whether, in addition to ongoing regulatory reforms, structural reforms of EU banks would strengthen financial stability and improve efficiency and consumer protection. Following on, the European proposal for structural reform aimed at minimizing the risky activities of the EU's 30 systemically important banks (European Commission 2014) bans proprietary trading for banks that are labeled by international regulators as too-big-to-fail in the global economy, or whose activities surpass certain financial thresholds. The EU reform would apply from 2017 in all 28 Member States.

The aim of this paper is to investigate if there are cost economies of scope in the European banking industry, how large they are (it may be the case that economies of scope are present but are economically insignificant), and how they vary across different bank sizes. For a sample of 779 banks from all the 28 EU countries between 2005 and 2014, we estimate cost economies of scope (WSCOPE) by employing several regression specifications in terms of cost function (SFA and SUR models) and functional forms (translog, generalized translog and Fourier Flexible). Overall, the results suggest evidence of scope economies in all European banking industries. Interestingly, scope economies are documented for all size deciles. Small, medium, large and giant banks enjoy economies of scope. In providing financial services jointly, banks may reduce costs due to production synergies (cost economies of scope); these production synergies enable banks to spread fixed expenses over a broader output mix, by exploiting complementarities in production, or by diversifying risks. Our empirical findings can contribute to the European banking regulatory debate, suggesting that such regulation might induce a loss of cost efficiency for banks that might harm banks' customers. Moreover, our findings seem to suggest that investor protection should not be taken as an absolute goal in banking regulation; it should instead be assessed against cost considerations such as economies of scope.

Section 7.2 discusses the relevant literature on economies of scope in banking, whereas Sect. 7.3 describes the methodology, the sample and the data sources. Section 7.4 provides the empirical evidence, and finally Sect. 7.5 concludes.

7.2 Literature Review

The post 2008 crisis regulatory trend clearly aims to separate banking from investment activity to create a banking system mainly composed by specialized banks. Gambacorta and van Rixtel (2013) report that the Volcker rule in the US, the Liikanen Report in the EU, the Vicker commission proposal in the UK and reform proposals in France and Germany, with differences among them, push to draw a line between loan generating activity and securities trading.

On economies of scope, there is a large body of research that mainly focuses on the US, providing unclear evidence on whether or not the potential benefits of functional diversification are larger than the costs. Overall studies on the US banking industry tend to document economies of scope in the pre-crisis period (Mester 1993; Pulley and Humphrey 1993; The Clearing House 2011) although several exceptions exist (Clark 1996; Mitchell and Onvural 1996; Jagtiani and Khanthavit 1996; Mester 1996; Stiroh and Rumble 2006). These studies also suggest that economies of scope are not constant throughout the US industry, but vary with bank sizes. Finally, regulations can influence scope economies.

The empirical studies on economies of scope for European banks instead are limited and they are all focused on the pre-crisis period. Altunbas and Molyneux (1996) provide the first empirical investigation on economies of scope in four different European countries in year 1988. They find limited evidence of scope economies, and document differences across countries. Diseconomies of scope appear in Italy for all bank sizes, whilst economies of scope are found in Spain for banks with total assets smaller than $1.5 billion only. Furthermore, economies of scope result for medium sized banks in France; in Germany scope economies are found for largest banks whereas smaller banks show scope diseconomies. Subsequent studies expand the time period and take into consideration more European countries. Vander Vennet (2002), using a panel of banks from 17 EU countries in the period 1995–1996, finds economies of scope in the European banking industry. The SCOPE measure spans between −1.6 and 6.5 for financial conglomerates, 1.1 and 18.1 for universal banks and −1.7 and 17.7 for specialized banks. Moreover, for financial conglomerates and universal banks, economies of scope tend to increase with bank size whereas for specialized banks diseconomies of scope are present for big-size banks and smaller specialized banks enjoy economies of scope. Another stream of literature investigates the impact of diversification on systematic risk for European banks.

Following on, in this paper we aim to empirically estimate different measures of economies of scope by using several methodologies (i.e. several cost functions and functional forms) with regard to European banks before and after the outbreak of the 2008 financial crisis.

7.3 Sample and Methodology

7.3.1 Sample

Our sample comprises banks operating in the 28 countries of the European Union (EU) over the period 2005–2014. Our final unbalanced panel database consists in 4610 observations from 779 EU banks. Consolidated statements are taken from Bankscope, and deflation indexes from the International Monetary Fund. Table 7.1 provides the number of banks within the sample per country and year.

Table 7.1 Number of banks in the sample (per year/country)

Country/Year	2005	2006	2007	2008	2009	2010	2011	2012	2013	2014	Total
Austria	11	8	8	17	19	22	26	24	27	25	187
Belgium	4	2	5	6	6	8	8	10	13	11	73
Bulgaria	2	1	4	4	5	5	11	12	11	9	64
Croatia	3	3	3	5	6	6	7	7	8	7	55
Cyprus	4	5	7	5	5	4	5	6	7	6	54
Czech Republic	8	6	7	8	8	8	8	7	7	7	74
Denmark	10	13	15	21	25	25	29	27	26	24	215
Estonia	3	3	3	2	1	2	3	3	3	3	26
Finland	3	5	5	7	5	8	8	13	11	7	72
France	48	55	60	86	87	87	102	109	110	106	850
Germany	18	26	31	33	35	41	47	50	52	39	372
Greece	7	5	7	7	10	11	8	8	6	4	73
Hungary	1	1	3	3	5	7	7	7	8	8	50
Ireland	9	13	14	12	10	10	9	8	7	7	99
Italy	28	26	33	45	42	45	51	56	54	53	433
Latvia	9	10	10	11	10	7	10	9	10	8	94
Lithuania	5	5	6	5	6	5	4	4	4	4	48
Luxembourg	5	5	7	8	8	9	12	14	13	12	93
Malta	1	1	1	1	2	1	3	4	2	2	18
Netherlands	12	13	14	14	16	16	17	23	26	22	173
Poland	4	6	9	12	14	14	14	14	14	14	115
Portugal	9	11	10	12	14	15	16	17	16	16	136
Romania	5	4	5	5	6	6	8	9	8	8	64
Slovak Republic	4	4	3	3	3	4	4	4	4	4	37
Slovenia	5	6	5	6	6	4	7	9	9	6	63
Spain	39	41	41	51	36	33	51	45	37	29	403
Sweden	6	6	9	12	11	12	15	15	15	12	113
United Kingdom	47	53	57	57	54	55	56	60	61	56	556
Total	310	337	382	458	455	470	546	574	569	509	4610

7.3.2 Economies of Scope Measure

In order to estimate economies of scope we employ the within SCOPE measure (WSCOPE hereafter), as in Mester (1993). WSCOPE compares a technical efficient multi-product bank with different technical efficient banks, each of them producing one output only and the minimum observed value for the other two outputs. In symbols:

$$COST\_WSCOPE_{i,t} = \frac{\sum_{j=1}^{3} TC_{j,i,t} - TC_{i,t}}{TC_{i,t}} = \frac{\sum_{j=1}^{3} TC\left(Q_1^{min}, \ldots, Q_{j,i,t} - Jq_j^{min}, \ldots, Q_J^{min}, P_{i,t}, Z_{i,t}; \widehat{\beta}\right) - TC_{i,t}}{TC_{i,t}} \tag{7.1}$$

where TC is the total cost of a technical efficient bank, $Q_{j,\,i,\,t}$ is the j-th output, Q_J^{min} is the observed minimum value of the j-th output, it can be considered as the minimum feasible amount of output that a bank should produce. P is a vector of inputs prices, Z is a vector of controls and $\widehat{\beta}$ is a vector of estimated parameters. If WSCOPE is greater than zero there are economies of scope because producing several outputs separately would result in an increase in costs. If WSCOPE is lower than zero there are diseconomies of scope: producing several outputs separately would be more efficient. If WSCOPE is equal to zero then there are neither economies nor diseconomies of scope: producing in the two ways would not change costs.

7.3.3 Econometric Specification

To estimate economies of scope we need to define the cost function, the functional form and the variables.

In this paper we employ both the Stochastic Frontier Analysis (SFA) and Seemingly Unrelated Regressions (SUR) to estimate cost functions.

SFA, introduced by Aigner et al. (1977) and Meeusen and Van der Broeck (1977), allows to estimate bank' technical inefficiency. The basic SFA framework is represented by Eq. (7.2):

$$TC_{i,t} == f\left(Q_{i,t}, P_{i,t}, Z_{i,t}; \beta\right) + v_{i,t} + u_{i,t}\, u_{i,t} \tag{7.2}$$

where TC are total operating costs; Q, P, Z, β are vector of outputs, inputs prices, control variables and parameters; i and t are indexes for bank and time specific observations; f (°) is a functional form to be determined. $v_{i,t}$ is idiosyncratic white noise; $u_{i,t}$ is the technical inefficiency component. Specifically, in this study we employ the technical inefficiency specification proposed by Battese and Coelli (1992). SFA models can be estimated through iterative log-likelihood procedure.

SUR, firstly introduced by Zellner (1962), allows to estimate a system of equations. In our case the system of equations is represented by Eq. (7.3):

$$S_{i,t} = \frac{\partial TC_{i,t}}{\partial P_{i,t}} + \omega_{i,t} \tag{7.3}$$

where $\omega_{i,t}$ is the idiosyncratic white noise for each additional equation in the system, representing allocative inefficiencies and $S_{i,t}$ is the share of input s on total operating costs.

Cost functions can assume different functional forms, in this work we employ three different functions: the Transcendental Logarithmic (translog), the Generalized Transcendental Logarithmic (generalized translog) and the Fourier Flexible.

In order to perform cost function estimates we collected data about banks total operating costs (TC), banks' outputs (Q), banks' inputs prices (P) and a set of control variables (Z). Total operating cost will be the dependent variable in all regressions. Banks outputs are gross loans (Q1), total securities (Q2) and off-balance sheet items (Q3), calculated as the difference between banks' total business volume and total assets. Banks inputs prices are price of labour (P1), price of loanable funds (P2) and price of capital (P3). Price of labour is calculated as the ratio between personnel expenses on total assets, price of loanable funds is expressed as the ratio between total interest expenses on total deposits and price of capital is the ratio between other operating expenses and fixed assets. Control variables are the ratio between loan loss reserve and gross loans (Z1) as a proxy of bank quality ratio (Mester 1996), the ratio between total equity and total assets (Z2) as a proxy of bank leverage and the ratio between liquid assets on deposits and short term funds (Z3) as a proxy for liquidity. Total cost and outputs are deflated with the IMF deflation index (using 2004 as base year).

Table 7.2 (Panel A) reports the descriptive statistics for the variables (including total assets). We divide the sample in deciles, in order to show how economies of scope change for banks of different sizes. Table 7.2 (Panel B) specifies the minimum level of assets of each of the ten size deciles.

Table 7.2 Summary statistics

Panel A				
Variable	**Mean**	**Std. Dev.**	**Min**	**Max**
TC	2.84E+09	7.34E+09	2050961	9.64E+10
TA	8.90E+10	2.44E+11	1.46E+07	2.41E+12
Q1	4.07E+10	9.75E+10	8061443	1.06E+12
Q2	3.30E+10	1.21E+11	82259.63	1.64E+12
Q3	1.68E+10	6.18E+10	97245.12	2.28E+12
P1	0.012	0.012	0	0.153
P2	0.043	0.084	0	2.453
P3	6.025	42.361	0.03	1609
Z1	3.924	5.051	0	77.626
Z2	8.801	6.826	−6.568	94.783
Z3	38.009	62.9	−6.584	977.311
Panel B				
1	**2**	**3**	**4**	**5**
1.46E+07	9.76E+08	2.06E+09	3.88E+09	6.93E+09
6	**7**	**8**	**9**	**10**
1.15E+10	1.82E+10	3.00E+10	6.61E+10	2.14E+11

7.4 Results

For each model (i.e. cost function and functional form) we report median values of WSCOPE[1] for the overall sample and for each size decile (defined according to bank total assets, from the smallest—decile 1—to the giant—decile 10). Table 7.3 reports the coefficients of the functions (translog, generalized translog, and Fourier Flexible) estimated by employing both SFA and SUR models (Panel A) and the additional regression specifications of the SUR model (Panel C). Panel B shows that, for all models, the parameter μ of the time invariant half-normal distribution is positive and statistically significant, whereas the parameter η is not statistically significant, meaning that inefficiency does not vary over time (assuming the time function as in Battese and Coelli 1992).

7.4.1 Translog

As for the translog function, only one out of the three output interactions term is statistically significant and negative: this means that producing together output 1 (loans) and 2 (total securities) can decrease total costs. However, the sign of cross coefficients is not sufficient to determine either economies or diseconomies of scope when outputs and input prices are non-separable, as it is here. Notice that

[1]Mean values qualitatively confirm median values results.

Table 7.3 Regressions results

Coefficients	Panel A					
	lnTC	lnTC	bcTC	bcTC	lnTC	lnTC
	Translog	Translog	Generalized translog	Generalized translog	Fourier flexible	Fourier flexible
	SFA	SUR	SFA	SUR	SFA	SUR
Austria	−0.136* 0.074	−0.128*** 0.032	−0.039 0.036	−0.071*** 0.02	−0.139* 0.073	−0.100*** 0.031
Belgium	0.013 0.095	−0.089* 0.046	−0.016 0.046	−0.055* 0.029	−0.053 0.093	0.009 0.045
Bulgaria	−0.273** 0.114	−0.146*** 0.051	−0.080 0.055	−0.12*** 0.031	−0.346*** 0.112	−0.085* 0.05
Croatia	−0.18 0.128	−0.131** 0.053	−0.059 0.061	−0.109*** 0.033	−0.170 0.124	−0.023 0.051
Cyprus	−0.178 0.123	−0.112** 0.054	−0.021 0.059	−0.17*** 0.033	−0.185 0.120	0.020 0.052
Czech Republic	−0.084 0.123	0.059 0.047	−0.025 0.058	0.088*** 0.029	−0.084 0.119	−0.033 0.045
Denmark	−0.409*** 0.073)	−0.409*** 0.031	−0.192*** 0.035	−0.201*** 0.019	−0.427*** 0.072	−0.339*** 0.03
Estonia	−0.38** 0.186)	−0.003 0.075	−0.151* 0.089	0.037 0.046	−0.389** 0.181	−0.118* 0.072
Finland	−0.348*** 0.106	−0.259*** 0.047	−0.162*** 0.051	−0.092*** 0.029	−0.359*** 0.103	−0.282*** 0.045
France	−0.058 0.05	−0.089*** 0.021	−0.030 0.024	−0.063*** 0.013	−0.069 0.049	0.001 0.021
Germany	0.132** 0.062	−0.025 0.026	0.033 0.030	−0.016 0.016	0.094 0.060	0.072*** 0.026
Greece	−0.049 0.113	0.051 0.047	−0.023 0.054	−0.057* 0.029	−0.050 0.110	0.117*** 0.045

Hungary	0.0178 0.134	−0.182*** 0.056	0.019 0.064	−0.165*** 0.035	0.057 0.131	0.020 0.053
Ireland	0.023 0.099	−0.049 0.042	−0.015 0.048	0.018 0.026	−0.014 0.097	−0.150*** 0.04
Italy	−0.269*** 0.058	−0.224*** 0.024	−0.127*** 0.028	−0.148*** 0.015	−0.267*** 0.057	−0.187*** 0.024
Latvia	−0.273** 0.11	0.063 0.044	−0.087* 0.052	0.051* 0.027	−0.300*** 0.107	−0.006 0.043
Lithuania	−0.298* 0.153	−0.126** 0.057	−0.089 0.073	−0.045 0.035	−0.287* 0.149	−0.102* 0.054
Luxembourg	0.214** 0.096	0.146*** 0.042	0.089* 0.046	0.063** 0.026	0.213** 0.093	0.224*** 0.041
Malta	−0.084 0.189	−0.232*** 0.09	−0.019 0.091	−0.066 0.056	−0.113 0.183	−0.235*** 0.087
Netherlands	−0.17** 0.077	−0.157*** 0.033	−0.085** 0.037	−0.08*** 0.02	−0.187** 0.075	−0.092*** 0.031
Poland	−0.195** 0.091	−0.178*** 0.039	−0.085* 0.044	−0.121*** 0.024	−0.175** 0.089	−0.083** 0.038
Portugal	−0.185** 0.087	−0.303*** 0.036	−0.079* 0.042	−0.191*** 0.023	−0.190** 0.085	−0.205*** 0.035
Romania	−0.18 0.128	−0.052 0.05	−0.050 0.061	−0.141*** 0.031	−0.177 0.124	0.127*** 0.048
Slovak Republic	−0.107 0.158	0.013 0.063	−0.023 0.075	0.042 0.039	−0.110 0.153	−0.014 0.061
Slovenia	−0.33*** 0.128	−0.158*** 0.051	−0.130** 0.061	−0.107*** 0.031	−0.307** 0.125	−0.116** 0.049
Spain	−0.084 0.058	−0.075*** 0.025	−0.051* 0.028	−0.056*** 0.016	−0.100* 0.057	−0.061** 0.025
Sweden	−0.214** 0.099	−0.609*** 0.039	−0.121*** 0.044	−0.192*** 0.024	−0.251*** 0.089	−0.465*** 0.038

(continued)

Table 7.3 (continued)

D06	0.011 0.016	−0.062** 0.029	−0.007 0.008	−0.061*** 0.018	0.011 0.016	−0.021 0.028
D07	0.081*** 0.018	−0.056** 0.028	0.024*** 0.009	−0.06*** 0.018	0.082*** 0.018	0.030 0.027
D08	0.127*** 0.021	−0.035 0.027	0.040*** 0.010	−0.052*** 0.017	0.132*** 0.020	0.060 0.026
D09	0.022 0.025	0.015 0.027	−0.015 0.012	0.026 0.017	0.030 0.024	−0.013 0.026
D10	−0.029 0.029	0.027 0.027	−0.042*** 0.014	0.067*** 0.017	−0.021 0.028	−0.054 0.026
D11	−0.005 0.033	0.021 0.027	−0.034** 0.016	0.047*** 0.016	0.001 0.032	−0.035 0.025
D12	0.018 0.037	0.052** 0.026	−0.032* 0.018	0.08*** 0.016	0.027 0.036	−0.023 0.025
D13	0.002 0.042	0.09*** 0.027	−0.043** 0.021	0.128*** 0.017	0.007 0.041	−0.037 0.026
D14	0.006 0.047	0.121*** 0.027	−0.050** 0.023	0.166*** 0.017	0.011 0.045	−0.039 0.026
Z1	−0.001 0.001	−0.004*** 0.001	0 0.001	−0.003*** 0.001	−0.001 0.001	−0.001 0.001
Z2	−0.002** 0.001	−0.003*** 0.001	0 0.001	−0.003*** 0.001	−0.002 0.001	−0.002** 0.001
Z3	0.000 0.000	−0.001*** 0	0 0	0*** 0	0.000 0.000	−0.001*** 0.000
lnQ1	−0.648*** 0.089	−0.851*** 0.071	–	–	0.165 1.100	0.260 1.19
lnQ2	0.326*** 0.052	0.748*** 0.044	–	–	1.615*** 0.468	0.652 0.532

lnQ3	0.214*** 0.052	0.037 0.047	–	–	−1.257 0.648	1.182 0.796
bcQ1	–	–	0.075*** 0.020	0.116*** 0.02	–	–
bcQ2	–	–	0.195*** 0.018	0.104*** 0.019	–	–
bcQ3	–	–	0.048*** 0.013	0.076*** 0.015	–	–
lnP1	0.438*** 0.018	0.296*** 0.005	0.558*** 0.012	0.432*** 0.007	0.450*** 0.018	0.212*** 0.005
lnP2	0.391*** 0.015	0.539*** 0.007	0.270*** 0.009	0.497*** 0.009	0.388 0.015***	0.472*** 0.007
lnP3	0.172*** 0.022	0.165*** 0.006	0.172*** 0.012	0.071*** 0.008	0.162*** 0.021	0.316*** 0.009
$(lnQ1)^2$	0.054*** 0.003	0.075*** 0.003	–	–	0.031 0.025	0.043 0.027
$(lnQ2)^2$	0.032*** 0.001	0.042*** 0.001	–	–	0.005 0.012	0.039*** 0.013
$(lnQ3)^2$	0.004*** 0.001	0.003** 0.001	–	–	0.032** 0.016	−0.032 0.02
lnQ1lnQ2	−0.064*** 0.004	−0.095*** 0.004	–	–	−0.077*** 0.004	−0.095*** 0.004
lnQ1lnQ3	−0.005 0.003	0 0.003	–	–	0.007** 0.003	0.007** 0.004
lnQ2lnQ3	0.001 0.002	−0.005** 0.002	–	–	0.006** 0.003	0.004 0.003
$(bcQ1)^2$	–	–	0.001** 0.001	0.007*** 0.001	–	–
$(bcQ2)^2$	–	–	0.016*** 0.000	0.018*** 0.001	–	–

(continued)

Table 7.3 (continued)

$(bcQ3)^2$	–	–	0.001*** 0.000	0.001*** 0	–	–
bcQ1bcQ2	–	–	−0.015*** 0.001	−0.022*** 0.001	–	–
bcQ1bcQ3	–	–	0.001 0.001	0 0.001	–	–
bcQ2bcQ3	–	–	−0.003*** 0.001	−0.004*** 0.001	–	–
$(\ln P1)^2$	0.002 0.001	0.018*** 0.001	0.000 0.001	−0.001* 0	0.003*** 0.001	0.001** 0
$(\ln P2)^2$	0.004*** 0.001	0.031*** 0.001	0.001 0.001	0.002*** 0.001	0.005*** 0.001	0.011*** 0.000
$(\ln P3)^2$	−0.001 0.001	0.007*** 0.000	0.001* 0.001	0.011*** 0.000	−0.001 0.001	0.000 0.000
lnP1lnP2	−0.013*** 0.004	−0.083*** 0.002	0.001 0.002	0.019*** 0.002	−0.018*** 0.003	−0.024*** 0.001
lnP1lnP3	0.006* 0.003	0.011*** 0.001	0.000 0.002	−0.015*** 0.001	0.004 0.003	0.020*** 0.001
lnP2lnP3	−0.004 0.003	−0.04*** 0.002	−0.003** 0.002	−0.028*** 0.002	−0.002 0.003	−0.019*** 0.002
lnQ1lnP1	−0.037*** 0.005	−0.006*** 0.001	–	–	−0.045*** 0.005	−0.020*** 0.002
lnQ1lnP2	−0.038*** 0.004	−0.014*** 0.002	–	–	−0.048*** 0.004	−0.016*** 0.002
lnQ1lnP3	−0.027*** 0.003	−0.074*** 0.003	–	–	−0.024*** 0.003	−0.078*** 0.003
lnQ2lnP1	0.014*** 0.004	0.008*** 0.001	–	–	0.018*** 0.004	0.011*** 0.001

lnQ2lnP2	−0.004 0.003	0.003* 0.002	–	–	0.001 0.003	0.005*** 0.002
lnQ2lnP3	0.008*** 0.002	0.032*** 0.002	–	–	0.005** 0.002	0.028*** 0.002
lnQ3lnP1	0.023*** 0.004	−0.002 0.001	–	–	0.027*** 0.004	0.010*** 0.001
lnQ3lnP2	0.042*** 0.004	0.011*** 0.002	–	–	0.047*** 0.004	0.011*** 0.002
lnQ3lnP3	0.018*** 0.003	0.042*** 0.003	–	–	0.018*** 0.003	0.050*** 0.003
bcQ1lnP1	–	–	−0.052*** 0.001	−0.018*** 0.001	–	–
bcQ1lnP2	–	–	−0.021*** 0.001	0.002* 0.001	–	–
bcQ1lnP3	–	–	−0.020*** 0.001	−0.031*** 0.001	–	–
bcQ2lnP1	–	–	0.051*** 0.001	0.016*** 0.001	–	–
bcQ2lnP2	–	–	0.013*** 0.001	−0.004*** 0.001	–	–
bcQ2lnP3	–	–	0.018*** 0.001	0.028*** 0.001	–	–
bcQ3lnP1	–	–	0.001 0.001	0.001** 0.001	–	–
bcQ3lnP2	–	–	0.007*** 0.001	0.002* 0.001	–	–
bcQ3lnP3	–	–	0.002** 0.001	0.002** 0.001	–	–
cos(z1)	–	–	–	–	0.558 0.475	0.672 0.506

(continued)

Table 7.3 (continued)

cos(z2)	–	–	–	–	1.068** 0.448	−0.094 0.503
cos(z3)	–	–	–	–	−1.252** 0.616	1.177 0.753
sin(z1)	–	–	–	–	−0.345*** 0.119	−0.448*** 0.118
sin(z2)	–	–	–	–	−0.087 0.112	−0.172 0.127
sin(z3)	–	–	–	–	−0.190 0.172	0.376** 0.172
cos(2z1)	–	–	–	–	−0.166*** 0.067	−0.132* 0.068
cos(z1 + z2)	–	–	–	–	0.030 0.046	0.208*** 0.05
co(sz1 + z3)	–	–	–	–	0.391*** 0.041	0.242*** 0.048
cos(2z2)	–	–	–	–	−0.005 0.062	−0.133* 0.071
cos(z2 + z3)	–	–	–	–	0.113** 0.044	−0.052 0.055
cos(2z3)	–	–	–	–	−0.329*** 0.081	0.087 0.097
sin(2z1)	–	–	–	–	−0.212*** 0.040	−0.072* 0.038
sin(z1 + z2)	–	–	–	–	0.316*** 0.045	0.027 0.045
sin(z1 + z3)	–	–	–	–	−0.021 0.045	−0.153*** 0.045

sin(2z2)	–	–	–	–	−0.147*** 0.035	0.015 0.039
sin(z2 + z3)	–	–	–	–	−0.218*** 0.044	−0.036 0.048
sin(2z3)	–	–	–	–	0.121*** 0.042	0.229*** 0.051
cons	13.441*** 1.067	15.134*** 0.55	7.588*** 0.001	9.068*** 0.217	8.579 12.110	–5.964 13.148
Panel B						
μ	1.737*** 0.659	–	0.675*** 0.11	–	1.588*** 0.440	–
η	0.004 0.003	–	−0.006 0.11	–	0.005 0.003	–
Panel C						
S1						
lnP1	–	0.036*** 0.001	–	−0.002* 0.001	–	0.001** 0
lnP2	–	0.042*** 0.001	–	0.009*** 0.001	–	−0.024*** 0.001
lnP3	–	0.006*** 0.001	–	−0.008*** 0.001	–	0.02*** 0.001
lnQ1	–	−0.006*** 0.001	–	–	–	−0.02*** 0.002
lnQ2	–	0.008*** 0.001	–	–	–	0.011*** 0.001
lnQ3	–	−0.002 0.001	–	–	–	0.01*** 0.001
bcQ1	–	–	–	−0.018*** 0.001	–	–

(continued)

Table 7.3 (continued)

bcQ2	–	–	–	0.016*** 0.001	–	–
bcQ3	–	–	–	0.001** 0.001	–	–
cons	–	0.296*** 0.005	–	0.432*** 0.007	–	0.212*** 0.005
S2						
lnP1	–	−0.042*** 0.001	–	0.009*** 0.001	–	−0.024*** 0.001
lnP2	–	0.062*** 0.002	–	0.004*** 0.001	–	0.011*** 0
lnP3	–	−0.02*** 0.001	–	−0.014*** 0.001	–	−0.019*** 0.002
lnQ1	–	−0.014*** 0.002	–	–	–	−0.016*** 0.002
lnQ2	–	0.003* 0.002	–	–	–	0.005*** 0.002
lnQ3	–	0.011*** 0.002	–	–	–	0.011*** 0.002
bcQ1	–	–	–	0.002* 0.001	–	–
bcQ2	–	–	–	−0.004*** 0.001	–	–
bcQ3	–	–	–	0.002** 0.001	–	–
cons	–	0.539*** 0.007	–	0.497*** 0.009	–	0.472*** 0.007

P-values have been calculated through t-test for statistical significance of mean values. ***p<0.01, **p<0.05, *p<0.1.

control variables Z2 is statistically significant at the 5% confidence level whereas Z1 and Z3 are not statistically significant, which implies that bank total costs are not determined by bank liquidity or asset quality and are mainly influenced by financial leverage, inputs and outputs. However, the variation of statistical significance of control variables is high across specifications, in general the impact of control variables on total costs appears to be negative.

Table 7.4 reports the median values of WSCOPE for each size decile and for the overall sample over the period 2005–2014. For all European banks during the period under observation, the median WSCOPE measure is equal to 2.534 when employing SFA and 2.806 when employing SUR (with both measures statistically significant at the 1% level). This evidence indicates that, on average, economies of scope exist in the European banking industry. These results are in-line with previous papers that analyze the EU industry and rely on the translog function (Altunbas and Molyneux 1996; Vander Vennet 2002). As for the evolution of economies of scope over time, there is not a clear time trend. Nevertheless in years 2009 and 2010 we observe the highest values of WSCOPE (when employing both SFA and SUR), suggesting that the effect of the outbreak of the financial crisis has been an increase in economies of scope for European banks. This would suggest that increasing the output mix enables banks to minimize total costs.[2] As for the levels of economies of scope for different size deciles, the median values of WSCOPE increase with bank size (when employing SFA from 0.352 of the smallest size decile to 20.715 of the giant banks; when employing SUR from 0.243 of the smallest size decile to 55.032 of the giant banks). This evidence means that the larger the size the larger the benefit in terms of economies of scope.

The evidence of economies of scope also for giant banks (i.e. systemically important banks) supports the arguments of some industry studies (Institute of International Finance 2010; The Clearing House 2011), that find substantial to very substantial benefits related to both size and diversification. Their argument is that larger banks and their scope for achieving greater diversification across business lines and geographies may realize significant synergies, promoting safer, more stable and ultimately more valuable banks. Our evidence on European banks goes in the same direction on which basis structural bank regulation initiatives would imply impairment costs, not only for banks and their shareholders, but for banks' customers and the economy as a whole.

Table 7.5 reports the median values of WSCOPE for each country when employing SFA. Economies of scope are documented for all EU countries both in the overall time period and in each year under observation, with the only exceptions of Malta where diseconomies of scope are reported in some years. The highest values of economies of scope are reported for the countries mostly affected by the

---

[2]An alternative explanation is that, as a result of the financial crisis, the banks' profit margins might have decreased, simply forcing them to offer a more differentiated output mix. Nevertheless market conditions after the financial crisis would be reflected in input prices, output quantities and control variables. Therefore, it seems plausible that our WSCOPE findings suggests that increasing the output mix enables banks to minimize total costs, given the existing market conditions.

Table 7.4 WSCOPE estimates

Size decile	Regression specification	2005	2006	2007	2008	2009	2010	2011	2012	2013	2014	Total
1	Translog SFA	0.43***	0.319***	0.352***	0.247***	0.347***	0.326***	0.34***	0.33***	0.391***	0.378***	0.352***
	Translog SUR	0.336***	0.298***	0.278***	0.235***	0.208***	0.234***	0.204***	0.291***	0.206***	0.238***	0.243***
	General translog SFA	0.201***	0.099***	0.174***	0.043**	0.208***	0.088***	0.129***	0.201***	0.218***	0.268***	0.16***
	General translog SUR	0.079***	0.035**	0.138**	0.092**	0.093***	0.096***	0.069***	0.085***	0.115***	0.086**	0.091***
	Fourier SFA	1.674***	1.396**	1.412**	1.280**	1.601***	1.691***	1.613***	1.673***	1.757***	1.769**	1.629***
	Fourier SUR	0.554***	0.449***	0.541***	0.387***	0.473***	0.487***	0.467***	0.481***	0.494***	0.436***	0.478***
2	Translog SFA	0.948***	0.969***	0.815***	0.731***	0.756***	0.879***	0.742***	0.819***	0.814***	0.794***	0.837***
	Translog SUR	0.838***	0.768***	0.631***	0.614***	0.613***	0.695***	0.698***	0.617***	0.64***	0.592***	0.646***
	General translog SFA	1.28***	0.993***	0.961***	0.672***	0.373***	0.66***	0.487***	0.602***	0.858***	0.716***	0.699***
	General translog SUR	0.673***	0.569***	0.338***	0.471***	0.397***	0.426***	0.546***	0.449***	0.411***	0.334***	0.443***
	Fourier SFA	1.503***	1.409***	1.321***	0.910***	1.132***	1.402***	1.276***	1.357***	1.448***	1.474***	1.322***
	Fourier SUR	0.518***	0.487***	0.325***	0.318***	0.304***	0.363***	0.391***	0.323***	0.359***	0.366***	0.363***
3	Translog SFA	0.974***	1.255***	1.151***	0.904***	0.796***	0.754***	1.018***	1.1***	0.853***	0.973***	0.938***
	Translog SUR	1.157***	1.266***	1.179***	1.085***	0.881***	0.759***	0.702***	0.835***	0.78***	0.825***	0.897***
	General translog SFA	1.001***	1.126***	1.098***	0.747***	0.767***	0.513***	0.956***	0.994***	0.687***	0.994***	0.912***
	General translog SUR	1.249***	1.481***	1.365***	1.624***	1.127***	0.864***	0.806***	0.709***	0.7***	0.724***	0.997***
	Fourier SFA	1.564***	1.627***	1.550***	1.226***	1.397***	1.425***	1.534***	1.773***	1.761***	1.556***	1.562***
	Fourier SUR	0.585***	0.813***	0.706***	0.525***	0.360***	0.376***	0.320***	0.403***	0.359***	0.413***	0.423***

4	Translog SFA	1.496***	1.599***	1.462***	1.623***	2.115***	2.168***	1.836***	1.831***	1.755***	1.725***	1.754***
	Translog SUR	1.812***	1.953***	1.624***	1.902***	2.148***	2.245***	1.925***	1.616***	1.552***	1.27***	1.768***
	General translog SFA	1.398***	1.87***	1.106***	1.512***	2.125***	2.779***	1.657***	1.402***	1.408***	1.974***	1.635***
	General translog SUR	1.934***	2.412***	1.808***	2.845***	2.877***	2.776***	2.441***	1.949***	1.449***	1.479***	2.121***
	Fourier SFA	2.178***	2.476***	2.123***	2.399***	3.199***	3.332***	2.812***	2.591***	2.586***	2.794***	2.588***
	Fourier SUR	0.993***	1.149***	0.981***	1.182***	1.331***	1.416***	1.211***	0.891***	0.978***	0.761***	1.100***
5	Translog SFA	2.247***	2.28***	1.701***	1.894***	2.026***	2.533***	2.615***	2.453***	2.583***	2.577***	2.41***
	Translog SUR	2.768***	2.824***	2.198***	2.498***	2.558***	2.493***	2.384***	2.063***	2.172***	2.214***	2.404***
	General translog SFA	2.284***	2.196***	1.87***	1.987***	2.283***	3.073***	3.129***	2.818***	3.048***	3.34***	2.503***
	General translog SUR	3.847***	3.626***	2.74***	3.477***	3.948***	3.499***	3.543***	3.23***	3.102***	3.172***	3.439***
	Fourier SFA	2.376***	2.319***	2.098***	1.952***	2.268***	2.667***	2.779***	2.679***	3.097***	3.191***	2.501***
	Fourier SUR	1.486***	1.303***	1.018***	1.047***	1.230***	1.214***	1.106***	1.083***	1.018***	1.014***	1.139***
6	Translog SFA	4.008***	3.341***	3.035***	2.924***	3.104***	3.753***	3.055***	3.466***	3.693***	4.079***	3.378***
	Translog SUR	5.518***	4.382***	4.007***	4.349***	4.001***	4.209***	4.068***	4.128***	4.234***	4.175***	4.214***
	General translog SFA	5.256***	3.796***	3.279***	3.256***	3.947***	5.092***	4.938***	5.019***	5.623***	6.314***	4.775***
	General translog SUR	10.26***	7.727***	8.44***	8.201***	7.314***	6.415***	7.508***	7.184***	7.241***	7.108***	7.489***
	Fourier SFA	2.913***	2.516***	2.107***	2.256***	2.407***	2.902***	2.722***	2.915***	3.168***	3.455***	2.776***
	Fourier SUR	2.942***	2.039***	2.173***	2.134***	1.846***	2.043***	1.972***	2.135***	2.141***	2.131***	2.134***

(continued)

Table 7.4 (continued)

Size decile	Regression specification	2005	2006	2007	2008	2009	2010	2011	2012	2013	2014	Total
7	Translog SFA	4.309***	3.797***	4.195***	4.115***	5.12***	5.04***	4.525***	3.832***	4.949***	3.96***	4.335***
	Translog SUR	7.801***	4.395***	7.178***	5.936***	6.214***	5.562***	4.747***	4.429***	4.355***	3.597***	4.999***
	General translog SFA	4.953***	5.607***	6.501***	6.707***	7.704***	7.169***	6.561***	6.485***	7.966***	6.954***	6.876***
	General translog SUR	15.223***	8.552***	16.355***	15.539***	15.744***	10.904***	11.203***	10.936***	10.372***	7.436***	11.262***
	Fourier SFA	4.076***	3.145***	3.575***	3.549***	5.204***	4.608***	4.142***	3.934***	4.875***	4.309***	4.027***
	Fourier SUR	4.481***	2.521***	4.208***	3.943***	4.243***	3.602***	2.816***	2.818***	2.943***	2.213***	3.167***
8	Translog SFA	5.918***	5.161***	5.314***	5.104***	6.083***	6.736***	6.418***	6.194***	6.483***	8.293***	6.214***
	Translog SUR	10.933***	11.759***	11.955***	8.881***	10.06***	12.019***	11.379***	9.749***	8.369***	8.585***	9.907***
	General translog SFA	13.038***	9.996***	8.462***	9.158***	12.767***	17.272***	13.891***	14.967***	15.224***	17.465***	14.297***
	General translog SUR	37.439***	43.127***	69.347***	47.245***	27.303***	47.842***	43.829***	40.644***	23.582***	24.44***	37.2***
	Fourier SFA	6.522***	5.213***	4.485***	5.024***	6.546***	7.363***	6.859***	7.104***	7.606***	8.584***	6.758***
	Fourier SUR	7.265***	8.168***	7.460***	6.241***	7.437***	8.574***	8.302***	7.259***	6.340***	6.483***	7.052***
9	Translog SFA	7.223***	7.709***	8.209***	7.004***	8.638***	8.793***	9.011***	8.67***	10.404***	11.559***	8.828***
	Translog SUR	14.334***	14.171***	18.032***	19.704***	16.646***	17.147***	15.592***	13.09***	14.458***	15.815***	15.445***
	General translog SFA	14.421***	27.368***	19.918***	15.577***	21.617***	23.043***	22.504***	19.761***	29.593***	34.463***	22.568***
	General translog SUR	68.306***	162.546***	179.327***	198.992***	153.344***	136.124***	157.344***	117.385***	127.147***	122.812***	147.838***
	Fourier SFA	4.883***	5.671***	5.584***	4.741***	6.097***	6.159***	5.774***	5.760***	7.427***	8.151***	6.094***
	Fourier SUR	8.404***	9.096***	10.246***	10.237***	11.204***	10.014***	9.898***	8.148***	8.755***	10.810***	9.646***

10	Translog SFA	20.897***	18.102***	17.031***	17.202***	20.207***	20.631***	23.058***	22.328***	23.401***	27.308***	20.715***
	Translog SUR	60.905***	52.641***	55.876***	48.37***	52.122***	48.39***	73.354***	56.015***	49.166***	55.082***	55.082***
	General translog SFA	114.971***	110.227***	84.045***	138.007***	153.649***	234.679***	171.977***	169.866***	137.879***	247.579***	151.152***
	General translog SUR	4274.727***	3506.414***	4964.522***	4359.801***	2144.172***	1496.445***	3675.931***	3366.355***	1859.011***	1899.26***	2911.646***
	Fourier SFA	10.984***	9.928***	8.429***	9.390***	13.295***	16.091***	16.866***	15.787***	20.182***	19.481***	14.926***
	Fourier SUR	33.359***	26.762***	31.725***	30.177***	33.408***	35.852***	45.593***	40.550***	37.684***	34.283***	34.216***
Panel	Translog SFA	2.31***	2.18***	2.442***	2.307***	2.485***	2.792***	2.584***	2.533***	2.734***	3.067***	2.534***
	Translog SUR	2.745***	2.764***	3.157***	2.788***	3.012***	3.241***	2.77***	2.528***	2.46***	2.799***	2.806***
	General translog SFA	3.022***	2.824***	2.99***	2.891***	3.347***	3.848***	3.45***	3.498***	3.662***	4.775***	3.452***
	General translog SUR	4.102***	3.999***	6.368***	6.08***	5.325***	5.081***	4.505***	4.343***	4.123***	4.394***	4.641***
	Fourier SFA	2.599***	2.491***	2.486***	2.375***	2.776***	3.135***	2.904***	2.978***	3.204***	3.429***	2.853***
	Fourier SUR	1.636***	1.490***	1.791***	1.683***	1.726***	1.833***	1.522***	1.402***	1.399***	1.515***	1.598***

P-values have been calculated through t-test for statistical significance of mean values. ***$p<0.01$, **$p<0.05$, *$p<0.1$.

Table 7.5 WSCOPE estimates by country

Country	2005	2006	2007	2008	2009	2010	2011	2012	2013	2014	Total
Austria	5.808***	3.14**	3.592**	2.753***	3.417***	3.756***	3.2***	3.369***	3.285***	3.529***	3.396***
Belgium	14.261*	15.748	9.176**	1.201**	9.685**	4.155**	5.004**	5.161***	3.7***	7.318***	6.189***
Bulgaria	0.938	1.943	1.089*	1.078*	1.586 **	1.341 **	1.033***	0.69***	0.829***	1.09**	1.033***
Croatia	0.967	1.115	0.965	1.336**	2.242**	2.543**	2.125**	1.638**	1.191**	1.536***	1.435***
Cyprus	1.079	0.799*	0.874**	2.087**	1.254**	1.561*	2.154	2.378	1.5*	2.58**	1.5***
Czech Republic	1.483**	1.98**	2.25**	2.038**	2.429**	2.316**	2.05**	2.189**	2.234**	5.905**	2.158***
Denmark	0.851***	1.361***	1.186***	0.727***	0.593***	0.527***	0.759***	0.76***	0.784***	0.891***	0.76***
Estonia	3.212	2.148	1.966	3.144	4.905	6.939	2.549	3.244	3.794	5.035	3.041***
Finland	4.245	4.199**	3.212**	2.959**	5.224**	1.676**	1.419**	1.473***	2.092***	3.224**	1.977***
France	1.575***	1.621***	1.848***	2.218***	2.688***	3.031***	3.02***	3.31***	3.693***	3.874***	2.847***
Germany	3.649***	3.724***	3.955***	5.284***	6.211***	4.46***	4.525***	4.085***	4.618***	5.142***	4.463***
Greece	2.01**	1.577*	2.367**	2.133**	6.567***	7.359***	7.531**	6.15**	10.429**	11.537*	5.704***
Hungary	1.148	1.577	1.434	1.331	1.196**	1.477**	1.419**	1.011**	0.636**	1.525**	1.357***
Ireland	6.922***	8.424***	6.202***	7.162***	6.093***	4.448***	3.823***	5.825**	9.148**	8.767**	7.088***
Italy	2.284***	1.5***	3.145***	1.681***	2.584***	3.526***	2.904***	2.698***	2.669***	2.471***	2.695***
Latvia	0.79**	0.79***	0.614***	0.602***	0.569***	1.308**	0.669***	0.633***	0.665***	1.228**	0.721***
Lithuania	1.236**	0.819**	0.912**	0.67**	0.612**	0.822**	0.705*	1.348*	1.466*	1.759*	0.858***
Luxembourg	2.443	2.213**	1.694**	1.319**	3.526**	2.961***	1.254***	1.466***	2.025***	2.487***	2.032***
Malta	0.015	−0.124	−0.208	−0.165	2.878	2.666	2.46	1.444*	1.504	0.358	0.446***
Netherlands	2.569***	2.28***	2.641***	1.733***	2.252***	2.386***	2.377***	2.194***	1.897***	2.144***	2.28***
Poland	0.493*	1.05**	1.129***	1.439***	1.384***	1.323***	1.557***	1.502***	1.778***	2.132***	1.378***
Portugal	4.024**	3.244***	3.138**	2.77***	3.183***	4.004***	3.07***	2.706***	3.662***	3.237***	3.247***
Romania	0.437**	1.833*	2.488**	2.307**	0.97**	1.085**	0.499**	0.426***	0.535**	0.614**	0.674***
Slovak Republic	1.281*	1.135	0.973	0.553	0.592	1.054*	1.098**	1.016**	1.542**	1.516**	1.202***
Slovenia	0.935**	1.26**	1.311**	1.079**	1.413**	2.18*	1.922**	0.969***	1.046***	1.574**	1.261***
Spain	5.861***	6.058***	5.771***	5.287***	8.026***	9.933***	8.372***	6.008***	6.589***	10.061***	6.607***
Sweden	8.779**	5.284**	3.679**	2.638***	4.723***	3.792***	1.442***	1.142***	1.004***	1.299***	2.485***
United Kingdom	2.152***	2.552***	2.498***	2.34***	2.55***	2.343***	2.535***	3.094***	3.151***	4.047***	2.594***
Total	2.31***	2.18***	2.442***	2.307***	2.485***	2.792***	2.584***	2.533***	2.734***	3.067***	2.534***

P-values have been calculated through t-test for statistical significance of mean values. ***p<0.01, **p<0.05, *p<0.1.

2008 financial crisis: Ireland (7.088 statistically significant at 1% level), Belgium (6.89 statistically significant at 1% level), Spain (6.607 statistically significant at 1% level) and Greece (5.704 statistically significant at 1% level). Economies of scope are spread out in European banking markets—this result differs from the one in Altunbas and Molyneux (1996) that document differences across the French, German, Italian and Spanish banking markets (i.e. diseconomies of scope for Italian banks and economies of scope for Spanish banks in year 1988). Our evidence of homogenous results across countries, differently from Altunbas and Molyneux (1996), might be due to the EU's single market program that increased the homogeneity in the production technologies across Europe.

7.4.1.1 Generalized Translog

As for the generalized translog function (Table 7.3, Panel A and C), the coefficients of the control variables are not statistically significant. This finding strengthens the hypothesis that banks total costs are mainly determined by input prices and outputs. As documented with the translog regression, only one out of three coefficient of cross outputs is statistically significant and negative, which is not sufficient for stating that there are economies of scope. The coefficient μ is statistically significant whereas η is not, which implies that there are technological inefficiencies which do not change over time.

WSCOPE median values (Table 7.4) confirm the translog findings: they are, on average, equal to 3.45 when employing SFA and to 4.461 when employing SUR (with both measures statistically significant at the 1% level). Also, as the same as with the translog, WSCOPE median values increase with size deciles: economies of scope increase when bank size increase.

7.4.1.2 Fourier Flexible

As for the Fourier Flexible (Table 7.4), WSCOPE median values are found to be positive and statistically significant (2.853 estimated through the SFA model and 1.598 with SUR model, both values are statistically significant at the 1% level) and increasing with total assets. As for the levels of economies of scale for different size deciles, both SFA and SUR models indicate that the path of scope economies across different bank size deciles is not monotonic.

7.5 Conclusions

Despite the importance of scope economies in light of the policy debate on the 2014 structural reform proposal on the EU banking industry, also for its implications in terms of social welfare and costs shifted on banks, no recent studies appear to have provided cross-country comparisons for European banks. This paper provides evidence on the need for regulators to assess the effect of regulation on banks efficiency, which could also impact customers. In order to contribute to the policy debate, this paper empirically investigates economies of scope for 779 banks located in 28 EU countries over the period 2005–2014. By using the WSCOPE measures for cost economies of scope and several regression specifications in terms of cost function (SFA and SUR models) and functional forms (translog, generalized translog and Fourier flexible), we document the presence of widespread economies of scope in all European banking industries. On average, to separate the three main banks outputs (loans, securities and off-balance sheet) might introduce economic inefficiency in the financial system. In providing financial services jointly, banks may reduce costs due to production synergies (cost economies of scope) because banks are able to spread fixed expenses over a broader output mix, by exploiting complementarities in production, or by diversifying risks. The highest values of economies of scope are reported for the countries mostly affected by the 2008 financial crisis (Ireland, Belgium, Spain and Greece) and after the outbreak of the financial crisis (years 2009 and 2010).

When investigating economies of scope for different size deciles, the WSCOPE measure reveals that economies of scope are documented across all size deciles, including gigantic, highly diversified, banking conglomerates. This evidence for SIFIs and other very large banks means that although they might increase systematic risk (as documented in Baele et al. 2007), they are economically efficient in comparison to large-non systemic banks.

Overall, these results suggest that allowing banks to jointly produce different outputs increase the cost efficiency of the banking system. Therefore, although a trade-off between financial stability and efficiency exists, the findings of this paper do not support the view of the 2014 European proposal for structural reform aimed at minimizing the proprietary trading activities of banks—our evidence implies that such a reform would impose additional costs for banks and their shareholders, and more in general for banks' customers and the economy as a whole. Our findings suggest that bank regulators should take into consideration an economic phenomenon like economies of scope in settling up and evaluating the suitability of a regulation, rather than focusing exclusively on investor protection. Our contribution goes in the direction of stating that such a regulation might increase end-user costs and harm banks' customers.

Acknowledgments We wish to thank Nikolaos Antypas, Mirco Balatti, Francisco Rodríguez Fernández, Philip Molyneux, Alessando Sbuelz, all participants at the SANFI workshop in Santander and an anonymous referee for their suggestions on a previous version of the paper.

References

Aigner, D. J., Lovell, C. A. K., & Schmidt, P. (1977). Formulation and estimation of stochastic frontier production function models. *Journal of Econometrics, 6*, 21–37.

Altunbas, Y., & Molyneux, P. (1996). Economies of scale and scope in European banking. *Applied Financial Economics, 6*, 367–375.

Altunbas, Y., Gardener, E. P. M., Molyneux, P., & Moore, B. (2001). Efficiency in European banking. *European Economic Review, 45*, 1931–1955.

Baele, L., De Jonghe, O., & Vennet, R. V. (2007). Does the stock market value bank diversification? *Journal of Banking & Finance, 31*(7), 1999–2023.

Battese, G. E., & Coelli, T. J. (1992). Frontier production functions, technical efficiency and panel data with application to paddy farmers in India. *Journal of Productivity Analysis, 3*, 153–169.

Beccalli, E., Anolli, M., & Borello, G. (2015). Are European banks too big? Evidence on economies of scale. *Journal of Banking and Finance, 58*, 232–246.

Berger, A. N., Hanweck, G. A., & Humphrey, D. B. (1987). Competitive viability in banking. Scale, scope and product mix economies. *Journal of Monetary Economics, 20*, 501–520.

Clark, J. A. (1996). Economic cost, scale efficiency, and competitive viability in banking. *Journal of Money, Credit and Banking, 28*, 342–364.

DeYoung, R., & Jiang, C. (2013). *Economies of scale and the economic role of banks*. Working Paper.

Dijkstra, M. A. (2013). *Economies of scale and scope in the European Banking Sector 2002–2011*. Amsterdam Law School Research Paper.

European Commission. (2014, January 29). *Proposal on banking structural reform*, Brussels.

Gambacorta, L., & van Rixtel, A. (2013). *Structural bank regulation initiatives: Approaches and implications* (BIS Working Papers 412).

Institute of International Finance. (2010). *Systemic risk and systemically important firms. An integrated approach.*

Jagtiani, J., & Khanthavit, A. (1996). Scale and scope economies at large banks. Including off-balance sheet products and regulatory effects (1984–1991). *Journal of Banking & Finance, 20*, 1271–1287.

Meeusen, W., & Van der Broeck, J. (1977). Efficiency estimation from Cobb-Douglas production functions with composed error. *International Economic Review, 18*, 435–444.

Mester, L. J. (1993). Efficiency in the savings and loan industry. *Journal of Banking and Finance, 17*, 267–286.

Mester, L. J. (1996). A study of bank efficiency taking in account risk preferences. *Journal of Banking and Finance, 20*, 1025–1045.

Mitchell, K., & Onvural, N. M. (1996). Economies of scale and scope at large commercial banks. Evidence from the Fourier flexible functional form. *Journal of Money, Credit and Banking, 28*, 178–199.

Pulley, L. B., & Humphrey, D. B. (1993). The role of fixed costs and cost complementarities in determining scope economies and the cost of narrow banking proposals. *The Journal of Business, 66*, 437–462.

Stiroh, K., & Rumble, A. (2006). The dark side of diversification. The case of US financial holding companies. *Journal of Banking and Finance, 30*, 2131–2432.

The Clearing House. (2011). *Understanding the economics of large banks*. New York: The Clearing House.

Vander Vennet, R. (2002). Cost and profit efficiency of financial conglomerates and universal banks in Europe. *Journal of Money, Credit and Banking, 34*, 254–282.

Zellner, A. (1962). An efficient method of estimating seemingly unrelated regressions and tests for aggregation bias. *Journal of the American Statistical Association, 57*(1962), 348–368.

7. [illegible]

References

Aiyar, [illegible] (19[illegible]). [illegible] production [illegible] *[illegible] of Econometrics*, [illegible].
Alaudin, [illegible] (19[illegible]). [illegible]
Baltagi, [illegible] *Economics*, [illegible]
Battese, G. [illegible] production [illegible] *Journal of Productivity Analysis*, [illegible]
Berger, [illegible] *Journal of Banking and Finance*, [illegible]
Berger, A. N., [illegible] (199[illegible]). [illegible] *Journal of Economic Perspectives*, [illegible]
Coelli, T. (199[illegible]). [illegible]
De Young, [illegible] (199[illegible]). [illegible] Paper.
Diewert, [illegible]
[illegible] Economic [illegible]
Gathergood, [illegible]
Institute of [illegible]
Kumbhakar, S. C. [illegible] (199[illegible]). [illegible]
[illegible] *Journal of Econometrics*, [illegible]
Kumbhakar, S. [illegible] & Van den Broeck, J. [illegible] (19[illegible]). [illegible] *Economic Review*, [illegible]
Mester, L. [illegible] (199[illegible]). [illegible] *Journal of Banking and Finance*, [illegible]
Mester, L. J. (199[illegible]). [illegible] *Journal of Banking and Finance*, [illegible]
Mitchell, K., & Onvural, N. M. (199[illegible]). Economies of scale and scope at large commercial banks: [illegible] *Journal of Money, Credit and Banking*, [illegible]
Sealey, C. W., & Lindley, J. T. (19[illegible]). [illegible] *Journal of Finance*, [illegible]
[illegible] *Journal of Banking and Finance*, [illegible]
The [illegible]
Vander Vennet, R. (200[illegible]). [illegible] *Journal of Money, Credit and Banking*, [illegible]
Zellner, A. (196[illegible]). [illegible] *Journal of the American Statistical Association*, [illegible]

Part II
Individual Country Studies About Corporate Governance in Banking and Investor Protection

Chapter 8
Corporate Governance of Financial Conglomerates in Indonesia: Legal Issues and Gaps

Tony Tony

8.1 Introduction

The Indonesian financial system has, in common with those of other countries, undergone significant structural change over the past few decades. Globalisation, deregulation, technology advancement, product innovation, and changing customers' preference in financial services have all induced financial institutions to expand their business activities beyond traditional sectoral boundaries and to engage in cross-sectoral consolidation. The financial institutions have apparently tended to become financial conglomerates, operating through networks of entities under common control to offer a broad range of services in banking, securities, insurance, and multi-financing, in various combinations. As combining different financial services into a group might produce diversification benefits and operational synergies, financial conglomerates have rapidly emerged and become the prevalent feature of the Indonesian financial system. Recently, the Indonesian Financial Services Authority (*Otoritas Jasa Keuangan*, OJK)[1] has recorded 97 financial conglomerates existing in Indonesia (see Rahadian and Kaihatu 2016). These conglomerates comprise 380 financial institutions and control approximately 77.1% of Indonesian financial sectors' total assets as of December 2015.

[1]The Indonesian Financial Service Authority (OJK) is an independent and integrated financial authority that established by the Law No.21 of 2011. It has authority to regulate, supervise, inspect, and investigate all financial activities and institutions in Indonesia. It is mandated to implement an integrated regulation and supervision towards all financial services activities, including to financial conglomerates.

T. Tony (✉)
Griffith Law School, Griffith University, Nathan, QLD, Australia
e-mail: tony.tony@griffithuni.edu.au

B. Díaz Díaz et al. (eds.), *Corporate Governance in Banking and Investor Protection*, CSR, Sustainability, Ethics & Governance,
https://doi.org/10.1007/978-3-319-70007-6_8

Financial conglomerates give rise to intricate corporate governance issues, which mostly stem from the fundamental nature of the financial conglomerates themselves (see Bank of Japan 2005; Lumpkin 2011). Given their inherent complex organisational structure and activities, financial conglomerates often come with lack of transparency, unclear managerial structures and accountability, inadequate consolidated risk management practices, intensified conflicts of interest, and moral hazard (see e.g., Blume 2014; Group of Ten 2001; Fanto 2010; Khanna and Yafeh 2007; Skippers 2000; Tripartite Group 1995; Walter 2004). Moreover, the concentrated ownership of financial conglomerate also makes it more susceptible to tunnelling (see e.g, Claessens et al. 2002; Johnson et al. 2000; Obata 2002; Nurazi et al. 2015). All these issues increase the likelihood of poor corporate governance practices, including expropriation of minority investors' interests. Despite these issues, there was no legal framework on corporate governance for financial conglomerates in Indonesia until a few years ago. Indeed, the legal framework has customarily been focused on financial institution as a single entity, with no or little contemplation of financial conglomerates, and thus, it has not addressed the corporate governance issues of financial conglomerates adequately. As Kirkpatrick (2004) argues, "there is strong evidence that, without appropriate regulatory framework, the undesirable effects of [financial conglomerates] do in fact represent cost for an economy" (p. 5). Numerous studies have also documented that the absence of sound regulation specifically governing financial conglomerates make it easy for them to confuse or defraud the investment communities or outside investors and disturb the well-functioning of financial systems (see e.g., Claessens et al. 2002; Farrar 2012; Hadden 1992; Nicoló et al. 2004; OECD 2003; Sun et al. 2011; Wilmarth 2009).

To address the issues and to endorse good corporate governance practices of financial conglomerates in Indonesia, the OJK enacted Regulation No. 18/POJK.03/2014 on the Implementation of Corporate Governance for Financial Conglomerates on November 2014, which is further implemented through the OJK Circular Letter No.15/SEOJK.03/2015 (hereinafter: the Integrated Regulation).[2] The Integrated Regulation is the first regulations in Indonesia that specifically address financial conglomerates in its entirety as a group. It sets out minimum regulatory requirements to be followed by financial conglomerates in establishing group-wide corporate governance arrangements in accordance with the principles of transparency, accountability, responsibility, and fairness. Since financial conglomerates comprise a number of separate legal entities, the Integrated Regulation requires it to appoint a lead entity, which is either the parent company or appointed sister company, to hold responsibility for implementing integrated corporate governance of the financial conglomerate as a group. It further stipulates that such responsibility rests with the

[2]It is worth noting here that the OJK also enacted Regulation No.17/POJK.03/2014 on the Implementation of Integrated Risk Management for Financial conglomerate, which further implemented through the OJK Circular Letter No.14/SEOJK.03/2015. This regulation is considered as an integral part of the Integrated Regulation.

boards of the lead entity. Accordingly, most of the requirements on integrated corporate governance for financial conglomerates stipulated in the Integrated Regulation aims at the lead entity and its boards.

This chapter critically evaluates the requirements on corporate governance for financial conglomerates, especially related to the lead entity, stipulated in the Integrated Regulation. It also considers the corporate governance issues in financial conglomerates and the regulatory requirements related to corporate governance specified in other prevailing laws in Indonesia (i.e., company law, banking law, and capital market law). We find that although the Integrated Regulation might minimise some major corporate governance issues of financial conglomerates, many requirements specified in the Integrated Regulation conflict with the regulatory requirements stipulated in other prevailing laws. These conflicting regulatory requirements might raise legal issues for the parties within the financial conglomerate. Furthermore, this chapter argues that the Integrated Regulation has not fully addressed the corporate governance issues of financial conglomerates. Thus, it suggests for further legal reform to address the legal issues and gaps by enacting a particular law for financial conglomerates. This chapter contributes to the existing literature on financial conglomerates and corporate governance in two main ways. First, this chapter explores the regulation on corporate governance of financial conglomerates in Indonesia, which is scarcely discussed in the literature. Second, this chapter adds to the sparse literature that discusses the corporate governance of financial conglomerates in developing countries from a legal perspective, in contrast to the abundant literature that covers financial conglomerates and corporate governance in developed countries from an economic perspective (see e.g., Adams and Mehran 2012; Boyd et al. 1993; Laeven and Levine 2007; Stiroh and Rumble 2006).

The remainder of this chapter is divided into five sections. Section 8.2 provides the definition and organisational structure of financial conglomerates with emphasis on the Indonesian context. Section 8.3 discusses corporate governance issues in financial conglomerates. Section 8.4 describes the regulatory requirements stipulated in the Integrated Regulation and discusses the legal issues and gaps. Section 8.5 offers suggestion for further legal reform. Last section provides the conclusions.

8.2 Definition and Structure of Financial Conglomerate in Indonesia

Many authors assert that the term financial conglomerate carries multiple meanings and interpretations (see e.g., Dierick 2004; Skippers 2000; Van de Berghe and Verweire 1998). They also find that financial conglomerates can be structured in various ways. Thus, it is important to provide a clear definition of the term and to describe the various organisational structures of financial conglomerate with emphasis on the Indonesian context before discussing further the issues of corporate governance in financial conglomerates.

8.2.1 What Is a Financial Conglomerate?

Generally, there is no single-agreed definition of the term financial conglomerate and the usage slightly differs between countries and regions (see e.g., Yoshino et al. 2007; Van de Berghe 1995). In the United States, Japan, and Korea, the term financial conglomerate often refers to a financial holding company, which is a non-operating company that owns or controls numerous financial institutions as its subsidiaries. In Continental European countries, the terms *allfinanz*, *bancassurance*, and universal bank are also used to denote financial conglomerate. Broadly, Van Lelyveld and Schilder (2003) define financial conglomerates as "a group of firms that engage in financial activities that have been kept separate, by law and regulation, for many years in many countries" (p. 197). The Staff of Bank of Japan (2005) defines financial conglomerate as "groups of financial institutions and firms that offer a wide range of services" (p. 6). In the international discourse, the Joint Forum[3] (2012) defines financial conglomerates as "any group of companies under common control or dominant influence, including any financial holding company, which conducts material financial activities in at least two of the regulated banking, securities or insurance sectors" (p. 5). Based on these definitions, financial conglomerates have three main characteristics, which: (1) relate to business group; (2) are formed by different types of financial institutions; and (3) conduct cross-sectoral financial activities (p. 19).

In Indonesia, the definition of a financial conglomerate is slightly different from the abovementioned definitions. The Integrated Regulation defines financial conglomerates as a group of financial institutions under common control or ownership (art 1 par. 2). Based on this definition, financial conglomerates can be groups of financial institutions with activities that span across financial sectors (*heterogeneous group*) or groups of financial institutions that confine their activities to a given financial sector (*homogenous group*). Further, the Integrated Regulation also specifies that the types of financial institutions in a group might include banks, securities companies, insurance companies, and multi-finance companies (art 3 par. 2). To provide a common understanding of the controlling party, the Integrated Regulation explains that control occurs when a party (i.e., a person, a non-financial company, or a financial institution) owns directly or indirectly more than 50% of the companies' shares with voting rights; or a party owns less than 50% of the companies' shares with voting rights but it meets one of the following conditions: (1) it has an agreement with other shareholders of the company, so that, it can control the exercise of more than 50% of the voting rights; (2) it has the authority to determine the financial policies and operations of the company based on the article of association or agreement; (3) it has the authority to appoint or to replace most members of the board of

[3]The Joint Forum was established in 1996 under the aegis of the Basel Committee on Banking Supervision (BCBS), the International Organization of Securities Commissions (IOSCO) and the International Association of Insurance Supervisors (IAIS) to deal with issues common to banking, securities, and insurance sectors, including the regulation of financial conglomerates.

commissioners and the board of directors (hereinafter: boards) or other units of equal level and control over the company; or (4) it has the ability to obtain majority votes in the boards' meetings (elucidation of art. 4 par. 2). The government is excluded from the controlling party, although it directly controls a number of large financial institutions in Indonesia (art. 50). Generally, when a number of financial institutions are controlled by a similar party, these financial institutions are considered as a financial conglomerates, and thus, they are subject to Integrated Regulation.

The term financial conglomerate should not be confused with the term mixed conglomerate or business group. The latter term refers to a group of companies under common control that has predominant commercial or industrial activities, despite that it might include financial institutions (see Tripartite Group 1995, p. 36). Although the financial conglomerate is often a sub-group of the mixed conglomerate or business group in Indonesia (see e.g., Daniel 2003; Sato 2004; Tabalujan 2001), the OJK focuses on financial conglomerates. Therefore, the Integrated Regulation is only aimed at financial conglomerates, not at mixed conglomerates or business groups.

8.2.2 Structure of Financial Conglomerates

Financial conglomerates can be formed in various organisational structures, which depend on the regulatory regime as well as the business decision (Dierick 2004, p. 17; Tripartite Group 1995, p. 14). For example, in Germany where the law allows the combination of banking and securities activities in a single entity, the integrated model or universal banking model evolved as the prevalent structural forms of financial conglomerate (Herring and Santomero 1990, p. 223). In the United States, Japan, and South Korea, the law requires the formation of a financial holding company to engage in different financial activities, and thus, the financial holding company model developed as the predominant structure of financial conglomerates (see Skipper 2000, p. 73). In Indonesia, the banking law prohibits the combination of banking, securities, and insurance activities in a single entity. In addition, the regulatory regime generally does not recognise financial holding companies (see Sulistiowati 2011). However, the financial laws generally allow a financial institution to own other financial institutions as subsidiaries. Moreover, there is no legal restriction for a party to directly own majority shares or to control a number of financial institutions. Many owners and managers of a financial institution then use these legal loopholes to form financial conglomerate by separating different financial activities into different legal entities under common control. Based on the control relationship of financial institutions and for its regulatory and supervisory purpose, the OJK differentiates the structure of financial conglomerates into three models: vertical, horizontal and mixed, as can be seen in Fig. 8.1. Based on data from the OJK, there are currently 31 financial conglomerates forming vertical models, 52 using the horizontal model, and 14 adopting the mixed model.

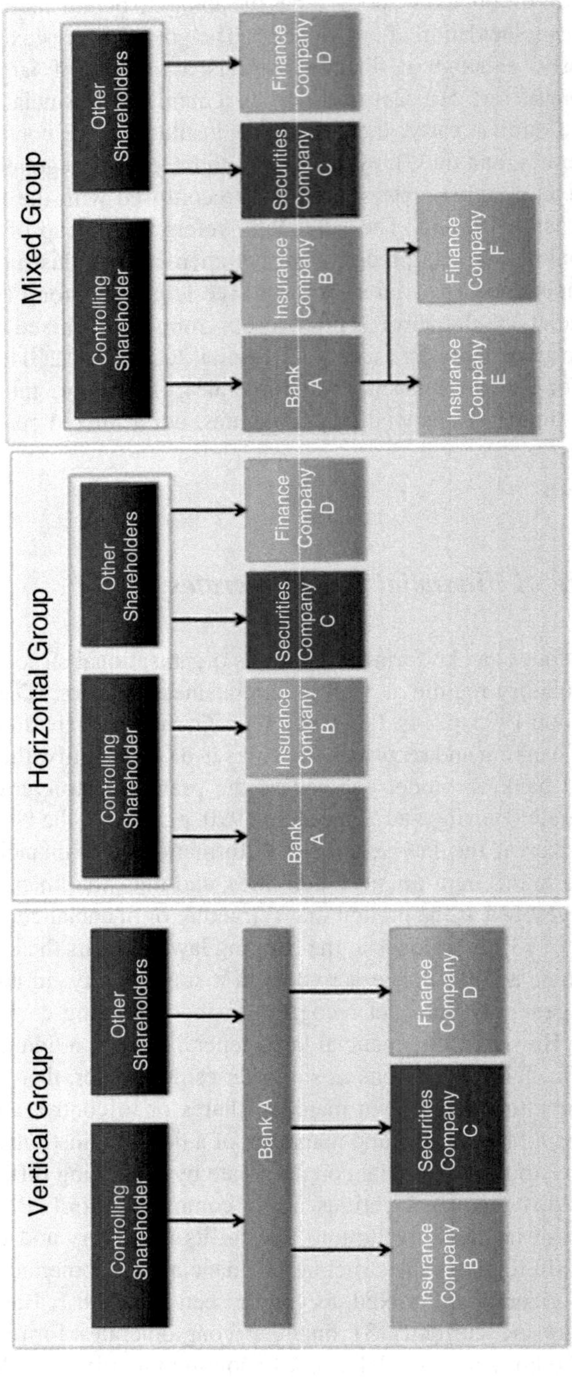

Source: Otoritas Jasa Keuangan (2014)

Fig. 8.1 Various structures of financial conglomerates in Indonesia

The vertical model is based on parent-subsidiary relationship. In this model, the managers of a financial institution decide to expand the business by establishing or acquiring other financial institutions. The financial institution then becomes the parent company that controls other financial institutions as its subsidiaries. From a company law perspective, the parent company and its subsidiaries are separate legal entities. Each of them has its-own assets, liabilities, capital, boards, and management. The parent company as a shareholder is shielded with the limited liability principle, under which it has no legal obligation for its subsidiary's liabilities beyond its shareholdings. Accordingly, this principle allows the parent company to protect its assets from any attempt of the creditors of its subsidiaries who want to seek recourse when subsidiaries get into financial trouble, while permitting it to take benefit from the positive returns of its subsidiaries (see also Herring and Santomero 1990; Yoo 2010). However, in business practice, the parent company may abstain from taking full advantage of the limited liability principle due to two main considerations. Firstly, Indonesian accounting standards require the parent company to present consolidated financial statements, in which the parent company must accrue the assets, liabilities, and profits or losses of its subsidiaries. Further, banking regulation requires the parent bank to fulfil minimum capital adequacy on a consolidated basis, including ensuring the fulfilment of minimum capital adequacy of its subsidiaries. Hence, the parent company's financial performance may adversely be impacted by the financial distress of its subsidiaries. Secondly, the parent company and its subsidiaries often use similar group brands or logos. Such practice often creates a public perception that the parent company and its subsidiaries are a single entity. As such, the parent company's reputation may falter when that of its subsidiary is damaged. Due to these considerations, the parent company may decide to cover the liabilities of its subsidiaries beyond its shareholdings and may be actively involved in its subsidiary's governance by determining their strategic plans, monitoring their risks, control, and performance, reviewing their strategic internal policies, and allocating resources.

The horizontal model is based on sister companies' relationships. In this model, a party (i.e., wealthy person, non-financial company, or foreign financial institution) already in ownership or controlling a financial institution decides to expand its business by establishing or acquiring other financial institutions. The former and latter financial institutions then become sister companies. Each sister company is independent of the other sister companies. It has no direct capital or control link with the other sister companies. Accordingly, it has no direct access to the profits or assets of the other sister companies. Yet, these sister companies are considered as a financial conglomerate due to the virtue of being controlled by a similar party. Dissimilar to the vertical model, Indonesian accounting standards do not require companies within this group to consolidate their financial statements, particularly when they are owned or controlled by a single person. The banking regulations also do not regulate this model as they focus on the parent bank-subsidiaries relationship. Besides, each financial institution within this group may use its own unique brand or logo. Based on these descriptions, principally, the problems of a sister company might not have a direct impact on other sister companies and might present a lesser threat to the group as a whole. However, in business practices,

Yiu et al. (2013) note that "the horizontal connections between sister group affiliates serve to facilitate coordination and resources sharing among group affiliates" (p. 467; see also Maman 1999). The sister companies may have arrangements in place among them for cross selling and bundling of different types of financial products and information sharing. Additionally, the controlling party may be involved in determining major business decisions and strategic plans of the companies. It may also place the same person to serve as a board member in many sister companies, which is known as interlocking directorates, to enhance coordination of the activities of various components of the group (see Claessens et al. 2002; Khanna and Rivkin 2006; Mizruchi and Marquis 2006). Accordingly, the sister companies in a financial conglomerate may have business interdependencies among one another and may be managed on a unitary basis through informal mechanisms.

The mixed model is the combination of vertical and horizontal models in a financial conglomerate. In this model, a party directly controls a number of financial institutions as sister companies. The financial institution further directly controls other financial institutions as its subsidiaries. The former corresponds to the horizontal model whereas the latter corresponds to the vertical model. Hence, this structure is called a mixed model.

8.3 Corporate Governance Issues in Financial Conglomerates

Having set out the definition and structure of financial conglomerates, this chapter now discusses the corporate governance issues. According to the Cadbury Report (1992), "corporate governance is the system by which companies are directed and controlled" (p. 11). Shleifer and Vishny (1997) state that "corporate governance deals with the ways in which providers of finance to corporations assure themselves of getting return on their investment" (p. 737). Ira Millstein (1998) argues that corporate governance "encompasses all the laws designed to hold the corporation accountable to shareholders and the public, as well as the workings of the market for corporate control." In a nutshell, good corporate governance is about how corporations promote the principles of transparency, accountability, responsibility, and fairness to safeguard the investors' interests in conformity with public interests on a sustainable basis (see BCBS 2015, p. 3; Fernando 2009, p. 11; Gregory and Simms 1999, p. 7). In the financial sector, good corporate governance is important as a precondition for effective financial supervision (BCBS 2015, p. 3).

Yet, good corporate governance is likely hard to achieve by financial conglomerates. As Clarke (2015) argues, "it is the level of scale, complexity, and sophistication [of the financial conglomerates] that poses greatest governance challenges" (p. 201). Similarly, Farrar (2012) asserts that "complex financial conglomerates give rise to difficult problems" (p. 521). The following discussions explore corporate governance issues in financial conglomerates, which have raised the concerns of financial regulators and market participants.

8.3.1 Complex Structure and Lack of Transparency

There has been a concern that "some financial conglomerates may choose a complex structure in order to make their operations opaque and to avoid regulation" (see Tripartite Group 1995, p. 29). In its report, the Associations of Supervisors of Banks of the Americas Working Group (2007) revealed that owners of a complex financial conglomerate might organise the group's structure and activities in such manner, so that market participants might find it difficult to obtain an accurate picture of its structure and risk profile (p. 26). It also stated that "the structure of financial conglomerate has become increasingly complex over the last decade and has made it difficult for supervisors to understand which companies belong to certain groups" (p. 29). Similarly, Avgerinos (2003) studied financial conglomerates in European countries and highlighted "the problem of complex and non-transparent group structure, which represents a supervisory obstacle with regard to all possible group-wide and cross-border risks" (p. 228). The lack of transparency of financial conglomerates also occurs in Indonesia. As discussed above, financial conglomerates may form in horizontal and mixed models. These structures are opaque and have created a problem for the OJK and market participants to get a complete picture of the structure of financial conglomerates and their member entities. Without a clear picture of the entire structure of a financial conglomerate, it would be difficult for OJK and market participants to properly monitor the financial conglomerate as a whole and each of it member entities.

This lack of transparency of financial conglomerates is also attributed to the limitations of the disclosure regime and accounting consolidation. As noted above, the current disclosure regime in Indonesia does not require the financial conglomerates to adopt a horizontal or mixed structure to provide consolidated financial statements. Although it requires financial conglomerates forming in vertical models to provide consolidated financial statements, the accounting consolidation process aggregates the accounts of the parent company and its subsidiaries and eliminates inter-company transactions. Such aggregation conceals the financial difficulties, potential insolvencies, and poor performance of the member entities (see Pierce and Brenan 2003, p. 17). The elimination process also diminishes detailed information about intragroup transactions and exposures, such as shared-services, cross-contribution arrangements, cross-guarantees, transfer pricing, and profit shifting. Additionally, the 2008 global financial crisis has exposed situations when the limitations of Generally Accepted Accounting Principles (GAAP), especially off-balance transactions, fair-value accounting, and loan loss provisioning, were used by complex financial conglomerates to conceal their large amount of complicated transactions, such as credit default obligations, credit default swaps, etc. (see Barth and Landsman 2010; Kirkpatrick 2009; Laux and Leuz 2009). All these limitations have created problems for regulators and market participants to get an overall picture of the financial performance of financial conglomerates and to make appropriate judgments about the riskiness of financial conglomerates as a whole and for each of its member entities.

8.3.2 Matrix Management and Less-Clear Accountability

The complex organisational structure of financial conglomerates often comes with complex management, in which the managerial structure of a financial conglomerate may be different from its legal structure. As Friedland (1994) notes, "a financial conglomerate may have adopted a matrix management whereby accountability is organised on a functional basis spanning a different number of corporate entities rather than following a pyramid structure within each corporate entity" (p. 38; see IOSCO 1992). In Indonesia, many financial conglomerates have also adopted matrix management. In matrix management, "individuals report to different senior managers on different aspects of their work" (Tripartite 1995, p. 30). In other words, the staff of a company within a group report to two bosses: the direct manager at the company and manager at the head of the group (see Davis and Lawrence 1987). Hence, matrix management might create many frustrations that stem from dual responsibilities and authority, divided loyalty, multiple and complex reporting lines, having too many people involved in decision making, unclear roles, conflicts of priorities and allocation of resources, and confusion over accountability (Burke and Baron 2014, p. 62; Ramanlingam 2013, p. 95). The use of matrix management by financial conglomerates has also been a concern of financial regulators as "they might not be able to fully understand the lines of accountability relevant to their tasks" (Ulst 2005, p. 37). More importantly, they might be unable to take prompt, adequate, and effective supervisory actions to address the issues in financial conglomerates.

8.3.3 Consolidated Risk Management Issues

The complex activities of financial conglomerates present consolidated risk management issues (see e.g., Berger et al. 1999; Delimatsis 2011; Santomero and Eckles 2000; Wilmarth 2009). As Kuritzkes et al. (2003) note, empirical studies "point out that the practicalities of achieving integrated risk management are daunting and appear to have discouraged firms from adopting consolidated risk management" due to several reasons (p. 3). *First*, there are different regulatory approaches between financial sectors for measuring similar types of risk. For example, a credit exposure to an A-rated customer requires 4% of capital outstanding when it was booked in a bank balance sheet; however, it may require only 0.16% of capital outstanding when it is booked in an insurance company balance sheet. This condition may increase the possibility for a financial conglomerate to conduct regulatory arbitrage. *Second*, it is also an issue to ensure "compatible and efficient information technology systems for data capture, data analysis, and data reporting that encompass the whole of their operations" (see Joint Forum 2003, p. 5). *Lastly*, combining the different risk factors is very difficult as they are often not perfectly correlated to one another, so it would be problematic to add them up together. Further, the risk aggregation model, which is a qualitative risk measure that incorporates multiple types or sources of risk, including risk concentration and intragroup transactions and exposure risks has not been well-developed until now, especially in Indonesia. All these issues have significantly contributed to non-existent or inadequate group risk profiling of financial conglomerates. The non-existence of group risk profiles is particularly profound in financial conglomerates formed in horizontal or mixed models as there is no institution that has clear responsibility to conduct consolidated risk management. Without adequate information on a group-wide risk profile of a financial conglomerate, it would be difficult for managers at the parent level, regulators, and interested external parties to conduct proper monitoring of the entire risks of a financial conglomerate as well as its member entities.

8.3.4 Moral Hazard

Financial conglomeration increases moral hazard problems that may arise in several ways. First, a financial conglomerate can become so large that it will be considered as "too big to fail" by the financial regulator and market participants (see Hashmall 2010; Wilmarth 2010). Second, non-bank financial institutions within the group may gain access to bank safety net programs, such as deposit insurance schemes, emergency lending facilities, and the lender of last resort. Particularly, "when the support by a parent to these groups affects regulated entities that end up drawing these facilities" (Dierick 2004, p. 15; IMF 2006, p. 87). Third, the risk tolerance of financial institutions within the group might significantly increase due to the expectation that it will be supported by the parent entity or other member entities in the event that problems occur (Lumpkin 2011; Wilmarth 2002). This condition is further encouraged by the existence of intra-group transactions between member entities, such as credit extensions, cross-guarantees, intra-group trading, centralized management of short-term liquidity, provisions of management and other services, and risk transfer through reinsurance (The Joint Forum 1999). All of these issues might eventually increase risk-taking behaviour of the member entities within a group as well as the financial conglomerate as a whole.

8.3.5 Conflicts of Interest

Conflicts of interest are pervasive in financial conglomerates because they comprise a number of separate legal financial institutions and offer a broad range of services to numerous clients, acting as principal and agents, simultaneously (see Cranston 1990; Crockett et al. 2003; Massa and Rehman 2008; McVea 1996). In fact, one scholar has identified 23 types of conflicts of interests in financial conglomerate (see Walter 2004). Generally, these conflicts can be differentiated into four categories based on the involved parties, as follows:

1. Conflict of interests between parent company or controlling party and subsidiaries or member entities. Teen and Bennett (2014) cited that "the most obvious situation [of this conflict] is where the group entity and the parent group engage in transactions with each other in a way that favours the parent entity at the expense of the group entity" (p. 6). Frederick (2014) also states that 'parent company may harm subsidiary in many way, some of which, such as intragroup transfers. Other less visible ways might include…low interest loans, uncollateralized liquidity pooling, pricing decisions for shared services that the group performs for subsidiary, and so on" (p. 30). Additionally, the parent company might also use the subsidiary assets for its own purposes at the expense of the subsidiary or charge its expenses to the subsidiaries. Moreover, the parent company might conduct tunnelling, as will be discussed below.
2. Conflict of interests among member entities. Van de Berghe and Verweire (1998) consider this category of conflict as an internal conflict that may occur due to several factors, including competition between the business units to get market share, struggle between different distribution outlets, market cannibalisation (the growth of one company by taking sales off other companies), and cross-subsidisation (the use of one product profits to subsidise other product losses) (p. 163).
3. Conflict of interests between member firms and customers. There are numerous situations, in which such conflict might occur, including: (1) tying practice, e.g., a bank may require mortgage customers to buy home insurance from its affiliated insurance companies; (2) misuse of customers' private information, such as a securities company uses debtors' information from its affiliated bank for proprietary trading; (3) misuse of a fiduciary role, for example, the mutual fund managers invest a large amount of the fund in shares of its affiliated companies; and (4) fraudulent financial misselling, which is deceptive and manipulative marketing, selling, or advising of a financial product or service to an end user, in the knowledge that the product or service is unsuitable for that specific end user's needs but it would create profits for the member firms or financial conglomerate as a whole (see Reurink 2016; Renda et al. 2009; World Bank 2006 for discussion on financial misselling). Furthermore, Herring and Santomero (1990) also argue that "by integrating commercial and investment banking activities, a conglomerate could use trust funds to mask bad underwriting decisions ("stuffing") or generate large brokerage commissions by excessive transactions in trust accounts ("churning")" (p. 230).
4. Conflict of interests between customers. This conflict occurs because a financial conglomerate has relationships with two or more customers that results in incompatible duties to the customers. The classic example is when one arm of a financial conglomerate acts as investment adviser that has fiduciary duty to keep confidential the information from its client while the other arm acts as broker-dealer that has fiduciary duty to disclose material information in its

possession to its clients. As Tuch (2014) puts it, "to satisfy a duty of disclosure to the latter client is to violate a duty of confidence to the former client." He also states that "the existence of incompatible duties occurs many times over in the financial conglomerate, considering that the firm will often represent many thousands of clients at any one time, owing manifold duties in doing so" (p. 574).

All in all, as Walter (2004) concludes:

> [w]hen those conflicts of interest are exploited, agency costs are imposed on all kinds of users of financial markets, from the smallest retail investor to the largest corporation—sometimes even multiple agency costs. As a result, both efficiency and fairness in financial markets suffer, and so does the effectiveness with which financial intermediaries engage in the corporate monitoring and governance process (p. 362).

8.3.6 Tunnelling

Financial conglomerates are susceptible to tunnelling since their ownership is highly concentrated. Johnson et al. (2000) define tunnelling as "the transfer of assets and profits out of firms for the benefits of those who control them" (p. 22). Tunnelling can be conducted through legal or illegal methods (see Faccio et al. 2001). For instance, the controlling party can increase its shares through dilutive share issues, minority freeze-outs, creeping acquisitions, and other legal transactions that result in expropriation of minority investors' interests. It can also conduct abusive self-dealing transactions, such as insider trading and non-arm's length intragroup pricing. Tunnelling can happen because the controlling party has power not only to determine the end result of the shareholders meeting, but also to appoint the board's members and senior management so that it can direct daily operations of each member entity within the group and financial conglomerate as a whole. In his article, Jackson (1994) considered the controlling party or parent company as "a hungry-wolf" that is prone to prey on its subsidiaries for its own benefits. Empirical studies show that tunnelling issues are more extensive in countries with weak legal investor protection, such as Indonesia (see Claessens et al. 2000; Friedman et al. 2003; LaPorta et al. 1998, 2000; Sato 2004). Indeed, Obata (2002) argues that in Indonesia, the large business groups often "intentionally keep their financial groups at the bottom of the pyramid of group structure as tools to expropriate outsiders because there is more room to manipulate accounting numbers in financial institutions and to conduct tunnelling through them" (p. 9). Recently, Nurazi et al. (2015) investigate the tunnelling activities in Indonesian public listed companies, including financial firms, and found that most of the companies "had experienced expropriation in the form of tunnelling, particularly expropriation from majority to minority shareholders, which can be identified through the related party transaction" (p. 127). They conclude that "the mechanism of good corporate governance is not well implemented. Therefore, a majority shareholder tends to expropriate the minority shareholder by transferring the welfare from the small firm to the larger firm in terms of financial support" (p. 148). In short, without a sound institutional and legal framework on corporate governance for financial conglomerates, tunnelling can be easily done by controlling parties, thus severely damaging the interests of outside investors, other recognised stakeholders, and overall financial system stability.

8.4 Regulatory Requirements of Integrated Corporate Governance for Financial Conglomerates

To minimise the issues discussed above and to endorse good corporate governance practices in financial conglomerates, the OJK enacted the Integrated Regulation in November 2014, as highlighted above. This is the first regulation that addresses financial conglomerates in their entirety as a group. Previously, corporate governance regulations have customarily been focused on a company as a single entity, with no or little contemplation of the financial conglomerate as a group. Although Bank Indonesia, which was responsible for banking regulation and supervision prior to the OJK, has enacted several regulations related to different aspects of corporate governance for banking groups, such as single presence policy, consolidated risk management, and bank report transparency and publication, these regulations have several shortcomings in addressing the financial conglomerates. First, they exclude insurance companies, which are often part of a banking group. Second, they do not address financial conglomerates that are formed in horizontal structures, which comprises sister companies in a group and mixed structure that involves parent-subsidiaries as well as sister companies in a group. Lastly, they do not provide comprehensive regulatory requirements on corporate governance for financial conglomerates. The Integrated Regulation thus intends to close the regulatory gaps and to enhance corporate governance regulations in addressing the financial conglomerates in Indonesia.

The Integrated Regulation purportedly aims at the financial conglomerate in its entirety as a group. It sets out minimum requirements to be followed by financial conglomerates in establishing its group-wide corporate governance arrangements in accordance with the principles of transparency, accountability, responsibility, and fairness. The Integrated Regulation is a delegated regulation. It is supplementary to and does not replace the prevailing laws and regulations relating to corporate governance in Indonesia. According to the OECD (2015), "if new laws and regulations [on corporate governance] are needed, such as to deal with clear cases of market imperfections, they should be designed in a way that makes them possible to implement and enforce" (p. 14). The new regulations should also avoid the potential regulatory overlaps and even conflicts that may frustrate the ability to pursue the corporate governance objectives (OECD 2015, p. 15). However, many requirements specified in the Integrated Regulation conflict with the requirements stipulated in other prevailing laws, particularly company law, banking law, and capital market law. These conflicting requirements might create legal issues for the parties within financial conglomerates in implementing the integrated corporate governance of the group. Furthermore, the Integrated Regulation has not fully addressed the problems of corporate governance in financial conglomerates. The following sub-sections first describe major regulatory requirements on corporate governance for financial conglomerates in the Integrated Regulation and afterwards discusses legal issues and gaps.

8.4.1 *Major Regulatory Requirements of the Integrated Regulation*

8.4.1.1 The Appointment of Lead Entity and Its General Responsibility

While financial conglomerates comprise a number of separate legal entities and can be formed in various organisational structures, the Integrated Regulation operates on the basis that there should be one entity to hold overall responsibility for implementing integrated corporate governance of the group. Dissimilar to other countries that adopted the financial holding company, the Integrated Regulation requires a financial conglomerate to appoint a lead entity to hold the mentioned responsibility (art. 2). As specified in the Integrated Regulation, the lead entity is the parent financial institution for financial conglomerates formed under the vertical model (art. 6 par. 3). For the financial conglomerate adopting horisontal and mixed models, the controlling shareholder must appoint a financial institution in the group (appointed sister company) as the lead entity. When the controlling shareholders of the financial conglomerate comprise two or more parties with equal ownership or control, these parties should approve the appointment of the lead entity. Furthermore, the Integrated Regulation requires that the lead entity should be a financial institution within the group that has the largest total assets and/or sound quality risk management practices (art. 6 par. 6). Thus, the lead entity is different from the financial holding company. Whereas the financial holding company is a non-operating firm that controls a number of financial institutions as its subsidiaries, the lead entity is an operating firm and can be the parent company or an appointed sister company. Furthermore, the financial holding company usually needs approval or particular license from the financial authority, while the Integrated Regulation only requires the appointed lead entity to report to the OJK after its appointment (art. 44). Additionally, the report should include the information about the member entities within the group, the financial conglomerate structure, and the larger business group structure (if any). The lead entity should also report to the OJK when there is a change in the member entities or dissolution of the financial conglomerate.

The Integrated Regulation stipulates that the lead entity is responsible for developing and ensuring the implementation of integrated corporate governance guidelines of the financial conglomerate as a group (art 7). The guidelines include integrated corporate governance framework for the lead entity itself and corporate governance framework for the member entities (art. 28). The integrated corporate governance framework for the lead entity must address minimum requirements for the candidate of the board of commissioners and the board of directors of the lead entity to ensure that they have knowledge and capability to conduct their duties for implementing integrated corporate governance for the entire group; responsibility and duties of the boards of the lead entity; responsibility and duties of the integrated corporate governance committee: responsibility and duties of the integrated internal audit unit, responsibility and duties of the integrated compliance unit; and implementation of integrated risk management for the entire group (art. 8; art. 29). The corporate governance framework for the member entities should include at least the requirements for the candidate of the board of commissioners and the board of directors; the requirements for the candidate of the Islamic supervisory board if the financial conglomerate includes Islamic financial institutions; the structure of the boards; the structure of the Islamic supervisory board; independency of the board of commissioners; the application of the tasks and responsibility of the board of directors, board of commissioners, and Islamic supervisory board; the application of the tasks and responsibility of the compliance and internal audit, functions, the implementation of external audit; the implementation of risk management, policy on remuneration, and management of conflict of interests (art. 30). Basically, the corporate governance framework for the member entities is adopted from the framework for commercial banks as specified in the Bank Indonesia Regulation No.8/4/PBI/2006. The main reasons behind such adoption are because there was no particular corporate governance regulation for insurance companies, securities firms, and multi-finance companies prior to the enactment of the Integrated Regulation, and there is a need to provide a common corporate governance framework for all types of financial institutions that are members of a financial conglomerate.

In establishing the integrated corporate governance guidelines, the Integrated Regulation also requires the lead entity to balance the diverging interests of the financial conglomerate as a group and each of its member entity. The lead entity must safeguard that the guidelines have considered and respected the interests of outside investors and other recognised stakeholders. It should also ensure that the guidelines have covered adequate policies and procedures for identifying, mitigating, and controlling potential conflicts of interests in the financial conglomerate. After developing the guidelines, the lead entity must deliver them to the member entities within the group (art. 28 par. 3), so that, they can adopt and implement the guidelines. The Integrated Regulation further requires the lead entity to ensure the implementation of integrated corporate governance guidelines by conducting a self-assessment at minimum every 6 months (art. 45). In this matter, the lead entity should refer to the working paper specified in the OJK Circular Letter No.15/SEOJK.03/2015. The Integrated Regulation also requires the lead entity to submit the self-assessment report to the OJK, for the period ending on June and on December and to be submitted by the 15th of the second month after a period ends. As will be discussed below, all the responsibilities of the lead entity rest with its boards.

Essentially, the lead entity is expected to minimise the corporate governance issues of financial conglomerates, especially the opacity issue of financial conglomerate structure, in several ways. First, it enables a complex financial conglomerate to exist as a single business entity, while financial conglomerates may freely set their hierarchical, functional, and business structure. Second, it provides the overall picture of the financial conglomerate structure. Third, it performs a holding company function for financial conglomerates that involves discharging the legal and regulatory obligations as well as meeting minimum standards of due diligence in corporate governance. Fourth, it is anticipated to add value to the implementation of good corporate governance of financial conglomerates by influencing and ensuring good corporate practices across entities within the group, establishing prudent group-wide guidelines that include policies and procedures, monitoring and advising the implementation of the guidelines, and providing centralised services for integrated risk management, integrated internal audit, and integrated compliance of the group. From the financial supervisor's point of view, the role of lead entity is vital since it acts a single point of contact for getting information and discussing supervisory concerns about corporate governance and other issues in financial conglomerates. However, from a legal perspective, the lead entity concept conflicts with the single entity concept adopted under company law, as will be discussed below.

8.4.1.2 The Responsibility of the Boards of the Lead Entity

In Indonesia, companies have a two-tier board structure, comprising the board of commissioners (supervisory board; hereinafter: BOC) and the board of directors (executive board; hereinafter: BOD). This chapter uses the term "boards" to refer to both the BOC and BOD. Each of these boards has its own responsibility and authority on their respective function as mandated by the laws, regulations, and articles of association of the company (see IFC and OJK 2014, p. 108). The BOD is responsible for day-to-day management of the company. The BOC has a general function to oversee the implementation of the duties of the BOD and to give advice to the BOD, and it is prohibited to make any operational decisions. However, they both have similar responsibility, which is to ensure the implementation of good corporate governance practices and the long-term sustainability of the company.

The Integrated Regulation stipulates that the BOD of the lead entity has responsibility for ensuring the implementation of integrated corporate governance of the financial conglomerate (art. 10). In conducting this responsibility, the BOD of the lead entity should: (1) develop and establish integrated corporate governance guidelines of the financial conglomerate, as discussed above; (2) direct, monitor, and evaluate the implementation of the guidelines; and (3) follow-up any direction and advice from the BOC of the lead entity for enhancing integrated corporate governance guidelines. It must also implement integrated risk management of the financial conglomerate as a group, as will be discussed below (art. 27). It should also establish an integrated risk management committee, integrated risk management unit, integrated compliance unit, and integrated internal audit to support in ensuring the effective implementation of the integrated corporate governance, as will be discussed below. Additionally, the BOD of the lead entity must ensure that audit findings and recommendations from integrated internal audit unit, external auditors, financial supervisors, and other authorities have been followed up by each member entity within the group (art. 11).

The Integrated Regulation stipulates that the BOC of the lead entity is responsible to oversee the implementation of integrated corporate governance (art. 12). In conducting its responsibility, the BOC must at least: (1) monitor the implementation of the integrated corporate governance guidelines in each member entity within the financial conglomerate; (2) supervise the implementation of the duty and responsibility of the BOD of the lead entity, including providing advice and recommendations to the BOD of the lead entity related to the implementation of integrated corporate governance guidelines; and (3) evaluate the integrated corporate governance guidelines and direct the necessary enhancements. The Integrated Regulation also stipulates that the BOC of the lead entity shall meet at least twice a year to discuss the implementation of integrated corporate governance of the financial conglomerate. Additionally, the BOC of the lead entity must also establish an integrated corporate governance committee to support in fulfilling its oversight responsibility, as will be discussed below.

Basically, the imposition of the boards of lead entity's responsibility for ensuring the implementation of integrated corporate governance is expected to minimise the problems of matrix management and less-clear accountability in financial conglomerates. The boards of the lead entity are expected to play a critical role for enhancing good corporate governance practices in financial conglomerate as a whole as well as in each of its member entities through several ways. First, they are expected to bring their skills, knowledge, and experience for policy-making at group level that includes strategies, policies, and procedures. Second, they are also expected to professionally judge, question, and supervise the boards and executive managers of the entities within the group in implementing integrated corporate governance framework. Third, they are expected to provide professional advice and suggestions for the boards and managers of the entities within the group to enhance the implementation of the integrated corporate governance framework. Fourth, they are also expected to be contact-persons that connect the boards and executive managers of entities within the group into a group-wide network. Fifth, they are also expected as catalysts and role models for the boards and executive managers of each entity in the group. Last, they are expected to act as the "figure-head" and "service provider" of the group, in which they represent a financial conglomerate as a whole in front of the financial supervisors and other recognised stakeholders. Yet, it is important to emphasis that the boards of the lead entity are also the boards of a particular company. The boards of a company are generally bound to the fiduciary duty as stipulated in company law. As such, the expanding responsibility of the boards of lead entity might conflict with their fiduciary duty as the boards of a company, as will be discussed below.

8.4.1.3 The Board Committees

As highlighted above, the Integrated Regulation requires the boards of the lead entity to establish two types of committees: an integrated corporate governance committee and an integrated risk management committee. These committees are necessary to support the boards of the lead entity in performing their responsibilities relating to the implementation of integrated corporate governance.

The integrated corporate governance committee has as a primary function to assist the BOC of the lead entity. It has general responsibilities to evaluate the implementation of integrated corporate governance guidelines and to provide recommendations for enhancing the guidelines to the BOC of the lead entity (art. 19). Since a financial conglomerate comprises a number of entities and each of them has its own BOC, the Integrated Regulation requires that the members of this committee should at least comprise: (1) an independent commissioner of the lead entity, who also acts as a chairman of one of committees in the lead entity, as the chairman of the integrated corporate governance committee; (2) independent commissioners, who have been appointed from each member entity, as the members of the committee; and (3) members of the Islamic supervisory board, who have been appointed from each member's Islamic financial institution, as the member of the committee when the financial conglomerate comprises Islamic financial institutions (art. 17). The number and composition of the independent commissioners as members of this committee can be adjusted in accordance with the need of the financial conglomerate and the effectiveness and efficiency of the committee in performing its responsibility. However, each member financial institution must be represented by at least one of its BOC members, so that this committee can assess the implementation of the guidelines at entity level and at group level effectively and comprehensively.

The integrated risk management committee's main function is to support the BOD of the lead entity in ensuring the implementation of integrated risk management in the financial conglomerate. Specifically, this committee has responsibilities for: (1) confirming that the financial conglomerate as a group has adopted an integrated and comprehensive view of all the risks, considers the interrelationships between these risks and manages these risks in accordance with their degree of importance; (2) monitoring the implementation of the integrated risk management policies and procedures, and periodically reviewing the overall integrated risk management framework; (3) ensuring that the risks to which the financial conglomerate is exposed are clearly identified and reviewing the measures taken by management to adequately manage them; and (4) recommending enhancement on the integrated risk management framework, including policies and procedures, to the BOD of the lead entity. The members of this committee should at least consist of: (1) a director of the lead entity who is responsible for risk management, as the chairman; (2) directors from each member financial institution, as the members; and (3) senior managers from each member financial institution, as the members. The number and composition of the members in this committee can be adjusted in accordance with the need of a financial conglomerate and the effectiveness and efficiency of the committee in performing its duties. However, it must at least include a member from each type of financial institution within the group, so that the committee can effectively assess the comprehensiveness, effectiveness, and consistency of the integrated risk management framework.

Principally, the committees enable the members of the boards in a financial conglomerate to exchange their views, to increase synergy, and to make full use of their expertise in handling a great number of complex corporate governance issues in the financial conglomerate effectively and efficiently. They also facilitate the member of the boards within a financial conglomerate in developing and ensuring the effective implementation of integrated corporate governance and integrated risk management guidelines across the entities within the group. Furthermore, by providing constructive recommendations, the committees might improve good corporate governance practices in accordance with the principles of transparency, accountability, responsibility, and fairness in the financial conglomerate as a whole and in each of its member entities. Yet, it is important to understand that the committees do not supplant the responsibility of the boards of the lead entity. They only provide recommendation to the boards of the lead entity in relation to the implementation of integrated corporate governance in a financial conglomerate. The ultimate responsibility still rests with the boards of the lead entity. Hence, the boards of the lead entity should be able to skilfully use the committees for supporting the implementation of their responsibility.

8.4.1.4 Integrated Risk Management

It has been well recognised that effective risk management is a cornerstone of good corporate governance practices, particularly in financial institutions (see e.g., OECD 2014; Group of Thirty 2012). Thus, it is not surprising that the Integrated Regulation requires the boards of the lead entity to implement integrated risk management in the financial conglomerate in accordance with the requirements stipulated in the OJK Regulation No.17/POJK.03/2014, which is further implemented through Circular Letter No. No.14/SEOJK.03/2015 (art. 27). The latter regulation specifies responsibilities of the BOD of the lead entity in integrated risk management that include:

- Establishing integrated risk management policies and procedures that cover risk strategy, risk appetite, risk tolerance, and risk limits of the entire group;
- Implementing the integrated risk management policies and procedures;
- Developing a strong risk culture and awareness in the entire group;
- Ensuring adequacy of human resources that include competency, qualification, and quantity for implementing integrated risk management;
- Ensuring the operational independence of the integrated risk management unit;
- Reviewing integrated risk management processes conducted by the integrated risk management unit periodically; and
- Evaluating and adjusting the risk management strategy and systems at least once a year.

It also stipulates that the BOC of the lead entity has the responsibility to direct, approve, and evaluate integrated risk management policies that have been developed by the BOD of the lead entity. The BOC of the lead entity is also responsible to evaluate the implementation of integrated risk management. In implementing these responsibilities, the BOC of the lead entity has to review the policies and implementation of integrated risk management at least once a year.

To effectively implement the responsibilities relating to integrated risk management, the boards of the lead entity should have sufficient knowledge of the business activities and risks of the member entities within the group. They must also understand the interaction between risks from different member entities or business lines in the financial conglomerate and the aggregation of the risks at the group level. Thus, they can establish and implement effective integrated risk management systems in a financial conglomerate as a whole. Furthermore, the boards of the lead entity need to establish an integrated risk management unit to support the implementation of integrated risk management. In this regards, the latter regulation mentioned above stipulates that the boards of the lead entity may also expand the duties and responsibilities of the existing risk management unit in its company to perform the integrated risk management function, so that it does not need to establish a new unit.

The integrated risk management unit or function unit has broad duties regarding the implementation of integrated risk management practices. Those duties include:

- Providing recommendations on the integrated risk management policies to the BOD of the lead entity;
- Monitoring the implementation of the integrated risk management policies;
- Developing tools and procedures for identifying, measuring, monitoring, and controlling the entire risks in the financial conglomerate (i.e., credit risk, market risk, liquidity risk, operational risk, legal risk, reputational risk, strategic risk, compliance risk, intra-group transactions and exposure, and insurance risk);
- Conducting stress testing periodically;
- Reviewing the accuracy of risk assessment methodology, the adequacy of management information systems, and the adequacy of policies, procedures, and limits periodically;
- Assessing new business activity or new products that might impact the risk exposures of the group;
- Reporting to the integrated risk management committee on the issues that need to be followed up based on the evaluation of the implementation of integrated risk management;
- Providing recommendations regarding the establishment and enhancement of integrated risk management policies to the integrated risk management committee; and
- Providing periodic reports on the implementation of integrated risk management processes to the assigned risk management director and to the integrated risk management committee.

In performing its duties, the integrated risk management unit should closely coordinate with the risk management unit at each member entity. The coordination should be aimed to ensure the accuracy, adequacy, and availability of information on the risk exposure as well as risk assessment at each member entity, so that, the integrated management unit might produce comprehensive group-wide risk profile adequately. Such a comprehensive group-wide profile is important for the boards of the lead entity and financial supervisors to decide appropriate prompt corrective actions to minimise the risks in financial conglomerates at group level as well as at the entity level. However, in practice, the integrated risk management unit or function might have difficulty in implementing those duties since it faces confidentiality issues surrounding data and information provisions stipulated in the banking law and capital market law, as will be discussed below.

8.4.1.5 Internal Control: Integrated Compliance and Internal Audit Units

Good corporate governance requires effective internal control to be in place to provide assurance of the effectiveness of corporate governance mechanisms, compliance with the laws, regulations, and internal policies and procedures, and the reliability of corporate reporting. Based on best practices, the internal control should be assigned to independent units that have direct access to the boards (see OECD 2015, p. 49). Thus, the Integrated Regulation requires the boards of the lead entity to establish an independent integrated compliance unit and integrated audit unit, as highlighted above. It, however, stipulates that the boards of the lead entity can expand the duties and responsibilities of the existing compliance unit and internal audit unit in its company to perform the integrated compliance and internal audit functions, so that, they do not need to establish new units. It also implicitly requires each of the member entities of the financial conglomerate through the integrated corporate governance guidelines to establish similar internal control units in its company. Although both the integrated compliance unit and integrated internal audit unit represent similar critical control components of the financial conglomerate, they serve two different roles.

The integrated compliance unit or function is meant to assure the compliance of the financial conglomerate as a group to the prevailing laws, rules, and regulations, as well as internal guidelines, policies, and procedures. These include the integrated corporate governance guidelines and integrated risk management policies and procedures. Broadly, it has responsibility to conduct periodic reviews for assessing the compliance of entire business products and activities of the financial conglomerate, identifying key areas where there is a high possibility of non-compliance, conducting internal investigations on compliance issues, and advising solutions to handle the compliance issues. It should also help to educate staff throughout the group about compliance matters, act as a single point of contact within the financial conglomerate for compliance queries, and provide written compliance guidelines and manuals on the appropriate implementation of laws, rules, and regulations as well as internal policies and procedures. It has also responsibility to monitor and evaluate the implementation of compliance in each of member entities within the group (art. 22). In this regards, the integrated compliance unit should cooperate with the compliance unit or function in each of member entities within the group. Furthermore, it should provide advice of the boards of the lead entity on the laws, rules, and regulations related to the financial conglomerate as well as its member entities and keep them updated on developments in the area. In conducting its duties, the integrated compliance unit reports to the compliance director of the lead entity or the appointed director who is responsible for supervising compliance functions of the member entities within a financial conglomerate (art. 23 par. 1). This director then informs the boards of the lead entity about the implementation of responsibilities and duties of the integrated compliance unit (art. 23 par. 2).

The Integrated audit unit function is largely devised to monitor and evaluate the internal control environment in the financial conglomerate as a whole to ensure its adequacy, efficiency, and effectiveness. As the Institute of Internal Auditors (2016) states, "the internal audit activity helps an organisation accomplish its objectives by bringing a systematic, disciplined approach to evaluate and improve the effectiveness of governance, risk management, and control processes" (p. 23). As such, the integrated audit unit or function should deliver independent, unbiased assessments of the operations of financial conglomerates as a whole; provide the boards of the lead entity with information of the effectiveness of integrated corporate governance as well as the integrated risk management framework, guidelines, policies, procedures, and processes; act as a catalyst for improving control, governance, and risk management in the financial conglomerate; and provide consultation to the management to improve performance and control. It has also responsibilities to conduct periodic reviews on the achievement of the financial conglomerate as a group, to assess if the decisions made by management are already properly authorised in accordance to the established policies and procedures, to assess the reliability and integrity of information, to review asset safeguards, to assess the compliance of management within the financial conglomerate with the applicable laws, rules, and regulations, to evaluate efficiency, effectiveness, and economy of business activities within the group, to investigate any misconduct and fraud, and to follow-up previous audit findings to ensure remedial actions have been effectively taken and implemented. The Integrated internal audit has also responsibility to monitor and to evaluate the effective implementation of internal audit in each of the member entities (art. 25). Therefore, it is important for the integrated internal audit to closely coordinate with the internal audit of each member entity within the group. The integrated internal audit reports to the appointed director of the lead entity who is responsible to oversee the member entities in the financial conglomerate, the BOC of the lead entity, and to the compliance director or appointed director of the lead entity who is responsible for the compliance functions (art. 25).

Accordingly, the effectual performance of integrated compliance and internal audit units or functions aim to provide assurance to the boards of the lead entity, financial supervisors, and other recognised stakeholders that the financial conglomerate is governed effectively and efficiently. They are also expected to minimise the multi-faceted problems of corporate governance in the financial conglomerate, as discussed above, and to improve transparency, accountability, responsibility, and fairness of financial conglomerates as a whole and its member entities. Yet, the integrated compliance and internal audit units or functions might face difficulties in performing their responsibilities effectively because of the legal separateness of entities within the group and non-existence of direct reporting lines to the integrated committees, as will be discussed further below.

8.4.1.6 Disclosure

Good corporate governance demands transparency through adequate public disclosure that may promote well functioning market discipline (see OECD 2015, p. 37). Such disclosure is typically required at minimum on an annual basis, although it may also be provided on quarterly or a semi-annual basis. Therefore, to promote transparency of financial conglomerates in Indonesia, the Integrated Regulation requires the lead entity to provide annual reports on the implementation of integrated corporate governance of the financial conglomerate (art. 46 par. 1). This report should cover at least (1) the result of the self-assessment on implementation of integrated corporate governance of the financial conglomerate that covers the components of integrated corporate governance framework, as mentioned above, (2) the financial conglomerate structure and its larger business group structure (if any), (3) ownership structure of the financial conglomerate including its ultimate shareholder that also includes each party who is the shareholder in the member entities, (4) management structure of the financial conglomerate and its member entities, and (5) policies and procedures on intragroup transactions and exposures. Such a report can be combined into the lead entity general annual report or can also be provided separately (art. 46 par. 4). The Integrated Regulation also stipulates that the lead entity must upload the report into its homepage at the latest 5 months after the end of a financial year (art. 46 par. 3), so that, stakeholders can easily access it.

The annual report on the implementation of integrated corporate governance is expected to be able to minimise the lack of transparency issue in financial conglomerates. It generally provides qualitative information on the governance policies, procedures, and processes in financial conglomerates. Yet, such mandatory disclosure is not enough and may not be able to promote well functioning of market discipline, as will be discussed below.

8.4.2 Legal Issues and Gaps

Although the requirements in the Integrated Regulation might minimise the problems of corporate governance in financial conglomerates and promote their transparency, accountability, responsibility, and fairness, those requirements may raise legal concerns and issues because they conflict with provisions in company law, banking law, and capital market law, as already highlighted above. Moreover, the Integrated Regulation has not fully addressed the corporate governance issues in financial conglomerates. Six major legal concerns, issues, and gaps will be discussed further below.

First and *foremost*, it is important to recall that the Integrated Regulation is a delegated regulation. Based on the Law No.12 of 2011 on the Establishment of Legislations, the provisions in a delegated regulation cannot override and should not contravene the provisions in the primary law that has higher legislative hierarchy. This law adopted the so-called principle of *lex superior derogate lex inferiori*, which means that the law in higher hierarchy repeals the lower one. Furthermore, this law also stipulates that in the event that an interested party considers the delegated regulation conflicts with the primary law, it may request judicial review by the Supreme Court. Hence, the Integrated Regulation may be annulled when an interested party submits a juridical review. Fortunately, there has been no legal dispute relating to the conflicting regulatory issues and there has been no interested party submit a case for judicial review to date.

Second, the lead entity concept conflicts with the single entity concept adopted in company law. Under the latter concept, a company is a separate legal entity distinct from its members. It has independency in performing its legal conduct and being held liable for any of its legal conduct. This also implies that "any conduct performed by the company is considered solely as the conduct of the company, the yields of which is being attributed as its properties. Similarly, losses and liabilities of such company are burdened to that company" (Sulistiowati 2011, p. 47). As such, a company could not be held liable or responsible for any legal conduct performed by other companies. It also cannot intervene to the business activities, including strategies, policies, and procedures, of other companies. Indeed, the close relationship between parent and its subsidiaries does not mean that the parent has a right to intervene into business activities of its subsidiaries or become fully liable for any legal conduct performed by them. Yet, the Integrated Regulation disregards the single entity concept and considers a group of financial institutions or a financial conglomerate as a single entity through its lead entity, as discussed above. It also upholds that the lead entity is responsible to establish and implement the integrated corporate governance of the financial conglomerate as a whole. Such responsibility includes the establishment of integrated corporate governance guidelines and integrated risk management strategies, policies, and procedures that should be adopted and implemented by each of member entity within the group and monitoring of the effective implementation of those guidelines, strategies, policies, and procedures. These conflicting regulatory concepts may raise legal concerns and issues for both the member entity within the group and the lead entity itself. The member entity concerns that the lead entity might misuse its authority and responsibility for its own benefits through integrated corporate governance guidelines and integrated risk management strategies, policies, and procedures. When such conditions occurr the member entity must bear all the losses while the lead entity can hide behind the single entity concept and does not have to compensate for those losses. The lead entity also concerns that the requirements of Integrated Regulation may increase its legal and compliance risks due to two main reasons. First, the creditors of the member entity may file a claim to the court against the lead entity for its losses when the member entity conducts inappropriate behaviour or activities by contending that the lead entity has failed to ensure the effective implementation of integrated corporate governance of the financial conglomerate and its member entity, although the lead entity had done the best to implement integrated corporate governance in accordance with the requirement stipulated in the Integrated Regulation. Second, the appointed sister company as the lead entity concerns that it might not be able to implement the integrated corporate governance effectively because it has no direct legal mechanism to influence the member entities' or sister companies' strategies, policies, procedures, and activities, which is different from the parent company as the lead entity that has a direct legal mechanism through general shareholder meetings to determine its subsidiaries' strategies, policies, procedures, and activities. Overall, these conflicting concepts may impede the effectiveness of Integrated Regulation to achieve its objectives in enhancing good corporate governance practices in financial conglomerates as a whole, including in its member entities.

Third, company law stipulates that the fiduciary duty of the boards of a company is to act for the best interests of the company, not for the interests of the controlling party or the group. Accordingly, the boards must act independently and objectively when making any decision for the company. As explained by Komite Nasional Kebijakan Governance (National Committee on Governance) in the Indonesian Code of Corporate Governance (2006), the boards of a company "must avoid the occurrence of domination by any party, must not be influenced by any certain interests, must be free from conflict of interests and any influence or pressure, so that the decision making can be carried out objectively" (p. 6). However, the Integrated Regulation implicitly requires that the boards of member entities should follow directions from the boards of the lead entity for the interests of the group relating to integrated corporate governance, including integrated risk management. These conflicting requirements have created legal ambiguity and uncertainty for the boards of the member entity, as they must choose which legislation to follow. When they chose to follow the company law requirements to act independently and objectively for the interest of the company, they may need to refuse the directions from the boards of the lead entity that aim to achieve the interests of the group. As such, it would become difficult for the boards of the lead entity to ensure the effective implementation of integrated corporate governance of financial conglomerates in their entirety as a group.

Fourth, Indonesian banking law and capital market law has adopted confidentiality provisions. The banking law requires that the boards, managers, and employees of a bank shall keep the information on deposit customers and their deposits confidential. The capital market law also requires the boards, managers, and employees of securities firms to keep the confidentiality of material information that includes data, events, and incidents that may affect the price of securities or that may influence the decision of investors, prospective investors or others that have interests in such information. Failure to do so may result in criminal penalties for each of the boards, managers, and employees of financial institutions. Yet, the Integrated Regulation requires the lead entity to conduct integrated risk management assessment that that takes into account all risks from different business lines or entities within the group and the relationship between those risks as mentioned. This requirement leads to a legal issue for the lead entity as well as member financial institutions. On the one hand, the lead entity would certainly need abundant material information and data from member financial institutions to properly assess the overall risk profile of the financial conglomerate. On the other hand, member financial institutions would not be able to provide confidential information and data, such as information on large deposits for assessing liquidity risk and/or sensitive non-public market information of a securities firm for assessing market risk and operational risk. Hence, the result of these conditions may be that either the lead entity would fail to properly assess the group-wide risk profile or the member financial institutions should this violate secrecy provisions. Furthermore, the lead entity may also find difficulties in conducting integrated risk management assessment because of the different regulatory approaches for measuring similar types of risk between financial sectors. Overall, all of these issues may impede the effectiveness of Integrated Regulation to achieve its objective in minimising the issue of consolidated risk management in financial conglomerates.

Fifth, the legal entity concept and confidentiality provisions on specific information might also present issues for the integrated compliance and internal audit units or functions. As mentioned above, the integrated compliance and internal audit units or functions are established at the lead entity to provide assurance of the effectiveness of internal corporate governance mechanisms, compliance with the laws, regulations, and internal policies and procedures, and the reliability of corporate reporting. Accordingly, they need direct access to all necessary information and explanation from the member entities within the group for conducting their responsibility effectively. However, a question arises is that to what extent a division in one company can get such access from other companies. Based on the legal entity concept, it is clear that a division in one company has no right to demand such direct access from another company without explicit assignment from its boards. Moreover, the confidentiality provisions also prohibit the bank and securities firm for providing specific information related to their customers to other parties, including the integrated compliance and internal audit units that might not be the divisions at the bank or securities firm. Thus, the integrated compliance and internal audit units may not easily gain direct access to necessary information and explanation from staff and management at the member entities. Although these units may finally get such direct access from the boards of the member entities, the Integrated Regulation only requires them to report to the boards of the lead entity. Hence, these units face a lack of legal basis for reporting directly to the boards of member entities to provide important information relating to compliance and control issues. Correspondently, the boards of member entities might not be able to immediately follow-up their findings. All these issues and gaps may eventually impede the effectiveness of integrated compliance and internal audit units in implementing their responsibilities effectively.

Last but not least, the Integrated Regulation requires the lead entity for disclosing annual report about the implementation of integrated corporate governance to promote transparency of financial conglomerate, yet it does not require the lead entity to provide consolidated financial statements nor to disclose intra-group transactions and exposures. It also does not require the lead entity to disclose the risk profile of the financial conglomerate to outside investors and other recognised stakeholders. As such, they may still find difficulty to comprehend the entire performance as well as risks of the financial conglomerate and its member entities. Such situations may decrease market discipline that is valuable to minimise the problems of corporate governance in financial conglomerates.

8.5 Suggestion for Further Legal Reform

The legal issues and gaps discussed above need legal solutions from the government. The conflicting regulations have created legal uncertainty and ambiguity for the parties within a financial conglomerate, as they must choose which regulations are most important to follow. Certainly, following the requirements of one regulation might result in non-compliance of other regulations. Moreover, the Integrated Regulation still lacks comprehensive requirements to promote transparency, accountability, responsibility, and fairness in financial conglomerates. Therefore, this chapter proposes the OJK as well as the government (the legislators) to conduct further legal reform to solve the issues and gaps in order to enhance the Integrated Regulation.

In conducting the legal reform, this chapter suggests the legislators to enact a particular primary law for financial conglomerates. The new law should establish clear legal relationships and liabilities between the lead entity and member entities. In this regard, the lead entity can intervene in other member entities' policies, procedures, and activities through particular legal agreements and it must compensate the losses when the intervention results in a detrimental impact to the member entities within a financial conglomerate or their outside investors. The new law should also clarify the fiduciary duty of the boards of companies within financial conglomerates. It must specify new fiduciary duty for the boards of the lead entity that annuls the fiduciary duty adopted in company law. Furthermore, the new law should annul the confidentiality provisions in the banking law and capital market law for the purpose of the integrated risk assessment of financial conglomerates. It should also mandate the OJK to harmonise the different regulatory treatment of risks of financial institutions. Finally, it must require the financial conglomerate to enhance its disclosure to include consolidated financial statements, detail intragroup transactions and exposures, and clearly present a detailed risk profile of the financial conglomerate and its member entities. Thus, this new law might minimise the legal issues and gaps as discussed above, enhance the Integrated Regulation, and promote good corporate governance practices in financial conglomerates as a whole.

8.6 Conclusion

This chapter has discussed that financial conglomerates as a corporate group pose particular corporate governance issues due to their complexity. The issues include complex organisational structures and a lack of transparency, the use of matrix management and less-clear accountability, consolidated risk management issues, moral hazard, conflicts of interests, and tunnelling. These issues might adversely impact outside investors' and other recognised stakeholders' interests. The OJK as the financial authority has addressed some of the issues through the enactment of Integrated Regulation. This regulation requires financial conglomerate to establish and to implement integrated corporate governance for the group that promotes principles of transparency, accountability, responsibility, and fairness. However, several major requirements have given rise to legal issues as they conflict with the provisions in company law, banking law, and capital market law. Several legal issues have been identified to include unclear legal relationships and liability between the lead entity and member entities, conflicting requirements related to the fiduciary duty of boards, and the confidentiality provisions in the banking law and company law that might create difficulty for conducting adequate risks assessment of financial conglomerates. Furthermore, the Integrated Regulation has not fully addressed financial conglomerates' corporate governance issues, particularly the lack of transparency of financial performance, risk profile, and intragroup transactions and exposures. Therefore, this chapter proposes that the OJK and Government need to collaborate to conduct further legal reform. Particularly, the Government needs to enact a specific law for financial conglomerates. The new law should be able to address the issues mentioned in order to strengthen the Integrated Regulation.

References

Adams, R. B., & Mehran, H. (2012). Bank board structure and performance: Evidence for large bank holding companies. *Journal of Financial Intermediation, 21*(2), 243–267. https://doi.org/10.1016/j.jfi.2011.09.002.

Associations of Supervisors of Banks of the Americas, Work Group No. 3. (2007). *Consolidated supervision*. Retrieved from http://www.asbasupervision.com/en/todos/biblioteca-virtual-esp/i-publicaciones-asba/i-1-grupos-de-trabajo/757-gt04-2/file

Avgerinos, Y. (2003). *Regulating and supervising investment services in the European Union*. New York: Palgrave MacMillan.

Bank of Japan. (2005). *The expansion of corporate groups in the financial services industry: Trends in financial conglomeration in major industrial countries*. Retrieved from https://www.boj.or.jp/en/research/brp/ron_2005/data/ron0512b.pdf

Bank Indonesia, *Peraturan Bank Indonesia No.8/4/PBI/2006 tentang Pelaksanaan Good Corporate Governance Bagi Bank Umum* [Bank Indonesia Regulation No.8/4/PBI/2006 on the implementation of good corporate governance for commercial banks].

Bank Indonesia, *Peraturan Bank Indonesia No.8/6/PBI/2006 tentang Penerapan Manajemen Risiko Konsolidasi Bagi Bank yang Mengendalikan Perusahaan Anak* [Bank Indonesia

Regulation No.8/6/PBI/2006 on the implementation of consolidated risk management for bank that controls subsidiaries companies].

Bank Indonesia, *Peraturan Bank Indonesia No.8/16/PBI/2006 tentang Kepemilikan Tunggal Pada Perbankan Indonesia* [Bank Indonesia Regulation No.8/16/PBI/2006 on single presence policy in Indonesia banking].

Bank Indonesia, *Peraturan Bank Indonesia No.14/14/PBI/2012 tentang Transparansi dan Publikasi Laporan Bank* [Bank Indonesia Regulation No.14/14/PBI/2012 on bank report transparency and publication].

Barth, M. E., & Landsman, W. R. (2010). How did financial reporting contribute to the financial crisis? *European Accounting Review, 19*(3), 399423. https://doi.org/10.1080/09638180.2010.498619.

Basel Committee on Banking Supervision [BCBS]. (2015). *Guidelines corporate governance principles for banks*. Bank for International Settlements, Basel, Switzerland. Retrieved from http://www.bis.org/bcbs/publ/d328.pdf

Berger, A. N., Demsetz, R. S., & Strahan, P. E. (1999). The consolidation of the financial services industry: Causes, consequences, and implications for the future. *Journal of Banking and Finance, 23*(2), 135–194. https://doi.org/10.1016/S03784266(98)001253.

Blume, D. (2014, November). *Corporate governance of company group: International and Latin America experience*. Paper presented at the Latin America Roundtable Task Force on Corporate Governance of Company Groups. Retrieved from https://www.oecd.org/daf/ca/2014LatinAmericaCorporateGovernanceRoundtableCompanyGroups.pdf

Boyd, J. H., Graham, S. L., & Hewitt, R. S. (1993). Bank holding company mergers with nonbank financial firms: Effects on the risk of failure. *Journal of Banking and Finance, 17*(1), 43–63. https://doi.org/10.1016/0378-4266(93)90079-S.

Burke, R., & Baron, S. (2014). *Project management leadership: Building creative teams* (2nd ed.). West Sussex: Wiley.

Claessens, S., Djankov, S., & Lang, L. H. P. (2000). The separation of ownership and control in East Asian corporations. *Journal of Financial Economics, 58*(1), 81–112. https://doi.org/10.1016/S0304405X(00)000672.

Claessens, S., Djankov, S., Fan, J. P. H., & Lang, L. H. P. (2002). Disentangling the incentive and entrenchment effects of large shareholdings. *The Journal of Finance, 57*(6), 2741–2771. https://doi.org/10.1111/1540 6261.00511.

Clarke, T. (2015). Systemic crises in global markets: In search of regulatory and sustainable solutions. In A. Gűler (Ed.), *Sustainable markets for sustainable business: A global perspective for business and financial markets* (pp. 191–218). Burlington: Gower Publishing.

Committee on the Financial Aspects of Corporate Governance. (1992). *Report with code of best practice (Cadbury Report)*. London: Gee Publishing.

Cranston, R. (1990). Conflicts of interest in the multifunctional financial institution. *Brooklyn Journal of International Law, 16*(1), 125–143.

Crockett, A., Harris, T., Mishkin, F. S., White, E., & Francis, J. (2003). *Conflict of interest in the financial service industry: What should we do about them?* London: Centre for Economic Policy Research.

Daniel, W. E. (2003). Corporate governance in Indonesian listed companies—A problem of legal transplant. *Bond Law Review, 15*, 345–375.

Davis, S. M. & Lawrence, P. R. (1987, May). *Problems of matrix management*. Retrieved from https://hbr.org/1978/05/problems-of-matrix-organizations

Delimatsis, P. (2011). Financial innovation and transparency in turbulent times. *Journal of Financial Transformation, 33*, 99–112.

Dierick, F. (2004). *The supervision of mixed financial services groups in Europe* (European Central Bank Occasional Paper No.20). Retrieved from http://www.ecb.europa.eu/pub/pdf/scpops/ecbocp20.pdf

Faccio, M., Lang, L. H. P., & Young, L. (2001). Dividends and expropriation. *The American Economic Review, 91*(1), 5478. https://doi.org/10.1257/aer.91.1.54.

Fanto, J. A. (2010). Breaking up is hard to do: Should financial conglomerates be dismantled? *University of Cincinnati Law Review, 79*(2), 553–586.

Farrar, J. (2012). The governance and regulation of complex conglomerates. In T. Clarke & D. Branson (Eds.), *The SAGE handbook of corporate governance* (pp. 520–529). London: Sage Publications.

Fernando, A. C. (2009). *Corporate governance: Principles, policies and practices*. New Delhi: Pearson Education.

Frederick, W. R. (2014). *Challenges in group governance the governance of cross-border bank subsidiaries*. Washington: International Finance Corporation.

Friedland, J. H. (1994). *The law and structure of the international financial system: Regulation in United States, EEC, and Japan*. Westport: Quorum Books.

Friedman, E., Johnson, S., & Mitton, T. (2003). Propping and tunneling. *Journal of Comparative Economics, 31*(4), 732–750. https://doi.org/10.1016/j.jce.2003.08.004.

Gregory, H. J., & Simms, M. E. (1999, October). *Corporate governance: What it is and why it matters*. Paper presented at the 9th International Anti-Corruption Conference, Kuala Lumpur.

Group of Ten. (2001, January). *Report on consolidation in the financial sector*. Bank for International Settlements, Basel, Switzerland. Retrieved from http://www.bis.org/publ/gten05.pdf

Group of Thirty. (2012). Toward effective governance of financial institutions. Retrieved from http://group30.org/images/uploads/publications/G30_TowardEffectiveGovernance.pdf

Hadden, T. (1992). The regulation of corporate groups in Australia. *University of New South Wales Law Journal, 15*(1), 61.

Hashmall, A. (2010). After the fall: A new framework to regulate "too big to fail" nonbank financial institutions. *New York University Law Review, 85*(3), 829–866.

Herring, R. J., & Santomero, A. M. (1990). The corporate structure of financial conglomerates. *Journal of Financial Services Research, 4*(4), 471–497. https://doi.org/10.1007/BF00122882.

IFC Advisory Service Indonesia and Otoritas Jasa Keuangan. (2014, January). *Indonesian corporate governance manual*. Retrieved from https://www.ifc.org/wps/wcm/connect/64185f0042cc3ab0b145fd384c61d9f7/Indonesia_CG_Manual_Feb2014. pdf?MOD=AJPERES

International Monetary Fund [IMF]. (2006, September). *South Africa: Selected issues*. IMF country report No.06/328. Retrieved from https://www.imf.org/external/pubs/ft/scr/2006/cr06328.pdf

International Organisation of Securities Commissions [IOSCO]. (1992). *Principle of supervision of financial conglomerates*. Retrieved from http://www.iosco.org/library/pubdocs/pdf/IOSCOPD23.pdf

Jackson, H. E. (1994). The expanding obligations of financial holding companies. *Harvard Law Review, 107*(3), 507.

Johnson, S., de Silanes, F. L., La Porta, R., & Shleifer, A. (2000). *Tunneling*. Paper presented at the American Economic Review Papers and Proceedings.

Joint Forum. (1999, February). *The supervision of financial conglomerates*. Bank for International Settlements, Switzerland. Retrieved from http://www.bis.org/publ/bcbs47.pdf

Joint Forum. (2003, August). *Trends in risk integration and aggregation*. Bank for International Settlements, Switzerland. Retrieved from http://www.bis.org/publ/joint07.pdf

Joint Forum. (2012, September). *Principles for the supervision of financial conglomerates*. Bank for International Settlements, Basel, Switzerland. Retrieved from http://www.bis.org/publ/joint29.pdf

Khanna, T., & Rivkin, J. W. (2006). Interorganizational ties and business group boundaries: Evidence from an emerging economy. *Organization Science, 17*(3), 333–352.

Khanna, T., & Yafeh, Y. (2007). Business groups in emerging markets: Paragons or parasites? *Journal of Economic Literature, 45*(2), 331372. https://doi.org/10.1257/jel.45.2.331.

Kirkpatrick, G. (2004, November). *Corporate governance and company groups: Considerations from the OECD Principles*. Paper presented at the KDI Conference on Corporate Governance of Company Groups, Seoul: South Korea.

Kirkpatrick, G. (2009). The corporate governance lessons from the financial crisis. *OECD Journal: Financial Market Trends, 2009*(1), 61–87.

Komite Nasional Kebijakan Governance [National Committee on Governance] (2006). Pedoman good corporate governance Indonesia [Indonesia code of corporate governance]. http://www.ecgi.org/codes/documents/indonesia_cg_2006_en.pdf

Kuritzkes, A., Schuermann, T., & Weiner, S. M. (2003). Risk measurement, risk management, and capital adequacy in financial conglomerates. *Brookings-Wharton Papers on Financial Services, 2003*(1), 141–193. https://doi.org/10.1353/pfs.2003.0005.

Laeven, L., & Levine, R. (2007). Is there a diversification discount in financial conglomerates? *Journal of Financial Economics, 85*(2), 331–367. https://doi.org/10.1016/j.jfineco.2005.06.001.

LaPorta, R., LopezdeSilanes, F., Shleifer, A., & Vishny, R. (2000). Investor protection and corporate governance. *Journal of Financial Economics, 58*(1), 3–27. https://doi.org/10.1016/S0304405X(00)000659.

LaPorta, R., Lopez-de-Silanes, F., Shleifer, A., & Vishny, R. W. (1998). Law and finance. *Journal of Political Economy, 106*(6), 1113–1155. https://doi.org/10.1086/250042.

Laux, C., & Leuz, C. (2009). The crisis of fairvalue accounting: Making sense of the recent debate. *Accounting, Organizations and Society, 34*(6), 826834. https://doi.org/10.1016/j.aos.2009.04.003.

Lumpkin, S. A. (2011). Risks in financial group structure. *OECD Journal: Financial Market Trends, 2*, 105–136.

Maman, D. (1999). Research Note: Interlocking ties within business groups in Israel—A longitudinal analysis, 1974–1987. *Organization studies, 20*(2), 323–339.

Massa, M., & Rehman, Z. (2008). Information flows within financial conglomerates: Evidence from the banks—mutual funds relation. *Journal of Financial Economics, 89*(2), 288–306. https://doi.org/10.1016/j.jfineco.2007.10.002.

Millstein, I. M. (1998, February 2). *The evolution of corporate governance in the United States.* Remarks at the World Economic Forum, Davos, Switzerland.

Mizruchi, M. S., & Marquis, C. (2006). *Interlocking directorates. International encyclopedia of economic sociology* (pp. 375–377). London: Routledge.

McVea, H. (1996). Financial conglomerates and conflicts of interest: Resolving a regulatory dilemma. *Northern Ireland Legal Quarterly, 47*(3), 239–259.

Nicoló, G. D., Bartholomew, P., Zaman, J., & Zephirin, M. (2004). Bank consolidation, internationalization, and conglomeration: Trends and implications for financial risk. *Financial Markets, Institutions & Instruments, 13*(4), 173–217. https://doi.org/10.1111/j.09638008.2004.00076.x.

Nurazi, R., Santi, F., & Usman, B. (2015). Tunneling: Evidence from Indonesia stock exchange. *Asian Academy of Management Journal of Accounting and Finance, 11*(2), 127–150.

Obata, Seki. (2002). *Pyramid business groups in East Asia: Insurance or tunneling?* (Working Paper No.2002–13) CEI Working Paper Series, Center for Economic Institutions, Institute of Economic Research, Hitotsubashi University. Retrieved from http://hermes-ir.lib.hit-u.ac.jp/rs/bitstream/10086/13923/1/wp2002-13a.pdf

OECD. (2003). *Experiences from the regional corporate governance roundtables.* Organisation for economic co-operation and development, Paris. Retrieved from http://www.oecd.org/daf/ca/corporategovernanceprinciples/23742340.pdf

OECD. (2014). Risk management and corporate governance. *OECD Publishing*. https://doi.org/10.1787/9789264208636-en.

OECD. (2015). G20/OECD Principles of corporate governance. Retrieved from http://www.oecd-ilibrary.org/docserver/download/2615021e.pdf?expires=1508980426&id=id&accname=guest&checksum=C273B20578846095080DE8CB6FDD243B

Otoritas Jasa Keuangan (OJK). *Peraturan OJK No.17/POJK.03/2014 tentang Penerapan Manajemen Risiko Terintegrasi Bagi Konglomerasi Keuangan* [OJK Regulation No.17/

POJK.03/2014 on the Implementation of Integrated Risk Management for Financial Conglomerates].

Otoritas Jasa Keuangan (OJK). *Peraturan OJK No.18/POJK.03/2014 tentang Penerapan Tata Kelola Terintegrasi Bagi Konglomerasi Keuangan* [OJK Regulation No.18/POJK.03/2014 on the Implementation of Integrated Corporate Governance for Financial Conglomerates].

Otoritas Jasa Keuangan (OJK). *Surat Edaran OJK No.14/SEOJK.03/2015 tentang Penerapan Manajemen Risiko Terintegrasi Bagi Konglomerasi Keuangan* [OJK Circular Letter No.14/SEOJK.03/2014 on the Implementation of Integrated Risk Management for Financial Conglomerates]

Otoritas Jasa Keuangan (OJK). *Surat Edaran OJK No.15/SEOJK.03/2015 tentang Penerapan Tata Kelola Terintegrasi Bagi Konglomerasi Keuangan* [OJK Circular Letter No.15/SEOJK.03/2016 on the Implementation of Integrated Corporate Governance for Financial Conglomerates]

Pierce, A., & Brennan, N. (2003). *Principles and practice of group accounts: A European perspective*. London: Thomson.

Rahadian, A., & Kaihatu, M. A. (2016). Tata kelola terintegrasi bagi konglomerasi keuangan dan kemandirian perseroan terbatas [Integrated corporate governance for financial conglomerates and independency of limited liability company]. *Jurnal Hukum dan Pasar Modal, 7*(12), 5–26.

Ramanlingam, B. (2013). *Aid on the edge of chaos: Rethinking international cooperation in a complex world*. London: Oxford University Press.

Renda, A., Ayadi, R., Lamandini, M., Cheliout, S., Mykolaitis, D., Naouar, A., & Valiante, D. (2009). *Tying and other potentially unfair commercial practices in the retail financial service sector*. Final Report submitted to the European Commission, DG Internal Market and Services. ETD/2008/IM/H3/78. Brussels: Centre for European Policy Studies. Retrieved from http://www.eurofinas.org/uploads/documents/policies/UCPD/report_en.pdf

Reurink, A. (2016). *Financial fraud: A literature review*. Max-Planck-Institut für Gesellschaftsforschung, Discussion Paper, No. 16/5. Retrieved from https://www.econstor.eu/bitstream/10419/141282/1/859161242.pdf

Santomero, A. M., & Eckles, D. L. (2000). The determinants of success in the new financial services environment: Now that firms can do everything, what should they do and why should regulators care? *Federal Reserve Bank of New York Economic Policy Review, 6*(4), 11–23.

Sato, Y. (2004). Corporate governance in Indonesia: A study on governance of business groups. In Y. Shimomura (Ed.), *Asian development experience 2* (pp. 88–136). Singapore: Institute of Southeast Asian Studies.

Shleifer, A., & Vishny, R. W. (1997). A survey of corporate governance. *The Journal of Finance, 52*(2), 737783. https://doi.org/10.1111/j.15406261.1997.tb04820.x.

Skipper, H. D. (2000). Financial services integration worldwide: Promises and pitfalls. *North American Actuarial Journal, 4*(3), 71–108.

Sulistiowati. (2011). *Extension of parent company's liability against third parties of subsidiary company*. Mimbar Hukum-Fakultas Hukum Universitas Gadjah Mada, pp. 40–58.

Sun, W., Stewart, J., & Pollar, D. (Eds.). (2011). *Corporate governance and financial crisis: International perspective*. Cambridge: Cambridge University Press.

Stiroh, K. J., & Rumble, A. (2006). The dark side of diversification: The case of US financial holding companies. *Journal of Banking and Finance, 30*(8), 2131–2161. https://doi.org/10.1016/j.jbankfin.2005.04.030.

Tabalujan, B. S. (2001). Corporate governance of Indonesian banks—The legal and business contexts. *Australian Journal of Corporate Law, 13*(1), 67.

Teen, M. Y. & Bennett, C. (2014). *Governance of company groups*. CPA Australia, The Iclif Leadership & Governance Centre. Retrieved from http://www.iclifgovernance.org/file/files/governance-co-groups.pdf

The Institute of Internal Auditor. (2016). *International standards for the professional practice of internal auditing (standards)*. Retrieved from https://na.theiia.org/standardsguidance/Public%20Documents/IPPF-Standards-2017.pdf

The World Bank (2006). Unlocking Indonesia's domestic financial resources: the role of Non-bank financial institutions. http://siteresources.worldbank.org/INTINDONESIA/Resources/Publication/280016-1168483675167/NBFIFinal_Ext.pdf

Tripartite Group. (1995, July). *The supervision of financial conglomerates: A report by the Tripartite Group of bank, securities and insurance regulators.* Bank for International Settlements, Basel, Switzerland. Retrieved from http://www.bis.org/publ/bcbs20.pdf

Tuch, A. F. (2014). Financial conglomerates and information barriers. *Journal of Corporation Law, 39*(3), 563–616.

Ulst, I. (2005). *Linkages of financial groups in the European Union: Financial conglomeration development in old and new member states.* Hungary: Central European University Press.

Van de Berghe, L., & Verweire, K. (1998). *Creating the future with all finance and financial conglomerates.* Dordrecht: Springer. https://doi.org/10.1007/978-1-4757-4881-9.

Van de Berghe, L. (1995). *Financial conglomerates: New rules for new players?* Dordrecht: Springer. https://doi.org/10.1007/978-94-011-0413-5.

Van Lelyveld, I., & Schilder, A. (2003). Risk in financial conglomerates: Management and supervision. *Brookings-Wharton Papers on Financial Services, 2003*(1), 195–224.

Walter, I. (2004). Conflicts of interest and market discipline among financial service firms. *European Management Journal, 22*(4), 361–376. https://doi.org/10.1016/j.emj.2004.06.004.

Wilmarth, A. E. (2002, July). *Controlling systemic risk in an era of financial consolidation.* Paper presented at IMF Seminar on Current Developments in Monetary and Financial Law, Washington, DC.

Wilmarth, A. E., Jr. (2009). The dark side of universal banking: Financial conglomerates and the origins of the subprime financial crisis. *Connecticut Law Review, 41*(4), 963–1050.

Wilmarth, A. E., Jr. (2010). Reforming financial regulation to address the toobigtofail problem. *Brooklyn Journal of International Law, 35*(3), 707–794.

Yiu, D. W., Chen, X., & Xu, Y. (2013). Corporate governance in business groups. In M. D. S. S. Wright, K. Keasey, & I. Filatotchev (Eds.), *The Oxford handbook of corporate governance* (pp. 465–488). Oxford: Oxford University Press.

Yoo, Y. E. (2010). Capital aadequacy regulation of financial conglomerates in the European union. (IMFS Working Paper Series No. 37).

Yoshino, N., Suzuki, K., Abe, K. & Kuhara, M. (2007). *Financial conglomeration in East Asian regional development.* Tokyo: Daiwa Institute of Research. Retrieved from http://www.asean.org/storage/images/archive/20738.pdf

Chapter 9
Does Diversity of Bank Board Members Affect Performance and Risk? Evidence from an Emerging Market

Bowo Setiyono and Amine Tarazi

9.1 Introduction

The financial crisis triggered in 2008 has called for further investigation on existing governance practices and board effectiveness in the banking industry. The poor performance of many banks has often been related to poor governance practices and the failure of board directors to perform in the best interest of stakeholders (Aebi et al. 2012; Beltratti and Stulz 2012; Berger et al. 2012; Erkens et al. 2012). Other papers have questioned whether board structure actually matters for firm performance (e.g., Adams and Ferreira 2007; Adams and Mehran 2012; Anderson et al. 2011; Ferreira 2010; Masulis et al. 2012; Pathan and Faff 2013). In this work, we look into various characteristics of board members such as gender, citizenship, age, experience, tenure, ethnicity, education level and type to investigate the impact of background diversity of board members on bank performance and risk.

Banks' performance is closely related to various factors such as regulatory scrutiny, the degree of financial development and the existence of public safety

This chapter is based on the second chapter of my Ph.D. dissertation. An earlier version of this working paper with Amine Tarazi (Setiyono and Tarazi 2014) appeared on as "Does Diversity of Bank Board Members Affect Performance and Risk? Evidence from an Emerging Market". Available at SSRN: https://ssrn.com/abstract=2491145

B. Setiyono (✉)
Université de Limoges, LAPE, 5 rue Félix Eboué, Limoges Cedex 87031, France

Universitas Gadjah Mada, Faculty of Economics and Business, Jl. Sosio Humaniora No. 1, Yogyakarta 55281, Indonesia
e-mail: bowo@ugm.ac.id

A. Tarazi
Université de Limoges, LAPE, 5 rue Félix Eboué, Limoges Cedex 87031, France
e-mail: amine.tarazi@unilim.fr

B. Díaz Díaz et al. (eds.), *Corporate Governance in Banking and Investor Protection*, CSR, Sustainability, Ethics & Governance,
https://doi.org/10.1007/978-3-319-70007-6_9

nets such as deposit insurance systems. It is well understood that the banking industry is characterized by higher opacity and more complex agency conflicts than other industries (Levine 2004; Morgan 2002). Also, because of deregulation and cross border expansion in most countries, banks have to deal with a more diverse environment to such an extent that it is imperative for them to consider a more diverse board. As such, board structure and its diversity can be crucial and significantly related to performance (Anderson et al. 2011). Furthermore, board structure is an important governance mechanism particularly in developing and emerging countries where other control mechanisms are commonly weaker (Claessens and Yurtoglu 2013). Hence, when directors are regarded as important resources to the firm, various dimensions regarding their background and skills clearly become important (Ferreira 2010).

Generally, board diversity refers to a situation in which members have different social, cultural and professional backgrounds (e.g., Milliken and Martins 1996; Erhardt et al. 2003). The main purpose of diversity is to enhance the ability of firms to tap into diverse markets and to increase market share within a global economy (Cox 2001). A more heterogeneous board offers benefits from diverse members' skills and experiences which serve as complementary sources to access resources and connections (Ferreira 2010). However, from another perspective, diversity (or heterogeneity) can be regarded as endogenous to the firm's characteristics and a way out when boards deal with agency problems. Increasing the level of diversity, for instance, does not necessarily bring in more benefits because of a failure to harmonize different backgrounds and mitigate potential conflicts among board members that could ultimately lead to negative net outcomes (e.g., Adams and Ferreira 2009; Baranchuk and Dybvig 2009). Also, it might only be regarded as an effort to comply with certain regulations (e.g. Davies et al. 2011, 2014) or to demonstrate an absence of discrimination and therefore its impact on organizational performance is unclear (Erhardt et al. 2003).

This study extends the existing literature on bank board governance in several ways. First, a large number of works on governance practices in non-financial firms find contrasting results and no clear-cut implication can therefore be drawn for banking (e.g., Campbell and Minguez-Vera 2008; Zhang 2007). Furthermore, the existing banking literature on emerging countries has paid more attention to institutional, regulatory and macroeconomic determinants of bank performance (e.g., Berger et al. 2010; Caprio et al. 2007; Chen and Kao 2011; Djankov et al. 2005). Second, unlike other studies on the banking industry (e.g., Adams and Mehran 2012; Liang et al. 2013; Mateos de Cabo et al. 2012; Pathan and Faff 2013), this paper considers not only a single measure of diversity (e.g. gender), but also other diversity indices that could potentially influence performance (i.e. citizenship, age, experience, tenure, ethnicity, nationality, education level and type) (Setiyono 2014). Third, Adams et al. (2010) note that the vast majority of the literature on board characteristics mainly focuses on Anglo-American firms and hence studies of boards in non-Anglo-American firms is an understudied area. We go beyond by using several diversity dimensions, particularly ethnicity and professional background, by focusing on an emerging country. Our study provides evidence on how diversity of board members affects bank performance in a relatively weak shareholder protection environment as highlighted by Claessens and Yurtoglu (2013). To our knowledge, this study is the first comprehensive study looking into the impact of board diversity on bank risk. We consider the case of Indonesia which is the fourth populated country in the world (250 million) with more than 1000 ethnic groups and 121 commercial banks including 10 foreign banks, making it an ideal laboratory to, furthermore, avoid cross country heterogeneity. In a country with weak investor protection rights, which is the case of this study, board structure and its diversity might have stronger effects in mitigating various incentive problems. This study also adds to the growing body of literature which investigates whether bank performance and risk during the global financial crisis of 2007/2008 can be partly explained by corporate governance mechanisms (Adams and Mehran 2012; Aebi et al. 2012; Beltratti and Stulz 2012; Erkens et al. 2012; Fahlenbrach and Stulz 2011). Moreover, in Asia, the less transparent process of nominating and appointing directors and scarce board evaluation increase the probability of poor-performing directors to be re-elected (OECD 2013). From this perspective, boards with a balanced diversity, and therefore presumably less prone to collusion of their members, are expected to more easily mitigate the lack of appropriate and sound external evaluation processes.

The rest of the paper is structured as follows. Section 9.2 shows how our work extends the current literature and provides a rationale for the tested hypotheses. Section 9.3 presents the Indonesian institutional setting and bank corporate governance. Data and the econometric specification are discussed in Sect. 9.4. Section 9.5 discusses the results. Section 9.6 concludes.

9.2 Related Literature and Research Focus

The board diversity literature is divided into various strands. The *resource based theory* argues that the board of directors (BOD) is a strategic resource by which a firm can get access to external sources such as funds, new skills or methods, and new opportunities. This theory is in-line with *human capital theory* suggesting that every person has unique and useful characteristics. Hence, a heterogeneous board also allows more and richer information to flow into the firm which can benefit from a broader information network. A more diverse board is regarded as positive for the firm and its financial performance (Carter et al. 2010; Fang et al. 2012; van der Walt and Ingley 2003). For non-financial firms, empirical studies have shown that heterogeneity is associated with positive outcomes such as more diverse perspectives, higher creativity and innovation, and better results in terms of risk and/or audit management (e.g., Brown et al. 2002; Robinson and Dechant 1997). In the banking industry, however, studies using board size to capture a higher-resourced Board of Directors (BoD) provide inconclusive results (e.g., Adams and Mehran 2012; Andres and Vallelado 2008).

Another large body of literature on board diversity is based on the *principal-agency theory*. Since the members of the board might have incentives to serve their own personal benefits and not those of shareholders, the board may need independent oversight (Adams et al. 2010; Fama 1980; Shleifer and Vishny 1997). Also, to conduct effective monitoring and advising roles, boards accordingly need the appropriate mix of experience and capabilities that can be achieved through a more diverse board (e.g., Hillman and Dalziel 2003) in the notion that a more diverse board will increase board independence (Carter et al. 2010, 2003). In contrast, Adams and Mehran (2012) find that board independence, which presumably is stronger as diversity increases, has no effect on bank performance.

Carter et al. (2010) argue that as a homogeneous group is built in a search of trust, any new member from the outside or from a different background might be considered as a threat. The addition of new a member might generate extra costs and reduce team cohesion and performance. Similarly, diversity could bring unintended consequences such as the lack of cooperation, inadequate qualifications, and conflicts of interest (Ferreira 2010). Nevertheless, *contingency theory* postulates that such diversity may still be desirable in some types of organizations and depending on specific circumstances at different times (Boyd 1990; Gabrielsson and Huse 2004). In other words, when board heterogeneity results in better outcomes (e.g. performance), it should be treated as imperative otherwise it should be reconsidered as unnecessary. For example, Pathan and Faff (2013) find that the excessive proportion of females on the board could adversely affect the possibility to catch more capable male directors.

Other studies argue that higher diversity could lead to negative outcomes (e.g., Ferreira 2010; Mueller 2003). To achieve optimal performance, the board not only needs better access to relevant information that could be brought by outside members, but also a timely and efficient decision making process. Heterogeneous boards may imply a trade-off between higher costs in terms of longer decision-making and the lower external costs associated with better information access (Mueller 2003). Elron (1997) observes that cultural heterogeneity and member diversity do not correlate with group cohesion although group cohesion is positively related to performance. This partly explains the fact that a heterogeneous board does not necessarily lead to better performance. In other words, while a more heterogeneous board might offer higher information efficiency it can hinder efficient decision-making. A heterogeneous board might also be superior in knowledge about the business environment and about other firms but does not necessarily come with superior knowledge about the firm itself. Other studies find that homogeneous teams outperform heterogeneous ones (e.g., Baranchuk and Dybvig 2009; Treichler 1995).

Similarly, previous studies find little evidence of any impact of gender heterogeneity on firm performance (see, e.g., Farrell and Hersch 2005; Terjesen et al. 2009; Darmadi 2011, 2013). Other studies have investigated other types of diversities with regard to expertise (Monks and Minow 2011), independent director characteristics (Anderson et al. 2004), minority group members (Westphal and Milton 2000) with various results.

In the case of emerging countries such issues can be further exacerbated by the lack of an appropriate institutional environment and protection for shareholders.

For instance, Khanna and Yafeh (2007) argue that the lack of transparency related to management structures often leads to worse corporate governance and expropriation of minority rights. Because ownership is often largely concentrated, the potential conflicts between majority and minority shareholders are generally more pronounced (e.g., Claessens and Fan 2002; Claessens and Yurtoglu 2013; Djankov et al. 2008). For this reason, Saito and Dutra (2006) argue that minority shareholders and the firm itself suffer from a dependency problem between the controlling shareholder and the board of directors. Hence, the structure and composition of board structures in such countries is crucial and there is a need for an appropriate mix (i.e., diversity) of board members combined with other governance mechanisms (e.g., independent directors, presence of block holders, *et cetera*).

There is much less research regarding the impact of board diversity on bank risk. Previous studies which are largely dedicated to non-financial firms suggest that women are more risk-averse than men and that their presence is associated with lower risk taking (e.g., Simpson et al. 2010; Mateos de Cabo et al. 2012). Adam and Ferreira (2004) argue that such a relationship might not be due to differences in gender risk aversion but, rather to a preference towards risk in homogenous environments—i.e. higher risk in a less diverse (fewer women) board. In contrast, Berger et al. (2012) provide evidence that a higher proportion of female executives in German banks leads to riskier activities.

A study by May (1995) suggests that older directors are more reluctant to take risk. Similarly, Berger et al. (2012) and Grable et al. (2009) find that younger teams are associated with higher risk-taking. Previous studies also consider the relationship between education level and risk to be either positive (Bertrand and Schoar 2003) or negative (Graham and Harvey 2001). Hence, how diversity could affect risk on this behalf remains an open question.

9.3 The Indonesian Institutional Setting and Bank Corporate Governance

Like others countries in Asia, Indonesia has experienced significant economic growth until the 1997 financial crisis hit the region. The crisis called for a review of the existing governance characteristics due to a high degree of ownership concentration by family/business groups (e.g., Claessens et al. 2000), excessive government-led growth (Hanazaki and Liu 2007), lack of transparency and control (Zhuang et al. 2000), and poor legal protection of investors (Obata 2003). Regarding the Indonesian banking sector, studies reveal that there is over reliance on external (foreign) funding in the corporate sector that in turn leads to vulnerable positions and higher credit risks (Batunanggar 2002). In addition, ineffective supervision by the two-tier board system and by creditors, as in Indonesia, has also contributed to the crisis (Asian Development Bank 2000; Claessens and

Yurtoglu 2013; Zhuang et al. 2000). In the post-crisis period (1997–2000), 61 banks were closed, 54 taken-over, and 39 recapitalized.

Accordingly, Bank Indonesia (BI) has introduced numerous regulations to promote good governance practices such as imposing a fit and proper test on bank board members, requiring a compliance director, and the introduction of independent board members (i.e., Bank Indonesia 2006). In the view of board diversity, however, there are only few regulations to address or encourage more diverse backgrounds of board members despite the fact that promoting diversity has proliferated particularly in the political context (i.e., 30% gender representation).

With regard to the board characteristics, there is only one regulation for Indonesian banking. The regulation on fit and proper tests for board candidates as stipulated by the regulation (PBI No.12/2010, which was latterly amended by the Indonesian Financial Service Authority/OJK Regulation No.27/POJK.03/2016) (Indonesian Financial Service Authority 2016a, b) sets the general procedures and targets of this test but does not specify detailed requirements for the candidate. Furthermore, it only suggests that the majority (more than 50%) of board members must have at least 5 years of banking experience. In relation to this, the current debate is on setting a minimum number of years of experience in the financial sector for board member candidates.

9.4 Data, Variables, and Empirical Setting

9.4.1 Sample

To perform our analysis, we use data from banks operating in Indonesia where there are 121 commercial banks and 1682 rural banks (Bank Indonesia 2010) serving more than 240 million people and more than 300 ethnic groups. Note that the Census 2010 by the Indonesia Central Bureau of Statistics (BPS), however, reveals there are 1128 ethnic groups that inhabit the country and speak more than 200 different local languages. There are more than 10 ethnic groups with population more than 1 million. However, because data on boards' profiles are rarely available our sample is limited to 38 commercial banks over the 2001–2011 period. Our sample banks nevertheless represent approximately 82.6% of aggregate bank assets during the period under study with 418 bank-year observations covering approximately 4200 individual-year observations and more than 21 ethnic groups. This includes state-owned banks, private banks and regional banks. We exclude rural banks because such banks operate in a very limited area and are very small. Due to data availability, we only have two foreign banks in our sample.

To construct our measures, we manually extract the profile of board members mainly from the annual reports, banks' web sites, and other relevant sources such as Indonesia Banking Institutes and news releases. Hence, when the first two sources do not provide sufficient information (e.g., the bank only provides the name and working experience of board members), we go to the next sources until we find the necessary information. For banks which are subsidiaries or owned by business groups, we are able to collect more detailed profiles of board members in the affiliated firm's reports/websites than in the bank's report itself to complete the data. We also retrieve data from particular columns of banking magazines and newspapers that publish bankers' profiles.

9.4.2 Variables Measurement

9.4.2.1 Measuring Diversity

Existing studies measure board diversity (heterogeneity) using two approaches—individual versus composite indices. In this study, we identify seven individual measures namely gender, nationality, ethnicity, experience, tenure, education level, and education type. We focus on our composite diversity measures based on ethnicity and nationality (Ethnog), experience and tenure (Professional), and education level and type (Education) in addition to gender diversity. Nevertheless, for robustness, we also use individual measures which we discuss later. Individual and composite measures are defined as follows.

To account for gender diversity, we calculate the proportion of women (Female) on the board as a proxy for gender diversity (see Appendix for detailed definition). Previous studies on diversity largely focus on gender as the main variable and show that stronger presence of women can either positively (e.g., Bilimoria 2000; Erhardt et al. 2003; Mattis 2000), negatively (Eklund et al. 2009), or non-significantly (Rose 2007) affect performance. Female directors commonly have higher expectations regarding their responsibility leading to better monitoring. Based on a sample of 612 European banks, Mateos de Cabo et al. (2012) conclude that the proportion of women on the board increases in lower-risk, larger boards and growth-oriented banks. In another study, Bellucci et al. (2010) find that Italian female loan officers are more risk-averse as they tend to restrict credit availability to new borrowers.

Studies on ethnic diversity have been less pronounced and virtually limited to certain countries due to ethnic characteristics in each country (e.g. too homogenous or unavailability of ethnicity data). Cox (2001) examines the quality of ideas generated by homogeneous groups of Whites and other groups comprising Asian Americans, Blacks, White, and Hispanics. They conclude that ideas generated by ethnically diverse groups were rated on average 11% higher than those of homogeneous groups both in terms of feasibility and effectiveness. Nevertheless, Carter et al. (2010) do not find any relation between ethnic heterogeneity on the boards of S&P 500 firms' performances. We measure ethnic heterogeneity (Ethnic diversity) based on the ethnicity of bank directors (e.g., Chinese, Javanese, Sundanesse, Batak, Malay, Caucasian, Minahasa, Bugis, Minang *et cetera*). We note that there are more than 1000 ethnic groups in Indonesia but we identify 21 ethnic groups that appear on the director profiles of this study. To compute ethnic diversity, we use Blau's index (see Harrison and Klein 2007) which is similar to the inverse of the Herfindal-Hirschman index (HHI) and formulated as follows:

$$\text{Diversity index} = 1/\sum_{\alpha}^{n}\left(\frac{N\alpha}{\mathrm{NT}}\right)^2 \tag{9.1}$$

Where Nα represents the number of directors in the αth category and NT represents the total number of directors. A higher value taken by the index represents a more diverse group (For further discussion, see Harrison and Sin 2006; Harrison and Klein 2007). Following Fang et al. (2012), for example, ethnic diversity = 1/[Chinese ratio^2 + Javanese ratio^2 + Sudanese ratio^2 + Bataknese ratio^2 + Malay ratio^2 + Minang ratio^2 + Javanese ratio^2].

Globalization and deregulation in banking have broadened the access of banks to various resources including foreign board members. One can argue that foreign board members will not only provide broader networks but also bring international perspective and experience to the recruiting banks. The bank could get advice on how the expansion to foreign markets should be established or how foreign banks operate in domestic markets. Liang et al. (2013) argue that foreign directors might bring new technology and managerial techniques, leading to better performance. In contrast, Masulis et al. (2012) find that foreign independent directors of the U.S. S&P-1500 firms is related to higher compensation, lower sensitivity of CEO turnover to performance and poorer firm performance. To account for this effect, we use Blau's index, based on the number persons who are foreign citizens and the others who are Indonesian. Each number is then divided by the total number of directors to compute the ratio of foreign directors (Foreign ratio) and the ratio of Indonesian directors (Indonesian ratio). Following Fang et al. (2012), Nationality diversity = 1/[Foreign ratio^2 + Indonesian ratio^2].

To consider ethnicity and nationality diversity as discussed above we build a variable named Ethnog diversity defined as the average of two components: Ethnic diversity and Nationality diversity. Hence Ethnog diversity = (Ethnic diversity + Nationality diversity)/2.

The resource dependent approach and human capital theory suggest that education and training can improve the value of people allowing them to have better knowledge and skills to achieve organizational goals. Simons et al. (1999) find that both educational and cognitive diversity are positively correlated with organizational performance. Following Anderson et al. (2011), we measure education heterogeneity based on its depth (education levels) and breadth (education types). For depth, we use the Blau index (Education level diversity) based on the highest degree of directors—i.e., whether he/she has no bachelor degree (S0), bachelor degree (S1), masters degree (S2), or doctoral degree/beyond (S3). We calculate the proportion of members in each educational level and measure the Blau index as formulated in Eq. (9.1). Specifically, education level diversity = 1/[S0 ratio^2 + S1 ratio^2 + S2 ratio^2 + S3 ratio^2]. While for breadth (Education type diversity), we divide the number of board members with education background other than economics, finance, accounting, and business by total board members. A higher figure indicates a more diverse board based on this background. To account for both diversities, we then measure education diversity as the average of education level and education type diversities.

Tenure essentially represents the length of time (e.g., years) a person has been sitting on the board and can be related to the business experience of a director. Hence, a longer-tenured director should lead to better performance. An increase in board tenure, however, is not only related to greater commitment but also more inflated CEO salaries (Vafeas 2003). In this study, tenure diversity (Tenure diversity) is measured by the standard deviation of tenure periods of board members. Next, working experience is important for directors to work effectively with other team members and to make better decisions. We measure the working experience by the length of time (years) a person has been working in the banking industry. This variable reflects the accumulated hand-on experience gained from the banking industry leading to higher human capital that in turn should allow the bank to achieve better performance. To estimate experience diversity (Experience diversity), we use the standard deviation of the years of banking experience. We compute the average of Tenure diversity and Experience diversity and name it Professional diversity.

9.4.2.2 Measuring Performance and Risk

This study uses several proxies to measure bank performance. First, we introduce the return on assets (ROA) of the bank that is defined as profits before taxes divided by its average assets (the mean value of bank's assets at time t and $t - 1$). We also consider the return on equity (ROE) defined as the ratio of profits before taxes to the average equity (the mean value of outstanding equity at time t and $t - 1$). Alternatively, we use two other measures of performance: (1) risk-adjusted return on assets (adjusted ROA) that is the ratio of ROA to its standard deviation calculated from the last three observations for the respective year; (2) risk-adjusted return on equity (adjusted ROE) that is the ratio of ROE to its standard deviation calculated from the last three observations for the respective year (i.e., t, $t - 1$ and $t - 2$).

In addition to the standard deviation of returns (SDROA and SDROE) to capture risk, we consider the Z-score (Goyeau and Tarazi 1992; Lepetit et al. 2008; Barry et al. 2011). This score is defined as (ROA + EA)/SDROA, where ROA is the bank's return on assets, EA is the ratio of equity to total assets. We also split the Z-score into its two components Z-score 1 defined as ROA divided by SDROA and Z-score 2 which is EA divided by SDROA. Z-score 1 is expected to measure asset risk and Z-score 2 leverage risk.

9.4.2.3 Control Variables

The size of the bank can be related to the bank's performance since a larger bank may be able to achieve cost reductions due to economies of scale. Hence, we consider the logarithm of total assets (e.g., Berger et al. 2005) to control for this dimension (Size). As size increases, banks may enjoy better portfolio diversification benefits leading to a negative relationship with risk. On the other hand, by increasing its size, a bank could also benefit from Too-Big-To-Fail (TBTF) safety net subsidies (De Nicolo 2000). Following Pathan and Faff (2013), we also include the total capital ratio defined as banks' total equity divided by its total assets (Capital). A well-capitalized bank is less likely to default and hence its cost of funding might be lower possibly leading to higher profitability (Berger 1995). Banks with higher levels of capital are able to sustain loss events more easily and hence avoid failure. Bank capital also determines the level of risk that banks might be willing to take. As such, this ratio is expected to capture the bank's degree of risk aversion.

A bank listed on a stock exchange is expected to be more closely monitored and subject to stronger market discipline leading to better performance. Following Liang et al. (2013), we include a dummy variable (Listed) that equals one (1) if the bank is listed and zero (0) otherwise. Publicly held banks should behave differently than their counterparts because they are subject to more stringent market discipline but at the same time they are able to raise additional equity at lower costs which allows them to invest in risky projects with higher returns. Hence, the effect of this variable is undetermined (Barry et al. 2011). We also use the loan to total assets ratio (Loan) to reflect the bank's strategy and its focus on traditional intermediation activities (Lin and Zhang 2009). On the one hand, banks with a lower loan to total assets ratio are less dependent on interest income and benefit more from diversification (DeYoung and Roland 2001). On the other hand, because regulators allow banks to hold less capital against non-interest activities, financial leverage will be larger which may raise earning volatility further (Demirgüç-Kunt and Huizinga 2010; DeYoung and Roland 2001). Banks with a higher share of loans in total assets can be more risky since they are more exposed to credit risk and therefore earning volatility (Maudos and Fernández de Guevara 2004). We further control for foreign ownership by considering a dummy variable (Foreign bank) which takes the value of 1 when foreign owners have stakes of at least 50% and zero otherwise (Barth et al. 2004). The presence of foreign owners could lead to lower cost of financial intermediation and thus lower profitability (Beck et al. 2008). Laeven (1999) argues that because foreign banks in South East Asia operate under more restrictions, particularly compared to state banks, they take less risk. We also consider if the bank is a member (subsidiary) of a business group by introducing a dummy variable (Business group) which takes the value of 1 if a bank belongs to a group and zero otherwise). A bank operating in a business group might be more inclined to serve the interests of its group and affiliated firms. Claessens and Fan (2002) argue that firms in a business group often deal with resource misallocation and poorer performance despite that such firms may be able to access funding at a lower cost. Claessens and Fan (2002) also highlight that a firm's risk strategy in East Asia is also influenced by group characteristics; group structure can be used to diversify risks internally. Eventually, to account for the global financial crisis of 2008 (Crisis) we introduce a dummy variable that takes the value of 1 for year 2008 and zero otherwise.

9.4.3 Empirical Model

We consider the following specification:

$$\text{Performance or Risk}_{i,t} = \alpha_0 + \beta_1 \text{Board Diversity}_{i,t} + \sum \beta_i \text{Controls}_{i,t} + \varepsilon_{i,t} \quad (9.2)$$

where Performance represents bank performance measured by either ROA, ROE, risk-adjusted ROA and risk-adjusted ROE. Risk is measured by either SDROA, SDROE, Z-score, Z-score 1, and Z-score 2. Board Diversity stands for the four categories of bank board heterogeneity that we consider in this study (i.e. Gender, Ethnog, Education, and Professional). Controls represent the matrix of control variables to account for bank characteristics and the financial crisis period.

Pathan et al. (2008) argue that empirical studies on board composition and performance suffer from endogeneity issues that partly come from the nature of the variables used in such studies. Board structure in a given year, for example, could be affected by the bank's performance in previous years. Hence, in their studies, Hermalin and Weisbach (2003), Adams et al. (2010), Carter et al. (2010), Anderson et al. (2011), Fang et al. (2012) use an instrumental variables/two-stage least-squares (IV/2SLS) specification. For this reason, we use the instrumental variables (IV) approach to deal with potential endogeneity as indicated by our reported tests in the following section.

9.5 Results

9.5.1 Descriptive Statistics

Before we go further, we exclude the extreme observations (1% lowest/highest values) to deal with possible outliers. We also drop negative values of capital as this implies that the bank is technically in default. Table 9.1 presents several descriptive statistics for the variables used in this study. Panel A describes the performance measures, ROA and ROE. The means of ROA and ROE during the 2001–2011 period are 2.2% and 18.5% respectively. We note that the average values of risk-adjusted ROA and risk-adjusted ROE are 5.4 and 5.1 respectively. The means of SDROA and SDROE are 1% and 9% respectively whereas those of Z-score, Z-score 1, and Z-score 2 are 9.9, 5.2, and 3.9 respectively.

As aforementioned, we calculate the diversity measures for each bank every year from 2001 to 2011. We note (Table 9.2), on average, a considerable increase in professional diversity, followed by Ethnog diversity (i.e., the sum of ethnicity and nationality diversity). Education diversity increases until 2004–2005 and decreases to 1.13 in 2011. Female members, however, only constitute around 8% (2001) to 10% (2011) of board members. Panel B of Table 9.1 shows the bank board characteristics that are used to measure diversity. Table 9.2 shows that Ethnog

Table 9.1 Descriptive statistics of performance, risk and diversity measures

Variable	Obs	Mean	Std. dev.	Min	Max
Panel A. Performance and risk measures					
ROA	395	0.022	0.013	0.001	0.084
ROE	394	0.185	0.115	0.000	0.612
Adjusted ROA	390	5.470	5.380	0.008	32.909
Adjusted ROE	390	5.135	5.274	0.007	29.573
SDROA	405	0.010	0.017	0.001	0.168
SDROE	405	0.090	0.179	0.005	2.213
Z-score	406	9.924	10.875	0.161	70.626
Z-score1	405	5.293	5.366	-0.527	32.909
Z-score2	405	3.956	5.839	0.017	48.853
Panel B. Board characteristics					
Female	414	0.094	0.100	0	0.4
Ethnog diversity	405	2.189	0.937	1	6.452
Professional diversity	393	5.942	1.453	1.938	9.313
Education diversity	395	1.220	0.386	0.556	4.010
Panel C. Control variables					
Capital	400	0.188	0.090	0.086	0.771
Loan	416	0.567	0.178	0.010	0.932
Foreign bank	418	0.227	0.420	0	1
Listed	418	0.474	0.500	0	1
Business group	418	0.589	0.493	0	1
Assets	418	40,100	72,700	105.55	424,000
Crisis	418	0.091	0.288	0	1

See Appendix for detailed descriptions

Table 9.2 Board diversity from 2001 to 2011

Year	Female div.	Ethnog div.	Professional div.	Education div.
2001	0.085	1.881	5.532	1.122
2002	0.084	2.086	5.599	1.312
2003	0.094	2.197	5.782	1.325
2004	0.083	2.200	5.763	1.334
2005	0.081	2.173	5.833	1.286
2006	0.093	2.206	5.804	1.250
2007	0.100	2.287	5.843	1.193
2008	0.104	2.220	6.060	1.150
2009	0.107	2.285	6.276	1.180
2010	0.107	2.246	6.303	1.148
2011	0.098	2.253	6.379	1.136
Total	0.094	2.189	5.942	1.220

diversity continuously increases over the sample period, although slowly, suggesting that banks tend to appoint more persons from other ethnicities or foreign countries.

Professional diversity measures the diversity in terms of working experience in the banking sector and tenure period acquired by the board member. A higher index indicates the richness of banking experience. Based on our results, it has an average of 5.9 years with minimum of 1.9 and maximum of 9. We note that this variable also increase considerably during the period 2001–2011 (Table 9.2).

Table 9.2 reports the mean values of diversity measures. Female is the percentage of female on the board. Ethnog diversity is the average diversity index of ethnicity and nationality. Professional diversity is the average index of banking experience and tenure diversity. Education diversity is the average diversity index of education level and education type.

Education diversity, measured by the average value of diversity by education level and education type has a mean value of 1.2. Most of the board members hold a masters or bachelors degree and almost every three of ten directors have a degree in fields other than economics or business.

Panel C presents the descriptive statistics of the control variables considered in our study. On average, the total assets (Assets) of our sample banks amount to 40.1 trillion rupiahs. The ratio of equity to total assets (Capital) has a mean of 18.8% with a minimum value of 8.6% and a maximum value of 77.1%. Foreign ownership increases from 0.13 (13.2%) in 2001 to 0.263 (26.3%) in 2011. Approximately 47% of the banks in our sample are listed on the stock exchange, but only 29% in 2001 while more than 60% in 2011. More than half of the banks (around 58.9% of our observations) belong to a business group.

9.5.2 Univariate Analysis

Table 9.3 presents the pair-wise correlation matrix between the considered variables. The proportion of females on the board is negatively correlated with ROA; ROE adjusted ROA and adjusted ROE in-line with the view that under certain circumstances the presence of females—as an additional/tougher monitor—may lead to a negative net effect (Adams and Ferreira 2009). Similarly, Ethnog diversity negatively correlates with performance.

Professional diversity is negatively correlated with ROA and ROE but positively with risk-adjusted ROA and risk-adjusted ROE. Education diversity is positively correlated with performance except for ROA. In terms of risk, we find that Ethnog diversity is positively correlated with SDROA and SDROE whereas the other diversity measures are negatively correlated with both of them. Ethnog diversity is also negatively related to all Z-score measures whereas the other diversity measures are positively correlated with them.

Table 9.3 Correlation matrix

No.	Variable	1	2	3	4	5	6	7	8	9	10	11	12	13	14	15	16	17	18	19
1	ROA	1																		
2	ROE	0.6156*	1																	
3	Adjusted ROA	0.2757*	0.2324*	1																
4	Adjusted ROE	0.3068*	0.2500*	0.5788*	1															
5	SDROA	0.3140*	0.0615	−0.6123*	−0.3951*	1														
6	SDROE	0.2275*	0.2717*	−0.4059*	−0.6085*	0.6492*	1													
7	Z-score	0.0722	0.0764	0.6699*	0.6306*	−0.6896*	−0.7807*	1												
8	Z-score1	0.0918*	0.3026*	0.7597*	0.5591*	−0.7561*	−0.5103*	0.8389*	1											
9	Z-score2	−0.0809	−0.3433*	0.3373*	0.5161*	−0.4473*	−0.8946*	0.7756*	0.4341*	1										
10	Female	−0.1793*	−0.2200*	−0.0147	−0.1057*	−0.1772*	−0.1034*	0.0247	0.0132	0.0267	1									
11	Ethnog diversity	−0.0821	−0.0556	−0.1963*	−0.2013*	0.1164*	0.1878*	−0.1984*	−0.1570*	−0.1752*	0.005	1								
12	Professional diversity	−0.1705*	−0.1901*	0.0453	0.0972*	−0.1168*	−0.2193*	0.1171*	0.0714	0.2540*	0.2591*	−0.1387*	1							
13	Education diversity	−0.0138	0.0741	0.2004*	0.1442*	−0.1545*	−0.0256	0.0757	0.1682*	−0.0095	−0.0064	0.0207	0.0117	1						
14	Capital	0.1798*	−0.2065*	0.0297	−0.0292	0.2295*	−0.0735	0.1680*	−0.0479	0.2871*	−0.1506*	−0.0755	0.0343	−0.1478*	1					
15	Loan	−0.002	−0.1577*	0.1442*	0.1585*	−0.1266*	−0.3013*	0.2381*	0.1471*	0.3577*	0.0705	−0.1272*	0.3296*	0.0592	0.0032	1				
16	Foreign bank	−0.1342*	−0.1475*	−0.0567	−0.1175*	0.0474	0.1022*	−0.1418*	−0.0990*	−0.1123*	0.1985*	0.4192*	0.0824	0.0867*	−0.0870*	0.0976*	1			
17	Listed	−0.1390*	−0.0539	−0.0241	0.042	−0.1085*	−0.1343*	0.0619	0.038	0.1077*	0.1691*	0.3136*	0.1244*	−0.0279	−0.0521	−0.0455	−0.0343	1		
18	Business group	−0.1795*	−0.2727*	0.0103	−0.0311	−0.1167*	−0.1706*	0.0928*	0.0263	0.2243*	0.1718*	0.0242	0.1670*	0.0942*	0.044	0.0174	0.0011	0.3649*	1	
19	Size	0.1368*	0.3061*	0.0872*	0.1436*	−0.1220*	0.0131	0.0976*	0.1905*	−0.1050*	−0.0771	0.2780*	−0.0675	−0.018	−0.0991*	−0.1789*	0.006	0.4011*	−0.2468*	1
20	Crisis	−0.0803	−0.0801	0.0517	0.0962*	−0.1121*	−0.1426*	0.0686	0.0299	0.1162*	0.0303	0.0104	0.0265	−0.0591	−0.031	0.1237*	0.0271	0.0667	0.0108	0.0715

Note: See Appendix for detailed descriptions

* represents the significance at the 10% level or smaller

9.5.3 Multivariate Analysis

In this section we run regressions of performance measures—ROA, ROE, adjusted ROA, and adjusted ROE—on the diversity measures and control variables. To deal with possible collinearity issues we introduce our main diversity variables one after the other in the regressions. Note also that the composite indices proposed in this study (see Sect. 9.4.2) are expected to better deal with collinearity concerns. For instance, it might be argued that there is possible strong correlation between ethnic diversity and nationality diversity because an incoming foreign director mostly means that she/he belongs to a different ethnic group. Furthermore, a foreign member might bring longer banking experience increasing the professional diversity score. As a further robustness check, we alternatively use orthogonalized variables for the presumably correlated variables. We also examine regressions with individual diversity dimensions run separately.

As discussed above, studies on board structure and performance often suffer from endogeneity that partly comes from the nature of the investigated variable (e.g., Carter et al. 2010; Fang et al. 2012; Pathan 2009). For instance, better performing banks are inclined to select more experienced board members. We check for endogeneity by running the Durbin Wu-Hausman Chi-sq test with the null hypotheses that the diversity variable is exogenous. The tests generally report that the diversity variables are endogenous except for model (1). Table 9.4 reports the results of IV/2SLS regressions with ROA, ROE, adjusted ROA, and adjusted ROE as the dependent variables.

Except for model 5 (ROE), our results show that almost all of the coefficients of gender diversity (Female) are not significant in our models. These results are in-line with those of Terjesen and Singh (2008) and Rose (2007) who find that women have little impact when sitting on the board in contrast with the findings of Erhardt et al. (2003). Despite the argument that a gender-diverse board is a tougher monitor, the net effect of gender heterogeneity (i.e. Female) is likely to disappear supporting the findings of Adams and Ferreira (2009) and Carter et al. (2010). This suggests that in the perspective of contingency theory, such additional monitoring might be counterproductive. Also, there is a possibility that banks appoint female directors only to follow the trend of inclusion of women and ethnic minorities on the board.

Our sample allows us to examine diversity based on ethnicity and nationality of board members (Ethnog diversity). Table 9.4 reports negative coefficients of Ethnog diversity in all the models (ROA, ROE, adjusted ROA, and adjusted ROE). This is surprising because the board could presumably get more benefits from this diversity. This effect is economically significant. For instance, an increase of one standard deviation in this diversity measure is associated with decreases in ROA by 1.11, ROE by −0.52, adjusted ROA by −0.39, and adjusted ROE by −1.51. In other words, Ethnog diversity is not only related to lower performance, but also simultaneously to higher risk with a greater increase in risk, leading to lower risk-adjusted returns.

Table 9.4 The impact of board diversity on bank performance: IV/2SLS models

Dependent var.	Return on assets (ROA)				Return on equity (ROE)				Adjusted ROA				Adjusted ROE			
Model	(1)	(2)	(3)	(4)	(5)	(6)	(7)	(8)	(1)	(2)	(3)	(4)	(5)	(6)	(7)	(8)
Female	−0.0206				1.087**				−17.41				−18.42			
	(−0.74)				(1.96)				(−1.28)				(−1.62)			
Ethnog diversity		−0.0265***				−0.102**				−2.261**				−8.302**		
		(−3.08)				(−2.41)				(−2.19)				(−2.00)		
Professional div.			0.00841***				0.0274*				5.155***				2.200**	
			(3.22)				(1.66)				(3.05)				(2.53)	
Education div.				0.0339**				0.573**				7.520*				8.397*
				(2.29)				(2.32)				(1.66)				(1.83)
Size	−0.00180*	−0.000895	−0.00228	0.00168	−0.0199	−0.0114	−0.0168	0.0376	1.173**	0.798	0.776	1.878***	0.985*	1.544*	0.594	1.514**
	(−1.66)	(−0.41)	(−1.42)	(0.93)	(−1.40)	(−1.06)	(−1.45)	(1.36)	(2.10)	(1.64)	(0.99)	(3.33)	(1.89)	(1.78)	(1.16)	(2.39)
Capital	0.0222**	0.0801***	0.0320**	0.0521***	−0.0642	−0.0292	−0.199**	0.0728	11.85**	12.85**	13.91**	12.34*	−5.441	6.243	−2.486	−0.458
	(2.16)	(2.95)	(2.43)	(3.20)	(−0.83)	(−0.27)	(−2.08)	(0.35)	(2.18)	(2.42)	(2.38)	(1.96)	(−1.18)	(0.88)	(−0.63)	(−0.08)
Loan	0.000611	0.00219	−0.0211**	−0.00858	−0.272**	−0.111*	−0.208***	−0.246**	6.024*	5.259*	−1.336	1.846	4.603	2.183	−0.0824	−0.171
	(0.08)	(0.20)	(−2.16)	(−0.93)	(−2.47)	(−1.79)	(−3.18)	(−1.97)	(1.70)	(1.80)	(−0.29)	(0.64)	(1.46)	(0.59)	(−0.03)	(−0.05)
Foreign bank	−0.00350	0.0101*	−0.000914	0.00807	0.0377	0.0330	−0.0385**	0.164*	−5.496***	−2.376	−4.630**	−1.929	−4.769***	−0.220	−4.305***	−2.187
	(−1.41)	(1.86)	(−0.25)	(1.27)	(0.77)	(1.11)	(−1.99)	(1.66)	(−2.94)	(−1.26)	(−2.02)	(−1.06)	(−3.20)	(−0.09)	(−3.08)	(−1.26)
Listed	0.00213	0.0109**	−0.00228	−0.000713	−0.0246	0.000226	−0.0184	−0.0587*	−1.615	−0.962	−1.553	−1.243	2.246**	4.528**	2.359**	2.187*
	(1.15)	(2.43)	(−1.14)	(−0.30)	(−1.00)	(0.01)	(−1.38)	(−1.93)	(−1.07)	(−0.61)	(−0.84)	(−0.91)	(2.49)	(2.53)	(2.35)	(1.89)
Group business	0.00975**	0.0328***	0.00432	0.0236***	0.176**	0.0926*	−0.00736	0.197**	−2.154	−1.691	−0.546	4.605***	2.321	−7.095	1.046	4.010
	(2.01)	(3.75)	(1.05)	(4.20)	(2.06)	(1.80)	(−0.18)	(2.41)	(−1.04)	(−0.66)	(−0.21)	(2.87)	(1.17)	(−0.77)	(0.52)	(1.57)
Crisis period	−0.00227**	−0.00414**	−0.00482	−0.000158	−0.0261*	−0.0277**	−0.0278	0.0157	0.524	0.325	0.293	1.111	1.010	0.452	0.820	1.622*
	(−2.26)	(−2.03)	(−1.38)	(−0.10)	(−1.74)	(−2.13)	(−1.12)	(0.65)	(0.63)	(0.37)	(0.22)	(1.21)	(1.13)	(0.45)	(0.91)	(1.75)
No. obs.	335	334	344	326	351	332	329	329	346	344	363	369	379	349	365	369
F-stat	5.23***	2.33**	3.84***	4.21***	2.267***	3.79***	5.17***	1.90*	2.63***	3.06***	2.82***	3.59***	4.69***	2.56***	4.62***	3.55***
Endog. test, Chi-sq:	0.109	10.471***	6.676***	7.471***	0.093	5.076**	3.560*	14.086***	2.558	4.237**	8.578***	0.198	4.071**	4.067**	3.003*	5.314**

Note: The table above reports IV/2SLS regression using ROA, ROE, adjusted ROA and adjusted ROE as the dependent variables. We utilize "xtivreg2" in Strata proposed by Schaffer (2010). It implements IV estimation of the fixed-effects and first-differences panel data models with possibly endogenous regressors. t-Statistics shown in parentheses are corrected for White heteroskedasticity. See Appendix for detailed descriptions

*, **, *** represent the significance at $p < 0.1$, $p < 0.05$, and $p < 0.01$ respectively

Our results are somewhat different from those of Carter et al. (2010) who find no significant link between U.S. S&P 500 firms' performance and the presence of ethnic minority directors and foreign directors. Theoretically, ethnic diversity would allow the board to better understand their customers and hence deliver better services. In practice, ethnicity diversity, if not well managed, may become a burden for board members because they often bring different values and norms that might be difficult to coordinate. Ethnic diversity might indicate diversity in other terms such as language, custom, behavior or even the specific perspectives of certain ethnic groups on conducting business activities. Working with persons belonging to different ethnic groups could pose challenges and not necessarily lead to better performance.

Regarding the presence of foreign members on the board, although their involvement presumably brings a broader international exposure, a weak knowledge of local market characteristics might outweigh the expected benefits. Our results support Masulis et al. (2012) who find that foreign directors often reduce the board's effectiveness leading to poorer performance.

Next, the coefficient of professional diversity is positive in all models, implying that an increase in professional diversity is likely to lead to higher performance. For instance, an increase in professional diversity by one standard deviation is associated to an increase of 0.55 and 0.21 times the current ROA and ROE respectively. Unlike Ethnog diversity, professional diversity is related to lower SDROA and SDROE. Hence, the effect of this type of diversity is economically more important when considering income volatility-adjusted performance as measured by risk-adjusted ROA and risk-adjusted ROE; an increase in professional diversity by 1% is associated with an increase in risk-adjusted ROA of 1.37 and risk-adjusted ROE of 0.62 times the current levels. Note that professional diversity is composed of diversity in working experience in the banking sector and of tenure periods. Longer experience in the banking sector should lead to higher capability in managing a bank. Hence, in the perspective of human capital theory, the presence of more experienced persons should lead to better decision making as supported by our results. Also, when we consider the second component (tenure period), a longer tenure may allow board members to learn from each other and exercise more skills. Our results support this argument.

The importance of education and training has been advocated particularly by the proponents of the resource dependent and human capital theories. With regard to education, our results show that education diversity is positively related to performance. All of the impacts on performance are significant despite that education diversity is only associated with risk-adjusted performance measures at the 10% significance level. Economically, an increase in education diversity by one standard deviation is related to an increase of ROA, ROE, adjusted ROA, and adjusted ROE by 0.58, 1.19, 0.53, and 0.63 of the existing level respectively (see model 4 and model 8 of Table 9.4).

Regarding control variables, we find Size to have little impact on ROA and ROE but it is significantly and positively correlated with risk-adjusted ROA and risk-adjusted ROE. Highly capitalized banks are likely to have a higher ROA and risk-adjusted ROA but a lower ROE. Such banks might be benefiting from lower funding costs. The coefficient of Loan is mostly negative for ROE in all models and for ROA in model (3). The coefficient is positive for risk-adjusted ROA.

Foreign ownership has a negative impact on risk-adjusted ROA and risk-adjusted ROE and little impact on ROE and ROA. Ceteris paribus, being listed on the stock exchange is associated with higher risk-adjusted ROE and banks belonging to a business group generally exhibit higher performance possibly because they benefit from better funding opportunities and/or support from their group.

With regard to risk, we find that the inclusion of a larger number of female members on the board is related to lower risk, particularly with regard to SDROA and SDROE (see Table 9.5). This is in-line with previous studies (see, e.g., Barber and Odean 2001; Mateos de Cabo et al. 2012). Economically, an increase in the ratio of female board members by one standard deviation reduces SDROA and SDROE by 71% and 14% respectively. In all models, Ethnog diversity is linked to higher return volatility (SDROA and SDROE) and higher default risk (Z-score, Z-score 1, and Z-score 2). For instance, an increase in Ethnog by one standard deviation is associated with approximately a 10% increase in SDROA and SDROE. Our results report that banks with professionally-diverse boards are likely to take less risk. Lastly, banks with more education diversity on the board exhibit higher returns variability, supporting Graham and Harvey (2001).

Bank size (measured by total assets) is negatively related to risk, suggesting that the risk diversification hypothesis is more effective than the moral hazard hypothesis (TBTF). Banks with a higher proportion of loans in total assets are those with lower risk, supporting the conjecture that such banks might benefit from more stable earnings.

9.5.4 Robustness Checks: Alternative Measurements and Models

We go further by conducting tests to examine the consistency of our results with those obtained with a more extensive breakdown of board diversity measures. Specifically, we separately consider the impact of gender (Female), nationality (National diversity), ethnicity (Ethnic diversity), experience (Experience diversity), tenure (Tenure diversity), education level (Education level diversity), and education type (Education type diversity) The results are reported in Tables 9.6 and 9.7 for performance and risk respectively. On the whole our main results remain unchanged.

To check for further robustness, we run regressions with alternative performance measures namely the net interest margin (NIM) defined as net interest income divided by average earning assets and the ratio of operating expenses to operating income (OEOI). We report the results in Table 9.8.

Table 9.5 The impact of board diversity on bank risk: IV/2SLS models

Dependent var.	SDROA				SDROE				Z-score				Z-score1				Z-score2			
Model	(1)	(2)	(3)	(4)	(1)	(2)	(3)	(4)	(1)	(2)	(3)	(4)	(5)	(6)	(7)	(8)	(9)	(10)	(11)	(12)
Female	−7.022***				−1.458*				1.020				3.175				1.079			
	(−2.64)				(−1.74)				(0.38)				(1.07)				(0.41)			
Ethnog diversity		1.043**				0.986**				−1.638***				−2.398***				−1.135**		
		(2.19)				(2.02)				(−3.00)				(−3.36)				(−2.09)		
Professional div			−0.399***				−0.435***				0.854***				0.873***				0.496***	
			(−2.82)				(−2.77)				(4.07)				(4.26)				(2.73)	
Education div				2.055*				2.251*				−0.199				1.450				−3.574*
				(1.76)				(1.87)				(−0.23)				(1.27)				(−1.91)
Size	−0.293***	−0.416***	−0.342***	−0.162	−0.256***	−0.330**	−0.303***	−0.100	0.216***	0.343**	0.314**	0.232*	0.241**	0.361*	0.260*	0.374**	0.282***	0.352**	0.315***	−0.0291
	(−2.87)	(−3.51)	(−3.50)	(−1.30)	(−2.71)	(−2.38)	(−2.97)	(−0.62)	(2.61)	(2.15)	(2.26)	(1.89)	(2.50)	(1.80)	(1.85)	(2.35)	(2.98)	(2.21)	(2.74)	(−0.13)
Capital	−0.556	−2.872*	−0.958	0.513	−0.159	−2.070	−0.836	0.521	0.831	4.248**	1.599	0.995	1.359	6.694***	2.544*	2.901*	2.640**	4.637***	2.815**	0.671
	(−0.52)	(−1.70)	(−0.85)	(0.45)	(−0.17)	(−1.44)	(−0.82)	(0.48)	(0.95)	(2.40)	(1.35)	(1.03)	(1.28)	(2.81)	(1.92)	(1.89)	(2.36)	(2.82)	(2.45)	(0.49)
Loan	0.170	−0.760	−0.215	−1.223*	−1.139**	−1.498***	−0.716	−1.714**	0.738	1.015	−0.441	0.904*	0.0331	1.200	−0.677	0.00249	1.584**	1.923***	0.985	2.355**
	(0.25)	(−1.35)	(−0.37)	(−1.87)	(−2.16)	(−2.66)	(−1.07)	(−2.42)	(1.19)	(1.50)	(−0.55)	(1.65)	(0.05)	(1.33)	(−0.84)	(0.00)	(2.10)	(2.99)	(1.33)	(2.49)
Foreign bank	−0.00450	−0.125	0.500**	1.068**	0.470**	0.0488	0.668***	1.257***	−0.488*	0.171	−0.876**	−0.638*	−0.534	0.437	−0.964***	−0.199	−0.361	0.0985	−0.608***	−1.590**
	(−0.01)	(−0.40)	(1.97)	(2.27)	(2.43)	(0.17)	(2.81)	(2.63)	(−1.89)	(0.49)	(−2.47)	(−1.70)	(−1.64)	(0.92)	(−2.63)	(−0.39)	(−1.43)	(0.31)	(−2.64)	(−2.25)
Listed	0.243	−0.0343	0.424*	0.177	−0.467***	−0.741***	−0.296	−0.559***	0.168	0.715**	−0.155	0.189	−0.108	0.623	−0.470	−0.151	0.608***	0.989***	0.478**	0.842***
	(1.08)	(−0.13)	(1.86)	(0.73)	(−2.74)	(−2.67)	(−1.59)	(−2.87)	(1.02)	(2.39)	(−0.59)	(1.09)	(−0.49)	(1.48)	(−1.45)	(−0.59)	(3.20)	(3.25)	(2.28)	(3.52)
Group business	−0.555	−0.389	0.890***	1.082***	−0.522	−0.537	0.698***	0.870**	0.267	1.351***	−0.915***	0.0640	0.544	1.864***	−0.924***	0.642	0.302	0.972**	−0.454*	−0.963
	(−1.37)	(−0.91)	(4.00)	(2.67)	(−1.33)	(−1.34)	(3.29)	(2.12)	(0.69)	(2.70)	(−2.83)	(0.21)	(1.26)	(2.76)	(−2.69)	(1.63)	(0.80)	(2.14)	(−1.88)	(−1.57)
Crisis period	−0.158	−0.0829	−0.123	−0.0418	−0.217**	−0.168	−0.181	−0.0627	0.101	0.0239	0.0937	0.0885	−0.0302	−0.185	−0.0409	0.0758	0.182	0.147	0.166	−0.0388
	(−1.25)	(−0.61)	(−0.91)	(−0.29)	(−2.15)	(−1.38)	(−1.46)	(−0.43)	(0.90)	(0.15)	(0.50)	(0.70)	(−0.21)	(−0.84)	(−0.18)	(0.47)	(1.58)	(1.06)	(1.19)	(−0.20)
No. obs.	357	341	337	348	356	353	334	336	354	352	345	338	344	343	336	328	343	352	334	336
F-stat	2.551***	3.010***	3.737***	2.933***	7.704***	6.799***	7.035***	6.1020***	5.141***	3.646***	4.515***	5.395***	2.242***	2.645***	3.707***	1.629***	8.605***	9.307***	11.61***	5.696 ***
Endog. test	2.532	7.500***	9.587***	3.662*	0.826	0.097	4.136**	4.267**	0.9325	6.462**	14.391***	0.001	1.005	18.081***	24.243***	2.471	1.634	0.662	4.285**	6.400**

Note: The table above reports IV/2SLS regression using SDROA, SDROE, Z-score, Z-score 1, and Z-score 2 as the dependent variables. t-Statistics shown in parentheses are corrected for White heteroskedasticity. See Appendix for detailed descriptions

*, **, *** represent the significance at $p < 0.1$, $p < 0.05$, and $p < 0.01$ respectively

Table 9.6 The impact of board diversity on bank performance: IV/2SLS models on individual diversity dimensions

Dependent var.	Return on asset (ROA)							Return on equity (ROE)						
Model	(1)	(2)	(3)	(4)	(5)	(6)	(7)	(1)	(2)	(3)	(4)	(5)	(6)	(7)
Female	−0.0206							1.087**						
	(−0.74)							(1.96)						
National diversity		−0.0534**							−0.608***					
		(−2.31)							(−2.99)					
Ethnic diversity			−0.00519*							−0.0688***				
			(−1.84)							(−3.13)				
Experience diversity				0.00434**							0.0214**			
				(2.61)							(1.96)			
Tenure diveristy					0.0122**							0.118**		
					(2.52)							(2.44)		
Education level diversity						0.0321*							0.255**	
						(1.80)							(2.47)	
Education type diversity							0.0483*							0.955***
							(1.69)							(3.14)
Size	−0.00180*	−0.000254	−0.00150	0.00121	−0.0102***	0.00298	0.000960	−0.0199	0.0227	−0.00239	0.00683	−0.0873**	0.0315	0.0443**
	(−1.66)	(−0.19)	(−1.14)	(0.74)	(−2.85)	(1.13)	(0.41)	(−1.40)	(1.20)	(−0.21)	(0.44)	(−2.29)	(1.24)	(2.03)
Capital	0.0222**	0.0495***	0.0204**	0.0267***	0.0155**	0.0197	0.0259***	−0.0642	0.0823	−0.0141	−0.0360	−0.0818	−0.0447	0.127
	(2.16)	(3.27)	(2.53)	(3.59)	(2.41)	(1.24)	(2.68)	(−0.83)	(1.26)	(−0.31)	(−0.64)	(−1.09)	(−0.44)	(1.24)
Loan	0.000611	−0.00487	−0.0112*	−0.0166*	−0.0278***	−0.0306**	−0.0201*	−0.272**	−0.112*	−0.164**	−0.167**	−0.313***	−0.284***	−0.318***
	(0.08)	(−0.59)	(−1.66)	(−1.86)	(−2.76)	(−1.97)	(−1.92)	(−2.47)	(−1.66)	(−2.29)	(−2.55)	(−2.76)	(−2.59)	(−2.85)
Foreign bank	−0.00350	0.0234**	0.000423	−0.00604*	0.000260	0.0174	−0.00102	0.0377	0.265**	0.0103	−0.0451*	−0.00209	0.129	0.00189
	(−1.41)	(1.99)	(0.18)	(−1.86)	(0.07)	(1.29)	(−0.39)	(0.77)	(2.50)	(0.41)	(−1.68)	(−0.05)	(1.57)	(0.05)
Listed	0.00213	0.00278	0.00500	0.00164	−0.00666	−0.00287	0.00283	−0.0246	−0.0381*	0.00701	−0.0362*	−0.119***	−0.0742**	−0.0132
	(1.15)	(1.01)	(1.48)	(0.49)	(−1.41)	(−0.69)	(0.95)	(−1.00)	(−1.76)	(0.34)	(−1.79)	(−2.64)	(−2.41)	(−0.41)
Group business	0.00975**	0.0528***	0.0173***	0.00586	0.00754	0.0399***	0.00586	0.176**		0.0728	−0.0169	−0.0378	0.228***	−0.134*
	(2.01)	(3.08)	(4.52)	(1.53)	(1.26)	(2.61)	(1.00)	(2.06)	(3.09)	(1.53)	(−0.44)	(−0.53)	(2.68)	(−1.88)
Crisis period	−0.00227**	−0.00256**	−0.00278**	−0.00233	−0.00198	0.00256	−0.00234*	−0.0261*	−0.0268**	−0.0296**	−0.0241*	−0.0207	0.0147	−0.0241
	(−2.26)	(−2.09)	(−2.07)	(−1.18)	(−1.25)	(0.77)	(−1.76)	(−1.74)	(−2.08)	(−2.10)	(−1.69)	(−1.23)	(0.73)	(−1.33)
No. obs.	335	339	352	349	348	348	348	351	357	357	351	348	348	350
F-stat.	5.230***	5.441***	3.945***	4.622***	3.565***	2.158***	3.794***	2.267***	3.774***	4.271***	3.342***	2.776***	2.202***	3.342 ***
Endog. test	0.109	12.629***	7.533***	15.799***	8.092***	7.700***	8.515***	0.093	4.923**	4.145**	4.132**	7.744***	9.823***	4.708**

Dependent var.	Adjusted ROA							Adjusted ROE						
Model	(1)	(2)	(3)	(4)	(5)	(6)	(7)	(1)	(2)	(3)	(4)	(5)	(6)	(7)
Female	−17.41							−18.42						
	(−1.28)							(−1.62)						
National diversity		−8.666*							−9.510**					
		(−1.65)							(−2.15)					
Ethnic diversity			−1.136**							−1.121**				
			(−2.26)							(−2.42)				
Experience diversity				3.488***							0.568**			
				(3.14)							(2.42)			
Tenure diveristy					1.283**							5.170**		
					(2.03)							(2.05)		
Education level						5.779*							3.538*	
diversity						(1.93)							(1.67)	
Education type diversity							22.48*							36.26*
							(1.96)							(1.88)
Size	1.173**	1.036**	0.752	2.769***	−0.0505	1.915***	2.286***	0.985*	0.913*	0.444	0.831	−2.913*	1.300**	2.477*
	(2.10)	(2.16)	(1.53)	(2.88)	(−0.08)	(3.14)	(3.01)	(1.89)	(1.76)	(0.81)	(1.61)	(−1.78)	(2.27)	(1.84)
Capital	11.85**	13.41**	12.15**	20.41***	9.109*	11.35*	17.71**	−5.441	0.931	−1.562	−2.947	−2.588	−2.463	11.18
	(2.18)	(2.38)	(2.31)	(2.73)	(1.83)	(1.84)	(2.37)	(−1.18)	(0.19)	(−0.34)	(−0.70)	(−0.52)	(−0.50)	(1.18)
Loan	6.024*	6.762**	5.023*	−0.611	2.732	1.754	0.489	4.603	4.441	3.604	2.734	−3.565	0.729	−2.217
	(1.70)	(2.16)	(1.71)	(−0.12)	(0.93)	(0.64)	(0.16)	(1.46)	(1.57)	(1.27)	(0.97)	(−0.65)	(0.23)	(−0.41)
Foreign bank	−5.496***	0.719	−2.949	−6.875**	−3.521**	−1.553	−2.551	−4.769***	0.567	−3.461**	−4.543***	−3.098	−2.629	−3.197
	(−2.94)	(0.22)	(−1.63)	(−2.21)	(−2.02)	(−0.86)	(−1.52)	(−3.20)	(0.22)	(−2.47)	(−3.37)	(−1.49)	(−1.64)	(−1.46)
Listed	−1.615	−1.612	−0.956	−1.338	−2.603	−1.503	−0.169	2.246**	1.927*	3.063***	2.276**	−1.436	2.118*	3.264*
	(−1.07)	(−1.14)	(−0.61)	(−0.56)	(−1.59)	(−1.09)	(−0.12)	(2.49)	(1.90)	(2.94)	(2.32)	(−0.59)	(1.88)	(1.97)
Group business	−2.154	6.660*	−2.545	−5.790***	−0.440	5.092***	3.541	2.321	7.083**	−2.907	−0.978	−3.332	3.843	−6.384*
	(−1.04)	(1.67)	(−0.93)	(−2.61)	(−0.51)	(3.11)	(1.51)	(1.17)	(2.02)	(−1.14)	(−1.02)	(−1.22)	(1.57)	(−1.83)
Crisis period	0.524	0.340	0.336	0.476	0.464	1.410	0.500	1.010	0.782	0.746	0.856	0.956	1.539*	0.836
	(0.63)	(0.41)	(0.38)	(0.33)	(0.54)	(1.46)	(0.54)	(1.13)	(0.94)	(0.87)	(1.06)	(0.94)	(1.73)	(0.77)

(continued)

Table 9.6 (continued)

Dependent var.	Adjusted ROA							Adjusted ROE						
Model	(1)	(2)	(3)	(4)	(5)	(6)	(7)	(1)	(2)	(3)	(4)	(5)	(6)	(7)
No. obs.	346	357	344	335	334	370	367	379	353	346	336	333	369	329
F−stat.	2.627***	3.495***	3.035***	2.367***	3.830***	3.032***	2.834***	4.690***	3.970***	4.721***	4.343***	2.092***	3.727***	1.752***
Endog. test	2.558	0.578	4.894**	21.742***	3.208*	2.877*	4.972**	4.071**	4.279**	4.519**	1.083	6.353**	4.150**	4.542**

Note: The table above reports IV/2SLS regression using ROA, ROE, adjusted ROA and adjusted ROE as the dependent variables. t-Statistics shown in parentheses are corrected for White heteroskedasticity. See Appendix for detailed descriptions

*, **, *** represent the significance at $p < 0.1$, $p < 0.05$, and $p < 0.01$ respectively

Table 9.7 The impact of board diversity on bank risk: IV/2SLS models on individual diversity dimensions

Dependent var.	SDROA							SDROE							Z-score		
Model	(1)	(2)	(3)	(4)	(5)	(6)	(7)	(1)	(2)	(3)	(4)	(5)	(6)	(7)	(1)	(2)	(3)
Female	−7.022***							−1.458*							1.942**		
	(−2.64)							(−1.74)							(2.21)		
National diversity		11.05***							4.274**							−11.71***	
		(3.29)							(2.40)							(−3.53)	
Ethnic diversity			0.660**							0.190**							−0.213**
			(2.41)							(2.02)							(−2.19)
Experience diversity				−0.327***							0.0974***						
				(−2.74)							(−2.63)						
Tenure diversity					−1.269**							−0.763***					
					(−2.09)							(−3.16)					
Education level diversity						0.301*							0.470***				
						(1.82)							(3.27)				
Education type diversity							7.869**							7.869**			
							(2.00)							(2.00)			
Size	−0.293***	−0.983***	−0.368***	−0.557***	0.451	−0.304***	−0.00231	−0.256***	−0.489***	−0.278***	−0.350***	0.209	−0.225**	−0.00231	0.209**	0.988***	0.243**
	(−2.87)	(−3.56)	(−2.85)	(−4.63)	(1.07)	(−3.22)	(−0.01)	(−2.71)	(−3.34)	(−2.66)	(−3.74)	(1.12)	(−2.21)	(−0.01)	(2.39)	(3.33)	(2.46)
Capital	−0.556	−7.625**	−2.802*	−1.027	−0.581	−0.289	3.014*	−0.159	−2.672*	−0.674	−0.335	−0.570	0.0790	3.014*	0.892	8.889***	1.452
	(−0.52)	(−2.53)	(−1.77)	(−0.84)	(−0.39)	(−0.28)	(1.72)	(−0.17)	(−1.66)	(−0.71)	(−0.35)	(−0.62)	(0.08)	(1.72)	(1.01)	(2.84)	(1.55)
Loan	0.170	−2.413*	−0.764	−0.281	1.278	−0.803	−2.166**	−1.139**	−2.102***	−1.396***	−1.259**	−0.302	−1.490***	−2.166**	0.800	2.554**	1.109**
	(0.25)	(−1.92)	(−1.25)	(−0.45)	(1.00)	(−1.60)	(−2.03)	(−2.16)	(−3.04)	(−2.82)	(−2.45)	(−0.40)	(−2.84)	(−2.03)	(1.63)	(2.07)	(2.23)
Foreign bank	−0.00450	−4.717***	0.0782	0.683**	0.182	0.609**	0.694*	0.470**	−1.624*	0.417**	0.627***	0.396	0.832***	0.694*	−0.402*	4.785***	−0.364
	(−0.01)	(−2.81)	(0.29)	(2.31)	(0.48)	(2.41)	(1.70)	(2.43)	(−1.73)	(2.05)	(3.38)	(1.51)	(3.60)	(1.70)	(−1.72)	(2.92)	(−1.46)
Listed	0.243	0.291	−0.190	0.235	1.166*	0.190	0.496	−0.467***	−0.409**	−0.565***	−0.435**	0.115	−0.503***	0.496	0.207	0.0403	0.309*
	(1.08)	(0.83)	(−0.62)	(0.84)	(1.94)	(0.83)	(1.46)	(−2.74)	(−2.05)	(−3.22)	(−2.53)	(0.44)	(−2.98)	(1.46)	(1.28)	(0.12)	(1.79)
Group business	−0.555	−7.373***	−0.115	1.026***	1.073*	0.658***	−0.724	−0.522	−3.618***	0.0383	−0.280	0.588*	0.569***	−0.724	0.420***	8.380***	−0.225
	(−1.37)	(−3.07)	(−0.35)	(4.19)	(1.72)	(3.66)	(−1.07)	(−1.33)	(−2.58)	(0.13)	(−0.56)	(1.90)	(3.29)	(−1.07)	(2.69)	(3.54)	(−0.55)
Crisis period	−0.158	−0.0958	−0.120	−0.164	−0.217	−0.131	−0.187	−0.217**	−0.180	−0.197*	−0.208**	−0.231*	−0.158	−0.187	0.0987	0.0255	0.0746
	(−1.25)	(−0.48)	(−0.84)	(−1.05)	(−1.20)	(−1.13)	(−1.07)	(−2.15)	(−1.56)	(−1.86)	(−2.02)	(−1.85)	(−1.54)	(−1.07)	(0.87)	(0.13)	(0.62)
No. obs.	357	363	351	344	345	343	350	356	352	352	345	345	343	350	355	360	351
F-stat.	2.551***	2.726***	3.873***	2.078***	4.134***	2.338***	8.025***	7.704***	15.11***	8.157***	6.260***	9.235***	2.338***	9.526***	2.892***	5.217***	4.673***
Endog. test	2.532	11.481***	8.955***	11.636***	10.261***	0.810	17.195***	0.826	7.024***	2.717*	1.435	8.552***	0.811	4.446**	4.156**	18.463***	6.096**

(continued)

Table 9.7 (continued)

Dependent var.	Z-score				Z-score 1							Z-score 2						
Model	(4)	(5)	(6)	(7)	(1)	(2)	(3)	(4)	(5)	(6)	(7)	(1)	(2)	(3)	(4)	(5)	(6)	(7)
Female					1.764*							1.458*						
					(1.73)							(1.68)						
National diversity						−12.82***							−8.406***					
						(−3.88)							(−3.02)					
Ethnic diversity							−0.278**							−0.198*				
							(−2.15)							(−1.75)				
Experience diversity	0.484***							0.685***							0.398***			
	(3.49)							(3.61)							(2.86)			
Tenure diversity		0.251***							0.238**							1.854***		
		(2.66)							(2.14)							(4.18)		
Education level diversity			−0.323**							1.794**							−2.494*	
			(−2.11)							(2.30)							(−1.83)	
Education type diversity				3.953*							5.312**							−4.597**
				(1.82)							(2.25)							(−2.05)
Size	0.620***	0.0812	0.186**	0.518***	0.203*	0.855***	0.225*	0.667***	0.0572	0.558***	0.621***	0.248**	0.776***	0.273**	0.573***	−0.886***	−0.0618	0.0886
	(4.08)	(0.69)	(2.00)	(3.41)	(1.94)	(3.09)	(1.91)	(3.43)	(0.40)	(2.98)	(3.37)	(2.36)	(3.26)	(2.28)	(3.90)	(−2.70)	(−0.23)	(0.57)
Capital	1.623	0.839	0.632	3.096**	0.948	10.47***	1.813	2.934*	0.915	2.073	3.493**	1.997*	7.641***	2.545**	2.787**	2.496	0.737	0.436
	(1.24)	(0.99)	(0.73)	(2.17)	(0.86)	(3.34)	(1.44)	(1.84)	(0.81)	(1.27)	(2.11)	(1.85)	(2.85)	(2.41)	(2.03)	(1.64)	(0.46)	(0.31)
Loan	0.131	0.641	1.209**	0.537	0.726	2.634**	1.173*	−0.321	0.686	0.471	0.373	1.537**	2.773***	1.789***	1.118	−1.055	2.614**	2.511***
	(0.17)	(1.28)	(2.42)	(0.80)	(1.10)	(2.01)	(1.67)	(−0.32)	(0.98)	(0.50)	(0.44)	(2.51)	(2.73)	(3.13)	(1.39)	(−0.85)	(2.38)	(3.10)
Foreign bank	−0.991***	−0.460*	−0.680**	−0.419*	−0.284	5.251***	−0.190	−1.186**	−0.329	0.236	−0.188	−0.356*	3.512**	−0.299	−0.780***	−0.0971	−1.986**	−0.614**
	(−2.75)	(−1.96)	(−2.51)	(−1.72)	(−0.73)	(3.11)	(−0.48)	(−2.46)	(−0.85)	(0.44)	(−0.47)	(−1.75)	(2.57)	(−1.38)	(−2.78)	(−0.21)	(−2.07)	(−2.00)
Listed	0.156	−0.00321	0.227	0.555**	−0.147	−0.0572	−0.00162	−0.0890	−0.333	−0.146	0.197	0.671***	0.534**	0.771***	0.621**	−0.717	1.011***	0.490**
	(0.54)	(−0.02)	(1.37)	(2.27)	(−0.66)	(−0.16)	(−0.01)	(−0.22)	(−1.36)	(−0.49)	(0.68)	(3.60)	(2.00)	(4.15)	(2.39)	(−1.44)	(2.98)	(2.05)
Group business	−0.801***	0.171	0.0998	1.520***	0.278	9.233***	−0.544	−1.142***	0.0307	2.518***	2.056**	0.808**	6.101***	0.228	−0.617**	−0.835	−1.861*	0.821**
	(−2.82)	(0.79)	(0.38)	(2.66)	(1.57)	(3.87)	(−0.92)	(−2.97)	(0.14)	(3.41)	(2.17)	(2.09)	(3.02)	(0.64)	(−2.07)	(−1.16)	(−1.70)	(2.00)

Crisis period	0.0792	0.100	0.0464	0.120	−0.0430	−0.124	−0.0764	−0.0738	−0.0485	0.235	−0.0450	0.203*	0.135	0.181	0.190	0.252	−0.142	0.218*
	(0.41)	(0.86)	(0.39)	(0.88)	(−0.30)	(−0.55)	(−0.49)	(−0.26)	(−0.33)	(1.12)	(−0.27)	(1.81)	(0.82)	(1.54)	(1.15)	(1.20)	(−0.53)	(1.71)
No. obs.	346	341	344	373	345	346	343	337	334	367	364	356	354	352	346	345	348	347
F-stat.	6.240***	4.884***	5.910 ***	5.564***	2.763***	2.699***	2.847***	3.383***	3.564***	3.787***	9.091***	5.701***	20.33***	6.789***	4.559***	4.390***	8.259***	***
Endog. test	12.513***	4.353**	0.743	0.951	1.346	27.666***	5.030**	24.071***	3.762**	7.154***	3.470*	0.2837	9.474***	3.088*	8.449***	22.830***	6.83***	2.304

Note: The table above reports IV/2SLS regression using SDROA, SDROE, Z-score, Z-score 1, and Z-score 2 as the dependent variables. t-Statistics shown in parentheses are corrected for White heteroskedasticity. See Appendix for detailed descriptions

*, **, *** represent the significance at $p < 0.1$, $p < 0.05$, and $p < 0.01$ respectively

Table 9.8 The impact of board diversity on bank performance: alternative performance measures

Dependent var.	NIM				OEOI			
Model	(1)	(2)	(3)	(4)	(1)	(2)	(3)	(4)
Female	0.0287*				−1.088**			
	(1.77)				(−2.29)			
Ethnog diversity		0.00371				0.176***		
		(1.11)				(3.06)		
Professional diversity			0.0287***				−0.0944***	
			(3.21)				(−3.93)	
Education diversity				0.0376**				−0.585***
				(2.15)				(−3.05)
Size	−0.00241	−0.00324*	−0.00313	0.00184	−0.00782	−0.0255	−0.00254	−0.0719***
	(−1.37)	(−1.74)	(−0.82)	(0.65)	(−0.60)	(−1.62)	(−0.16)	(−2.89)
Capital	−0.0154*	−0.0206**	0.0178	−0.00678	−0.230***	−0.300***	−0.252***	−0.284
	(−1.95)	(−2.36)	(1.03)	(−0.50)	(−3.19)	(−2.66)	(−3.26)	(−1.61)
Loan	0.0211*	0.0272**	−0.00782	0.00262	0.119	0.0775	0.148*	0.264**
	(1.92)	(2.36)	(−0.38)	(0.18)	(1.39)	(1.04)	(1.95)	(2.12)
Foreign bank	0.00799*	0.00482	−0.000949	0.0160**	−0.0277	−0.0622	0.0424	−0.162*
	(1.92)	(1.05)	(−0.10)	(2.09)	(−0.76)	(−1.61)	(1.27)	(−1.73)
Listed	−0.0000488	−0.000913	−0.0124*	−0.00230	−0.0308	−0.0750**	0.00381	0.0150
	(−0.01)	(−0.25)	(−1.68)	(−0.56)	(−1.23)	(−2.26)	(0.13)	(0.48)
Business group	0.0240***	0.0272***	−0.00855	0.0435***	−0.173**	−0.253***	0.0268	−0.313***
	(3.38)	(4.64)	(−0.72)	(5.99)	(−2.30)	(−4.04)	(0.58)	(−3.89)
Crisis period	−0.000204	−0.0000708	−0.000757	0.00282	0.0258*	0.0280*	0.0207	−0.0231
	(−0.14)	(−0.05)	(−0.16)	(1.28)	(1.79)	(1.88)	(1.05)	(−0.97)
N	352	348	348	349	389	355	348	350
F-stat	4.18***	6.25***	3.50***	10.12***	2.40**	2.81***	3.17***	2.49**
Endog. Test (Chi-sq)	12.92***	13.77***	6.95***	7.33***	2.72***	9.44	7.00***	9.13***

Note: The table above reports IV/2SLS regression using net interest margin (NIM) and the ratio of operating expense-to-operating income (OEOI) as the dependent variables. t-Statistics shown in parentheses are corrected for White heteroskedasticity. See Appendix for detailed descriptions

*, **, *** represent the significance at $p < 0.1$, $p < 0.05$, and $p < 0.01$ respectively

The coefficients of Female in both models show that the presence of women on the board is related to better performance—i.e. higher NIM but only at the 10% significance level and lower OEOI in-line with the argument of stronger monitoring. We do not find any significant impact of Ethnog diversity on NIM. Nevertheless, it has a positive impact on OEOI.

Table 9.8 reports that professional diversity is associated with higher NIM and lower OEOI, confirming that such diversity is associated with better performance. Consistently, higher education diversity leads to higher NIM and lower OEOI. These results confirm the findings obtained in the previous section.

In addition, we run regressions by excluding certain variables to deal with possible multicollinearity issues. First, we drop foreign bank from our models because it is considerably correlated with Ethnog diversity. This correlation is naturally understandable considering that banks owned by foreign investors are more likely to appoint foreign board members. Second, in our sample, around 60% of group-member banks are also listed on the stock exchange (the correlation coefficient between Listed and Business Group is equal to 0.36). Hence, we exclude Business group from the regressions. Next, we also exclude Listed because listed banks are more likely to be larger banks. On the whole our main results remain unchanged. Alternatively, we orthogonalize Foreign bank, Business group and Listed with respect to Size. Again, our main findings remain the same.

9.6 Conclusion

Board structure has received increasing attention by researchers, regulators and practitioners. Specifically, the presence of diverse board members is expected to affect performance through various channels. On the one hand board diversity is expected to enrich decision-making processes leading to better performance. On the other hand, diversity could become a burden to integrate and coordinate different views leading to poorer performance.

We conduct our study in one of the most fast-growing and diverse countries; Indonesia. The results show that female presence does not strongly impact performance and that the presence of more diverse ethnic groups is associated with lower performance. Professional diversity that measures diversity in working experience and tenure periods is linked to higher performance. Lastly, education diversity has a positive and significant impact on performance. Furthermore, female presence has a negative impact on risk. Banks with diverse nationalities and ethnic groups on the board exhibit higher risk whereas those with higher professional diversity take less risk. Education diversity leads to higher income volatility and leverage risk.

On the whole, our results show that looking into the diversity of board members is crucial for a better understanding of bank performance, supporting Claessens and Yurtoglu (2013) who argue that board composition is an important mechanism in emerging markets where corporate governance codes are relatively weak.

Our findings suggest that the design and choice of board structure is critical in the Indonesian banking sector, as in other emerging countries, which is undergoing a notable improvement in corporate governance mechanisms. For example, regulators are aiming to set longer years of experience for director candidates. Regulatory bodies and stakeholders should also limit the possible downside effect while promoting more diverse boards. As argued by Ferreira (2010), firms should be able to identify the trade-offs of diversity in order to increase their performance and values. Therefore, drawing any firm conclusion on how board characteristics will eventually affect performance and risk is hazardous. Nevertheless, our study sheds light on specific factors and possible tracks for future policies aimed at improving board effectiveness and efficiency.

Appendix: Definition of Variables

Variable	Definition	Source
Panel A. Performance and risk measures		
ROA	Profits before taxes divided by average assets	Annual reports
ROE	Profits before taxes divided by average equity	Annual reports
Adjusted ROA	The ratio of ROA to its standard deviation calculated from the last three observations for the respective year	Annual reports
Adjusted ROE	The ratio of ROE to its standard deviation calculated from the last three observations for the respective year	Annual reports
SDROA	Standard deviation of last 3-year returns on average assets (i.e., t, $t-1$ and $t-2$)	Annual reports
SDROE	Standard deviation of last 3-year return on average equity (i.e., t, $t-1$ and $t-2$)	Annual reports
Z-score	Return on average assets (ROA) plus equity to total assets ratio, divided by the standard deviation of last 3-year ROA	Annual reports
Z-score 1	Return on average assets (ROA) divided by the standard deviation of last 3-year ROA	Annual reports
Z-score 2	Equity to total assets ratio, divided by the standard deviation of last 3-year ROA	Annual reports
Panel B. Diversity (Heterogeneity) measures		
1. Female	The ratio of female on the board, that is the number of female divided by total number of directors	Annual reports, News releases, Bank's website
2. Ethnog diversity	Ethnog diveristy = (Ethnic diversity + nationality diversity)/2	
# Ethnic diversity	The Blau's index (inversed HHI) based on the ethnicity	Annual reports, News releases, Bank's website

(continued)

Variable	Definition	Source
# Nationality diversity	The Blau's index (inversed HHI) based on the nationality, ranging from 0 (no diversity) to 0.5 (the number of local is the same as that of foreign directors)	Annual reports, News releases, Bank's website
3. Professional diversity	Professional diversity = (Tenure diversity + Experience diversity)/2	
# Experience diversity	The standard deviation of the number of years of banking experience	Annual reports, News releases, Bank's website, Indonesia Banking Institute
# Tenure diversity	The standard deviation of the number of years (tenure) the person serving the directorship	Annual reports, News releases, Bank's website, Indonesia Banking Institute
4. Education diversity	The average of education level and education type diversities. Education diversity = (education level diversity + education level diversity)/2	
# Education level diversity	The Blau's index based on the highest education degree of directors: (1) no bachelor degree (S0), (2) bachelor degree (S1), (3) master degree (S2), and (4) doctoral degree or beyond (S3)	Annual report, News releases, Bank's website
# Education type diversity	The number of board members with education background other than economics, finance, accounting, and business divided by total board members	Annual report, News releases, Bank's website
Panel C. Control variables		
Size	The logarithm of total assets	Annual reports
Capital	Total equity divided by total assets	Annual reports
Loan	Total loan divided by total assets	Annual reports
Foreign bank	Dummy takes one if the bank is owned by foreign investors, zero otherwise	Annual reports
Listed	Dummy takes one if the bank is publicly listed, zero otherwise	Annual reports
Business group	Dummy takes one if the bank is a member of a business group, zero otherwise	Annual reports, Bank's website
Crisis	Dummy takes one for year 2008, zero otherwise	Annual reports, Central Bank of Indonesia

References

Adams, R. B., & Ferreira, D. (2004). Gender diversity in the boardroom. *European Corporate Governance Institute, Finance Working Paper, 58*(58).

Adams, R. B., & Ferreira, D. (2007). A Theory of friendly boards. *The Journal of Finance, 62*(1), 217–250. https://doi.org/10.2307/4123461.

Adams, R. B., & Ferreira, D. (2009). Women in the boardroom and their impact on governance and performance. *Journal of Financial Economics, 94*(2), 291–309. https://doi.org/10.1016/j.jfineco.2008.10.007.

Adams, R. B., Hermalin, B. E., & Weisbach, M. S. (2010). The role of boards of directors in corporate governance: A conceptual framework and survey. *Journal of Economic Literature, 48*(1), 58–107.

Adams, R. B., & Mehran, H. (2012). Bank board structure and performance: Evidence for large bank holding companies. *Journal of Financial Intermediation, 21*(2), 243–267. https://doi.org/10.1016/j.jfi.2011.09.002.

Aebi, V., Sabato, G., & Schmid, M. (2012). Risk management, corporate governance, and bank performance in the financial crisis. *Journal of Banking & Finance, 36*(12), 3213–3226. https://doi.org/10.1016/j.jbankfin.2011.10.020.

Anderson, R. C., Mansi, S. A., & Reeb, D. M. (2004). Board characteristics, accounting report integrity, and the cost of debt. *Journal of Accounting and Economics, 37*(3), 315–342. https://doi.org/10.1016/j.jacceco.2004.01.004.

Anderson, R. C., Reeb, D. M., Upadhyay, A., & Zhao, W. (2011). The economics of director heterogeneity. *Financial Management, 40*(1), 5–38. https://doi.org/10.1111/j.1755-053X.2010.01133.x.

Andres, P. d., & Vallelado, E. (2008). Corporate governance in banking: The role of the board of directors. *Journal of Banking & Finance, 32*(12), 2570–2580. https://doi.org/10.1016/j.jbankfin.2008.05.008.

Asian Development Bank. (2000). *Corporate governance and finance in East Asia: A consolidated report*. Manila, Philippines: Asian Development Bank (ADB).

Bank Indonesia. (2010). *Peraturan Bank Indonesia tentang uji kemampuan dan kepatutan (Fit and proper test)*. Indonesia: Jakarta.

Bank Indonesia (BI). (2006). *Peraturan Bank Indonesia tentang pelaksanaan good corporate governance bagi bank umum*. Indonesia: Jakarta.

Baranchuk, N., & Dybvig, P. H. (2009). Consensus in diverse corporate boards. *Review of Financial Studies, 22*(2), 715–747. https://doi.org/10.1093/rfs/hhn052.

Barber, B. M., & Odean, T. (2001). Boys will be boys: Gender, overconfidence, and common stock investment. *The Quarterly Journal of Economics, 116*(1), 261–292. https://doi.org/10.1162/003355301556400.

Barry, T. A., Lepetit, L., & Tarazi, A. (2011). Ownership structure and risk in publicly held and privately owned banks. *Journal of Banking & Finance, 35*(5), 1327–1340. https://doi.org/10.1016/j.jbankfin.2010.10.004.

Barth, J. R., Caprio, G., Jr., & Levine, R. (2004). Bank regulation and supervision: What works best? *Journal of Financial Intermediation, 13*(2), 205–248. https://doi.org/10.1016/j.jfi.2003.06.002.

Batunanggar, S. (2002). *Indonesia's banking crisis resolution: Lesson and the way forward*. Paper presented at the The Banking Crisis Resolution Conference – CCBS, London.

Beck, T., Demirguc-Kunt, A., Laeven, L., & Levine, R. (2008). Finance, firm size, and growth. *Journal of Money, Credit and Banking, 40*(7), 1379–1405. https://doi.org/10.2307/25096315.

Bellucci, A., Borisov, A., & Zazzaro, A. (2010). Does gender matter in bank–firm relationships? Evidence from small business lending. *Journal of Banking & Finance, 34*(12), 2968–2984. https://doi.org/10.1016/j.jbankfin.2010.07.008.

Beltratti, A., & Stulz, R. M. (2012). The credit crisis around the globe: Why did some banks perform better? *Journal of Financial Economics, 105*(1), 1–17. https://doi.org/10.1016/j.jfineco.2011.12.005.

Berger, A. N. (1995). The relationship between capital and earnings in banking. *Journal of Money, Credit and Banking, 27*(2), 432–456. https://doi.org/10.2307/2077877.

Berger, A. N., Clarke, G. R. G., Cull, R., Klapper, L., & Udell, G. F. (2005). Corporate governance and bank performance: A joint analysis of the static, selection, and dynamic effects of domestic, foreign, and state ownership. *Journal of Banking & Finance, 29*(8–9), 2179–2221. https://doi.org/10.1016/j.jbankfin.2005.03.013.

Berger, A. N., Hasan, I., & Zhou, M. (2010). The effects of focus versus diversification on bank performance: Evidence from Chinese banks. *Journal of Banking & Finance, 34*(7), 1417–1435. https://doi.org/10.1016/j.jbankfin.2010.01.010.

Berger, A. N., Kick, T., & Schaeck, K. (2012). Executive board composition and bank risk taking. *Deutsche Bundesbank Research Centre Papers, 3*.

Bertrand, M., & Schoar, A. (2003). Managing with style: The effect of managers on firm policies. *The Quarterly Journal of Economics, 118*(4), 1169–1208. https://doi.org/10.2307/25053937.

Bilimoria, D. (2000). Building the business case for women corporate directors. In R. Burke & M. Mattis (Eds.), *Women on corporate boards of directors* (Vol. 14, pp. 25–40). Netherlands: Springer.

Boyd, B. (1990). Corporate linkages and organizational environment: A test of the resource dependence model. *Strategic Management Journal, 11*(6), 419–430. https://doi.org/10.1002/smj.4250110602.

Brown, D. A. H., Brown, D. L., & Anastasopoulos, V. (2002). *Women on boards: Not just the right thing ... but the 'bright' thing*. Canada: The Conference Board of Canada.

Campbell, K., & Mínguez-Vera, A. (2008). Gender diversity in the boardroom and firm financial performance. *Journal of Business Ethics, 83*(3), 435–451. https://doi.org/10.2307/25482388.

Caprio, G., Laeven, L., & Levine, R. (2007). Governance and bank valuation. *Journal of Financial Intermediation, 16*(4), 584–617. https://doi.org/10.1016/j.jfi.2006.10.003.

Carter, D. A., D'Souza, F., Simkins, B. J., & Simpson, W. G. (2010). The gender and ethnic diversity of US boards and board committees and firm financial performance. *Corporate Governance: An International Review, 18*(5), 396–414. https://doi.org/10.1111/j.1467-8683.2010.00809.x.

Carter, D. A., Simkins, B. J., & Simpson, W. G. (2003). Corporate governance, board diversity, and firm value. *Financial Review, 38*(1), 33–53. https://doi.org/10.1111/1540-6288.00034.

Chen, A., & Kao, L. (2011). Effect of collateral characteristics on bank performance: Evidence from collateralized stocks in Taiwan. *Journal of Banking & Finance, 35*(2), 300–309. https://doi.org/10.1016/j.jbankfin.2010.08.001.

Claessens, S., Djankov, S., & Lang, L. H. P. (2000). The separation of ownership and control in East Asian corporations. *Journal of Financial Economics, 58*(1–2), 81–112. https://doi.org/10.1016/S0304-405X(00)00067-2.

Claessens, S., & Fan, J. P. H. (2002). Corporate governance in Asia: A survey. *International Review of Finance, 3*(2), 71–103. https://doi.org/10.1111/1468-2443.00034.

Claessens, S., & Yurtoglu, B. B. (2013). Corporate governance in emerging markets: A survey. *Emerging Markets Review, 15*, 1–33. https://doi.org/10.1016/j.ememar.2012.03.002.

Cox, T. (2001). *Creating the multicultural organization: A strategy for capturing the power of diversity* (1st ed.). Jossey-Bass.

Darmadi, S. (2011). Board diversity and firm performance: The Indonesian. *Corporate Ownership and Control Journal, 8*.

Darmadi, S. (2013). Do women in top management affect firm performance? Evidence from Indonesia. *Corporate Governance: The international journal of business in society, 13*(3), 288–304.

Davies, L., Ducas, A., Mackenzie, A., Parker, S. J., Casserley, D., Vinnicombe, S., & Bott, S. (2011). *Women on boards*. London: The Women on Boards Steering Board, UK.

Davies, L., Ducas, A., Mackenzie, A., Parker, S. J., Casserley, D., Vinnicombe, S., & Bott, S. (2014). Women on boards: Davies review – Annual report 2014.

De Nicolo, G. (2000). Size, charter value and risk in banking: An international perspective. *International Finance Discussion Papers, 689*.

Demirgüç-Kunt, A., & Huizinga, H. (2010). Bank activity and funding strategies: The impact on risk and returns. *Journal of Financial Economics, 98*(3), 626–650. https://doi.org/10.1016/j.jfineco.2010.06.004.

DeYoung, R., & Roland, K. P. (2001). Product mix and earnings volatility at commercial banks: Evidence from a degree of total leverage model. *Journal of Financial Intermediation, 10*(1), 54–84. https://doi.org/10.1006/jfin.2000.0305.

Djankov, S., Jindra, J., & Klapper, L. F. (2005). Corporate valuation and the resolution of bank insolvency in East Asia. *Journal of Banking & Finance, 29*(8-9), 2095–2118. https://doi.org/10.1016/j.jbankfin.2005.03.010.

Djankov, S., La Porta, R., Lopez-de-Silanes, F., & Shleifer, A. (2008). The law and economics of self-dealing. *Journal of Financial Economics, 88*(3), 430–465. https://doi.org/10.1016/j.jfineco.2007.02.007.

Eklund, J. E., Palmberg, J. K., & Wiberg, D. (2009). Ownership structure, boardcomposition and investment performance. *Working Paper Series in Economics and Institutions of Innovation, 172*.

Elron, E. (1997). Top management teams within multinational corporations: Effects of cultural heterogeneity. *The Leadership Quarterly, 8*(4), 393–412. https://doi.org/10.1016/S1048-9843(97)90021-7.

Erhardt, N. L., Werbel, J. D., & Shrader, C. B. (2003). Board of director diversity and firm financial performance. *Corporate Governance: An International Review, 11*(2), 102–111. https://doi.org/10.1111/1467-8683.00011.

Erkens, D. H., Hung, M., & Matos, P. (2012). Corporate governance in the 2007–2008 financial crisis: Evidence from financial institutions worldwide. *Journal of Corporate Finance, 18*(2), 389–411. https://doi.org/10.1016/j.jcorpfin.2012.01.005.

Fahlenbrach, R., & Stulz, R. M. (2011). Bank CEO incentives and the credit crisis. *Journal of Financial Economics, 99*(1), 11–26. https://doi.org/10.1016/j.jfineco.2010.08.010.

Fama, E. F. (1980). Agency Problems and the Theory of the Firm. *Journal of Political Economy, 88*(2), 288–307. https://doi.org/10.2307/1837292.

Fang, Y., Francis, B., & Hasan, I. (2012). More than connectedness – Heterogeneity of CEO social network and firm value. *Bank of Finland Research Discussion Paper, 26*.

Farrell, K. A., & Hersch, P. L. (2005). Additions to corporate boards: The effect of gender. *Journal of Corporate Finance, 11*(1–2), 85–106.

Ferreira, D. (2010). Board diversity. In H. K. Baker & R. Anderson (Eds.), *Corporate governance: A synthesis of theory, research, and practice*. Hoboken, NJ: Wiley.

Gabrielsson, J., & Huse, M. (2004). Context, behavior, and evolution: Challenges in research on boards and governance. *International Studies of Management & Organization, 34*(2), 11–36. https://doi.org/10.2307/40397590.

Goyeau, D., & Tarazi, A. (1992). Evaluation of risk of failure banking in Europe. *Journal of Political Economy, 102*(3), 249–280.

Grable, J. E., McGill, S., & Britt, S. L. (2009). Risk tolerance estimation bias: The age effect. *Journal of Business & Economics Research, 7*(7), 1–12.

Graham, J. R., & Harvey, C. R. (2001). The theory and practice of corporate finance: Evidence from the field. *Journal of Financial Economics, 60*(2–3), 187–243. https://doi.org/10.1016/S0304-405X(01)00044-7.

Hagendorff, J., & Keasey, K. (2012). The value of board diversity in banking: Evidence from the market for corporate control. *European Journal of Finance, 18*(1), 41–58.

Hanazaki, M., & Liu, Q. (2007). Corporate governance and investment in East Asian firms—empirical analysis of family-controlled firms. *Journal of Asian Economics, 18*(1), 76–97. https://doi.org/10.1016/j.asieco.2006.12.003.

Harrison, D. A., & Klein, K. J. (2007). What's the difference? diversity constructs as separation, variety, or disparity in organizations. *Academy of Management Review, 32*(4), 1199–1228. https://doi.org/10.5465/amr.2007.26586096.

Harrison, D. A., & Sin, H.-P. (2006). What is diversity and how should it be measured? In A. M. Konrad, P. Prasad, & J. K. Pringle (Eds.), *Handbook of workplace diversity* (pp. 192–218). London: SAGE Publications Ltd..

Hermalin, B. E., & Weisbach, M. S. (2003). Boards of directors as an endogenously determined institution: A survey of the economic literature. *Economic Policy Review, 9*, 7–26.

Hillman, A. J., & Dalziel, T. (2003). Boards of directors and firm performance: Integrating agency and resource dependence perspectives. *The Academy of Management Review, 28*(3), 383–396. https://doi.org/10.2307/30040728.

Indonesian Financial Service Authority (Otoritas Jasa Keuangan, OJK). (2016a). Regulation No.27/POJK.03/2016 on fit and proper tes.

Indonesian Financial Service Authority (Otoritas Jasa Keuangan, OJK). (2016b). Circular Letter No.31/SEOJK.05/2016 on fit and proper tes for financial service institutions primary parties.

Khanna, T., & Yafeh, Y. (2007). Business groups in emerging markets: Paragons or parasites? *Journal of Economic Literature, 45*, 331–372.

Laeven, L. (1999). Risk and efficiency in East Asian banks. Research Working Paper Series, The World Bank, 2255. https://doi.org/10.1596/1813-9450-2255

Lepetit, L., Nys, E., Rous, P., & Tarazi, A. (2008). Bank income structure and risk: An empirical analysis of European banks. *Journal of Banking & Finance, 32*(8):1452–1467.

Levine, R. (2004). The corporate governance of banks: A concise discussion of concepts and evidence. *World Bank Policy Research Working Paper, 3404*.

Liang, Q., Xu, P., & Jiraporn, P. (2013). Board characteristics and Chinese bank performance. *Journal of Banking & Finance, 37*(8), 2953–2968. https://doi.org/10.1016/j.jbankfin.2013.04.018.

Lin, X., & Zhang, Y. (2009). Bank ownership reform and bank performance in China. *Journal of Banking & Finance, 33*(1), 20–29. https://doi.org/10.1016/j.jbankfin.2006.11.022.

Masulis, R. W., Wang, C., & Xie, F. (2012). Globalizing the boardroom—The effects of foreign directors on corporate governance and firm performance. *Journal of Accounting and Economics, 53*(3), 527–554. https://doi.org/10.1016/j.jacceco.2011.12.003.

Mateos de Cabo, R., Gimeno, R., & Nieto, M. (2012). Gender diversity on European banks' boards of directors. *Journal of Business Ethics, 109*(2), 145–162. https://doi.org/10.1007/s10551-011-1112-6.

Mattis, M. C. (2000). Women corporate directors in the United States. In R. Burke & M. Mattis (Eds.), *Women on corporate boards of directors* (Vol. 14, pp. 43–56). Netherlands: Springer.

Maudos, J. N., & Fernández de Guevara, J. (2004). Factors explaining the interest margin in the banking sectors of the European Union. *Journal of Banking & Finance, 28*(9), 2259–2281. https://doi.org/10.1016/j.jbankfin.2003.09.004.

May, D. O. (1995). Do managerial motives influence firm risk reduction strategies? *The Journal of Finance, 50*(4), 1291–1308. https://doi.org/10.2307/2329353.

Milliken, F. J., & Martins, L. L. (1996). Searching for common threads: Understanding the multiple effects of diversity in organizational groups. *The Academy of Management Review, 21*(2), 402–433. https://doi.org/10.2307/258667.

Monks, R. A. G., & Minow, N. (2011). *Corporate governance* (5th ed.). Hoboken, NJ: Wiley.

Morgan, D. P. (2002). Rating banks: Risk and uncertainty in an opaque industry. *The American Economic Review, 92*(4), 874–888. https://doi.org/10.2307/3083285.

Mueller, D. C. (2003). *Public choice III* (3rd ed.). Cambridge: Cambridge University Press.

Obata, S. (2003). Pyramid business groups in East Asia: Insurance or tunneling? *CEI Working Paper Series, 2002-13*.

OECD. (2013). Corporate Governance: Better policies for board nomination and election in Asia: OECD Publishing. http://dx.doi.org/10.1787/9789264204386-en.

Pathan, S. (2009). Strong boards, CEO power and bank risk-taking. *Journal of Banking & Finance, 33*(7), 1340–1350. https://doi.org/10.1016/j.jbankfin.2009.02.001.

Pathan, S., & Faff, R. (2013). Does board structure in banks really affect their performance? *Journal of Banking & Finance, 37*(5), 1573–1589. https://doi.org/10.1016/j.jbankfin.2012.12.016.

Pathan, S., Skully, M., & Wickramanayake, J. (2008). Board size, independence and performance: An analysis of Thai banks. *Asia-Pacific Financial Markets, 14*(3), 211–227. https://doi.org/10.1007/s10690-007-9060-y.

Robinson, G., & Dechant, K. (1997). Building a business case for diversity. *The Academy of Management Executive, 11*(3), 21–31. https://doi.org/10.2307/4165408.

Rose, C. (2007). Does female board representation influence firm performance? The Danish evidence. *Corporate Governance: An International Review, 15*(2), 404–413. https://doi.org/10.1111/j.1467-8683.2007.00570.x.

Saito, R., & Dutra, M. G. L. (2006). Board of directors of publicly-held companies in Brazil: Profile and implications for minority shareholders. *Corporate Governance: An International Review, 14*(2), 98–106.

Schaffer, M. E. (2010). XTIVREG2: Stata module to perform extended IV/2SLS, GMM and AC/HAC, LIML and k-class regression for panel data models. Vol. S456501. Statistical Software Components: Boston College Department of Economics.

Setiyono, B. (2014). *Essays on bank corporate governance in Asia and emerging markets*. Unpublised Dissertation. Université de Limoges, France.

Setiyono, B., & Tarazi, A. (2014). *Does diversity of bank board members affect performance and risk? Evidence from an emerging market*. Available at SSRN: https://ssrn.com/abstract=2491145.

Shleifer, A., & Vishny, R. W. (1997). A survey of corporate governance. *Journal of Finance, 52*(2), 737–783.

Simons, T., Pelled, L. H., & Smith, K. A. (1999). Making use of difference diversity, debate, and decision comprehensiveness in top management teams. *The Academy of Management Journal, 42*(6), 662–673.

Simpson, W. G. C., David, A., & D'Souza, F. (2010). What do we know about women on boards? *Journal of Applied Finance, 20*(2), 27–39.

Terjesen, S., Sealy, R., & Singh, V. (2009). Women directors on corporate boards: A review and research agenda. *Corporate Governance: An International Review, 17*(3), 320–337.

Terjesen, S., & Singh, V. (2008). Female presence on corporate boards: A multi-country study of environmental context. *Journal of Business Ethics, 83*(1), 55–63. https://doi.org/10.1007/s10551-007-9656-1.

Treichler, C. M. (1995). Diversity of board members and organizational performance: An integrative perspective. *Corporate Governance: An International Review, 3*(4), 189–200. https://doi.org/10.1111/j.1467-8683.1995.tb00116.x.

Vafeas, N. (2003). Length of board tenure and outside director independence. *Journal of Business Finance & Accounting, 30*(7-8), 1043–1064. https://doi.org/10.1111/1468-5957.05525.

van der Walt, N., & Ingley, C. (2003). Board dynamics and the influence of professional background, gender and ethnic diversity of directors. *Corporate Governance: An International Review, 11*(3), 218–234. https://doi.org/10.1111/1467-8683.00320.

Westphal, J. D., & Milton, L. P. (2000). How experience and network ties affect the influence of demographic minorities on corporate boards. *Administrative Science Quarterly, 45*(2), 366–398. https://doi.org/10.2307/2667075.

Zhang, P. (2007). Top management team heterogeneity and firm performance: An empirical research on Chinese listed companies. *Frontiers of Business Research in China, 1*(1), 123–134. https://doi.org/10.1007/s11782-007-0008-x.

Zhuang, J., David, E., Webb, D. C., & Capulong, M. V. (2000). *Corporate governance and finance in East Asia: A study of Indonesia, Republic of Korea, Malaysia, Philippines, and Thailand* (Vol. 1). Manila, Philippines: Asian Development Bank.

Chapter 10
Insider Trading and Corporate Governance in the Banking Sector. New Lessons on the Entrenchment Effect

Esther B. del Brio, Javier Perote, Alberto de Miguel, and Gerardo Gómez

10.1 Introduction

Corporate governance at the banking industry has become one of the main research topic in recent times due not only to the financial crisis that affected Europe and Western countries in the beginning of the twenty-first century, but also to the fact that the available literature is somewhat scarce when compared to the literature on corporate governance for non-financial firms. In this sense, if we come to analyze the goodness of the corporate governance system as control mechanism that prevents a variety of opportunistic behaviors in the banking sector, the available literature is very scarce. That is the case for the analysis of banking insider trading and the effects of control mechanisms as its deterrents.

In fact, little can be said about insider trading in the bank industry since financial firms are usually dropped from the studies on insider trading due to their particular characteristics (as in Seyhun 1988; Del Brio et al. 2002; Hillier and Marshall 2002; or Del Brio and Miguel 2010). Baesel and Stein (1979), Lee and Bishara (1989) and Madura and Wiant (1995) found that banking insiders obtained abnormal returns when trading in their own firms' shares on the Canadian and US markets, concluding that purchases have greater informational content than sales. Baesel and Stein (1979) analyse bank insider trading for Canadian markets. More recently, Bhattacharya and Daouk (2002, 2009), Lo et al. (2006), Friedrich (2016) or Ali et al. (2011), for mutual funds, Cline et al. (2014), for REITS, Verstein (2016) for

E.B. del Brio (✉) • J. Perote • A. de Miguel
University of Salamanca, Salamanca, Spain
e-mail: edelbrio@usal.es; perote@usal.es; amiguel@usal.es

G. Gómez
Universidad de Piura, Piura, Peru
e-mail: lgomezj@unp.edu.pe

B. Díaz Díaz et al. (eds.), *Corporate Governance in Banking and Investor Protection*, CSR, Sustainability, Ethics & Governance,
https://doi.org/10.1007/978-3-319-70007-6_10

commodity markets, or Ryan et al. (2016) for securization and insider trading, have advanced research in the topic. The empirical analyses conclude that bank directors have unbeatable access to private information, and are in a better position than corporate insiders in other industries' firms. The reasoning being, among other things, that they control a substantial portion on the bank's ownership and are members of the boards of directors of other non-financial companies.

Still, most research on bank insider trading applies the event study's methodology to calculate the abnormal returns associated with insider dealings, and unanimously conclude that bank insiders obtain abnormal returns in their open-market transactions thanks to their access to relevant private corporate information (Baesel and Stein 1979; Madura and Wiant 1995; Jordan 1999; Ramirez and Yung 2000; Slovin et al. 1991; and Madison et al. 2004, among others). Abnormal profits are also detected for the banking industry when analyzing insider trading around corporate announcements such as mergers and acquisitions (Madison et al. 2004), when analyzing investment banking reputation in initial public offerings (Ramirez and Yung 2000) and when analyzing sales of corporate assets (Hirschey et al. 1990).

To approach the analysis of the factors triggering insider trading, we apply the agency theory of insider trading (Beny 2007; 2008), which holds that the manager-shareholder conflict is the core theoretical lens through which to analyse the positive and negative externalities of insider trading. Unlike Zhang (2001), who states that insider trading mitigates the problem of information asymmetry and allows shareholders to better control management, most of the financial literature supports the opposite idea, and analyses insider trading as a manifestation of the lack of control shareholders have on managers and, thus, a source of agency costs due to the need to monitor opportunistic managers. As a result, a negative relationship is commonly expected between the convergence of property and control interests and insider trading activity.

Conversely, Jordan (1999) concludes that trading by bank insiders helps to reduce the agency problem, since, by exploiting specific private information, bank directors increase the rate of return and reduce the riskiness of their investments in their bank. If we can consider that it exits widespread literature that detects that bank insiders obtain abnormal profits from their private information, then it would be worthy to analyze how internal control mechanisms in the financial firms could be mitigating insider trading, its intensity and its profitability.

To clarify these issues, we next examine the effects on insider trading activity of several factors that are crucial to understanding managers' behaviour in the banking sector, and which are mainly related to the behaviour and monitoring of bank management. Among them, we highlight bank reputation, bank risk, bank capitalisation and insider ownership. Some of these are analysed for the first time in the insider trading literature or on the banking insider trading literature (charter value, risk-taking incentives, entrenchment and capitalisation).

We also followed, however, previous literature, such as Madura and Wiant (1995), who single out bank size as one of the main variables since small banks are less controlled by analysts and investors, so that their directors can have access to a greater volume of reserved information than large banks. Ramirez and Yung (2000) on a different topic show that the bank's reputation is such an important asset for an investment bank that it can restrict the trading behaviour of the insider. Thus, the insiders of the most prestigious banks are less likely to trade on private information.

The aim of the current paper is focused on the first target: to determine how control internal mechanisms may reduce the propensity of insiders to invest on their own firms' shares. For that purpose, firstly we calculate the ratio and intensity of banking insider trading activity and secondly we analyze the relationship between insider trading intensity and several internal control mechanisms. Based on the agency theory of insider trading, a negative relationship is commonly expected between insider trading activity and the convergence of property and control interests, since insider trading is considered as an abuse of private knowledge and a proof of distrust of the firms' managers versus the proprietors of the firms' capital. Nevertheless, the entrenchment theory and some stakeholders' oriented theories are capital for developing our hypotheses and will be more deeply analyzed in the hypotheses section.

Thus, this research tells us about the factors which enhance bank insider trading and those which help to diminish it. Using a sample of Spanish banking insider trading and robust panel data methodology, we find evidence that insider trading is positively correlated with larger bank size, less prestige, lower charter values for high levels of ownership and entrenched directors. Entrenchment seems to be clearly related to insider trading, thus indicating that managers may extract two-fold private benefits. Furthermore, entrenchment modifies the risk-taking incentives of managers, which in turn has a direct effect on financial costs, bank performance and firm value. In this sense, our results provide evidence against the lower monitoring of small caps. Actually, the positive relationship between insider trading activity and size could be understood as an achievement of entrenched managers, that not only invest based on private information, but also reach one of their main perquisites—firm growth. We also find that banks are much aware of their corporate reputation and, thus, more prestigious banks usually prevent their managers from trading based on private information.

The remainder of the chapter is organized as follows: Sect. 10.2.1 presents a review of the literature on bank insider trading and poses the hypotheses to be tested to identify the factors that explain insider trading in the Spanish banking industry. Section 10.2.2 describes the sample and methodology used. Section 10.2.3 presents the model estimation and results, and Sect. 10.3 presents and discusses the estimation results and gives conclusions.

10.2 Corporate Governance, Firm-Specific Factors and Insider Transactions

10.2.1 Hypotheses

As stated before, the agency theory of insider trading holds that the manager–shareholder conflict is the lens through which to analyze insider trading. Insider trading is thus as a manifestation of the lack of control shareholders have over managers and a source of agency costs due to the need to monitor opportunistic managers. As a result, a negative relationship is commonly expected between insider trading activity and the convergence of property and control interests (as in Fidrmuc et al. 2006; Betzer and Theissen 2009).

Under this assumption, we next examine the effects on insider trading activity of several factors that are crucial to understanding manager behavior and corporate governance in the banking sector: the level of manager entrenchment, the level of manager discretion, the level of managers' risk-taking incentives and the effects of self-regulation and external regulation.

Jensen and Meckling (1976) defined ownership by directors as an efficient mechanism to more closely align managers' interests with those of shareholders. The higher the director ownership, the higher the alignment of interests among control and property groups. Jordan (1999) shows that bank directors who own a high percentage of the firm's shares tend to trade less opportunistically on private information, thus assuming that the alignment of interests is a prelude for less insider trading activity.

Nevertheless, the entrenchment literature (Shleifer and Vishny 1989) has brought to light the fact that, when insider ownership surpasses an optimal threshold, an increase in insider ownership makes managers entrenched and allows them to satisfy their non-value-maximizing objectives without endangering their employment and status. However, although the relationship between entrenchment and firm value is well documented, no evidence has yet been found regarding the level of director entrenchment and bank insider trading. Since entrenchment usually exacerbates both information asymmetry and non–value-maximizing behaviors, we expect a positive relationship between insider trading activity and the level of entrenchment. Therefore, a cubic relationship is expected between bank insider ownership and bank insider trading intensity, i.e., we expect a negative relationship for low and very high levels of insider ownership and a positive relationship for moderate and high stakes, due to the entrenchment effects. In short, we expect a non-linear relationship between insider trading and insider ownership, which is based on the non-linear relationship between insider ownership and firm value already documented by Shleifer and Vishny (1989) for the US case and Miguel et al. (2004) for the Spanish non-financial firms.

To properly examine this relationship, we construct the variable insider ownership (IO), its square (IO^2) and its cubic (IO^3). IO is measured as the number of shares held by bank directors at the end of the previous period divided by the total number of outstanding shares, as developed in Jordan (1999) and Lee (2002), He and Rui (2016), among others. We use these to test the following hypothesis:

Hypothesis 1 The more entrenched the bank director, the higher the intensity of bank insider trading.

Despite the crucial influence of charter value on bank risk and bank performance, no evidence has yet been found regarding the relationship between charter value and insider trading. Charter value (understood as the value of the right to continue to operate) has traditionally been used as an indicator of risk-taking incentives for bank directors. In fact, we use charter value in this study as a proxy for risk-taking incentives in order to understand how the level of risk that managers are willing to take on enhances insider trading. Since no evidence has been uncovered in the existing literature regarding this relationship within the bank industry, this remains an open empirical question.

According to Keeley (1990), Demsetz et al. (1996) or González (2005), for the Spanish market, lower charter values are traditionally associated with greater risk-taking incentives. However, Gorton and Rosen (1995), Jordan (1999) and Cebenoyan et al. (1999) acknowledge that as long as insiders increase their proportion of the firm's wealth, they increase their exposure to undiversifiable risk in such a way that, when property and control interests are aligned, insiders will attempt to take on only profitable risks, thus modifying the expected relationship between charter value and risk-taking incentives. Therefore, according to these authors, to determine the effects of managers' risk aversion, we first should determine how the alignment (or lack of alignment) of interests is affecting risk-taking incentives.

According to González (2005), lower charter values are traditionally associated with greater risk-taking incentives. However, Gorton and Rosen (1995) and Cebenoyan et al. (1999) acknowledge that, as long as insiders increase their proportion of the firm's wealth, they increase their exposure to undiversifiable risk in such a way that, when property and control interests are aligned, insiders will attempt to take on only profitable risks, thus modifying the expected relationship between charter value and risk-taking incentives. Therefore, according to these authors, to determine the effects of managers' risk aversion, we first should determine how the level of alignment of interests is affecting risk-taking incentives.

For that reason, we follow Cebenoyan et al. (1999) and create the slope interaction variable between charter value (proxying risk-taking incentives) and inside ownership, which indicates how the impact of risk incentives on insider trading is correlated to insider ownership. However, as an increase in insider ownership beyond an optimal level may produce entrenchment problems, we go further and examine the relationship between risk-taking incentives and insider trading by controlling the effects of entrenchment. In this case, lower charter values should still lead to greater risk-taking incentives and higher insider trading activity—the reason why a negative relationship is thus expected between the variables.

For this purpose, we construct the slope interaction variable between charter value and the square of inside ownership. To proxy charter value, we used Tobin's Q, previously used by González (2008), which modifies the traditional market-to-book value of equity by proxying the market value of assets by the book value of assets minus the book value of equity plus the market value of common stocks.

Hypothesis 2 The lower the charter value at entrenchment levels, the higher the intensity of bank insider trading.

As noted by Furfine (2001), in the presence of a supervisory discipline effect, excess capital increases, since banks attempt to avoid costs related to market discipline and supervisory intervention if they approach or fall below the regulatory minimum capital ratio. Since supervisors and market discipline help to reduce information asymmetry, the increase in excess capital may lead to less control and thus more severe insider trading activity. Therefore, a positive relationship could be expected between these variables. In the literature, however, lower capitalization has been shown to be related to more opportunistic behavior from managers, probably because, under the bad management hypothesis, managers have over-invested in non-valuable investment projects, thus reducing bank capital (Williams 2004). According to this reasoning, a negative relationship should be expected between insider trading activity and excess capital.

In fact, when excess capital is considered a proxy of external regulation, a positive relationship is expected. However, when it is considered as a proxy of the level of manager discretionality, a negative relationship is expected. Since no evidence has yet been found regarding this relationship and different theories support contradictory expectations, we consider it an open empirical question.

To proxy excess bank capital, we follow Furfine (2001) and use the excess capital-to-asset ratio, measured as the difference between the ratio of the book value of equity to the book value of risky assets minus the regulatory minimum capital ratio (8%).

Hypothesis 3 The lower the excess capital, the higher the intensity of bank insider trading.

Reputation, together with size, media attention and analyst interest, is usually considered a proxy for the firms' transparency or visibility, as in Dyck et al. (2008). Bad management, opportunistic behavior and rent-expropriation by managers erode bank reputation, which is one of the firm's main assets. Therefore, much effort should be devoted to protecting the firm from being the subject of bad news, misleading rumors and financial scandals, among them insider trading. When reputation matters, firms usually dissuade their managers from severely trading on their own bank shares so as not to attract the attention of the media and to avoid the negative impact that profitable trading by insiders might have on future share prices.

Ramirez and Yung (2000) analyze the influence of reputation on insider trading behavior for a sample of investment banks and conclude that the insider trading activities of the more prestigious investment banks are less likely to show systematic patterns of abnormal profits since their reputation will exert a constraint on improper insider trades. Although no evidence has been documented regarding the relationship between insider trading and commercial bank reputation, a negative relationship would be expected.

Reputation for US investment banks is usually proxied by way of the Carter and Manaster (1990) underwriter prestige ranking; however, it is difficult to measure reputation for commercial banks outside the US. Furthermore, our study focuses on Spanish commercial banks, for which no prestige ranking mechanism exists. However, investors usually react positively to any Spanish bank belonging to the Forbes Global 2000, a list of the world's two thousand largest companies based on a composite ranking of sales, profits, assets and market value.

Therefore, we construct a dummy variable that takes the value of 1 for Spanish banks ranking among the first 2000 firms within the Forbes Global 2000 (which we consider prestigious), and takes the value of zero, otherwise. About 40% of the banks in the sample ranked among the first 2000 firms in at least one year within the sample period.

Hypothesis 4 The worse a bank's reputation, the higher the intensity of bank insider trading.

10.2.2 Sample and Methodology

This study analyses the legal open market transactions carried out by presidents, vice-presidents and directors in Spanish commercial banks between January 1994 and December 2003, that were reported by the insiders themselves to the Comisión Nacional del Mercado de Valores (CNMV) as required by the Spanish Securities Market Law. The data were obtained from the Insiders Dealings Records provided by the CNMV. The sample analyzed comprises 4623 insider transactions in 18 commercial banks quoted on the continuous market. Out of these transactions, 3089 were purchases and 1534 were sales. Stock prices and other data needed to construct the insider trading indexes, as well as the explanatory variables of the model estimated in Eq. (10.1), were obtained from the Datastream and Bankscope databases.

Table 10.1 gives the descriptive statistics of the banks in our sample.

The annual financial data from 1994 to 2003 were averaged and the mean, median, standard deviation, and maximum and minimum values of these averaged values were obtained. Results are shown in Panel A. Panel B shows the estimations of the annual stock returns and insider transactions from 1994 to 2003. The stock returns during this period were generally positive, with the highest average returns in 1997 and negative average returns in 1994 and 2003. The average number of purchase transactions by insiders was substantially lower in 1997 and 1998 than in the rest of the study period, while the average number of sale transactions was significantly lower from 1997 to 2000 compared to the rest of the study period. The average number of shares bought by bank insiders increased tenfold from 1994 to 2003. Likewise, the average number of shares sold increased almost 14-fold over the study period.

Since the aim of this paper was to analyze the effects of corporate governance on the propensity of banking insiders to use and abuse of private information, our target was not to measure abnormal returns and profitability but just to measure the intensity and frequency of bank insider transactions. For this purpose, we rely on the insider trading measures which has been found to better explain insider trading in Spain (Del Brio 2006) and other contexts (Karpoff and Lee 1991; Yur-Austin 1998).

Table 10.1 Descriptive statistics

Thousands of euros	Mean	Median	Standard deviation	Minimum	Maximum
Panel A. Financial data					
Total assets	32,572,691	6,413,236	63,881,435	851,607	224,032,798
Net income	2,694,051	439,618	5,698,630	33,164	20,499,721
Net result	231,341	52,192	425,886	−6186	1,408,294
Return-on-assets (%)	0.95	0.74	0.76	−0.83	2.27

Panel B. Mean values of stock returns and indexes of insider trading for the banks in the sample

		Average number of transactions by insider		Average number of shares traded		Insider trading index
Year	Return	Purchases	Sales	Purchases	Sales	*SNVI*
1994	−0.038	29	20	1,817,849	697,812	5,182,307
1995	0.042	32	18	2,860,639	1,798,237	4,380,712
1996	0.090	34	28	4,776,971	1,812,055	2,062,939
1997	0.184	14	12	1,858,119	464,307	4,357,295
1998	0.091	2	1	457,106	2,547,833	588,730
1999	0.006	29	5	9,060,779	988,973	19,140,555
2000	0.010	40	7	3,183,494	5,527,863	2,969,734
2001	0.008	32	21	4,272,089	4,730,692	476,474
2002	−0.036	28	26	35,303,462	50,386,384	940,440
2003	0.129	26	26	18,326,734	10,079,396	17,207,039

This table reports descriptive statistics for the banks in the sample each year from 1994 to 2003. Panel A displays the mean, median, standard deviation, minimum and maximum values for the variables total assets, net income, net results and return on assets over the study period. Panel B displays the yearly average number of insider transactions, total number of shares traded by insider and values for the four indexes of insider trading. *SNVI* and *NVI*. $SNVI_{it}$ represents the EPS Standardized Net Euro Volume Index for period t, and is defined as $SNVI_{it} = NVI_{it}/EPS_{it}$, where NVI_{it} is the net volume index for firm i and period t and is measured as $NVI_{it} = NV_{it}/(P_{it} + S_{it}) = (P_{it} - S_{it})/(P_{it} + S_{it})$, and EPS_{it} is the earnings-per-share ratio for firm i at period t. P_{it} is the volume of purchases for month t and firm I and S_{it} is the volume of sales in firm i and month t.

The insider trading index is thus calculated as the absolute value of the difference between the euro volume of insider purchases minus sales, standardized by the earnings-per-share ratio in a certain month, as in Eq. (10.1):

$$SNVI_{it} = NV_{it}/EPS_{it}, \tag{10.1}$$

where $SNVI_{it}$ represents the EPS Standardized Net Euro Volume Index for period t, NV_{it} is the difference between purchases and sales for period t (also referred to as volume of net purchases) and EPS_{it} is the earnings-per-share ratio for period t. Karpoff and Lee (1991) and Del Brio (2006) support the standardization of insider trading indexes by EPS, since it has been proven to be the main feature of the firm that should be controlled for when measuring the severeness of insider trading.

Table 10.2 Descriptive statistics and Pearson's correlations of the variables in the models

	Mean	Median	Standard deviation	*LSNVI*	*REPU*	*IO*	*CV*	*BC*	*SIZE*
LSNVI	11.82	12.40	3.71	1.00					
REPU	0.42	0.00	0.50	0.12	1.00				
IO	51.44	49.43	33.14	−0.45	−0.59	1.00			
CV	49.92	41.85	38.27	−0.46	−0.64	−0.64	1.00		
BC	0.08	0.07	0.04	−0.52	−0.42	−0.42	0.55	1.00	
SIZE	14.03	13.54	1.57	0.29	0.57	0.57	−0.29	−0.47	1.00

This table reports the mean, median, standard deviation and Pearson's correlations for the following variables: $LSNVI_{it}$ is the natural logarithm of the absolute value of the *EPS*-standardized net volume of insider transactions; REPU_{it} is the bank reputation; IO_{it} is the percentage of shares in the hands of bank directors; CV_{it} is the charter value, as measured by Tobin's Q; $CV{*}IO^2$ is the slope interaction variable between charter value and the entrenchment effect; BC_{it} is the ratio of excess equity to total assets; and $SIZE_{it}$ is the natural logarithm of the market value of outstanding firms.

Taking this index as dependent variable of our model, we next examine which firm corporate governance characteristics may be triggering insider transactions, applying Generalized Least Squares panel data estimation for a complete unbalanced panel composed of 18 banks and a 10-year time series running from 1993 to 2004.

Controlling for time-specific effects in our study is of great importance due to possible changes in the macroeconomic environment or regulation affecting Spanish banks, as well as changes in technology, as noted by Williams (2004), among others. We use GLS estimation and included T − 1 lags as instrumental variables for the explanatory variables in order to control for endogeneity. Table 10.2 shows the descriptive statistics and Pearson's correlation for the explanatory variables.

Thus, the estimated model is expressed according to Eq. (10.2):

$$\begin{aligned} LSNVI_{it} = \beta_0 + \beta_1 IO_{it} + \beta_2 IO_{it}^2 + \beta_3 IO_{it}^3 + \beta_4 CV_{it}{*}IO_{it}^2 + \\ + \beta_5 BC_{it} + \beta_6 REPU_{it} + \beta_7 SIZE_{it} + u_{it} \end{aligned} \tag{10.2}$$

where $u_{it} = \eta_i + \delta_t + \varepsilon_{it}$, η_{it} corrects for bank-specific effects and δ_t for time-effects, and ε_{it} is the disturbance of the model. The dependent variable in our study is the absolute value of the logarithm conversion of the *SNVI* index, measured as the net euro volume of insider purchases standardized by the earnings-per-share ratio. This index is chosen as the dependent variable in our model because it is found to be the most significant measure of insider trading among the four indexes tested in this paper. We use the absolute value of the index since it is used as an index of severeness of insider trading regardless of the sign of the transaction.

Finally, bank size is used as a control variable since it is often correlated with other unobserved variables (such as managerial abilities and asset diversification). The description and measurement of different variables is displayed in Appendix.

10.2.3 Results

Results of the estimation are shown in Table 10.3. The variables *IO*, IO^2 and IO^3, which capture the non-linear expected relationship between insider trading and insider ownership, are all significant and the signs are as expected. *IO* is negatively related to insider trading, which means that, as insider ownership increases, directors are more aligned with shareholder interests and they trade less severely on private information. At the same time, IO^2 is positively related to insider trading at the 1% significance level, which means that, above a certain threshold, the higher the inside ownership, the higher the insider trading activity. Finally, IO^3 is negatively related to insider trading activity.

This confirms that, at moderate-to-high levels of insider ownership, the convergence of interests is not guaranteed and insiders behave opportunistically by increasing their insider trading activity. We are unaware of any previous paper analyzing the combined effects of insider trading and entrenchment for the banking

Table 10.3 Factors triggering insider trading in the Spanish banking industry: Panel data estimation

Explanatory variables	Coefficient	t-Ratio	p-Value
IO	−0.013	−1.84*	0.072
IO^2	0.008	2.88**	0.004
IO^3	−0.000	−1.98**	0.087
$CV{*}IO^2$	−0.009	−3.43**	0.001
BC	−1.638	−3.14**	0.002
REPU	−4.726	−2.83**	0.005
SIZE	1.289	0.05	0.958
CONSTANT	−6.701	−0.86	0.388
Wald test (p-value)	52.18 (0.0001)		
R^2	0.66		
Number of observations: 798			

This table reports coefficients, t-statistics and Wald tests for the GLS estimation of the parameters of a panel data model with random effects. $LSNVI_{it}$ is the natural logarithm of the absolute value of the EPS standardized net volume of insider trading; $SIZE_{it}$ is the natural logarithm of the market value of outstanding firms; IO_{it}, $IO^2{}_{it}$ and $IO^3{}_{it}$ are the percentage of shares in the hands of bank directors, its square and its cubic, respectively; CV_{it} is the charter value, as measured by Tobin's Q; $CV{*}IO^2$ is the slope interaction variable between charter value and the entrenchment effect; BC_{it} is the ratio of excess equity to total assets; $REPU_{it}$ is the bank reputation; η_{it} corrects for bank-specific effects and δ_t for time-effects; and ε_{it} is the disturbance of the model.

$$LSNVI_{it} = \beta_0 + \beta_1 IO_{it} + \beta_2 IO^2{}_{it} + \beta_2 IO^3{}_{it} + \beta_3 CV^{*}IO^2{}_{it} + \beta_4 BC_{it} + +\beta_5 REPU_{it} + \beta_6 SIZE_{it}$$
$$+\eta_i + \delta_t + \varepsilon_{it}$$

Panel data model is estimated using GLS panel data. Model is estimated after taking first differences of the variables so as to eliminate the individual effect, and lags t − 2 have been used as instruments for the explanatory variables in order to control for endogeneity. Heteroskedasticity-consistent asymptotic standard error in parentheses. Wald test is the tests the joint significance of the reported coefficients, asymptotically distributed as χ^2 under the null of no relationship, degrees of freedom in parentheses. * and ** stand for 5% and 1% level of significance, respectively

sector, but this first insight seems to indicate that as directors get more entrenched and shareholder control is less efficient, managers trade more severely on private information.

The slope interaction variable CV^*IO^2, which captures the effects of risk-taking incentives on insider trading when controlling for its correlation with the level of entrenchment, is significant and negatively related to insider trading activity, as expected. This variable is tested for the first time in the insider trading literature, and it corroborates the position in Klock (1994) that, when managers are allowed to trade on private corporate information, they usually take on too much risk, although we should specify that this happens only when managers are entrenched. The obtained relationship indicates that risk-taking incentives are higher for managers trading on their own firms as long as the level of insider ownership departs from control levels.

The evidence shown in this paper clearly supports that a lack of alignment of interests leads to managers behaving opportunistically and, more specifically, managers trading on private information. This fact is also corroborated by the coefficient obtained for excess capitalization (*BC*), which is negative and significant, suggesting that, for the Spanish banks, thin capitalization works as an indicator of opportunistic behaviors from the side of managers. These managers are not only more likely to over-invest in non-profitable projects, but they are also more likely to increase their insider trading activity. We may also conclude that this result supports the philosophy behind the Basel I Capital Accord, which advocates close surveillance of thin capitalized banks under the presumption that these banks are the most likely to incur in opportunistic behavior.

Finally, reputation is also significant and negatively related with insider trading activity, which confirms the expectation that, when firms care about their collective reputation, they provide incentives to their managers not to trade on the basis of private information as a way of protecting the firm from financial scandals. Size, considered as a control variable, is significant and positive, in contradiction to previous literature. This suggests that small firms are usually less monitored and insiders are more camouflaged when trading on their own bank's shares.

10.3 Discussion of Results and Conclusions

This paper uses panel data estimation under the assumptions of the agency theory to identify the factors enhancing bank insider trading. We conclude that the more entrenched the directors, the less prestigious the bank, the bigger the firm and the lower the charter values for high levels of ownership, the higher the intensity of insider trading activity.

Thus, the emerging picture is of a scenario where insider trading activity is triggered by the absence of efficient control mechanisms, either external (regulators control the level of bank capitalization but it is not easy for them to also control other opportunistic behaviors) or internal (shareholders fail to control managers when managers' stakes are very low or very high).

Entrenchment is clearly related to insider trading, thus indicating that managers may extract private benefits through different manifestations of opportunistic behavior. Furthermore, entrenchment modifies managers' risk-taking incentives, which in turn has a direct effect on financial costs, bank performance and firm value (Lee 2002), an association that will be much interested to analyze in future research. We thus agree with Sánchez-Ballesta and García-Meca's (2007) assessment that it is still an open question whether insider ownership helps to address agency problems.

Our results also provide evidence against the lower monitoring of small caps—small size banks are not associated with higher insider trading, as hypothesized by Madura and Wiant (1995), Jordan (1999) and Madison et al. (2004). Thus, the positive relationship between insider trading activity and size could be understood as the achievement of entrenched managers who not only invest based on private information, but are also able to achieve one of their main perquisites—firm growth.

Finally, this investigation has implications for bank regulation, insider trading regulation and the design of corporate governance mechanisms within the firm. It is worthwhile noting that one factor that dissuades insiders from trading on private information is bank reputation, which results from the management's effort to preserve the firm's public image from any kind of financial scandal. It brings to light the relevance and efficacy of internal ethical codes of conduct, which could be more suitable for enforcing insider trading than external or governmental rules—an idea also proposed by Bris (2005), who believes that harsher laws are not usually good for reducing the profitability of insider trading. Although our results are mainly attributable to countries characterized by low shareholder protection, such as Spain, they are easy to extend to most countries where the subprime crisis has demanded higher harmonization between the regulatory institutions of different countries.

Still, we agree on the fact that there is not a universal corporate governance system and that different peculiarities should be taken into account. In this case, Spain represents a weak shareholder protection and French-law origin country and our results could be easily applied in this scenario.

We also want to insist on the difficulty of getting proper datasets to address these issues, reason why further research could be also based on the use of experimental markets, such as in Del Brio et al. (2016).

Acknowledgments Part of this research was undertaken while one of us was visiting the University Carlos III (Madrid) & the University of Piura. Research Agency of the Spanish Ministry of Economics and Competitiveness (Grants ECO2013-4561P and ECO2016-75631P).

Appendix

Variables	Description	Measurement
$LNSVI_{it}$	Insider trading intensiveness	Absolute value of the logarithm conversion of the *SNVI* index, measured as the net euro volume of insider purchases standardized by the earnings-per-share ratio
IO_{it}	Insider ownership	Percentage of shares in the hands of bank directors
IO_{it}^2	Quadratic insider ownership	Square of insider ownership
CV_{it}	Charter value	Tobin's Q
BC_{it}	Bank capital	Ratio of excess equity to total assets
$REPU_{it}$	Reputation	Dummy variable that takes the value of 1 for Spanish banks ranking among the first 2000 firms within the Forbes Global 2000, and takes the value of zero, otherwise
$SIZE_{it}$	Bank size	Natural logarithm of the market value of outstanding firms

References

Ali, A., Wei, K. D., & Zhou, Y. I. (2011). Trading and option grant timing in response to fire sales (and purchases) of stocks by mutual funds. *Journal of Accounting Research, 49*(3), 595–632.

Baesel, J., & Stein, G. R. (1979). The value of information, inferences from the profitability of insider trading. *Journal of Financial and Quantitative Analysis, 14*(3), 553–571.

Beny, L. (2007). Insider trading laws and stock markets around the world: An empirical contribution to the theoretical law and economics debate. *Journal of Corporation Law, 32*(2), 237–300.

Beny, L. (2008). Do investors in controlled firms value insider trading laws? International evidence. *Law, Economics and Policy, 4*(2), 267–310.

Bhattacharya, U., & Daouk, H. (2002). The world price of insider trading. *Journal of Finance, 57*, 75–108.

Bhattacharya, U., & Daouk, H. (2009). When no law is better than a good law. *Review of Finance, 13*, 577–627.

Betzer, A., & Theissen, E. (2009). Insider trading and corporate governance: The case of Germany. *European Financial Management, 15*, 402–429.

Bris, A. (2005). Do insider trading laws work? *European Financial Management, 11*(3), 267–312.

Carter, R. B., & Manaster, S. (1990). Initial public offerings and underwriter reputation. *Journal of Finance, 45*, 1045–1067.

Cebenoyan, A., Cooperman, E., & Register, C. (1999). Ownership structure, charter value and risk-taking behaviour for thrifts. *Financial Management, 28*(1), 43–60.

Cline, B., Fu, X., Springer, T. M., & Tang, T. (2014). Insider trading in REITs: Evidence form informed stock option exercise around seasoned equity offerings. *Journal of Real Estate Research, 36*(4), 511–540.

Del Brio, E. B. (2006). Measuring insider trading in the Spanish stock market (Spanish). *Spanish Review of Finance and Accounting, 128*, 115–136.

Del Brio, E. B., Lopes e Silva, I., & Perote, J. (2016). Effects of opportunistic behaviors on security markets: An experimental approach to insider trading and earnings management. *Economia Politica, 33*, 379–402.

Del Brio, E., & Miguel, A. (2010). Dividends and market signalling: An analysis of corporate insider trading. *European Financial Management, 16*(3), 480–497.

Del Brio, E. B., Miguel, A., & Perote, J. (2002). An investigation of insider trading profits in the Spanish market. *Quarterly Review of Economics and Finance, 42*(1), 73–94.
Demsetz, R., Saidenberg, M., & Strahan, P. (1996). Banks with something to lose: The disciplinary role of franchise value. *Federal Reserve Bank of New York Economic Policy Review, 2*, 1–14.
Dyck, A., Volchkova, N., & Zingales, L. (2008). The corporate governance role of the media: Evidence from Russia. *Journal of Finance, 63*(3), 1093–1135.
Fidrmuc, J., Goergen, M., & Renneboog, L. (2006). Insider trading, news releases and ownership concentration. *Journal of Finance, 61*(6), 2931–2973.
Friedrich, E. K. (2016). Insider trading after newman: The impact on financial institutions. *Journal of Taxation and Regulation of Financial Institutions, 29*(4), 23–30.
Furfine, C. (2001). Bank portfolio allocation: The impact of capital requirements, regulatory monitoring and economic conditions. *Journal of Financial Services Research, 20*, 33–56.
González, F. (2005). Bank regulation and risk-taking incentives: An international comparison of bank risk. *Journal of Banking and Finance, 29*, 1153–1184.
González, F. (2008). The relationship between charter value and bank market concentration. The influence of regulations and institutions. *Applied Financial Economics, 18*(2), 153–172.
Gorton, G., & Rosen, R. (1995). Corporate control, portfolio choice and the decline of banking. *Journal of Finance, 50*, 1377–1421.
He, Q., & Rui, O. (2016). Ownership structure and insider trading: Evidence from China. *Journal of Business Ethics, 134*(4), 553–574.
Hillier, D., & Marshall, A. P. (2002). Are trading bans effective? Exchange regulation and corporate insider trading. *Journal of Corporate Finance, 8*, 393–410.
Hirschey, M., Slovin, M., & Zaima, J. (1990). Bank debt, insider trading, and the return to corporate selloffs. *Journal of Banking and Finance, 14*(1), 85–98.
Jensen, M., & Meckling, W. (1976). Theory of the firm: Managerial behavior, agency costs and ownership structure. *Journal of Financial Economics, 3*, 305–360.
Jordan, J. (1999). Bank managers opportunistic trading of the firms shares. *Financial Management, 28*(4), 36–51.
Karpoff, J. M., & Lee, D. (1991). Insider trading before new issue announcements. *Financial Management, 20*(1), 18–26.
Keeley, M. C. (1990). Deposit insurance, risk, and market power in banking. *The American Economic Review, 80*, 1183–1200.
Klock, M. (1994). Mainstream economics and the case for prohibiting insider trading. *Georgia State University Law Review, 10*, 297–317.
Lee, S. (2002). Insider ownership and risk-taking behaviour at bank holding companies. *Journal of Business Finance and Accounting, 27*(7&8), 989–1005.
Lee, M. H., & Bishara, H. (1989). Recent Canadian experience on the profitability of insider trades. *Financial Review, 24*(2), 235–249.
Lo, K.-H., Wang, K., & Liao, T. L. (2006). Insider transfer trading of banking companies around exchange listing. *Journal of Financial Intermediation, 15*(2), 215–234.
Madison, T., Roth, G., & Saporoschenko, A. (2004). Bank mergers and insider nontrading. *Financial Review, 39*(2), 203–229.
Madura, J., & Wiant, K. (1995). Information content of bank insider trading. *Applied Financial Economics, 5*(5), 219–227.
Miguel, A., Pindado, J., & De la Torre, C. (2004). Ownership structure and firm value: New evidence from Spain. *Strategic Management Journal, 25*(12), 1199–1207.
Ramirez, G., & Yung, K. (2000). Firm reputation and insider trading: The investment banking industry. *Quarterly Journal of Business and Economics, 39*, 49–67.
Ryan, S. G., Wu Tucker, J., & Ying, Z. (2016). Securization and insider trading. *Accounting Review, 91*(2), 649–675.
Sánchez-Ballesta, J. P., & García-Meca, E. (2007). A meta-analytic vision of the effect of ownership structure on firm performance. *Corporate Governance: An International Review, 15*(5), 879–893.

Seyhun, H. N. (1988). The information content of aggregate insider trading. *Journal of Business, 618*(2), 1–24.

Shleifer, A., & Vishny, R. W. (1989). Managerial entrenchment: The case of manager-specific investments. *Journal of Financial Economics, 25*(1), 123–139.

Slovin, M., Sushka, M., & Polonchek, J. (1991). Restructuring transactions by bank holding companies: The valuation effects of sale-and-leasebacks and divestitures. *Journal of Banking and Finance, 15*(2), 237–255.

Verstein, A. (2016). Insider trading and commodity markets. *Virginia Law Review, 102*(2), 447–500.

Williams, J. (2004). Determining management behaviour in European banking. *Journal of Banking and Finance, 28*(10), 2427–2460.

Yur-Austin, J. (1998). Can insiders bail themselves out before private renegotiation? *Review of Financial Economics, 7*(2), 197–211.

Zhang, G. (2001). Private information production, public disclosure, and the cost of capital: Theory and implications. *Contemporary Accounting Research, 18*(2), 363–384.

Chapter 11
Inside the Board of Spanish Saving Banks

Pablo de Andrés, Iñigo García-Rodríguez, M. Elena Romero-Merino, and Marcos Santamaría-Mariscal

11.1 Introduction

Spanish Saving Banks (hereinafter SSBs) have had almost 200 years of history—*the Caja de Ahorros de Jerez de la Frontera* was the first saving bank founded in 1834. SSBs are private financial intermediaries with special operational and governance characteristics. In their origins, they were born to educate the most modest classes on "the virtue of saving" (García-Roa 1994). The nonexistence of public aids left families in poverty in difficult times (e.g., unemployment or retirement). Only if they had previously saved money were these economic difficulties were mitigated. Inherited from their origin, focused on these families' needs, the SSBs continued to save and finance families and, in certain cases, the small businesses that they started. The foundation of the SSBs was also closely linked to the town or city in which they began their activity. This fact determines that the name of several SSBs include the name of the town (e.g., CajaMadrid and CajaBurgos). This linkage was reinforced because the savings banks used part of their profits to promote cultural, educational and social projects (social work or 'Obra Social') in the town where they developed their activity. These close ties with the community supposed an important competitive advantage because it was difficult for new competing banks to enter.

However, instead of their competitive advantage and market share, SSBs have virtually vanished. Currently, only 2 out of 45 entities from 2004 (Caixa Colonya

P. de Andrés • I. García-Rodríguez
Autonoma University of Madrid, Madrid, Spain
e-mail: p.andres@uam.es; inigo.garcia@uam.es

M.E. Romero-Merino • M. Santamaría-Mariscal (✉)
University of Burgos, Burgos, Spain
e-mail: meromero@ubu.es; msanta@ubu.es

B. Díaz Díaz et al. (eds.), *Corporate Governance in Banking and Investor Protection*, CSR, Sustainability, Ethics & Governance,
https://doi.org/10.1007/978-3-319-70007-6_11

Pollença in Baleares and Caixa de Ontinyent in Valencia) maintain the juridical status of savings bank. Although the causes of the Spanish savings banks withdrawals are multiple, their special organizational form with no ownership rights (and therefore no owners of residual rights) is one of them. First, the nonexistence of ownership rights limits the possibilities for the bank to increase its equity in order to absorb possible losses. Second, when there are no ownership rights, there is a great incentive for managers to use decision rights for their own benefit and make decisions that could have a negative impact on the performance or increase the risk of the entity.

The weakness of this corporate governance model has been shown in several papers (Melle and Maroto 1999; Azofra and Santamaría 2004; Crespí et al. 2004; Fonseca Díaz 2005; García-Marco and Robles-Fernandez 2008). In general, the SSBs' control mechanisms seemed to be ineffective. On the one side, the legal and institutional framework of a civil law country like Spain determines a lower level of legal protection for the investor rights and it also supposes a higher State intervention in the country economy (La Porta et al. 1998, 2000). All these issues limit the role of banking regulation as a monitoring mechanism (Caprio et al. 2007). This arguments have been recovered by the Governor of the Bank of Spain, who has recently admitted (Linde 2017) that the regulation and supervision of the Bank of Spain did not act as a control mechanism during the financial crisis due to its own shortcomings, political and institutional constraints, or information deficiencies.

On the other side, the specific idiosyncrasy of the SSBs also conditions the governance mechanisms. So, their legal form, without ownership rights, avoided the discipline of the corporate control market since the SSBs could not be acquired by other entities. The market for financial products discriminated among entities because the products that financial intermediaries offered were very similar (both in product offerings and in commissions' charges) (Melle and Maroto 1999). All this leaved to the internal control mechanisms the weight of the SSBs' supervision. These were weakened because of the lack of owners and especially of strong boards with power incentives to monitor and advise the managers. As it is well-known in corporate governance literature, a board of directors is a vital mechanism because it is "*at the apex of the internal control system*" and it had "*the final responsibility for the functioning of the firm*" (Jensen 1993).

The structure and composition of SSBs' board of directors is exogenous, since it was regulated through different (state and regional) laws. These laws assigned the power of control among different stakeholders (depositors, employees, public administrations) under a quota system. Following this regulation, politicians acquired a leading role in the boards of savings banks because they acted as representatives of the different local governments. The representatives of the institutional founders were elected by their institutions. Employee representatives are elected by trade unions. Finally, depositors' representatives were elected through a process in two stages. First, some of them were elected by a public draw process. Then, those of them who wished to participate in the SSBs' governing bodies presented a candidature and were designated by an election process.

This quota system of board composition conditions the effectiveness of the board in at least two senses. On the one hand, the board's response to any problem could be slower since board members' renewal occurred according to the legally established time limits (usually every 4 or 6 years). On the other hand, this directors' designation prioritizes the representation of the different SSBs' stakeholders to the specific characteristics of the director himself. In addition, this kind of composition may not respond to real needs of saving banks but to the aim of local and regional governments to obtain the control rights in order to manage the entity. It seems clear the SSBs' designation system is far from considering the recommendations established in the academic literature to achieve an effective board or the specific governing needs derived from the entity's idiosyncrasy.

Precisely, the aim of this paper is to offer a deeper view of boards of Spanish Saving Banks for the period 2004–2010. This paper confronts its composition and characteristics with those recommendations coming from the corporate governance literature and the international regulators, and with different characteristics of the bank business as size, profitability, capital adequacy, lending activity and social work. This aim requires a deep analysis of corporate governance reports of 45 saving banks operating in Spain, and collects biographical information around more than 1500 directors of Savings banks. We propose different classifications of directors and boards.

Our results show that on average, the board of SSBs was larger with less knowledge in business and less professional experience in banking but more gender diversity than the private banks analyzed in other studies. These characteristics almost did not change during the period we study, which seems to confirm that the board is an exogenous governance mechanism set by laws. Along these years, there are more politicians on boards than the laws allow governments to designate (approximately 52%). Finally, we find some important differences in board composition, depending on the SSBs' idiosyncrasy, such as a higher presence of directors with experience in finance in the most profitable SSBs, a higher percentage of businessmen in the SSBs' with higher levels of lending activity, or higher politicizing of the board in those SSBs' with more social work.

The chapter proceeds as follows. First, we review the academic literature about an effective board composition in the financial industry. Next, we introduce the sample, variables, and methodology we use. Following that we explain the results of our descriptive analysis. Finally, we close the paper with a brief discussion of our results and the most relevant conclusions.

11.2 In Search of an Optimal Banking Board of Directors

The literature about board of directors has evolved considerably during the last several decades (see John et al. 2016 for an excellent review). Traditional research on boards has gone from an external, purely quantitative approach of their composition (size and independence) to an internal, qualitative approach of their members (directors' knowledge, experience, diversity). This evolution is in line with the approach that the role of the board is not only disciplinary but also advisory. Contrary to the traditional disciplinary view, directors as advisors take on a much more dynamic and proactive role. When considering the advisory role of the directors, variables such as learning, knowledge, and experience acquires special importance. The analysis of these internal features of the board has helped to better explain the corporate decision-making. We describe on the following lines some of the most relevant board characteristics that the academic literature has studied.

11.2.1 Board Size and Independence

From a traditional disciplinary perspective, a bigger board results in a slowdown of the decision making and an increase in its costs (Jensen and Meckling 1976). In the banking industry, though some authors find evidence to support this statement (Pathan et al. 2007; Staikouras et al. 2007; Agoraki et al. 2010), others seem to find the opposite (Adams and Mehran 2003, 2008; Belkhir 2009) or complementary results (Andrés and Vallelado 2008). These last results suggest that the benefits of better monitoring or an advisory role by larger boards outweighs its costs. Both roles are particularly important in the banking industry in which the complexity of its activities requires a high level of cognitive resources to effectively fill the advisory role and its opacity requires substantial knowledge and information to effectively fill the monitoring role.

Regarding board independence, codes of good governance and prior theoretical arguments both emphasize the benefits of increasing the number of outsiders on the board. Fama (1980) argues that outsiders are more objective when monitoring the management, they add value by providing expert knowledge, and they have more incentives to protect shareholders' interests to maintain their reputation. In the banking industry, empirical studies also show that outsiders add value to the bank (Busta 2007; Pathan et al. 2007), although its significance seems to be fairly poor (Staikouras et al. 2007; Adams and Mehran 2008).

11.2.2 Knowledge and Experience in the Board

Boards of directors benefit from the different kinds of knowledge and experience that individual board members bring to the board (Boeker and Goodstein 1991). The recent recommendations from regulators and policy makers also highlights the importance in including expertise in the board (e.g., the Walker Review of Corporate Governance of United Kingdom Banking Industry and the Banking Code (Code Banken) drawn up by the Netherlands Bankers Association, both of them published in 2009). However, the empirical evidence on this issue is somewhat muddled. Performance is positively related to directors' banking experience

(Hau and Thum 2009 for a sample of German banks) and to directors' financial expertise (Minton et al. 2014 for a sample of US banks). Berger et al. (2014) find that the presence of executives with a PhD degree is associated with a decrease in portfolio risk. Also Cuñat and Garicano (2010), García-Cestona and Sagarra (2014), and García-Meca and Sanchez-Ballesta (2014) find that board chairs' human capital is directly related to the performance of the SSBs.

11.2.3 Board Diversity

Finally, it is also important to consider not only the accumulation of knowledge or expertise but also their heterogeneity. Cognitive diversity in terms of knowledge and skills increases the solving abilities of a group and favors the creativity its decision making (Bantel and Jackson 1989). Heterogeneous groups may take advantage of their differences because they can offer many possible solutions to a problem due to the many different sources from which to gather information (Hambrick and Mason 1984). The scarce literature about this matter in the banking sector supports these arguments (Bantel and Jackson 1989; Mamoghli and Dhouibi 2009).

During recent years the issue of gender diversity has become more important in the policy debate. Some authors have begun to analyze the link between this kind of diversity and corporate governance (Fields and Keys 2003; Adams and Ferreira 2009). The presence of women in the boardroom enriches board information, perspectives, and decision-making leading to better governance (Adams and Ferreira 2009).

After reviewing what the literature considers as an effective board composition in the financial industry, it would be necessary to analyze to what extent all the SSBs were conforming their boards according to these characteristics and whether this composition was significantly different depending on some of their intrinsic features.

11.3 Data

In this study, we analyze the 45 savings banks that operated in Spain during the 2004–2010 period. We have chosen this period because 2004 was the first year in which the savings banks were required to issue an annual corporate governance report and 2010 was the last year prior the sharp reduction in the number of entities (due to mergers and acquisitions). In this way, our database has 296 savings banks observations.

We analyze the board composition of the sample and some financial variables that allow us to compare and explain the results (see Table 11.1 for a full variable description). We obtained the list of directors from the annual corporate governance

Table 11.1 Variables description

Variables	Definition
Board size and independence	
SIZE	Number of directors
EMPLOYEES	% employees' representatives (we assimilate this variable to the insiders in the SSBs' boards)
DEPOSITORS	% depositors' representatives
GOVERNMENTS	% local and regional governments' representatives
OTHER ENTITIES	% other general interest entities' representatives
Knowledge of directors (percentage of directors with specific studies of. . .)	
ARTS	Art and humanities
BUSINESS	Business and economics
ENGIN	Engineering
HEALTH	Health sciences
LAW	Law
SCIENCES	Sciences
SOCIAL	Social sciences
Industry experience of directors (percentage of directors' experience in the industry following the Spanish National Classification of Economic Activities (CNAE))	
PRIMARY	Agriculture, forestry and fishing
EXTRACTIVE	Extractive industries
MANUFACTUR	Manufacturing
ENERGY	Electricity, gas, steam, and air conditioning supply
WATER	Water supply, sanitation activities, waste management and decontamination
CONSTRUCTION	Construction of buildings
TRADE	Wholesale and retail trade, repair of motor vehicles, and motorcycles
TRANSPORT	Transport and storage
HOSTELRY	Hostelry
INFORMATION	Information and communications
FINANCE	Financial and insurance
REAL ESTATE	Real estate activities
PROFESSIONAL	Professional, scientific, and technical
ADMINISTRATIVE	Administrative and support service activities
PUBLIC_SECT	Public administration and defense, social security
EDUCATION	Education
HEALTH SOCIAL	Human health and social services
ENTERTAIN	Arts, entertainment, and recreation
OTHER_SERV	Other services
Professional Experience of Directors (percentage of directors with experience in particular relevant positions).	
POLITICIAN	Representatives of local and regional governments (not only those appointed by local and regional governments but also those that are members of political parties though they formally represent other group of stakeholders in the SSBs' board)

(continued)

Table 11.1 (continued)

Variables	Definition
BUSINESSMAN	Entrepreneurs and businessmen
ACADEMIC	Academics in universities and research centers
Board diversity	
DIV_KNOW	Index of knowledge diversity estimated by adding the number of different branches of knowledge in which at least one of the directors of the board has studies and divided by the total number of branches
DIV_INDUST	Index of industry diversity calculated by considering the number of different industries in which directors have experience divided by the total number of industries
DIV_GENDER	Blau's (1977) index, $1-\sum(Pi)^2$, being Pi the proportion of men and women (so, 0.50 represents a board in which there are the same number of men and women)
SSBs' Financial characteristics from the Uniform Financial Institutions Rating System (the system became internationally known with the abbreviation CAMEL) that US Federal Reserve applied to supervise the U.S. banking institutions	
TOT_ASSETS	Total assets
LOANTA	Amount of loans granted in relation to its size
ROA	Return on assets
CAR	Capital Adequacy Ratio
SOC_WORK	Percentage of the net income allocated to social projects

report of each savings bank, forming up a database of 1525 different directors (5359 observations). We build a handmade, original biographical database that collected information for each director from publicly available sources, financial press, LinkedIn, Facebook, and SABI and BoardEx, where possible. Financial variables were collected from the annual report published by the Spanish Confederation of Savings Banks (CECA).

With all these variables, we describe the sample of SSBs', trying to determine whether their composition is in line with the academic recommendations regarding an effective board. Then, we evaluate the differences between the board composition in 2004 and the board composition in 2010 to check the temporal evolution of the SSBs' boards. To assess the significance of such differences, we will use the non-parametric Mann-Whitney test, which is especially recommended when the size of the subsamples are reduced. Finally, we analyze the existence of differences in the board composition depending on several SSBs' financial characteristics: size (TOT_ASSETS), lending activity (LOANTA), profitability (ROA), capital adequacy (CAR) and social work (SOC_WORK). To this end, we consider the mean values of each savings bank (44 observations). We divide the sample in quartiles (11 observations each one) and will statistically compare the differences between the extreme groups (first versus fourth). Again, we use the Mann-Whitney test to check the significance of these differences.

11.3.1 Board Composition of SSBs

In Table 11.2 we can observe the descriptive statistics of the variables described above. During the last decade, the average board size has risen from 16 directors (Azofra and Santamaría 2004) to 17 directors. This figure has an elevated deviation, as it goes from 7 members up to 40. It is far from the average we can find in the commercial banks (below 13 board seats according to Minton et al. (2014) and García-Meca et al. (2015)). In addition, 17 directors are well above the 14 members that some authors find as a limit to the effectiveness of board size (Wang and Hsu 2013; De Haan and Vlahu 2016).

The local and regional governments occupied more than the 40.6% of the board seats in the savings banks, which went in line with Law 44/2002 that indicated a maximum of 50% for them. (This percentage was reduced to 40% by the Royal Decree-Law 11/2010, but our sample only goes to 2010). Also according to the Law, the depositors' representation on the board was between 25 and 50% (35.6%) and the employees' representation was between 5% and 15% (9.6%). Finally, the percentage of other general interest entities on the board was 9.3%. There was no provision in Law 31/1985 for these entities. However, Royal Decree-Law 11/2010 indicated a maximum of 10% for them on the board in order to implicate more stakeholders in the governance of SSBs.

Regarding the composition of board, we focus on the employees' representation as the percentage of insiders in the board. Therefore, we consider that approximately 90% of the SSBs' directors are outsiders. This figure exceeds the 79% of outsiders found in an international sample of commercial banks by Andrés et al. (2012) or the 69% of outsiders found by Adams and Mehran (2003) in their sample of US banks. However, it is difficult to interpret this result in a positive sense, since the outsiders in the SSBs are neither owners with real incentives to control nor prestigious independent professionals as could occur in the commercial banking industry.

Regarding directors' knowledge (Table 11.3), we observe that business and law studies are the most common ones (15% of directors each of them), followed by engineering (10%), social sciences (7%), health sciences (6%), arts and humanities (5%) and sciences (2%) studies. The proportion of directors with knowledge in business goes in line with that of the German State banks but it is below the 19% of directors with business knowledge of the German private banks (Hau and Thum 2009).

Table 11.2 Board size and independence

Variable	Mean	Median	St. Dv.	Min.	Max.
Size	17.38	17.00	4.08	7.00	40.00
Employees	0.09	0.10	0.03	0.05	0.16
Depositors	0.36	0.38	0.09	0.06	0.50
Governments	0.41	0.47	0.11	0.17	0.67
Other entities	0.09	0.06	0.11	0.00	0.33
Obs.	296				

Table 11.3 Knowledge of directors

Variable	Mean	Median	St. Dv.	Min.	Max.
ARTS	0.05	0.00	0.06	0.00	0.33
BUSINESS	0.15	0.14	0.09	0.00	0.45
ENGIN	0.10	0.08	0.09	0.00	0.50
HEALTH	0.06	0.05	0.07	0.00	0.29
LAW	0.15	0.14	0.10	0.00	0.57
SCIENCES	0.02	0.00	0.04	0.00	0.24
SOCIAL	0.07	0.06	0.07	0.00	0.29
Obs.	296				

Table 11.4 Industry experience of directors

Variable	Mean	Median	St. Dv.	Min.	Max.
PRIMARY	0.02	0.00	0.04	0.00	0.19
EXTRACTIVE	0.01	0.00	0.01	0.00	0.06
MANUFACTUR	0.10	0.07	0.10	0.00	0.42
ENERGY	0.01	0.00	0.02	0.00	0.12
WATER	0.01	0.00	0.02	0.00	0.10
CONSTRUCTION	0.03	0.00	0.04	0.00	0.18
TRADE	0.04	0.00	0.06	0.00	0.25
TRANSPORT	0.02	0.00	0.03	0.00	0.18
HOSTELRY	0.02	0.00	0.03	0.00	0.09
INFORMATION	0.02	0.00	0.03	0.00	0.12
FINANCE	0.13	0.13	0.06	0.05	0.29
REAL ESTATE	0.03	0.00	0.05	0.00	0.25
PROFESSIONAL	0.15	0.13	0.09	0.00	0.40
ADMINISTRATIVE	0.01	0.00	0.02	0.00	0.12
PUBLIC_SECT	0.42	0.44	0.17	0.00	0.75
EDUCATION	0.16	0.14	0.10	0.00	0.43
HEALTH SOCIAL	0.05	0.05	0.05	0.00	0.21
ENTERTAIN	0.01	0.00	0.03	0.00	0.12
OTHER_SERV	0.04	0.00	0.06	0.00	0.47
Obs.	296				

When considering the directors' industry experience, we can observe in Table 11.4 that there are five industries that stand out from the rest. 42% of directors have experience in public administration (including politicians and civil servants), 16% in education, 14% as professionals (including economists, lawyers, consultants, etc.), 13% (including savings bank own employees) worked in the banking and finance industry, and 10% of directors have professional experience in the manufacturing industry. Again, regarding to the banking and finance experience, our sample shows similar figures (even higher) to those of the German State banks (11.1% according to Hau and Thum 2009), but in this case they are ever further

Table 11.5 Professional experience of directors

Variable	Mean	Median	St. Dv.	Min.	Max.
POLITICIAN	0.52	0.55	0.16	0.17	0.88
BUSINESSMAN	0.33	0.29	0.17	0.00	0.83
ACADEMIC	0.09	0.06	0.08	0.00	0.35
Obs.	296				

from reaching the proportion of directors with banking experience in the private banks (31.6% according to Hau and Thum (2009) for German Banks and approximately 20% according to Minton et al. (2014) for US banks).

In relation to the directors' experience in relevant positions (Table 11.5), we observe that 33% of directors are businessmen, 9% are academics and 52% are politicians. This last figure includes those directors directly designated by local and regional governments and those that are affiliated with a political party. This variable even reaches 88% in some savings banks, which shows the high (risk of) politicization of these organizations. Furthermore, it is important to note that, on average, local and regional governments could formally appoint only 41% of the board members (as we explained when we introduced the stakeholders' representation). The extra 11% notes how political parties tried to influence on the savings bank's decision-making by including their affiliates among the directors that represented other groups. If we consider that all of them had political links (even though not directly representing local and regional governments), the SSBs' board composition is clearly breaking the spirit of the Law that limited it to 50% (40% after 2010) participation of politicians on the board.

Moreover, we analyze the boards' diversity according to three issues. Regarding knowledge, we observe in Table 11.6 that boards accumulate almost five of the seven branches of knowledge, although there are savings banks with only one branch and others with all seven. However, it is important to note that none of the branches of knowledge is present in all the boards, so there were savings banks whose boards did not have members with economic or business studies. In relation to the diversity of industry experience, we obtain that, on average, boards accumulate experience in more than eight of the 19 considered industries. Lastly, there is an appreciable majority of men on the SSBs' boards. Female directors only represent 18% of the board, and few entities achieve the gender equality goal (each gender should represent between 40% and 60% of directors). Though this figure could seem too low, it is much higher than their counterparts in banks (10% in the international sample and 6% in Spanish banks according to García-Meca et al. 2015).

In short, although there are few studies with which to compare, we can say that the board of SSBs were larger, with less knowledge in business and less professional experience in banking, but more gender diversity than private banks. In fact, the SSBs' figures are in line with those of the German State Banks that, as Hau and Thum (2009) evidence, had a systematic underperformance during the financial crisis.

Table 11.6 Board diversity

Variable	Mean	Median	St. Dv.	Min.	Max.
DIV_KNOW	0.66	0.71	0.17	0.14	1.00
DIV_INDUST	0.44	0.42	0.11	0.21	0.74
DIV_GENDER	0.27	0.28	0.12	0.00	0.50
Obs.	296				

Table 11.7 Mean values and significant differences of board and financial variables in 2004 and 2010

Variable	Year 2004	Year 2010
SIZE	16.9773	18.0333
EMPLOYEES	0.0958	0.0921
DEPOSITORS	0.3567	0.3617
GOVERNMENTS	0.4019	0.4205
OTHER ENTITIES	0.0959	0.0721
BUSINESS	0.1439	0.1506
ENGIN	0.1505	0.1602
HEALTH	0.0578	0.0518
LAW	0.1009	0.0770
SOCIAL	0.0568	0.0729
MANUFACTUR	0.1035	0.0818
FINANCE	0.1302	0.1270
PROFESSIONAL	0.1374	0.1522
PUBLIC_SECT	0.4137	0.4186
EDUCATION	0.1568	0.1772
POLITICIAN	0.5150	0.5402
BUSINESSMAN	0.3458	0.2825
ACADEMIC	0.0935	0.0978
DIV_KNOW	0.6494	0.6714
DIV_INDUST	0.4462	0.4070
DIV_GENDER**	0.2499	0.3099
No. observations	44	30

**, significant difference at 95% level of confidence respectively

11.3.2 Evolution of the SSBs' Board Composition

To study whether savings banks have modified their board composition during the period, we compare the mean value of each variable in 2004 and 2010. The main conclusion we can extract from Table 11.7 is the static character of the board composition of SSBs'. In spite of being a difficult period in the SSBs', there were hardly any changes in their boards' compositions. This goes in line with the idea that board is an exogenous element because it is modified mainly through laws. As an example of this kind of "legal adaptation", we observe that the gender diversity is the only board variable that has changed significantly. Boards have become more diverse in terms of gender during the period we analyze (the proportion of women has increased from 16% to 21%). This is because they follow the recommendations given by several corporate governance codes and the Spanish Gender Equality Law (Law 3/2007).

11.3.3 Differences in the Board Composition Depending on the SBBs' Financial Characteristics

A descriptive analysis of the financial variables we use to split up the sample shows the high deviation of savings bank sizes. Although the mean value of their total assets is 23 million euros, this variable ranges from 0.228 to 270 million euros. In fact, only ten savings banks are above the mean value. On average, savings banks allocate almost a third of their net income to social, cultural, educational and health activities. Their lending activity represents 74% of their total assets, ranging from 66% to 86%. We can also observe that their profitability has been quite reduced (on average, 1%), with some savings banks in negative terms and never exceeding 5%. To end, the mean value of the capital adequacy (CAR) is 6%, although values show a high variability from 1% to 16%.

As we can see in Table 11.8, almost all the financial variables significantly changed during the analyzed period. Savings banks increased their size and the proportion of net income allocated to social issues (which could be explained by the reduction of such net income). These entities also reduced their profitability and solvency during the period, which denotes a worsening of their financial condition. Their lending activity was the only financial variable that did not change, although it significantly increased until 2007 and then declined.

Regarding the analysis of the board composition depending on the financial variables, it is important to highlight that we are not proposing any causal relationship, but we simply evaluate the existence of significant differences among the

Table 11.8 Mean values and significant differences of board and financial variables in 2004 and 2010

Variable	Mean 2004	Mean 2010	Full Sample Mean	Median	St. Dv.	Min.	Max.
TOT_ASSETS[a] **	13,873	32,722	23,375	11,020	40,010	227	269,757
LOANTA	0.7309	0.7227	0.7447	0.7520	0.0448	0.6644	0.8613
ROA***	0.0152	0.0038	0.0110	0.0118	0.0072	−0.0289	0.0492
CAR**	0.0648	0.0523	0.0625	0.0576	0.0242	0.0069	0.1592
SOC_WORK***	0.2784	0.5095	0.3263	0.2892	0.1838	0.0000	1.4068
No. observations	44	30	296				

[a]Total assets in millions of euros

,*, significant difference at 95% and 99% level of confidence respectively

savings banks due to their idiosyncrasy. In this study, we introduce the differences between the higher and lower quartile of the sample when we divide it according to some relevant SSBs' financial variables. In this section, we only report in tables those knowledge and experience variables whose mean value is above the 5% of the board.

As we can see in Table 11.9, the boards of bigger savings banks are significantly larger, with a higher knowledge diversity and a higher proportion of directors with business studies, finance experience, or academics. These outcomes seem to support the idea that the board composition is different depending on the organizational size. This could be because higher visibility allows entities to attract more valuable and diverse directors (as Andrés et al. 2012 found for commercial banks) or because this more effective board composition allows the SSBs to grow more.

When referring to the lending activity of the SSBs', we observe that those entities that extend more loans have smaller boards with a higher proportion of businessmen and directors with experience in manufacturing industry. However, they have a lower presence of directors who work in the public industry (most of them civil servants) and a less degree of knowledge diversity. These results can be explained by the risk profile of some types of directors. Thus, businessmen (many of them concentrated in the manufacturing industry) are less risk averse than the civil servants (those who work in the public industry) could be.

We also find some differences when we face the more and the less profitable entities. In general, the most profitable entities have larger boards, with more professional experience in finance and public sector, but less presence of businessmen and directors with experience in the manufacturing industry. A possible explanation of these results can be found in the existence of an inverse relationship between performance and lending activity. Credit growth leads to an increase in the risk of default, which can result in lower profitability (Climent-Serrano and Pavía-Miralles 2014). In this analysis, most of the board significant variables have been previously introduced when assessing the differences among those SSB with higher and lower ratio of loans to total assets. In this sense, the only new variable is the finance experience of directors, which is reasonably related with higher performance. In addition, the boards of the most profitable SSBs present a less diverse board in terms of gender but are more diverse when considering the directors' educational background. The unexpected negative relationship between diversity of gender and profitability might be explained by the fact of the increasing presence of women has coincided with the worsening of the financial situation and, therefore, with the reduction of ROA.

The SSBs' solvency gives us two samples that do not present many significant differences. Those better financial positions only present a higher proportion of professionals and directors with experience in public administrations. In contrast, businessmen seem to be more present in the SSBs' with less financial health. Again, the risk appetite of businessmen (versus those who work in the public sector) can be a potential explanation for these results.

Finally, when we divide the sample depending on the proportion of the net income that is allocated to social, cultural, educational and health projects

Table 11.9 Mean values of the significant differences of board depending on SSBs' size, lending activity, profitability, capital adequacy, and social work

		Size		Lending activity		Profitability		Capital adequacy		Social work	
		Low	High	Low	High	Low	High	Low	High	Low	High
Board characteristics		2,978,745	65,710,796	0.6822	0.7973	0.0080	0.0143	0.0414	0.0922	0.1973	0.4657
Size	SIZE	15.0519***	20.7727***	19.1039***	14.7792***	15.0000**	19.2576**	–	–	–	–
Knowledge	BUSINESS	0.1172**	0.1984″**	–	–	–	–	–	–	–	–
	ENGIN	–	–	–	–	–	–	–	–	0.1546**	0.1296**
Industry experience	FINANCE	0.1395*	0.1741*	–	–	0.1169*	0.1536*	–	–	–	–
	PUBLIC_SECT	–	–	0.4955**	0.3026**	0.3914*	0.5203*	0.3888*	0.5131*	0.3446**	0.5211**
	MANUFACT	–	–	0.0634**	0.1743**	0.1643*	0.0593*	–	–	–	–
	PROFESSIONAL	–	–	–	–	–	–	0.0977**	0.1580**	–	–
Professional experience	POLITICIANS	–	–	–	–	–	–	–	–	0.4360**	0.6117**
	BUSINESSMAN	–	–	0.2870*	0.4526*	0.4143**	0.2747**	0.3175*	0.2245*	0.3931*	0.2647*
	ACADEMIC	0.0317***	0.0884***	–	–	–	–	–	–	–	–
Diversity	DIV_KNOW	0.6296*	0.7515*	0.7270**	0.5795**	0.5306**	0.7257**	–	–	–	–
	DIV_GENDER	–	–	–	–	0.3537*	0.2107*	–	–	–	–

*,**,***, significant difference at 90%, 95% and 99% level of confidence respectively

(SOCIAL_WORK), we observe that those entities with more social work have a board with great importance of the directors' public experience (measured by proportions of politicians and directors with experience in the public sector). Therefore, they seem to be aware of this important social side of savings banks. In contrast, the presence of businessmen is significantly lower in those savings banks more socially oriented.

11.4 Discussion and Conclusions

A developed banking system is essential for the economy of a country. To achieve this, the existence of governance mechanisms that protect the interests of depositors (as the main investors in credit institutions) is a key variable. The weaknesses in the regulatory and institutional framework of the SSBs left their monitoring mainly in the hands of internal governance mechanisms such as the board of directors. That is why we focus here on the study of this particular mechanism. So, in this chapter we present the first in-depth descriptive analysis of the SSBs' boards in terms of size, independence, and quality (knowledge, experience and diversity). This whole report goes beyond the figure of the board chairman as some previous studies have done (Cuñat and Garicano 2010; García-Cestona and Sagarra 2014; García-Meca and Sanchez-Ballesta 2014; Martín-Oliver et al. 2017). To do this, we build a unique database with the profile of 1525 different directors of the whole population of SSBs during the period 2004–2010.

Our results show that the composition of the boards is far from the effectiveness parameters indicated by the literature. On the one side, when looking at the board structure, we find that SSBs' boards were larger (17 members) and apparently more independent (90%) than the commercial private banks. However, as we said before, these outsiders lack the incentives (no ownership rights) or the information necessary to effectively monitor or advice the savings banks' managers. On the other side, the SSBs' board quality is somewhat weak as they accumulate little banking experience or business knowledge and more politicians than might be expected. We find that only 15% of directors have business studies and only 13% have experience in banking. In addition, this limited bank experience would be even lower if we used, as other authors do, only independent directors, since in our sample the insiders (9% of SSBs' directors were employees) have been logically considered as advisers with banking experience. These percentages are lower than those found in other studies in private banks (Hau and Thum 2009; Minton et al. 2014) and similar to those found in the German State Banks that experienced difficulties during the crisis. Additionally, these board characteristics have not changed along the analyzed period despite going through an unstable period. This seems to confirm that the exogenous setting of the board by laws (as in the case of Spanish savings banks) limits their adaptation in times of change.

Regarding the role of politicians, we have obtained that political parties were present not only through those directors directly designated by local and regional governments (on average, 41%) but also by an extra 11% of directors that formally represented other groups of stakeholders. These data seems to confirm that, although the Spanish savings banks had the status of private entities, the real fact is that they were controlled mainly by politicians (52% of the board members).

When we study the potential differences among the boards of the SSBs' depending on the entity's idiosyncrasy, we find that the board politicizing, contrary to what other studies find (Azofra and Santamaría 2004; Illueca et al. 2014), is not significantly different in the SSBs with lower and higher performance. This lack of significance does not imply that there is no political influence on performance (or resources expropriation) but it is articulated through other direct measures, such as loans to regional government, political parties, etc. In this comparative analysis we also find that those directors with experience in public sector have more presence in the SSBs with higher levels of social (investment in social work) and economic behavior (profitability and solvency) and lower lending activity (possibly due to a risk aversion behavior). Contrary to them, the presence of businessmen in the board is higher in those SSBs' with lower values of profitability, capital adequacy and social work but higher lending activity. The risky decision making in which the businessmen are usually involved may suppose that they are especially comfortable in these types of SSBs or, when they are in the boards, they advocate an SSBs' riskier strategy with poorer results. Finally, we find a higher presence of directors with experience in finance in the more profitable savings banks. This finding is supported by prior banking literature, suggesting the great importance of the financial expertise in this particular industry.

Nevertheless, this study has some limitations that we note below. In this chapter we have not analyzed direct effects. Instead, we have performed an in depth descriptive analysis that allows us to suspect some relations but prevent us from confirming the direction of such relations. Moreover, due to the methodology we have used, the level of detail of the biography of each director differs depending on their public relevance. Additionally, the comparisons were made based on mean values of each savings bank.

Finally, this chapter suggests several lines of future research. First, it would be advisable the study of several relationships that our results make us intuit. In this way, it would be interesting to analyze the effect of the knowledge of the directors or their experiences in each industry on savings banks' performance measures, both financial (profitability, financial exposure, risk) and social (social work, branch offices in rural areas), and on strategic policies (expansion).

In sum, despite the disappearance of the SSBs' subsector itself, this fact suggests several lines of research that could be applied to other countries (e.g., Germany) where these types of entities coexist with commercial banks.

References

Adams, R. B., & Ferreira, D. (2009). Women in the boardroom and their impact on governance and performance. *Journal of Financial Economics, 94*(2), 291–309.

Adams, R., & Mehran, H. (2003). Is corporate governance different for bank holding companies? *Economic Policy Review, 9*(1), 123–142.

Adams, R. B., & Mehran, R. (2008). *Corporate performance, board structure, and their determinants in the banking industry*. Federal Reserve Bank of New York Staff Report no. 330.

Agoraki, M. E. K., Delis, M. D., & Staikouras, P. K. (2010). The effect of board size and composition on bank efficiency. *International Journal of Banking, Accounting and Finance, 2*(4), 357–386.

Andrés, P., & Vallelado, E. (2008). Corporate governance in banking: The role of the board of directors. *Journal of Banking & Finance, 32*(12), 2570–2580.

Andrés, P., Romero-Merino, M. E., Santamaría, M., & Vallelado, E. (2012). Board determinants in banking industry. An international perspective. *Managerial and Decision Economics, 33*(3), 147–158.

Azofra, V., & Santamaría, M. (2004). El gobierno de las cajas de ahorro españolas. *Universia Business Review, 2*(2), 48–59.

Bantel, K. A., & Jackson, S. E. (1989). Top management and innovations in banking: Does the composition of the top team make a difference? *Strategic Management Journal, 10*(S1), 107–124.

Belkhir, M. (2009). Board of directors' size and performance in the banking industry. *International Journal of Managerial Finance, 5*(2), 201–221.

Berger, A. N., Kick, T., & Schaeck, K. (2014). Executive board composition and bank risk taking. *Journal of Corporate Finance, 28*, 48–65.

Blau, P. M. (1977). *Inequality and heterogeneity*. New York: Free Press.

Boeker, W., & Goodstein, J. (1991). Organizational performance and adaptation: Effects of environment and performance on changes in board composition. *Academy of Management Journal, 34*(4), 805–826.

Busta, I. (2007). *Board effectiveness and the impact of the legal family in the European banking industry*. In FMA European Conference, Barcelona–Spain. Available at: www.fma.org/Barcelona/Papers/BustaFMA2007.pdf

Caprio, G., Laeven, L., & Levine, R. (2007). Governance and bank valuation. *Journal of Financial Intermediation, 16*(4), 584–617.

Climent-Serrano, S., & Pavía-Miralles, J. M. (2014). Determinantes y diferencias en la rentabilidad de cajas y bancos [Determinants and differences in the profitability of saving Banks and commercial Banks]. *Revista de Economía Aplicada, 65*(12), 117–154.

Code Banken (Dutch Banking Code). (2009). Netherlands Bankers' Association.

Crespí, R., García-Cestona, M. A., & Salas, V. (2004). Governance mechanisms in Spanish banks. Does ownership matter? *Journal of Banking & Finance, 28*(10), 2311–2330.

Cuñat, V., & Garicano, L. (2010). Did good Cajas extend bad loans? Governance, human capital and loan portfolios. Working paper, FEDEA no. 2010-08.

de Haan, J., & Vlahu, R. (2016). Corporate governance of banks: A survey. *Journal of Economic Surveys, 30*(2), 228–277.

Fama, E. F. (1980). Agency problems and the theory of the firm. *Journal of Political Economy, 88*(2), 288–307.

Fields, M. A., & Keys, P. Y. (2003). The emergence of corporate governance from Wall St. to Main St.: Outside directors, board diversity, earnings management, and managerial incentives to bear risk. *Financial Review, 38*(1), 1–24.

Fonseca Díaz, A. R. (2005). El gobierno de las cajas de ahorros: influencia sobre la eficiencia y el riesgo [The governance of savings banks: Influence on the efficiency and risk]. *Universia Business Review, 4*(8), 24–37.

García-Cestona, M., & Sagarra, M. (2014). *Good and bad Banks? Governance, human capital of top managers and performance.* Working paper, Accessed 23 Jan, 2016, from http://ssrn.com/abstract=2504593

García-Marco, T., & Robles-Fernández, M. D. (2008). Risk-taking behaviour and ownership in the banking industry: The Spanish evidence. *Journal of Economics and Business, 60*(4), 332–354.

García-Meca, E., & Sánchez-Ballesta, J. P. (2014). Politicization, banking experience and risk in savings banks. *European Journal of Law and Economics, 38*(3), 535–553.

García-Meca, E., García-Sánchez, I. M., & Martínez-Ferrero, J. (2015). Board diversity and its effects on bank performance: An international analysis. *Journal of Banking & Finance, 53*, 202–214.

García-Roa, J. (1994). *Las cajas de ahorros españolas: cambios recientes, fusiones y otras estrategias de dimensionamiento. [The Spanish savings banks: Recent changes, mergers and other oversizing strategies]*. Madrid: Civitas.

Hambrick, D. C., & Mason, P. A. (1984). Upper echelons: The organization as a reflection of its top managers. *Academy of Management Review, 9*(2), 193–206.

Hau, H., & Thum, M. (2009). Subprime crisis and board (in-)competence: Private vs. public banks in Germany. *Economic Policy, 24*, 701–751.

Illueca, M., Norden, L., & Udell, G. (2014). Liberalization and risk taking: Evidence from government-controlled Banks. *Review of Finance, 18*(4), 1217–1257.

Jensen, M. C. (1993). The modern industrial revolution, exit, and the failure of internal control systems. *Journal of Finance, 48*(3), 831–880.

Jensen, M. C., & Meckling, W. H. (1976). Theory of the firm: Managerial behavior, agency costs and ownership structure. *Journal of Financial Economics, 3*(4), 305–360.

John, K., De Masi, S., & Paci, A. (2016). Corporate governance in banks. *Corporate Governance: An International Review, 24*(3), 303–321.

La Porta, R., Lopez de Silanes, F., Shleifer, A., & Vishny, R. W. (1998). Law and finance. *Journal of Political Economy, 106*, 1113–1155.

La Porta, R., Lopez de Silanes, F., Shleifer, A., & Vishny, R. (2000). Investor protection and corporate governance. *Journal of Financial Economics, 58(1–2)*, 3–27.

Law 3/2007, of 22 March, for the effective equality of women and men.

Law 31/1985, of 2 August, regulating the basic rules on governing bodies of savings banks.

Law 44/2002, of November 22, on measures to reform the Financial System.

Linde, L. M. (2017, February 10). El Banco de España en la crisis. *El País*. Retrieved from http://economia.elpais.com/economia/2017/02/09/actualidad/1486671538_959492.html

Mamoghli, C., & Dhouibi, R. (2009). *Bank corporate governance and insolvency risk: Evidence from an emerging market.* Working paper, Accessed Aug 4, 2000, from http://ssrn.com/abstract=1391878

Martín-Oliver, A., Ruano, S., & Salas-Fumás, V. (2017). The fall of Spanish cajas: Lessons of ownership and governance for banks. *Journal of Financial Stability*. https://doi.org/10.1016/j.jfs.2017.02.004.

Melle Hernández, M., & Maroto Acín, J. A. (1999). Una aplicación del gobierno de empresas: incidencia de las Administraciones Públicas en las decisiones asignadas de las Cajas de Ahorro españolas [An application of corporate governance: The impact of government on allocative decisions of the Spanish savings banks]. *Revista Europea de Dirección y Economía de la Empresa, 8*(2), 9–35.

Minton, B. A., Taillard, J. P., & Williamson, R. (2014). Financial expertise of the board, risk taking, and performance: Evidence from bank holding companies. *Journal of Financial and Quantitative Analysis, 49*(2), 351–380.

Pathan, S., Skully, M., & Wickramanayake, J. (2007). Board size, independence and performance: An analysis of Thai banks. *Asia-Pacific Financial Markets, 14*(3), 211–227.

Royal Decree-Law 11/2010, of 9 July, about governing bodies and other aspects of the legal regime of savings banks.

Staikouras, P. K., Staikouras, C. K., & Agoraki, M. E. K. (2007). The effect of board size and composition on European bank performance. *European Journal of Law and Economics, 23*(1), 1–27.

Walker, D. (2009). *A review of corporate governance in UK banks and other financial industry entities – Final recommendations*. HM Treasury Archives, United Kingdom.

Wang, T., & Hsu, C. (2013). Board composition and operational risk events of financial institutions. *Journal of Banking & Finance, 37*(6), 2042–2051.

Chapter 12
Italian Banks' Ownership, Governance and Performance: The Evolving Role of Foundations

Giuliana Birindelli and Paola Ferretti

12.1 Background[1]

With the aim of promoting the modernization and competitiveness of the banking system and overcoming the anomaly of the public ownership of banks, in the Nineties the Italian government came to the decision on the privatization of banks (both savings banks and stated-owned banks) and their transformation into joint-stock companies. To address the limited availability of domestic capital, the Italian government created 88 community-owned non-profit Banking Foundations (hereinafter BFs) to serve as trustees for the capital of the lately privatized banks (IMF 2014).

The BFs represented, and continue to represent, an Italian peculiarity in the wider European field of foundations, generally defined (given the national specific characteristics) as non-profit entities with their own source of income and governing bodies, which use their financial resources for educational, social, religious, cultural or other public benefit purposes (among others, Schlüchter et al. 2001; Barbetta 2013). Indeed, in Italy the BFs were constituted as a new kind of non-profit organisation charged with philanthropic activity (previously assigned to the public banks) even if they held the majority shareholding of the spin-off banks; from these latter the BFs obtained the resources needed for carrying

[1]Even if the study reflects a common view, Giuliana Birindelli mainly contributed to Sects. 12.1, 12.3 and 12.4.3; Paola Ferretti to Sects. 12.2, 12.4.1, 12.4.2, and 12.5.

G. Birindelli (✉)
"G. d'Annunzio" University of Chieti-Pescara, Pescara, Italy
e-mail: giuliana.birindelli@unich.it

P. Ferretti
University of Pisa, Pisa, Italy
e-mail: paola.ferretti@unipi.it

B. Díaz Díaz et al. (eds.), *Corporate Governance in Banking and Investor Protection*, CSR, Sustainability, Ethics & Governance,
https://doi.org/10.1007/978-3-319-70007-6_12

out their philanthropic activity. As stated by Bassanini (2003), in Italy the BFs have been set in a border area between public and private, politics and economics, central powers and local authorities; that is one of the reasons why the BFs have been highly debated (and continue to be debated) in political and legislative-juridical terms.

In detail, the creation of the BFs was the result of the Amato Law no. 218/90, which initiated (but did not complete) the reform process of the Italian banks (Sect. 12.2). The first goal was to separate the banking functions from the philanthropic activities, by creating on one side private profit making credit institutions subject to the regulation as other banks and on the other side non-profit philanthropic institutions as a guidance force for voluntary organisations and for all the third sector. The link between BFs and banks was initially very close, because, as mentioned above, the BFs were the major shareholders in the newly created banks.

Over the years, legislation on the BFs has been extensive (Sect. 12.2), even if sometimes overlapping and producing elements of ambiguity and/or contradiction (among others, Clarich and Pisaneschi 2001). Equally broad was the debate among academics, politicians and lawyers with regard to the identity of the BFs, which have been frequently identified as hybrid entities covering roles, which are often difficult to reconcile (Faravelli and Clerici 2013), on the one hand being institutional investors who financially support banks with a medium-to-long term perspective and on the other being grant-making non-profit organisations. From this dual liaison between BFs-banks and BFs-community some distortions have derived, as in the case BFs had to undergo a drastic reduction in dividends received by investee banks in years in which banking profitability dropped. This also resulted in a decrease of the ability to support public benefit activities, as well to carry out capital injections for banks. Other negative impacts were on banks' governance and performance as evidenced by several studies (Sects. 12.4.2 and 12.4.3). Indeed, BFs, which tended to interpret shareholder rights quite broadly, exerted a negative influence on banking governance, hampering the needed turnover of banking bodies and orienting the selection of managers towards criteria not linked to professional skills. As stated, among others, by Fubini (2014) and Perotti and Zingales (2012), the strong BFs' domination by local politicians created situations of conflicts of interest and negatively impacted on the banking efficiency. Ultimately, such phenomenon impaired banks' performance as well as their ability to finance the economy.

Concluding, BFs exerted an important role in the reform process of banks. Particularly, they supported large processes of consolidations of the Italian banking sector (a national consolidation in the late 1990s, then more international acquisitions; see IMF 2014). Therefore, the change in equity investments portfolio of the BFs—characterized by the disposal of shares held in the "original" banks since the early 1990s—gave rise to new banking groups. In particular, three Italian large international banking groups are worth mentioning: Unicredit, Intesa Sanpaolo and Monte dei Paschi di Siena (ACRI, Fondazioni di origine bancaria. Annual Reports). The process of privatization and consolidation deeply changed the banking system, also in terms of figures: the number of banks dropped greatly, from 1064 in 1990 to

643 in 2015 (Banca d'Italia, Annual Reports). Closely linked to this aspect was the BFs' contribution in terms of financial support to banks also in more recent years when a strong recapitalization was needed.

However, the BFs' shareholding in the banks entailed also negative drawbacks, especially on the governance of the latter, and accordingly, on their performance.

Shedding light on the reverberation of the relationship between banks and foundations is therefore very interesting in order to understand whether, in the interest of banks' efficiency, this bond needs to be broken or, at least, requires provisions to loosen it further. For this aim, the chapter develops in the following Sections: Sect. 12.2 traces the evolution of legislation from the Nineties to date, Sect. 12.3 highlights the evolution occurred in the shareholdings in the banks held by the foundations, Sect. 12.4 delves into the aspects of banking management in terms of (i) financial support, (ii) impact on governance and (iii) impact on performance; finally, Sect. 12.5 draws some conclusions.

12.2 An Overview of the Legislation on Banking Privatization

Amidst a strongly competitive and an ever more globalized setting, the Nineties set the beginning of a reform process of the Italian banking system aiming to overcome the deficiencies and flaws banks featured at international level (Birindelli and Ferretti 1997). Accordingly, the urge to open the market for new capital, to increase the size of banks, and to withdraw banks from public control thus became the driver for this process towards modernization which was based on reinforcing the distinction between the public-interest functions and the business functions. The objective was thus to achieve a way of managing credit business exclusively according to business principles, in agreement with prudential criteria, and without interferences other than those of the business itself (Signorini 2015).

As already said, the kick off for such reform occurred with the so-called Amato Laws (Law no. 218/90 and Decree no. 356/90), which separated the philanthropic activities of the banks and the credit functions, which were originally carried out jointly within the public savings banks (Casse di Risparmio and Monti di Credito). Such provisions established that banks were to be separated from public institutions and turned into join stock companies, pursuing a profit intent. On the other hand, all activities focusing on social, cultural, and economic development were assigned to new entities—first known as transferor entities and later (from 1998 on) as BFs,—in the role of non-profit entities called to administer the controlling shareholdings in the transferee banks.

The need to speed up the privatization of the Italian banks, and at the same time assign BFs a well-defined role, required further regulatory measures. In this respect, it is worth recalling the Law no. 474/1994 and the Directive of the Minister for the Treasury of November 1994 (Dini Directive), which cancelled the requirement for

BFs to maintain the majority control of banks. The diversification of asset investments was facilitated through fiscal measures in those cases in which the value of the investments in shareholdings in banks (following the transfers) did not exceed the 50% of the assets of the transferor entity. This facilitated the diversification of corporate structures of the investee banks and hence the increase in their size. The renovation process of the Italian banking system continued with the Law no. 461/1998 (Ciampi Law), Decree no. 153/1999, and Recommendation of 5 August 1999. The 1998–1999 Ciampi Reform attributed to the renovation of the Italian credit system a greater strength than that bestowed by the Dini Directive (Guzzetti 2015a). Indeed, the Ciampi Law ended the controversy on the juridical and institutional nature of BFs, establishing that these operate mainly on their local territory in pursuit of two main objectives: social interest and promotion of the economic development. While placing the obligation for BFs to follow a certain course of action, by defining a range of possible intervention areas (eligible areas), the norm stated the BFs' autonomy in the identification of strategies and modes of action (statutory and management autonomy). In addition to this, the norm substituted the original requirement (ex Amato Laws) of keeping the majority of the capital of transferee banks with its opposite—i.e. drop of control—which provided further impulse to the consolidation process of the banking system. In order to encourage BFs to give up their control over banks, the law established a tax neutrality regime (extended to 31 December 2005) for capital gains realized on the disposal. Other measures related to the BFs concerned the profitability and use of income, the institutional organizational model, the requirements for the appointment of members within the governing bodies, and transparency policies. In sum, the Ciampi Law stated the BFs as private entities, defined their structural features (objectives, sectors, and resources that can be allocated), as well as their functional characteristics and recognized the supervisory authority the power to intervene on their operation.

The underlying principles of the above provisions were drastically hit with the Law 448/2001 (Tremonti Law) and Decree 217/2002. These provisions in fact blunted the essence of the previous norms (primarily the Ciampi Reform), inasmuch as the state's intervention was made more intrusive to the detriment of the autonomy of the BFs. Challenging the decision before the Regional Administrative Court (Tribunale Amministrativo Regionale—TAR) of Lazio, the BFs, however, were able to have a revision of the decision. Following the appeal, the TAR of Lazio found issues of constitutional illegitimacy and resubmitted the acts to the Constitutional Court to verify their consistency with the Constitution. The final decision was reported in Judgements no. 300-301/2003, in which the Constitutional Court definitively ruled on the legal status of foundations, placing them among the actors operating in the interest of the community, in agreement with their definition as private legal entities having full statutory and management autonomy and with the recognition of their social interest objectives. The Constitutional Court also declared as unconstitutional the prevalence of Regions, Provinces, Cities, Metropolitan Areas representatives within the foundations' governing bodies, which instead should leave place to qualified representatives of public and private entities characterizing the local reality, thus underlining the Ciampi Law dispositions (among others Caputo Nassetti 2015).

The principles of the Ciampi Reform have been further confirmed by the Law no. 122/2010, which made clear that the supervision of BFs was up to the Ministry of Economy and Finance (Ministro dell'Economia e delle Finanze—MEF), regardless of whether the BFs, directly or indirectly, own the majority of banks' capital or exercise the control through shareholders' agreements or other pacts. The issue of incompatibility of offices of managers taken in BFs and banks (issue already addressed by the Ciampi Law) has been strengthened too. Law no. 27/2012 has introduced indeed the incompatibility between the office in bodies of BFs and the office in management, supervisory and control bodies and/or functions of competitor companies of the bank or its group companies (the so-called prohibition of interlocking directorates, principle introduced into Italian law by Decree no. 201/2011).

The relevance of the Ciampi Reform in the evolutionary path of the subject matter is clear also from the two recent closely-linked self-regulatory interventions, namely: the Charter of the BFs (approved unanimously on 4 April 2012 by the Assembly of ACRI—Associazione di Fondazioni e di Casse di Risparmio Spa, a representative organization of the Italian BFs) and the Agreement Protocol (signed on 22 April 2015 by ACRI and MEF).

Although binding, the first is a voluntary document aiming to support the evolutionary process undertaken by the BFs. In fact, the changed historical, economic, and financial context unveiled the need for defining the specific scope of application of the principles decreed in the Ciampi Law. Such objective is achieved through the definition of standards for governance and accountability, institutional activity, and asset management. In particular, the document recommends transparency in the criteria and procedures for the BFs' board appointment, establishing temporal discontinuity and incompatibility with previous political assignments, while requiring expertise and autonomy of representatives of the BFs and of the investee banks (Visco 2013). As for the institutional profile, it emphasizes the mainstay of management being inspired by criteria of economy, effectiveness and efficiency, as well as specific criteria for the identification and selection of initiatives to be funded. As for the purposes of asset management, it requires there must be in place a strategic investment planning, which takes into account the principles of diversification and risk control. Such premises are fundamental for generating the profitability needed to conduct institutional activities, ensuring continuity of disbursements, and supporting initiatives consistent with the objectives pursued.

The path of strengthening the governance and management processes of the BFs, traced by the Charter, is further clarified in the 2015 Agreement Protocol (approved by 83 BFs out of the 86 BFs members of the ACRI), which confirms the validity of the regulatory framework of the Ciampi Law and, in doing so, explains its operational scope with regard to specific aspects.

Specifically, the implementation of the Protocol on behalf of the BFs decrees the commitment to implement and comply with standards of efficiency and operational and management effectiveness more stringent compared to the past, in the name of shared rules, which can be traced to the following key principles (Guzzetti 2015b): (i) the diversification of portfolio, that is assets cannot be engaged—directly or indirectly—in exposures to the individual subject for a total amount of more than a third of the total assets of the BFs; (ii) the reporting, focused on a timely, complete, transparent and adequate communication for promoting a genuine dialogue with the stakeholders; (iii) the autonomy and independence from third parties, with respect to which governance is crucial. This intends to address the duration of office and any conditions of incompatibility.

12.3 Banking Foundations: How Shareholdings Evolved from 1990 to Date

The disposal of the shareholdings held by foundations featured a fluctuating trend, being intense in some years, while moderate in others (Table 12.1 shows the time series of data from 1990, the year in which the foundations held total control of transferee banks). The process of shareholding disposal, which had shown a stark increase between 1996 and 2000, soon came to a pause in 2001 following a EU decree suspending tax benefits on disposal of shareholdings in banking, as foreseen by law 474/1994. The EU Commission, indeed, believed that such exemptions could represent the case of state aid, which contrasted with the principle of free competition. The investigation launched by the EU Commission resolved favourably for the foundations in August 2002, moment from which the process of shareholding disposal is resumed.

Data from the only official source available (ACRI) show, among others, the consequences of the legislative changes, which allowed/forced BFs to decrease their shareholdings. In particular, the foundations with shareholdings of more than 50% declined sharply, going from 88 in 1990 to 10 in 2015 (such foundations, as it is widely acknowledged, are those with assets of less than 200 million euros or having headquarters in regions with special statute). Those no longer with shareholdings were 31 in the last year of observation. Their number has increased gradually over time, showing some setbacks (see, for example, 2008–2011) and then a sustained acceleration especially from 2013 to 2015 (during which the number rose from 21 to 31). Finally, the foundations with shareholdings lower or equal to 50% are mostly made up by foundations with shareholdings of less than 5% (57% in 2015). These foundations rose from 2004 to 2015 (from 11 to 27); instead, the number of foundations with shareholdings between 5 and 20% decreased (from 21 in 2004 to 10 in 2015), similarly to those with shareholdings between 20 and 50% (from 26 in 2004 to 10 in 2015).

Overall, there is a growing "separation" between foundations and banks (Table 12.1). The bond between them has clearly loosened, although some foundations still maintain control and the influences exerted on banks are still profound and numerous, and—as we shall see—worrying, in such a way that it is desirable

Table 12.1 Shareholdings held by foundations in Italian banks (1990–2015)

	1990	1995	1996	1998	1999	2000	2001	2002	2003	2004	2005	2006	2007	2008	2009	2010	2011	2012	2013	2014	2015
(A) Foundations with shareholdings >50%	88	62	56	47	44	23	22	20	15	16[a]	16	15	15	15	15	15	14	13	13	12	10
(B) Foundations with no shareholding	0	1	3	6	9	9	10	10	11	14	15	17	17	18	18	18	18	22	21[b]	26	31
(C) Foundations with shareholdings < or equal to 50%, of which:	0	26	30	36	36	57	57	59	63	58	57	56	56	55	55	55	56	53	54	50	47
C.1 below 5%										11	11	12	18	16	17	21	20	22	26	26	27
C.2 between 5 and 20%										21	17	15	13	16	15	14	16	17	14	12	10
C.3 between 20 and 50%										26	29	29	25	23	23	20	20	14	14	12	10
Total foundations	88	89	89	89	89	89	89	89	89	88	88	88	88	88	88	88	88	88	88	88	88

Source: ACRI, Fondazioni di origine bancaria. Annual reports

Note: Data for 1997 are not available. The split-down for point (C) is available starting 2004. From the survey referring to 2006 the foundations at point (A) are those with an asset below 200 million euros or having headquarters in regions with special statutes, for which the provision at art. 25, comma 3bis of Decree 153/99 applies

[a]In 2004 the Fondazione Cassa di Risparmio di Bolzano has bought back shares from the Cassa di Risparmio di Bolzano Spa held by Bayerische Landesbank, obtaining again the control over the transferee bank

[b]The decrease of one unit compared to 2012 derives from the different classification of shareholdings in banking, already owned, made by a foundation

Table 12.2 Dividends paid to foundations/Foundations' shareholdings (percentage values)

Year	Dividends/Shareholdings
2008	15.7
2009	3.1
2010	2.9
2011	2.9
2012	2.3
2013	1.9
2014	2.2
2015	2.9

Source: ACRI, Fondazioni di origine bancaria. Annual reports

Table 12.3 Foundations' grant-making activity (million euros)

Year	Grant-making activity
2008	1676.7
2009	1386.5
2010	1366.6
2011	1092.5
2012	965.8
2013	884.8
2014	911.9
2015	936.7

Source: ACRI, Fondazioni di origine bancaria. Annual reports

that there will be a total and definitive separation, in accordance with the existing literature (Sect. 12.4).

This separation is able to mitigate the link between dividends paid by the banks to foundations and foundations' profitability. In fact, the sharp reduction in bank profitability that occurred with the outbreak of the financial crisis in Italy (in 2008) caused a substantial cut in dividends paid to foundations (Sect. 12.4.1); to this end Table 12.2 reports the dividends on BFs shareholdings, as this ratio is indirectly linked to the banks' profitability. Consequently, as confirmed by ACRI, the foundations suffered a deterioration in profitability, which reduced, among other things, their grant-making activity in favour of the community (Table 12.3). Only in the years 2014–2015 there was a slight increase in both the dividends and the grant-making activity.

12.4 Foundations' Shareholdings in Banks: Strengths and Weaknesses

Below we shall focus on the advantages and disadvantages arising from the shareholdings of foundations in banks. In particular, we will refer to the financial support to banks, the impact on banks' governance, as well as on their performance.

12.4.1 Financial Support to Banks

Foundations have confirmed their nature of long-term investors during the crisis years. Indeed, they not only have kept the shareholdings in portfolio, but have also injected considerable resources into Italian banks as capital, contributing extensively to their recapitalization. In particular, from the beginning of the international financial crisis to 2012, the foundations have provided about 8.6 billion euros to the major Italian banks, enabling them to achieve higher capital ratios as required by the European Banking Authority (ACRI, Fondazioni di origine bancaria, XVIII Report). The foundations have subscribed partly the capital issues in more recent years as well. For example, the Fondazione Monte dei Paschi di Siena subscribed 1.55% of the capital increase, whose amount was of 3 billion euros, made by the Banca MPS in May 2015. Besides, some foundations (Fondazione del Monte di Bologna e Ravenna, Fondazione Cassa di Risparmio di Modena, Fondazione Cassa di Risparmio di Torino, and Fondazione Cariverona) subscribed part of the capital increase, which amounted to 13 billion euros, carried out by Unicredit in February 2017, paying out 11 million euros, 85 million euros, 210 million euros, and 220 million euros respectively. By taking on the role of "lender of last resort", the foundations supported banking management's choices aiming to increase the level of capitalization through the subscription of an increase in capital and bond issues, enduring the consequences of the crisis of financial markets especially in terms of waiver of dividends. This way, the foundations contributed to the soundness and stability of the banks, and to their ability to grant loans to businesses and households (Saccomanni 2012; Banca d'Italia 2013a). Support for the development of the territory, among other things, is enshrined in the Charter of the foundations: "...Foundations pursue the aim of contributing to the promotion of economic development, in the awareness that a sound financial institution rooted in the territories constitutes a growth and stabilization flywheel of the local and national financial system". This interesting statement shows the role of foundations as subjects who help the banks—including those with a wide range of operations, such as Unicredit and Intesa Sanpaolo group—to be anchored in their birthplaces (Faravelli and Clerici 2013).

However, it is reasonable to assume that foundations will no longer be able to adequately support the banks. In fact, the financial position of several foundations weakened and currently shows operational deficits. Their profitability was affected primarily by the fall of bank profits, and thus the fall of the dividends paid by banks. At the same time, the operational costs of the foundations increased, further lowering their profitability (IMF 2014). In part, foundations have also compromised their relationships with stakeholders: the financial returns from bank stakeholdings cannot meet the foundations' demand for cash flow to put towards grants (Mediobanca Securities 2012). Moreover, some foundations have made use of bank credit (mortgages and credit lines) to fund expenditures such as bank capital increases or real estate acquisitions. Others have invested in risky products (derivatives and structured investments). These activities have increased their portfolio risk and raised the pressure on banks to generate dividends in a time of general cuts of dividends and of need for bank recapitalization (IMF 2014). Hence, by supporting the credit system foundations have weakened their financial health and profitability, affecting their ability in supplying any further financial aid.

12.4.2 Impact on Governance

Although over time BFs have significantly decreased the weight of their shareholdings in banks, they still exert a dominant influence in designing banking strategies and in implementing the related management decisions. Such influence leads to distortions in the governance of banks, as the foundations have always been characterized by the presence of bodies of political issuing and, therefore, by the pursuit of a primary objective far from the efficiency of banking business and the maximization of the economic value of the investee banks (see, among the others, Mediobanca Securities 2012; Boeri 2013).

The political influence on foundations produces negative impacts on the governance of banks. Indeed, foundations rarely monitor investee institutions deeply, directing them towards strategies that are non-compatible with the maximization of economic value, hampering the turnover of their governing bodies and orienting the choice of their directors and managers towards criteria other than professionalism and expertise (Costi 2007; Boeri and Guiso 2012). All this occurring despite several recommendations from all quarters; among all, remember those of the Governor of the Bank of Italy: the foundations, "…like any other shareholder, should promote the selection of managers on the basis of competence and professionalism, through transparent criteria" (Banca d'Italia 2013a).

In the absence of empirical studies, a study by Mediobanca based on company data (Mediobanca Securities 2012), focusing on the six Italian largest foundations, confirms the prevalence of local politicians within the board of directors of foundations: 47% is elected by local authorities (the Region, the Province or the City mayor), stressing the interest of local politicians and community (Campedelli et al. 2016), and 21% is directly appointed by the board of directors, implying that local politicians have indirect control. Further proof of the prevalence of politicians can be seen in Table 12.4, which reports the percentages of politicians on the boards of 18 foundations (Boeri 2013): the percentage is equal to or above the 50% in up to 10 of the foundations, and above the 70% in two cases.

Even in case of lack of controlling shareholdings, foundations often appoint the majority of the board of directors of Italian banks through shareholder agreements: some foundations signed specific shareholder agreements in which they commit to vote for a common list of board members. Foundations also exercise a significant influence on the Italian financial system through a complex network of cross shareholdings. They hold shares in several financial companies that are themselves interlinked by cross shareholdings (IMF 2014). Such interconnections are a

Table 12.4 Politicians within the boards of foundations (%)

Foundation	Percentage
Fondazione Monte dei Paschi di Siena	60
Fondazione Cassamarca	50
Fondazione Cassa di Risparmio in Bologna	25
Fondazione Cariparma	25
Fondazione Cassa di Risparmio delle Provincie Lombarde	55
Fondazione Cassa di Risparmio di Torino	45
Fondazione Banco di Sicilia	12
Fondazione Cassa di Risparmio di Alessandria	62
Fondazione Cassa di Risparmio di Fossano	75
Fondazione Cassa di Risparmio di Cuneo	71
Fondazione Cassa di Risparmio di Biella	57
Ente Cassa di Risparmio Firenze	15
Fondazione Cassa di Risparmio di Asti	55
Fondazione Cassa di Risparmio di Gorizia	30
Fondazione Cassa di Risparmio di Modena	58
Fondazione Cassa di Risparmio di Saluzzo	50
Fondazione Cassa dei Risparmi di Forlì	22
Fondazione Banca del Monte di Lombardia	28

Source: Boeri (2013)

potential source of financial contagion from one bank to the others and thus may contribute to triggering systemic crises.

Self-regulatory initiatives outlined in Sect. 12.2 will help to mitigate the risk that the political sphere influence investee banks through the foundations. In fact, as previously stated, in order to safeguard the autonomy of foundations and avoid conflicts of interest, the Charter of the foundations claims the participation in the bodies of the foundations as incompatible with any office or political candidacy. In addition, the MEF-ACRI Protocol enshrines the discontinuity of at least 1 year between the terms of office held in the foundation and those that may be covered in the transferee bank, and vice versa.

Conflicts of interest arising from former appointments and temporal discontinuity are important principles that should be fully implemented. Actually, more stringent governance requirements would be desirable, in order to avoid the switching of members of governing bodies between foundations and banks (IMF 2014).

12.4.3 Impact on Performance

Over the past decades many governments, such as the Italian one, have decided to undertake large bank privatization programs in order to ensure these contributed effectively to economic growth and to financial development, to increase the performance of the credit system and to enhance the effectiveness of financial intermediation (Caprio and Cull 2000). The concept behind the call for shareholding from the private sector was that state-owned banks are less profitable and efficient, because they maximize social objectives rather than profit: in fact, their managers are oriented to serve the politicians' objectives rather than to maximize the country's value and welfare (Barth et al. 1999; La Porta et al. 2002). Although the privatization of the Italian banks through the foundations represents a sui generis privatization, as an Italian peculiarity, we think it is possible to extend the considerations on the public ownership to the BFs shareholdings because of the political influence on foundations.

Hence, many studies have come to cross-country and bank-level findings that highlight the poor performance of government-owned banks, especially in developing countries, and their lower efficiency compared to privately-owned banks (Roe 1998; Caprio and Martinez Peria 2000). These findings appear to be partly due to the fact that state-owned banks often fund inefficient state-owned enterprises or governance deficits, thus misallocating capital within the economy. Moreover, several studies (IMF 2005) demonstrate that state-owned banks are more vulnerable to macroeconomic shocks mainly due to their low profits and the entailed lack of ability to generate capital through retained earnings.

However, evidence from studies on single countries is mixed. For example, the study by Haber (2005) finds that the outcome of privatization in Mexico in the early and mid-1990s was so disappointing that required a renationalization. Similar results were obtained from the early attempts of bank privatization in the Czech Republic, and to a lesser extent in Poland (Bonin et al. 2005). Conversely, Beck et al. (2005) find evidence of an improved performance in Nigerian banks that have been privatized. Similarly, Mohieldin and Nasr (2007) find that in Egypt the private banks outperform state-owned banks in terms of profitability and efficiency. Also Nakane and Weintraub (2005) and Gilbert and Wilson (1998) report positive performance development following privatization of state-owned banks, in Brazil and Korea, respectively. As to the Italian banks, Sapienza (2004) reports that public sector banks conduct inefficient capital allocation and may thus depress financial development, output, and productivity. Fiorentino et al. (2009), who consider a bank to be public if the foundation owns more than 50% of the bank's shares, find that Italian banks that underwent privatization had a strong immediate positive effect on the growth of their productivity. More precisely, this effect seemed to be driven by those banks that were involved in a merger after their privatization.

Other studies on Italian banks in which foundations hold shareholdings followed. Despite these have assessed many profiles (profitability, asset quality, financing to the economy, and so on) in relation to other banks, literature on this line of research is still mostly lacking. Among the few studies, noteworthy are the analyses performed by the Bank of Italy, which highlight that the performance of Savings banks that have become part of large banking groups and in which the foundations own minority shareholdings are on average better than the performance of those Savings banks entirely controlled by the foundations. This trend appears due to the smaller increase in funding costs, resulting from the centralized treasury management, and to the improved skill in screening the customers to whom grant loans, linked to the use of rating systems developed within the groups of belonging (Saccomanni 2012).

Moreover, the Bank of Italy performed a quality asset assessment updated to June 2012: the findings are that Italian banks in which foundations hold shareholdings have weaker asset quality metrics, on average, than other banks. In particular, in the case of a majority control by foundations, banks have a lower provision coverage, approximately 10% points below the system average (IMF 2014). Another study (Mediobanca Securities 2012) compares the banks participated by foundations with non-participated banks in different research profiles. Among the most relevant findings, we report those linked to granting loans to customers: surveys conducted in 2010 show that the former banks had reduced loans to Italian customers since the 2008 peak by cumulative EUR 32 billion (for example, −8% at UniCredit and −6% at Intesa Sanpaolo). This trend contrasts with 22% cumulative increase by banks non-participated by foundations, suggesting that large banks in Italy deleveraged balance sheets, while smaller competitors were increasing financing to the economy.

Finally, in early 2013, IMF completed the assessment of the Italian financial system under the Financial Sector Assessment Program (FSAP). IMF stressed that the system had shown significant resilience, despite the severe and prolonged recession of the world and national economy. The preliminary results of stress tests in fact show that the Italian banking system should be able to handle both a severe recession scenario, and one with idle growth, in virtue of its large capital base and the liquidity provided by the Eurosystem. Solvency stress tests, however, evidence that the banks in which one single foundation controls at least 20% of shares are less resilient to macroeconomic shocks: in the "adverse" scenario (simulating a double dip over a 3-year period (2012–2015), with growth declining by 5.6%), the Tier 1/RWAs ratio of these banks would have fallen from 8.8% in December 2012 to 2.5% in 2015, far below the Basel III minimum of 6%. The capital shortfalls of this category of banks would have accounted for almost half of the shortfalls of all Italian banks in the stress test (IMF 2014). On the regulatory side, although IMF recognizes the important role played by foundations as stable bank shareholders, it also evidences there should be a more stringent supervision over their diffuse presence among shareholders and the peculiarities of their governing bodies. In addition, it calls for regulatory measures to improve transparency and governance, to strengthen management and encourage greater investment diversification (Banca d'Italia 2013b).

In general, studies show that the shareholdings held by foundations, especially the substantial ones, worsen the performance of banks. Loosening of the bond between foundations and banks would increase profit, credit quality, and resilience to shock and bring more financing to the economy. On the other hand, the negative effects on governance—described in Sect. 12.4.2—cannot leave performance unaffected: relocating banks on the objective of maximizing their economic value can only occur through interventions aiming to guarantee a sound governance structure.

12.5 Conclusions

The birth of the BFs in Italy has triggered a great debate and an intense evolution of legislation, which aimed on the one hand to loosen the bond with investee banks, and on the other to implement the role these organisms have in non-profit activities in favour of the community.

Recently, such legislation has been flanked by self-regulatory measures, which set the premises for attenuating the vicious circle between banks and foundations.

Other aspects of the self-regulation that are worth appreciating are (i) the enhancement of the obligation on relinquishing control—also if joint or in fact—over investee banks; (ii) the provisions on the matter of governance with the aim of promoting the quality of bodies, favouring their turnover, and strengthening their autonomy; and (iii) greater transparency and accountability policies.

According to a survey on a sample of foundations shareholders of the major Italian banks, in the case of the significant institutions (that is, directly supervised by ECB within the Single Supervisory Mechanism) the total capital exceeding the threshold to be transferred would amount to 4.8 billion euros (Signorini 2015). According to another estimate given at the end of 2015 (ACRI, Fondazioni di origine bancaria, XXI Report), which takes into account the accounting data, the foundations whose investment in the transferee banks exceeds one third of their assets are 29, with an accounting exposure of over 3.78 billion euros.

This further loosening of the foundations-banks bond should have positive consequences on both of them. It is very likely that this will improve the banks' governance, determine a broader opening to the markets for their shareholdings, favour the opening to new investors, making the Italian financial system more soundness and more fitting to the needs of the real economy. On the other hand, the foundations will loosen their ties to the economic results of the investee banks and be able to allocate their resources to projects and initiatives in favour of the community, strengthening their grant-making activities.

In short, all this seems to be the prerequisite for a more developed Italian financial market where banks are more oriented to efficiency objectives, also thanks to an improved governance, and foundations are encouraged to emphasize their non-profit role in favour of all the market players (investors included).

References

ACRI-Associazione di Fondazioni e di Casse di Risparmio Spa. *Fondazioni di origine bancaria, Annual reports*, Roma.

Banca d'Italia. (2013a, Maggio 31). *Considerazioni finali*. Roma: Assemblea Ordinaria dei Partecipanti.

Banca d'Italia. (2013b, Maggio 31). *Relazione sulla gestione e sulle attività della Banca d'Italia*. Roma.

Banca d'Italia. *Annual reports*, Roma.

Barbetta, G. P. (2013). *Le fondazioni*. Bologna: Il Mulino.

Barth, J., Caprio, G., & Levine, R. (1999). *Banking systems around the globe: Do regulation and ownership affect performance and stability?* World Bank Policy Research Working Paper No. 2325.

Bassanini, A. (2003). Fondazioni bancarie e ammodernamento dello Stato: Riforma, controriforma o trionfo di Penelope? *Il Ponte, 5*, 11–24.

Beck, T., Cull, R., & Jerome, A. (2005). Bank privatization and performance: Empirical evidence from Nigeria. *Journal of Banking and Finance, 29*, 2355–2379.

Birindelli, G., & Ferretti, P. (1997). Profili evolutivi della privatizzazione del sistema bancario: limiti ed opportunità per le fondazioni e le aziende di credito. *Il Risparmio, 3*.

Boeri, T. (2013, Gennaio 27). *I politici ai vertici delle fondazioni bancarie*. Lavoce.info.

Boeri, T., & Guiso, L. (2012, Gennaio 13). *Quell'abbraccio mortale fra fondazioni e banche*. Lavoce.info.

Bonin, J. P., Hasan, I., & Wachtel, P. (2005). Bank privatization and performance: Evidence from transition countries. *Journal of Banking and Finance, 29*, 31–53.

Campedelli, B., Zanin, L., Moggi, S., Rossi, G., & Leardini, C. (2016). La governance delle fondazioni di origine bancaria italiane sancisce il modello della community-owned foundation. *Il Risparmio, gennaio-marzo*.

Caprio, G., & Cull, R. (2000). Bank privatization and regulation for Egypt, distinguished lecture series. *Cairo: Egyptian Center for Economic Studies, 15*.

Caprio, G., & Martinez, Peria M. (2000, November). Avoiding disaster: Policies to reduce the risk of banking crises. *Cairo: Egyptian Center for Economic Studies*, Working Paper No. 47.

Caputo, Nassetti F. (2015, Febbraio 2). *Fondazione bancaria che cambia: evoluzione normativa dal 1990 ad oggi. Intervento alla Conferenza "Banche e Fondazioni che cambiano: una occasione per la crescita delle comunità locali"*, organizzata dalla Associazione Attiva Ferrara e dalla Confartigianato di Ferrara, Ferrara.

Clarich, M., & Pisaneschi, A. (2001). *Le fondazioni bancarie. Dalla holding creditizia all'ente non-profit*. Bologna: Il Mulino.

Costi, R. (2007, Giugno 12). *Fondazioni e banche, quel legame che non si spezza*. Lavoce.info

Faravelli, M. L., & Clerici, M. A. (2013). *Economic crisis and new challenges for banking foundations*, IV EUGEO Congress, Rome, 5–7 September.

Fiorentino, E., De Vincenzo, A., Heid, F., Karmann, A., & Koetter, M. (2009, September). *The effects of privatization and consolidation on bank productivity: Comparative evidence from Italy and Germany*, Temi di discussione. Working Papers No. 722.

Fubini, F. (2014, ottobre 6). Fondazioni e banche, il sonno della politica. *Affari & Finanza*.

Gilbert, R. A., & Wilson, P. (1998). Effects of regulation on productivity of Korean banks. *Journal of Economics, 50*, 133–155.

Guzzetti, G. (2015a, Aprile 15). *Ruolo delle Fob nel processo di ristruttrazione, sviluppo e consolidamento del settore bancario nazionale*. Roma: Audizione – Senato della Repubblica.

Guzzetti, G. (2015b, Giugno 18). *Intervento al XXIII Congresso Nazionale delle Fondazioni di Origine Bancaria e delle Casse di Risparmio Spa*, Lucca.

Haber, S. (2005). Mexico's experiments with bank privatization and liberalization, 1991–2003. *Journal of Banking and Finance, 29*, 2325–2353.

IMF-International Monetary Fund. (2005, January). *State-owned banks, stability, privatization, and growth: Practical policy decisions in a world without empirical proof*, Prepared by Andrews, M. Working Paper No. 10.

IMF-International Monetary Fund. (2014, September). *Reforming the corporate governance of Italian banks*, Prepared by Jassaud, N., Working Paper No. 181.

La Porta, R., Lopez-de Silanes, F., & Shleifer, A. (2002). Government ownership of banks. *Journal of Finance, 57*, 265–301.

Mediobanca Securities. (2012, May 28). *Italian Banking Foundations*.

Mohieldin, M., & Nasr, S. (2007). On bank privatization: The case of Egypt. *The Quarterly Review of Economics and Finance, 46*, 707–725.

Nakane, M. I., & Weintraub, D. B. (2005). Bank privatization and productivity: Evidence for Brazil. *Journal of Banking and Finance, 29*, 2259–2289.
Perotti, R., & Zingales, L. (2012, febbraio 26). Quei pasticci tra le banche e la politica. *Il Sole 24 Ore*.
Roe, A. R. (1998, June). *The Egyptian banking system: Liberalization, competition and privatization*. Cairo: Egyptian Center for Economic Studies, Working Paper No. 28.
Saccomanni, F. (2012, Giugno 7). *Intervento al XXII Congresso Nazionale delle Fondazioni di Origine Bancaria e delle Casse di Risparmio Spa,* Palermo.
Sapienza, P. (2004). The effects of government ownership on bank lending. *Journal of Financial Economics, 72*, 357–384.
Schlüchter, A., Then, V., & Walkenhorst, P. (Eds.). (2001). *Foundation in Europe. Society, management and law*. London: Directory of Social Change.
Signorini, L. F. (2015, Giugno 19). *Intervento al XXIII° Congresso nazionale dell'ACRI*, Lucca.
Visco, I. (2013, Luglio 10). *Intervento all'Associazione Bancaria Italiana*. Roma: Assemblea Ordinaria.

Chapter 13
Corporate Governance in the Nigerian Banking Sector: A Bounded Rationality Conundrum

Franklin Nakpodia

13.1 Introduction

Allen et al. (2015) examined the significance of banks along two constructs. First, Allen et al. (2015) enlightened that banks ameliorate the information challenges inherent in the relationship between lenders and borrowers. This is achieved by ensuring that borrowers use depositor's funds appropriately. Second, Allen et al. (2015) also indicated that banks enable the intertemporal smoothing of undiversifiable risk while providing facilities to depositors to guide against unexpected consumption shocks. These expectations have not only heightened scholarship examining the role of banks as vehicles for economic development (Mayer 1990; Levine 1997) but have also persuaded governments and countries to channel resources towards preserving the health of its banking sector. It is imperative, therefore, to acknowledge that the role of banks in supporting economic growth is enhanced when it (banks) retains its ability to meet the expectations of its stakeholders i.e. the maximisation of stakeholder's wealth.

The capacity of corporations (such as banks) to maximise shareholder wealth links to the existence of a robust corporate governance framework (Sharfman 2014). While the literature reinforces the foregoing position, corporate governance has been challenged by infractions often triggered by corporate agents (i.e. management). Erkens et al. (2012) explained that this development has substantially provoked many of the disasters witnessed in the global business environment. The 2007–2008 financial crisis, for instance, provides ample evidence of the implications of a weak corporate governance architecture in the financial system. The crisis, which not only resulted in the collapse of an unprecedented number of financial institutions

F. Nakpodia (✉)
Newcastle Business School, Northumbria University, Newcastle, UK
e-mail: f.nakpodia@northumbria.ac.uk

B. Díaz Díaz et al. (eds.), *Corporate Governance in Banking and Investor Protection*, CSR, Sustainability, Ethics & Governance,
https://doi.org/10.1007/978-3-319-70007-6_13

(Erkens et al. 2012) also precipitated the financial meltdown that subsequently morphed into a global recession (Conyon et al. 2011). As Kirkpatrick (2009) infers, failures and weaknesses in corporate governance arrangements, which failed to protect against excessive risk taking in financial institutions, provoked the financial crisis. This resulted in enormous economic costs in many countries and also provided the basis for questioning some corporate governance theories and concepts (Conyon et al. 2011).

While the announcement of losses linked to the US subprime mortgage market by HSBC in February 2007 signalled the formal beginning of the crisis, Acharya et al. (2009) contended that the financial crisis originated in the first quarter of 2006 with the collapse of the US housing market. This collapse arose from the mortgages designed for the subprime market (a subset of the housing market) which required that mortgages are refinanced within a short period to counter increases in mortgage rates. This followed the assumption that there would be a continuous appreciation in property prices. Crouhy et al. (2008) note that interest rate during the period was relatively low, which contributed to the crisis. The prevailing low interest rates coupled with the abundance of available credit compelled credit suppliers to relax lending standards. This prompted increased borrowing activity in the housing market such that borrowers could acquire properties they hitherto could not afford despite the sizable surge in property prices. The desire to take advantage of the thriving market persuaded investors to seek subprime mortgages which offered higher yields than standards mortgages at the time. However, when prices began to fall, borrowers could not refinance nor honour their payment obligations, thereby provoking an unprecedented default rate in the system.

The collapse of the subprime mortgage market had severe implications for various industries and market participants (Crotty 2009) but the damage to the banking system was far-reaching. In the short term, Crouhy et al. (2008) stated that many banks lost money due to widespread mortgage defaults. Furthermore, interbank lending stalled and the creation of risk asset (loan) in favour of individuals and businesses was restricted. The impact of this problem was severe in other countries as many foreign banks invested in US collateralized debt obligations (CDOs). Thus, as mortgage defaults intensified, U.S. banks and those in other countries lost money on the loans. With the US experiencing recession, demand for imported goods plummeted, helping to ignite a global recession. These problems provoked a response from local and global regulatory bodies. In the US, the government introduced the Dodd-Frank Wall Street Reform and Consumer Protection Act whereas, on the international horizon, regulations regarding capital and liquidity standards were established, especially with the introduction of Basel III (Acharya et al. 2009).

Given the problems encountered by countries during the most recent global financial recession, it is crucial to examine how the impact of a similar future crisis can be managed particularly in developing countries. Consequently, the focus of this chapter is to extend the frontiers of understanding by exploring bounded rationality concerns that impact corporate governance practices amongst Nigerian banks. To achieve this objective, the chapter proceeds by undertaking a review of the Nigerian banking system, highlighting the impact of the global financial crisis on Nigerian banks and the policy responses implemented by regulators in the Nigerian banking sector. The chapter then explores the connection between corporate governance and bounded rationality in the context of Nigerian banks. It concludes by stressing that attempts at addressing corporate governance issues in the Nigerian banking sector must acknowledge that corporate governance is an information-based mechanism.

13.2 The Nigerian Banking Industry

According to Soludo (2004), the Nigerian banking landscape has experienced remarkable changes over the years, in terms of the number of institutions, ownership structure, as well as depth and breadth of operations. Soludo (2004) explained that these transformations resulted from complications instigated by the deregulation of the banking sector, globalisation of operations, advances in technology, and adoption of prudential guidelines that are consistent with international benchmarks. Given the preceding view, it is imperative to examine the evolution of the Nigerian banking system.

13.2.1 A Chronological Account of the Nigerian Banking Industry

The literature (Soyibo and Adekanye 1992; Uche 1999; Oluduro 2015) examining the origin of the Nigerian banking system has acknowledged various phases of development of the country's banking sector. Three distinct phases are identified and briefly discussed in this chapter. The first phase represents the period from 1892 to 1952. The history of banking in Nigeria dates back to 1892 following the establishment of the African Banking Corporation (ABC) (Oluduro 2015). However, in 1884, the operation of ABC was absorbed by the British Bank of West Africa (BBWA). A major feature of this era was that the sector was not regulated. This contributed to an influx of new entrants into the system, but these new entrants were mostly foreign-owned banks. Soyibo and Adekanye (1992) noted that the dominance of foreign banks prompted discriminatory practices against Nigerians. This problem acted as a catalyst for the establishment of indigenous banks, but the local banks offered little or no competition to the overseas banks due to their weak capital base and low managerial capacity (Oluduro 2015). Uche (1999) also reported that variety of malpractices were evident during this period, notably the increasing incidence of bad debts, the preference of foreign banks to lend to Europeans more than they did to Africans, among others. The desire to address these concerns triggered the developments that ushered in the second phase of banking evolution in the country.

The second phase (1952–1985) began with the enactment of the Nigerian Banking Ordinance (Oluduro 2015). The main purpose of the legislation was to regulate the sector, especially in setting standards, instituting reserve funds, establishing bank examinations, providing assistance to indigenous banks, among others (Uche 1999). This phase is prominent for three major developments. The first development was the banking boom witnessed in the sector as the 1952 legislation offered incentives for incorporating more local banks, but many of these banks failed due to the monopoly of the British banks as they enjoyed exclusive patronage from British and foreign companies (Soyibo and Adekanye 1992). The second development that characterised the second phase was the promulgation of the Central Bank of Nigeria Act of 1959, which resulted in the establishment of the Central Bank of Nigeria (CBN) (Uche 1999). The 1959 Act authorised the CBN to design and implement appropriate regulatory interventions, to accelerate the development of the country's banking sector. The final major development in this phase was the introduction of Nigerian Enterprises Promotion Act of 1977 (i.e. the Indigenization Act). According to Ugoani (2013), the 1977 Act demanded that should sell the ownership interests in their businesses to Nigerian citizens. This regulation had considerable implications for the banking system. For instance, the foremost bank in Nigeria (BBWA) metamorphosed to become First Bank of Nigeria (FBN) in 1979. The change in name was a reaction to government's Indigenisation policy (Soyibo and Adekanye 1992).

The final phase (1986–date) also witnessed regulatory interventions, incorporating a cycle of deregulation and regulation. In 1986, the government introduced the Structural Adjustment Programme (SAP) which allowed the government to transfer more responsibility to the market in the allocation of resources (Soyibo and Adekanye 1992). This resulted in the liberalisation of banking license and the deregulation of interest rates as CBN ceased to prescribe interest rates charged on loans and deposits. These developments triggered a second banking boom as the industry witnessed massive expansion such that by 1991, there were about 121 commercial and merchant banks in the sector (Oluduro 2015). The proliferation of banks regrettably produced distress and failures in the sector (Daodu et al. 2017), some of which relate to insider abuses, mismanagement, under-capitalisation, bad loans, among others. These problems resulted in the erosion of public confidence in the system thereby necessitating another round of government intervention in the shape of Banks and Other Financial Institutions Act (BOFIA) of 1991. This Act, updated in 2004, reinforced the functions and powers of the CBN, provided modalities for opening and closing of branches, revocation of bank licence, among several other important areas of banking operations. This phase also ushered in other regulatory frameworks notably in corporate governance with the introduction of the Securities and Exchange Commission (SEC) Code of Corporate Governance in 2003 (updated in 2011), and the CBN Code of Corporate Governance launched in 2006.

There is no doubt that the third phase of banking evolution in Nigeria brought considerable stability and direction to banking business in the country. Nonetheless, it is imperative to acknowledge that despite these improvements, the system remains confronted by a variety of challenges. These challenges were summarised in Soludo (2004) to include weak corporate governance, gross insider abuses, insolvency, weak capital base, over-dependence on government funds, among others. To address these problems, the CBN embraced a recapitalisation and consolidation policy. This policy meant that the minimum capitalisation for banks increased to N25billion (about $80 million), and banks were also encouraged to explore consolidation opportunities via mergers and acquisitions (Soludo 2004). Upon implementation of the recapitalisation and consolidation policy in January 2006, Sanusi (2010) affirmed that the Nigerian banking sector witnessed dramatic improvements post-consolidation. However, as the undesirable effects of the global financial crisis of 2007–2008 gathered momentum in various markets across the globe, the Nigerian banking system exhibited a lack of robustness needed to insulate itself from the consequences of the crisis.

13.2.2 The Global Financial Crisis and Its Impact on Nigerian Banks

Like in many countries of the world, Umanhonlen and Lawani (2015) explained that the global financial crisis had a considerable impact on the Nigerian economy, and particularly, its banking industry. Umanhonlen and Lawani (2015) added that the crisis exerted demand pressure on the foreign exchange market. This resulted from the divestment and repatriation of capital and dividends by foreign investors who were equally experiencing liquidity squeeze in their respective countries. This led to increased demand for forex and provoked a depletion of the country's foreign reserve (Ashamu and Abiola 2012). For the Nigerian banking industry, increased outflow of forex imposes liquidity mop-up which translates to the scarcity of liquidity in the country's financial system.

Regarding the impact of the global financial crisis, there was a further contraction in liquidity as lines of foreign credits enjoyed by many Nigerian banks were called in (Soludo 2009). This meant that many banks lost significant incomes typically generated from international trade finance deals. Indeed, Egbulonu and Okonkwo (2015) report that the reduction of credit lines or re-pricing (pushing up the interest rates) of existing credit lines from foreign banks were rife. In some cases, such credit lines were outrightly frozen. This led to substantial foreign exchange and counterparty risks as banks had to embrace techniques such as hedging to mitigate the effects of such risks on their profit levels.

Soludo (2009) added that the collapse of commodity prices especially oil (which is Nigeria's top forex earner) in the international market intensified the narrow liquidity problems. This not only led to a reduction in forex inflows from oil revenue but a corresponding reduction in export earnings and government revenue (Ashamu and Abiola 2012). The government resorted to increased borrowing activities to manage revenue shortfalls. In relation to falling oil prices, Ngwube and Ogbuagu (2014) also specified that banks incurred heavy losses from loans granted to oil companies as they could not repay the loans. These developments impacted the growth rate of money supply in the system and exposed the Nigerian currency (Naira) to severe pressure which it is yet to recover from till date. Umanhonlen and Lawani (2015) stated that the Naira lost more than 25% of its value between 2008 and 2015. The liquidity problem also meant that banks increased lending rates to cope with the increasing demand for liquidity. The approach however stifled investment initiatives, resulting in slower economic growth.

The impact of the crisis was also extended to the Nigerian capital market, as the reduction in capital inflow and divestments by foreign investors from the capital markets was instrumental to the crash of the market. This resulted in the loss of investor's confidence in the market. There was a growing incidence of nonperforming loans as stock market participants found it increasingly difficult to meet their maturing debt obligations. These failures have obligated increased loan-loss provisioning by banks which reduces profitability and lending (Ashamu and Abiola 2012). Okafor (2009) observed that low profitability represents a key factor driving the rising unemployment rate in the sector. Furthermore, the impact of the crisis is unforgiving on the income generation prospects of financial institutions that are directly dependent on the stock market, such as investment and asset management companies, stock broking firms, among others.

13.2.3 Policy Interventions by Nigerian Banking Regulators

Consequent upon the effects of the 2007–2008 global financial crisis on the Nigerian banking structure, regulators in the financial system reacted by implementing policies designed to ameliorate the impact of the crisis. Charles Soludo (a former governor of the CBN) articulated government policies for tackling the effects of the crisis on Nigerian banks along five core constructs; liquidity management, foreign exchange/exchange rate management, tightening of regulation and supervision, interest rate regime and confidence building initiatives (Soludo 2009).

As Soludo (2009) remarked, the central focus of CBN's intervention strategies was to boost systemic liquidity by engaging sound liquidity management techniques. These strategies started with the suspension of its aggressive mop up of liquidity to increase money in circulation. This compelled the reduction in some key ratios. For instance, the liquidity ratio reduced from 40 to 30% (and subsequently to 25%), the Monetary Policy Rate (MPR) also reduced from 10.25 to 9.75% (and later to 8%), and the Cash Reserve Ratio equally reduced from 4 to 2%. The objective underlying these reductions was to improve the capacity of banks to create loans. The CBN also extended the discount window, thereby allowing banks to borrow funds for up to 360 days.

As previously indicated that the crisis had ominous implications on foreign exchange in the sector, it is not surprising that financial regulators injected various tools to improve forex management. The CBN jettisoned the Whole Dutch Auction System (WDAS) and embraced the Retail Dutch Auction System (RDAS) to control the speculative demand for foreign exchange. In relation to RDAS and with the aim of boosting activity in the forex market, the CBN revised and enlarged transactions that are eligible under the RDAS. To increase the volume of forex, the CBN implemented a regulated forex management strategy which allowed it to adjust exchange rates as appropriate towards preserving foreign reserves.

Ailemen (2012) also enlightened that Nigerian banks were severely exposed to the crisis given the existing weak regulation and supervision framework. Consequently, various policies were introduced to tighten regulation and supervision of Nigerian banks. This meant that increased resources were committed to the enforcement of corporate governance. Resident examiners were assigned to banks for increased monitoring, to ensure the implementation of timely regulatory actions as deemed necessary. Credit bureaus were also introduced to ensure that stakeholders can access quality information to enhance their decision-making. The CBN also acknowledged the history of distress in the sector and consequently embarked on a review of the existing contingency planning framework to minimise systemic distress in banks.

The interest rate regime was also overhauled. The CBN, seeking to ease pressure on interbank rates, reduced the rates on Expanded Discount Window (EWD) to a maximum of 500 basis points above the MPR with effect from March 2009 (Soludo 2009). Further, interest rates were adjusted, with the maximum deposit and lending rates pegged at 15 and 22% respectively until the end of 2009. This was intended to relieve the liquidity pressure, to stimulate activity in the real economy.

Soludo (2009) also noted that as confidence in the banking sector has waned following the crisis, there was a need to resuscitate the confidence of the banking public by implementing confidence building initiatives. Thus, it was critical to provide assurances that the government and the CBN would not allow any bank to fail. This prompted greater disclosure requirements to both the banking public and the CBN (Okike et al. 2015). Additionally, it encouraged the strengthening of the operations of the Nigerian Deposit Insurance Corporation (NDIC) (saddled with the responsibility of protecting depositor's funds in the event of failure of insured institutions).

13.2.4 Outstanding Problem: A Corporate Governance Perspective?

Apparently, there is no doubt that regulators in the Nigerian banking sector have spared no effort in ensuring that adequate strategies are established to combat the challenges brought on the system by the global financial crisis. However, it is important to record that the effectiveness and success of these policy interventions have attracted substantial debate amongst scholars and practitioners. For instance, Nwankwo (2013) and Odeleye (2014) indicated that the Nigerian banking sector has recorded notable improvements post global financial crisis, but the generality of the literature suggests otherwise. Notably, findings in Adeusi and Oke (2013) and Alajekwu and Obialor (2014) are inconsistent with the outcomes in Nwankwo (2013) and Odeleye (2014). Reports from the CBN suggest that the banking system continues to experience several unethical practices. In August 2010, the CBN announced the sacking of the Chief Executive Officers (CEOs) of five major banks (Okafor 2013).

Furthermore, a recent report by Bonorchis (2016) informed that the Nigerian banking is experiencing a full-blown financial crisis. In understanding the problems confronting Nigerian banks, Okafor (2013) and Garuba and Otomewo (2015) explained that the majority of the challenges relate to weak corporate governance. This is reflected in the high turnover in board and management staff, inaccurate reporting, non-compliance with regulatory standards, deteriorating ethical principles, late or non-publication of annual reports, among others. Ehimare et al. (2013) and Adeyemi and Olowu (2013) shared similar sentiments. In line with the focus of this chapter and in recognition of the identified challenges linked to corporate governance amongst Nigerian banks, the next section examines these problems and proceeds by making a case for bounded rationality.

13.3 Drivers of Governance Challenges in Nigerian Banks: The Bounded Rationality Conundrum

The literature examined the many corporate governance challenges bedevilling the operations of Nigerian banks. These challenges are driven by endogenous and exogenous factors which include:

Corporate Corruption Scholarly outputs have demonstrated that a negative relationship exists between governance and corruption (Jain 2001). Equally, Caron et al. (2012) suggest that in countries with high levels of corruption, corporate governance practices are affected in organisations domiciled in such countries. Corruption has been severally identified as the bane of the Nigerian economy (Akindele 2005; Lawal 2007) and has seeped into every facet of the country's economic horizon (Okike 2007). Therefore, corporate governance in banks is exposed to the destructive effects of corruption. Okafor (2013) identified corruption as one of the reasons for the sacking of executives of five banks by CBN in 2010.

Weak Enforcement of Regulations Nmehielle and Nwauche (2004) note that the principal problem of corporate governance in Nigeria is the disconnection between the law and its enforcement. Afolabi and Amupitan (2015) agree that enforcement of regulations constitutes a major challenge to corporate governance amongst

Nigerian banks. The inability to enforce is an indication of the disequilibrium that exists between the authority of regulators and the power of operators. Weak enforcement suggests that the power of operators overwhelm the authority of regulators. Okaro and Tauringana (2012) acknowledged that Nigerian regulators lack the requisite capacity to perform their assigned responsibilities.

Weak Institutional Arrangements Aidt (2003) and Nakpodia et al. (2016) explained that weak institutions accelerate the problems of corruption and weak enforcement. Adegbite et al. (2012) and Nakpodia et al. (2016) argue that a country's institutional arrangement shapes its corporate governance regulation but added that the institutional elements in Nigeria are weak. In Hodgson (2006), institutions were expected to regulate the behaviour of economic actors, but Adegbite and Nakajima (2011) indicated that the institutions in Nigeria lack the robustness required to control the economic decisions of key agents in Nigeria.

The Multiplicity of Governance Codes Corporate governance in Nigerian banks is regulated using two codes; CBN Code of Corporate Governance (2006) and SEC Code of Corporate Governance (2011). However, Osemeke and Adegbite (2016) highlight the problems created by a multiple code regime. For example, there are variations in the operating mechanisms of the codes. Whereas the SEC code (2011) considerably reflects a principles-based approach (see Sect. 1.3 of the code), the CBN code (2006) is wholly rules-based (Nakpodia et al. 2016). This creates confusion and potentially provides opportunities for manipulation.

Governance Regulatory Model The SEC Code of Corporate Governance (2011), which is the foremost corporate governance regulation in Nigeria, has been criticised for adopting a substantially principles-based model (Nakpodia et al. 2016; Osemeke and Adegbite 2016; Daodu et al. 2017). In contrast, the CBN Code adopts a largely rules-based model for Nigerian banks, but Arjoon (2006) highlights the drawbacks of an excessive reliance on rule-based regulatory approach, as it increases the potential for legal absolutism, with stakeholder's actions not reflecting the 'spirit of the law.' This problem has been reported among Nigerian banks (see Keatinge 2016). As a result, Nakpodia et al. (2016) articulated an integrated regulatory strategy that combines the elements of both rules-based and principles-based regulation.

13.4 Corporate Governance: An Information-Based Mechanism?

In the previous section, it is apparent that regulation contributes to the challenges confronting corporate governance in Nigerian banks (see Osemeke and Adegbite 2016; Nakpodia et al. 2016). This is predicted as the literature has demonstrated that corporate governance is a regulation-driven mechanism (La Porta et al. 2002; Levine 2004). The concern is that regulation thrives on effective enforcement, thereby compelling the establishment of a framework that can induce compliance amongst stakeholders. The achievement of the preceding depends on the volume of information available to stakeholders. In other words, while stakeholder decisions are a reflection of the information at their disposal, Armstrong et al. (2010) suggests that the informational demands of contracting parties are characteristically heterogeneous. They (Armstrong et al. 2010) also indicated that corporate governance is significantly an information mechanism. These perspectives have been employed to enhance the understanding of the bounded rationality concept.

Bounded rationality suggests that as economic agents engage in decision making, the information they possess challenges their rationality (Simon 1972). While rationality illustrates a state of being reasonable, based on facts or reason, Case (2012) contends that the possession of (varying degrees of) information could stimulate alternative rational behaviours. Precisely, while extensive information could drive a more robust decision-making, scant information, on the contrary, provokes irrational behaviour. Greenwald and Stiglitz (1986) for instance, argued that equilibrium is rarely attained when the activities of economic agents are evaluated with respect to available information. As a result, various implications of a weak information structure were observed to include adverse selection practices, moral hazard, signalling, incomplete contingent claims markets, among others. Following from this, corporate governance practitioners and scholars, particularly in developing countries, are increasingly acknowledging the importance of information as central to attempts at improving corporate governance. Further arguments regarding the relevance of quality information in corporate governance have also enhanced scholarship in areas such as corporate disclosure (Hermalin and Weisbach 2012), information asymmetry (Cai et al. 2015), information efficiency (Cai et al. 2006), among others.

In developing economies such as Nigeria, the availability of sufficient quality information has remained problematic (Akpan-Obong 2009). As a result, decision-making relies on incomplete information which subsequently impacts the outcome generated from an action. Sanchez-Pages (2009) admits the potentials of conflicts and inefficiencies when the available information lacks completeness. Taking the above position into context, developing economies provide a peculiar scenario. While stakeholders widely acknowledge the relevance of information, its availability is limited, as issues ranging mainly from illiteracy hamper its production (of information).

Low literacy levels rank amongst the well-known attributes of less developed economies. Edem et al. (2011) enlightened that Nigeria has an illiteracy rate of 25.6% adult males and 40% adult females. The prevailing degree of literacy in the country has affected financial literacy among corporate stakeholders. For example, this problem has influenced shareholder activism as many shareholders are ignorant of their rights and would prefer to remain passive (Adegbite et al. 2012; Daodu et al. 2017). Additionally, the weak functionality of institutions (e.g. legal institution) (Nakpodia et al. 2016) to provide the necessary support for the emergence of a robust corporate governance is linked to low literacy. These problems not only affect the motivation of stakeholders in acquiring relevant information but also deny shareholders the opportunity to access the benefit of complete information, especially in investment decisions.

Another concern that emanates from the preceding is corporate disclosure. The culture of disclosure among Nigerian companies is not impressive. It is inconsistent with observable practices in the developed countries, and worryingly as testified in Isukul and Chizea (2016), the information collated by Nigerian banks that is expected to form the basis of corporate disclosure often reveals no link to the overall corporate strategy. The existence of this problem is not only connected to the poor quality of available information, but it is also promoted by the inability of directors to appreciate the value of quality information. According to the Summary of Progress Report on Corporate Governance in Africa (2005) and Okike et al. (2015), corporations must appreciate that disclosure is an asset, and should not be perceived as a burden or a cost-inefficient activity.

In relation to the above, information asymmetry issues inform the rationality of Nigerian corporate agents. Information problems in Nigerian corporate domain are underlined by, among other things, a lack of transparency (Adegbite et al. 2013; Okike et al. 2015). However, Ball et al. (2003) demonstrates that improvements in firm transparency through quality disclosure can reduce information asymmetry. Okike et al. (2015) added that avoidance of information asymmetry requires not only adequate but also reliable disclosure. Pandey (2015) defined information asymmetry as the gap between information possessed by managers and what they (managers) shared with shareholders. In the Nigerian stock market, Okpara (2010) stressed that some markets participants possess private information about the firm's value which other stakeholders are unable to access. Similarly, Ogun and Ofonyelu (2012) provide further evidence of asymmetric risks in the Nigerian banking sector. The hoarding of information restricts the robustness of the decision-making process of a wider range of stakeholders that would otherwise enhance their wealth maximisation objectives.

13.5 Conclusion and Areas for Further Research

This chapter extends the frontiers of the several challenges impacting the practice of corporate governance amongst Nigerian banks. This chapter identified the under-researched information-driven problems as a matter provoking the majority of the governance challenges confronting the governance of Nigerian banks. It is apparent that attempts by policy makers to promote good corporate governance practices must incorporate a strategy that would not only improve the availability of quality and reliable information, but it must also identify and implement strategies that would encourage stakeholders to understand the benefits inherent in actively sourcing and integrating quality information in their decision-making activities. The decision to adopt sound corporate governance practices link to the knowledge possessed by operators, determined by the level of information such operators can access.

Notably, the attainment of the preceding argument will benefit from further research in some specific areas. First, there is the need for an empirical research that examines the relationship between (available) information and corporate governance in developing economies. The increasing role of developing economies in the global corporate governance environment demands the deepening of the corporate governance literature in developing economies. Limited studies have explored this relationship in developed economies but the peculiarities often associated with developing economies demand research that incorporates these idiosyncrasies. The second area proposed for further research, which seeks to extend the boundaries of the first proposed research, is that scholars should seek to generate insights that would help policy makers identify appropriate strategies for increasing the desire for, and use of, information by relevant stakeholders. Corporate governance practices in developing economies will remain a problem as long as stakeholders desire to generate quality information is restricted.

References

Acharya, V., Philippon, T., Richardson, M., & Roubini, N. (2009). The financial crisis of 2007–2009: Causes and remedies. *Financial Markets, Institutions and Instruments, 18*(2), 89–137.

Adegbite, E., & Nakajima, C. (2011). Corporate governance and responsibility in Nigeria. *International journal of Disclosure and Governance, 8*(3) 252–271.

Adegbite, E., Amaeshi, K., & Amao, O. (2012). The politics of shareholder activism in Nigeria. *Journal of Business Ethics, 105*(3), 389–402.

Adegbite, E., Amaeshi, K., & Nakajima, C. (2013). Multiple influences on corporate governance practice in Nigeria: Agents, strategies and implications. *International Business Review, 22*(3), 524–538.

Adeusi, S. O., & Oke, M. O. (2013). Impact of bank consolidation on Nigeria economy growth. *International Journal of Innovative Research and Development, 2*(5), 1196–1212.

Adeyemi, B., & Olowu, A. O. (2013). Corporate governance: Has the Nigerian banking sector learnt any lesson? *International Journal of Business and Social Research, 3*(2), 49–59.

Afolabi, A., & Amupitan, M. D. (2015). Corporate governance in the Nigerian banking sector: Issues and challenges. *European Journal of Accounting Auditing and Finance Research, 3*(5), 64–89.

Aidt, T. S. (2003). Economic analysis of corruption: A survey. *The Economic Journal, 113*(491), F632–F652.

Ailemen, I. A. (2012). *Issues in banking and finance*. Lagos: The Chartered Institute of Bankers of Nigeria.

Akindele, S. T. (2005). A critical analysis of corruption and its problems in Nigeria. *Anthropologist, 7*(1), 7–18.

Akpan-Obong, P. I. (2009). *Information and communication technologies in Nigeria: Prospects and challenges for development*. New York: Peter Lang.

Alajekwu, U. B., & Obialor, M. C. (2014). Nigerian bank recapitalisation reforms: Effect on the banks and the economy (2000–2012). *International Journal of Managerial Studies and Research (IJMSR), 2*(2), 48–56.

Allen, F., Carletti, E., & Gu, X. (2015). The roles of banks in financial systems. In A. N. Berger, P. Molyneux, & J. O. Wilson (Eds.), *The oxford handbook of banking* (2nd ed.). Oxford: Oxford University Press.

Arjoon, S. (2006). Striking a balance between rules and principles-based approaches for effective governance: A risks-based approach. *Journal of Business Ethics, 68*(1), 53–82.
Armstrong, C. S., Guay, W. R., & Weber, J. P. (2010). The role of information and financial reporting in corporate governance and debt contracting. *Journal of Accounting and Economics, 50*(2), 179–234.
Ashamu, S., & Abiola, J. (2012). The impact of global financial crisis on banking sector in Nigeria. *British Journal of Arts and Social Sciences, 4*(2), 251–257.
Ball, R., Robin, A., & Wu, J. S. (2003). Incentives versus standards: Properties of accounting income in four East Asian countries. *Journal of Accounting and Economics, 36*(1), 235–270.
Bonorchis, R. (2016). *Nigerian banking industry seen in 'full-blown' credit crisis*. Bloomberg. Retrieved February 20, 2017, from https://www.bloombergquint.com/business/2016/10/10/nigerian-banking-industry-seen-in-full-blown-financial-crisis
Cai, C. X., Keasey, K., & Short, H. (2006). Corporate governance and information efficiency in security markets. *European Financial Management, 12*(5), 763–787.
Cai, J., Liu, Y., Qian, Y., & Yu, M. (2015). Information asymmetry and corporate governance. *The Quarterly Journal of Finance, 5*(3), 1550014.
Caron, M. I., Ficici, A., & Richter, C. L. (2012). The influence of corruption on corporate governance standards: Shared characteristics of rapidly developing economies. *Emerging Markets Journal, 2*(1), 21–37.
Case, D. O. (2012). *Looking for information: A survey of research on information seeking, needs and behavior*. Bingley: Emerald Group.
Conyon, M., Judge, W. Q., & Useem, M. (2011). Corporate governance and the 2008–09 financial crisis. *Corporate Governance: An International Review, 19*(5), 399–404.
Crotty, J. (2009). Structural causes of the global financial crisis: A critical assessment of the 'new financial architecture'. *Cambridge Journal of Economics, 33*(4), 563–580.
Crouhy, M. G., Jarrow, R. A., & Turnbull, S. M. (2008). The subprime credit crisis of 2007. *The Journal of Derivatives, 16*(1), 81–110.
Daodu, O., Nakpodia, F., & Adegbite, E. (2017). Institutional perspectives on corporate governance reforms in Nigeria. In F. Ngwu, O. Osuji, & F. Stephen (Eds.), *Corporate governance in developing and emerging markets*. London: Routledge.
Edem, E., Mbaba, U. G., Udosen, A., & Isioma, E. P. (2011). Literacy in primary and secondary education in Nigeria. *Journal of Languages and Culture, 2*(2), 15–19.
Egbulonu, K. G., & Okonkwo, O. N. (2015). A critical review of the effect of the global financial melt-down on the Nigerian banking sector. *Research on Humanities and Social Sciences, 5*(2), 109–117.
Ehimare, O. A., Taiwo, N. J., & Uche, O. (2013). The role of corporate governance in the growth of Nigerian banks. *Journal of Business Law and Ethics, 1*(1), 44–56.
Erkens, D. H., Hung, M., & Matos, P. (2012). Corporate governance in the 2007–2008 financial crisis: Evidence from financial institutions worldwide. *Journal of Corporate Finance, 18*(2), 389–411.
Garuba, A. O., & Otomewo, G. O. (2015). Corporate governance in the Nigerian banking industry: Issues and challenges. *African Research Review: An International Multidisciplinary Journal, 9*(2), 104–117.
Greenwald, B. C., & Stiglitz, J. E. (1986). Externalities in economies with imperfect information and incomplete markets. *The Quarterly Journal of Economics, 101*(2), 229–264.
Hermalin, B. E., & Weisbach, M. S. (2012). Information disclosure and corporate governance. *The Journal of Finance, 67*(1), 195–233.
Hodgson, G. M. (2006). What are Institutions?. *Journal of Economic Issues, 40*(1), 1–25.
Isukul, A. C., & Chizea, J. J. (2016). A comparative analysis of corporate governance disclosure in Nigerian and South African Banks. *Asian Journal of Economics, Business and Accounting, 1*(3), 1–15.
Jain, A. K. (2001). Corruption: A review. *Journal of Economic Surveys, 15*(1), 71–121.

Keatinge, T. (2016). Banking sector collaboration is needed to tackle Nigerian corruption. *RUSI Newsbrief, 36*(6), 26–28.

Kirkpatrick, G. (2009). *Corporate governance lessons from the financial crisis financial market trends* (Vol. 1). Paris: OECD.

La Porta, R., Lopez-de-Silanes, F., & Shleifer, A. (2002). Government ownership of banks. *The Journal of Finance, 57*(1), 265–301.

Lawal, G. (2007). Corruption and development in Africa: Challenges for political and economic change. *Humanity and Social Sciences Journal, 2*(1), 1–7.

Levine, R. (1997). Financial development and economic growth: Views and agenda. *Journal of Economic Literature, 35*, 688–726.

Levine, R. (2004). *The corporate governance of banks: A concise discussion of concepts and evidence* (Vol. 3404). Washington, DC: World Bank Publications.

Mayer, C. (1990). Financial systems, corporate finance, and economic development. In R. G. Hubbard (Ed.), *Asymmetric information, corporate finance, and investment* (pp. 307–332). Chicago: University of Chicago Press.

Nakpodia, F., Adegbite, E., Amaeshi, K., & Owolabi, A. (2016). Neither principles nor rules: Making corporate governance work in Sub-Saharan Africa. *Journal of Business Ethics*. doi: https://doi.org/10.1007/s10551-016-3208-5

Ngwube, A., & Ogbuagu, M. (2014). Global financial crisis and Nigeria economy. *Global Journal of Management and Business Research, 14*(4), 24–30.

Nmehielle, V., & Nwauche, E. (2004). *External-internal standards in corporate governance in Nigeria*. Paper presented at the Corporate Governance and Accountability in Sub-Saharan Africa, George Washington University Law School.

Nwankwo, O. (2013). Impact of pre and post bank consolidation on the growth of Nigeria economy. *International Journal of Business and Management, 8*(13), 73–82.

Odeleye, A. T. (2014). Pre-consolidation and post-consolidation of Nigerian banking sector: A dynamic comparison. *International Journal of Economics and Financial Issues, 4*(1), 27–34.

Ogun, O., & Ofonyelu, C. (2012). Determinant of asymmetric risks in Nigerian loan market: Any dichotomy between the banks and borrowers' perspectives? *African Journal of Economic Policy, 19*(2), 27–40.

Okafor, E. E. (2009). Post-consolidation challenges and strategies for managing employees' resistance to change in the banking sector in Nigeria. *Journal of Social Sciences, 19*(2), 129–139.

Okafor, E. E. (2013). Reforms in the Nigerian banking sector and strategies for managing human resource challenges. *European Journal of Business and Management, 5*(18), 127–137.

Okaro, S. C., & Tauringana, V. (2012). From SAS to IFRS: An investigation of Nigeria transition road map implementation problems. In V. Tauringana & M. Mangena (Eds.), *Accounting in Africa (research in accounting in emerging economies)* (Vol. 12, pp. 155–176). Bingley: Emerald Publishing.

Okike, E. (2007). Corporate governance in Nigeria: The status quo. *Corporate Governance: An International Review, 15*(2), 173–193.

Okike, E., Adegbite, E. A., Nakpodia, F. A., & Adegbite, S. (2015). A review of internal and external influences on corporate governance and financial accountability in Nigeria. *International Journal of Business Governance and Ethics, 10*(2), 165–185.

Okpara, G. C. (2010). Asymmetric information and dividend policy in emerging markets: Empirical evidence from Nigeria. *International Journal of Economics and Finance, 2*(4), 212–220.

Oluduro, O. F. (2015). History and evolution of banking in Nigeria. *Academia Arena, 7*(1), 9–14.

Osemeke, L., & Adegbite, E. (2016). Regulatory multiplicity and conflict: Towards a combined code on corporate governance in Nigeria. *Journal of Business Ethics, 133*(3), 431–451.

Pandey, I. M. (2015). *Financial management* (11th ed.). Ahmedabad: Vikas.

Sanchez-Pages, S. (2009). Bargaining and conflict with incomplete information. In M. R. Garfinkel & S. Skaperdas (Eds.), *The Oxford handbook of the economics of peace and conflict*. Oxford: Oxford University Press.

Sanusi, L. (2010). *The Nigerian banking industry – what went wrong and the way forward*. Paper presented at the lecture delivered to mark the Annual convocation ceremony of Bayero University, Kano, Nigeria.

Sharfman, B. S. (2014). Shareholder wealth maximization and its implementation under corporate law. *Florida Law Review, 66*(1), 389–431.

Simon, H. A. (1972). Theories of bounded rationality. *Decision and Organization, 1*(1), 161–176.

Soludo, C. C. (2004). *Consolidating the Nigerian banking industry to meet the development challenges of the 21st century*. Paper presented at the Special Meeting of Bankers' Committee, Central Bank of Nigeria, Abuja, Nigeria.

Soludo, C. C. (2009). *Banking in Nigeria at a time of global financial crisis*. Paper presented at the Special interactive session on the banking system, Lagos, Nigeria.

Soyibo, A., & Adekanye, F. (1992). The Nigerian banking system in the context of policies of financial regulation and deregulation (Vol. Research Paper Seventeen). Nairobi: African Economic Research Consortium.

Uche, C. U. (1999). Foreign banks, Africans, and credit in colonial Nigeria, c. 1890–1912. *The Economic History Review, 52*(4), 669–691.

Ugoani, J. N. (2013). Power of bank credit on economic growth: A Nigerian perspective. *International Journal of Financial Economics, 1*(3), 93–102.

Umanhonlen, O. F., & Lawani, I. R. (2015). Effect of global financial meltdown on the Nigerian banking industry and economy. *Management, 5*(3), 63–89.

Chapter 14
Ensuring Sanity in Ghana's Financial Sector: A Focus on Ghana's Microfinance Institutions

Sam Sarpong

14.1 Introduction

Ghana's financial sector has undergone drastic changes in recent years (Ackah and Asiama 2014; Diaz-Serrano and Sackey 2015). Apart from the 34 traditional banks, there are almost 500 microfinance institutions (MFIs) registered in the country today (BoG 2017). The banks do not only compete among themselves, but also with non-banking entities such as savings and loans companies, finance houses, rural and community banks and other MFIs (Asiama 2016). The situation has created a healthy competitive landscape in the drive for customers in the banking industry (PWC 2016; Diaz-Serrano and Sackey 2015) as many of these institutions now court customers with very interesting packages (PWC 2016).

Despite the new lease of life, a significant portion of people detest the banks because of the perception that banks do not provide helpful, proactive and customised financial services to them (Asiama 2016; Business Day 2015). On the contrary, MFIs have, in recent times, received huge patronage among a large number of the people, in view of their informality, flexibility and adaptability (Armendariz and Morduch 2000; Collins et al. 2009; Ghate 1990). With promises of high interest rates, many Ghanaians are being lured to deposit their lifelong savings at some of these MFIs, but the outcomes of such ventures have been devastating. Many depositors have lost their monies as a result of the phoney deals that some MFIs have been engaged in. The plethora of illicit activities within the MFI set-up has since compelled the central bank, Bank of Ghana (BoG), to act against the recalcitrant MFIs.

S. Sarpong (✉)
University of Mines and Technology, Tarkwa, Ghana
e-mail: ssarpong@umat.edu.gh

B. Díaz Díaz et al. (eds.), *Corporate Governance in Banking and Investor Protection*, CSR, Sustainability, Ethics & Governance,
https://doi.org/10.1007/978-3-319-70007-6_14

The chapter provides an overview of the situation regarding the MFIs in Ghana. It adopts an analytical approach to identify and analyse the key issues within the MFIs. The challenges within the sector are explored as well as the measures being undertaken by the BoG, which has the oversight responsibility, to sanitise the financial sector. A general insight is also provided into the corporate governance issues and the financial sustainability of MFIs in Ghana. Finally, the chapter suggests ways that can be adopted in order to overcome the current challenges.

The chapter is organised as follows: Firstly, it begins with a discussion on the financial sector reforms in Africa, as a whole and Ghana, in particular. It then looks at the whole gamut of microfinance, the recent incidents that have befallen it, its sustainability and the role of BoG in this. It concludes with recommendations for a healthier financial system for the MFI sector.

14.2 Reforms in the Financial Institutions in Sub-Saharan Africa

In the 1980s, when many African countries adopted an IMF/World Bank supported Structural Adjustment Programme (SAP), a major component of this was the financial sector reforms. The reforms involved institutional restructuring, the enhancement of the legal and regulatory framework for banking operations and liberalising interest rates (Sowa 2003). Many sub-Saharan Africa (SSA) countries have since liberalised their financial systems in order to create a conducive environment to enhance institutions and markets to support economic growth (Moyo et al. 2014). The increasing development of capital markets and accelerated financial sector reforms have been vital avenues for integrating Africa into the global financial economy and attracting international capital (Senbet and Otchere 2006). This has helped in no small measure to offset the huge difficulties experienced in the past, primarily due to the deficiencies in the financial system.

The reforms have since recorded considerable successes, in terms of the large numbers of financial institutions, increased competition and improved efficiency in the sector (PWC 2016). Despite that, financial systems in Africa still exhibit substantial degrees of inefficiencies in their savings mobilisation and allocations of resources into productive activities (Munyambonera 2013; Senbet and Otchere 2006). The commercial banks generally do not appear to have any proven lending methodologies for financing the poor, and rather underestimate businesses' demand for credit because they have not developed techniques for overcoming high transaction costs and risks (Opare 2001; Aryeetey et al. 1994).

According to Robinson (2001), about 90% of people in developing countries lack access to financial resources from formal institutions. The problem, meanwhile, is particularly acute in sub-Saharan Africa, where Kendall et al. (2010) claim only 20% of households in Sub-Saharan Africa has a formal relationship with a financial institution. Despite the healthy economic prospects in the region, SSA has the lowest share of banked households in the world (12%) and the highest share of poor people, with 50% of the population living on $1.25 a day or less (Glisovic et al. 2012). As such, the advent of MFIs has provided a respite for the poor in places where lack of access to finance has been a concern (Wampah 2014).

14.3 Ghana's Financial Reform Programme

Like many other African countries, Ghana's financial sector has undergone various changes over the years (Asiama 2016). The transformation, started as part of the Financial Sector Adjustment Programme, which was implemented in phases from the late 1980s under the SAP (Ackah and Asiama 2014). Prior to the financial sector reforms, banks in Ghana were dominated by non-performing state-owned ones whose weaknesses included low profitability resulting from high non-performing loan assets, less liquidity, low capital reserve, low level of technology and lack of competition (Antwi-Asare and Addison 2000; Brownbridge and Gockel 1996). The banking sector had also been characterised by limited innovation and poor governance structures (Ackah and Asiama 2014). In many instances, credit decisions lacked commercial considerations, resulting in failures in banking operations.

The key focus of the financial reforms was, therefore, to restructure the financially distressed banks, to improve the regulatory and supervisory framework, to develop fully liberalised money and capital markets in Ghana and to ensure the effective mobilisation of domestic savings and the promotion of non-bank financial institutions (Brownbridge and Gockel 1996). As part of the reforms, in 2004, the country introduced a new Banking Act. The new Act also saw the introduction of the universal banking licence, which allowed the banks to engage in some or all permissible banking business activities without restrictions (Asiama 2016). The Act, thus, created room for diversification of a range of financial services that a bank can provide.

Currently, a number of local banks have merged or have been acquired by others largely on account of the measures taken to make the banks more prudent (Ackah and Asiama 2014). Ghana has since moved from the time of severe distress and dysfunction in the banking system, illiquidity and insolvency, interest rate controls and credit rationing to a market-based regime. Processes, policies and stringent measures have been introduced and directed at improving the regulatory framework and the strengthening of bank supervision to ensure increased efficiency and profitability of banks in the country (Asiama 2017; Wampah 2014). There is now a more diversified financial system resulting from the privatisation of state-owned banks and the increased competition occasioned by the licensing of several new banks, including many foreign ones (Ackah and Asiama 2014). The pace of financial sector development has been strong and the sector continues to attract a lot of foreign direct investment, especially from other banks in the West African sub-region (PWC 2016). The sustained financial sector restructuring and transformation has since made Ghana one of the most vibrant financial services centres in the sub-region (Ackah and Asiama 2014; Quartey and Afful-Mensah 2014).

But, in spite of the current increase in formal banking infrastructures, traditional banks only serve a small number of the Ghanaian populace (Amesimeku 2014; Basu et al. 2004). The banks, therefore, still remain largely out of reach for the poor (Spencer and Wood 2005). Ghana has an unbanked population of over 80% and in terms of geographical spread, banking operations in Ghana are urban-based and highly concentrated in the southern part of the country (Wampah 2014). Stringent requirements for loans have systematically also kept low income households out of the credit delivery network of commercial banks. Typically, formal banks do not target the poor because lending without collateral is considered too risky (Field et al. 2016). As Field et al. note, poor households seeking credit are, therefore, forced into informal markets where the costs are exorbitant and the methods of repayment quite an uphill task. Dispensing with the elaborate requirements and paperwork of conventional banking, informal suppliers of money have devised their own methodologies which have worked to suit the conditions and positions of its low income clientele (Srinivas 2016).

Since the poor arguably need credit and other financial assistance much fervently, their impaired credit access is quite disturbing (Field et al. 2016). Hence, the vacuum created by their lack of access to credit and other banking services, is being filled by the MFIs and the informal *susu* system.[1] With a large unbanked population at its disposal, the MFIs have made substantial inroads into the populace. They now complement the formal banking sector in providing financial services to the poor (Basu et al. 2004).

Most of the unbanked tend to shun banks due to the lack of trust, difficulties in accessing funds, the strenuous requirements and procedures in opening accounts, and the fact that they are generally unable to access loans from them (Asiama 2016). Others, meanwhile, are generally disinterested in the high interest charges that they have to pay when they go for loans at the banks. The banks currently pay an average of 11.9% per annum as interest on deposits but charge their borrowers an average of 33.4% as nominal interest on loans annually, a situation that simply put, puts many depositors off (Adombila 2017).

The resort to MFIs, as Adams and Fitchett (1992) sum up, is boosted by the fact that the informal sector is more dynamic than the formal or semi-formal financial sectors because of some of the range of services provided by the former, especially small daily deposits, short-term loans, small loans, financial innovations that engender flexibility, speed and suppleness, the proximity of the service provider to the clients, among others. These and other related issues have pushed the microfinance agenda on the minds of Ghanaians. The warm embrace Ghanaians have accorded MFIs has turned the sector into one of the big successes of Ghana's liberalisation policies, reflecting a wider boom in financial services in the country (Amesimeku 2014).

[1]Susu is a traditional way of savings with several variants, the most common of which is where an individual known in the community collects periodic savings from other individuals on the understanding that the total savings will be returned at the end of the specified period, less a commission of a day's savings. In other variants, people may agree to contribute a specified amount and give the total to one member of a group repeating same by rotation till every member is served each time (Belnye 2012).

14.4 Microfinance Institutions in Ghana

The microfinance sector in Ghana comprises of four tiered ranges: *formal suppliers*, which include the savings and loan companies and rural and community banks; *semi-formal suppliers*, including credit unions, financial non-governmental organisations (FNGOs) and cooperatives; *informal suppliers*, including *susu* collectors and clubs and rotating and accumulating savings and credit associations (ROSCAs and ASCAs); and *government-sponsored microfinance schemes and programmes*, the current scheme being the Micro and Small Loans Centre (MASLOC) which is the apex body responsible for implementing the government's microfinance programme targeted at reducing poverty and creating jobs and wealth.

Micro-financing in Ghana has developed in stages over the years from the traditional informal groups, known as *susu*, through the stage where the government had to come in to formalise the process, to this very day where there is domination by the private sector, which owns and manages most of the MFIs. As such, the MFIs in Ghana are essentially a commercialised venture driven primarily by profit making rather than poverty alleviation. Historical analysis of this sector shows that the original proposition has gradually transformed into a standardised, highly commercial platform, at least for the larger MFIs (Roy 2010). The lucrative nature of the sector has drawn in many investors who have moved in to cash in on its prospects. Although it has traditionally been seen as a poverty reduction tool and an instrument to support economic development, increasingly, it is now recognised as a valuable financial service and a good business opportunity with a large chunk of microfinance companies being concentrated in the urban centres (Conroy 2003; Otero 1999).

For some years now, the sector has shown positive signs of growth. This is largely seen in the number of microfinance companies that have sprung up in recent times. Some commercial banks have even entered into the fray, taking advantage of the enormous business that can be made in the sector. Another trend has been the conversion of smaller traditional lenders into MFIs in what is seen as a 'promotion league.' Some have even moved on to become fully-fledged banks.

But with its core objectives bordering on helping the poor and/or less educated low income micro-entrepreneurs, often times, it seems inexcusable for MFIs to concentrate on major urban areas rather than the rural areas where they could be mostly needed. The expectation has been that they would help reduce poverty, which is considered as the most important development objective (World Bank 2000), especially for the rural economic players, who are constrained in credit accessibility to transform their subsistence operations. However, for now, the rural penetration has been quite negligible in Ghana (Wampah 2014). Despite that, there can be no doubt that for many in the informal sector, the MFIs remain the only hope for financial support, while their very presence, enables those who are not even their customers, to gain quicker access to financial products and services (Amesimeku 2014).

14.5 Fraudulent Issues Among MFIs

The drive to mobilise deposits from the unbanked population and to encourage savings habits has, however, faced serious challenges from the activities of some unscrupulous microfinance firms. Cases involving the swindling of depositors by MFIs have made the headlines on numerous occasions for the past 5 years. More recently, in February 2017, customers of an MFI, *Vision Gate Microfinance*, had their investments locked up because the owners of the company bolted after collecting GHC2.3 billion from more than 400 depositors. The latest case comes on the heels of similar occurrences in the last few years. These incidences arise principally because of imprudent use of mobilised resources and reflect a lack of expertise on the part of the collectors; other times, it is sheer fraud that is perpetrated. The developments do not only cost patrons their hard earned savings, but also hurt confidence in the wider financial system (Belnye 2012).

More serious issues arose within the MFI network in 2015. In that year alone, well over 100 microfinance companies folded up due to mismanagement of funds and other irregularities (Appiah 2016). Prominent among the issues they had to contend with were liquidity challenges, the posting of fictitious credits, fraudulent transfers or withdrawals and plain thievery. That year, the BoG also discovered a number of unlicensed MFIs in the system. Many of those MFIs had manipulated depositors to part with various sums of money. Whilst some MFIs were paying 30–35% interest on deposits (far in excess of the 24% interest that even the government pays on treasury bills), others were tripling 3 months-deposits as loans for customers. Meanwhile, more than 40 microfinance institutions also collapsed in 2013, and this together with other fraudulent acts within the sector, led to enormous concerns being expressed by the public over MFIs.

Major incidents over the years have been perpetrated by 'unregulated' MFIs (those unlicensed and operating illegally), together with some licensed ones which veered off their legitimate course of duty to lure unsuspecting customers into their fold under the pretext of providing them with high interest rates on their savings. Some depositors were also led into phoney investments. The management of these MFIs then either bolted with the monies they secured from the unsuspecting depositors or diverted the proceeds from their activities to acquire assets for themselves. Hundreds of account holders have since lost their savings and investments to these MFIs. Some depositors who lost most of their lifelong savings reportedly committed suicide. There are those who, up till this very day, are still pressing charges against MFIs in the law courts.

In the past, the BoG took the position that the MFIs were insignificant relative to the wider financial sector and therefore did not pose any risks to the financial system (Belnye 2012). In addition, as Belnye notes, regulating such small-scale operators was thought to be costly and a waste of scarce supervisory resources. However, as the spate of reported collapses increased from 2008 and the headlines became rampant, the bank moved in to close down a number of operations countrywide.

In 2011, it finally published new guidelines on the setting up of MFIs as a means to stop the continuous abuse in the system. Despite this and other measures, the sector still records pockets of malfeasance now and then.

14.6 Key Regulatory Requirements for the Licensing of MFIs

The BoG has now reviewed the entire process of licensing new microfinance institutions in the country. It has also resourced all its regional offices with the requisite staff to improve surveillance on MFIs (Wampah 2014). Regulated activities include an increase in paid up capital for the various tiers of non-bank financial institutions. The capital requirements for Non-Bank Financial institutions now stands at GHC15.0 million, up from GHC7.0 million while the minimum capital for rural banks has been pegged at GHC300,000. The microfinance sector investors now require GHC500,000 and GHC300,000 to obtain a Tier2 and Tier3 Microfinance company licence respectively. The objective of this exercise is to sanitise their operations and to safeguard the interest of their patrons (Wampah 2014). Currently, rural and community banks are regulated under the Banking Act 2004 (Act 673) as amended by the Banking Act 2007 (Act 738), while the Savings and Loans Companies are currently regulated under the Non-Bank Financial Institutions (NBFI) Act 2008 (Act 774). Until July 2011, there had been no regulatory framework for the rest of the players such as the financial non-governmental organisations or money lenders.

The central bank has also intensified public education on financial literacy in line with its desire to inform and educate the public on the activities of unlicensed MFIs (Issahaku 2016a, b). It has advised the public to deal only with licensed institutions which display their operating licenses, certificates of incorporation and certificates of commencement of business on their premises. Many victims of financial scams tend to lack information on the credibility of operators, hence the need for education on the dangers of dealing with unauthorised financial institutions (Issahaku 2016a, b). In the wake of the recent crises, the BoG has also instituted measures to protect depositors from and mitigate default risks from MFIs.

14.7 BoG's Supervision and Regulation of MFIs

The BoG has the role of nurturing the microfinance sector in order to realise its huge potential (Issahaku 2016a, b). In spite of that, for years, the MFI sector was left on its own with little or inadequate supervision until the last few years. Although the BoG put in the right measures in 2011 to institutionalise its supervisory and regulatory role, it failed woefully to enforce its own regulations. This was largely due to the fact that it lacked the logistic support for such operations (Belnye 2012).

The BoG, to say the least, had been ill-equipped to monitor effectively the huge numbers of MFIs in the country. However, it has recently intensified its efforts in response to public outcry against the incidences of criminality being perpetrated by some unruly MFIs. Whilst the monitoring of licensed MFIs could be said to be somehow appreciable, a considerable number, meanwhile, remained outside the monitoring system. Unlicensed, unregulated and unsupervised, they operated with impunity and posed the greatest danger to the MFI concept.

Usually, the only time the activities of these unregulated MFIs activities got to the attention of BoG was when things went wrong and depositors were unable to receive their monies. Considerable debate has since ensued among analysts as to whether the BoG has the resources to monitor the more than 500 MFIs in the country today. Although the BoG might not have control over some 'private' savings schemes that often spring up now and then, the law clearly states that any unlicensed institution engaging in deposit mobilisation or any other activity akin to banking would be in breach of Section 4 of the Banking Act, 2004 (Act 673). The BoG has since been closing down or suspending some of these MFIs.

The current measures initiated by the BoG has, meanwhile, affected several depositors some of whom have not been able to access their savings and investments because of the freeze on the assets of defaulting MFIs. Since there is no deposit insurance in Ghana, when MFIs collapse, customers irretrievably lose their working capital, savings and their sources of livelihood, which further predispose them to indebtedness and impoverishment. Consequently, the BoG is putting in measures to ensure depositors are cushioned off from any financial displacement. Now a Deposit Protection Act and the Banks and Specialised Deposit-taking Institutions Act have been initiated by the BoG to ensure a stronger and user-friendly regulatory regime and to avoid situations where depositors lose out when financial institutions fail. Both Acts, currently awaiting Presidential assent, are meant to serve as frameworks for the conduct of bank and non-bank businesses in promoting efficient savings mobilisation in the country (Asiama 2016).

14.8 Current Measures to Ameliorate Fraudulent Practices

The recent crises in the MFIs operations provided the basis for the saver protection scheme and the crucial need to define adequate protection for depositors. The BoG, therefore, in 2014 put in place measures to introduce the savings protection scheme in order to consolidate its mission of promoting confidence in the financial system, especially in relation to protecting the savings of all depositors, while encouraging financial inclusion and access to formal financial services (Wampah 2014).

A Deposit Insurance Corporation is also to be established under the Deposit Protection Act with the BoG providing the initial capital of GH26 million for the corporation. The scheme is expected to function as a 'pay box' with compensation to be paid to customers in the event of a bank failure. It would eventually be transformed into a fully-fledged deposit insurance scheme with a broader mandate to engage in risk-minimisation and other roles. Under the Specialised Deposit-Taking Institutions Act, all deposit-taking institutions are mandated to be members of the deposit insurance scheme which will provide a safety net for depositors in the event of bank failures of systemic nature. The objective of the legislation is to protect small savers from a loss incurred as a result of the occurrence of an insured event. The new frameworks are being complemented by a number of regulations and directives by the BoG.

14.9 The Challenges and Prospects of MFIs

Events unfolding in Ghana point to a serious crisis within the MFI set-up in spite of attempts to sanitise it. Although the sector is growing at a faster pace, questions regarding its sustainability continue to linger on. The threats MFIs face can be seen in their poor infrastructure, poor corporate governance and their inability to find, afford, train and retain high quality staff. The lack of basic infrastructure and the high cost of utilities serve as a severe drawback too, especially when weighed against the 'small' nature of their business. Small-scale businesses like the MFIs have had cause to complain of late about high operational costs because of the hikes in taxes, office accommodation and utility bills. Power supply too is quite erratic of late adding to the numerous problems besetting the sector.

The under-mentioned issues also present formidable challenges to the MFIs.

14.9.1 Staff

In a number of cases, MFIs are staffed by inadequately trained staffs who are mostly relatives and or close friends of the owners. What most of the MFIs do is to recruit recent young senior high school graduates who then move from door-to-door in savings mobilisation exercises. Those recruited often lack adequate training and their poor conditions of service also act as a disincentive. As a result, there is a high staff turn-over rate. Again, some MFIs ignore the relevance of other non-financial services like training for their staff, customer care, relationship marketing and other business measures that help in sustaining a good relationship with their clients.

Aside from the afore-mentioned, one considerable feature of the Ghanaian MFIs is that they have failed to recognise and assess the risks involved in new products and activities. They have also not done much in terms of improving their internal control mechanisms. Staff do not even abide by the policies and procedures that have been developed to integrate risk management. Many MFIs are suffering because they lack the required institutional capabilities and controls after expanding too quickly and rolling out new products or expanding into different markets.

14.9.2 Corporate Governance

The rapid growth in the MFIs has not been accompanied by an equal improvement in the operational environment of the MFI. Rather, it seems, many boards and managements of MFIs have failed on numerous occasions to develop a strong culture to maintain successful operations. In the wake of this, a number of MFIs have collapsed or are collapsing because they do not have stringent measures in place to ensure they thrive in the competitive environment. The infractions of inadequate checks and balance of executives, lack of transparency in reporting, lack of independent board nomination, insufficient transparency about ownership and conflict of interest at various levels of management, have all had an impact on the performances of some MFIs.

Some board members and management even acquire facilities from these MFIs which are misused; some do not even pay back what they owe. A whole array of irregularities, lack of business acumen and sheer disregard for laid-down procedures, have often bedevilled the MFIs, which subsequently reflect on their poor performances and high levels of fraudulent deals. As Issahaku (2016b) notes, weaknesses in corporate governance still remains a challenge in the non-bank financial institution sector in Ghana. Applying high business standards not only increases the accountability towards investors, but it also encourages MFIs to prevent and control corruptible practices.

14.9.3 Operational Issues

Some of the owners of the MFIs are also more inclined towards making brisk business and profit within a relatively short time of their operation. This, therefore, leads them to indulge in some unfair practices and risks. Consequently, they give out loans for which they are often not in a position to recover. Those MFIs which are bent on exacting huge deposits from clients, often resort to the ponzi schemes in order to make much money for themselves. Another issue worth considering is the quality of leadership provided by the MFIs, which to say the least, is sometimes quite disingenuous. People without the requisite qualifications are often at the helm of affairs. Generally, many of these are unable to set the ethical tone for their businesses. As such, not much effort is made to shore up the ideals of integrity, culture of hard work and meritorious services in such businesses.

Although the chapter has dwelt extensively on the fraudulent deals perpetrated by MFI, it is also pertinent to realise that delinquent loans are also part of the issues facing the MFIs in Ghana. In recent times, multiple borrowing and over-indebtedness have constituted severe challenges to the MFIs. Some clients intentionally borrow from multiple MFIs with no intention of repaying these monies. Oftentimes, the MFIs do not have a means of knowing about such predispositions because the activities of the MFIs are not coordinated in a manner that can provide information on clients. The situation is now being remedied by the Ghana Association of Microfinance Companies, an umbrella grouping of all MFIs, which is taking steps to prevent multiple borrowing by clients. To support its members to deal with this, the association has introduced a biometric verification system to help improve due diligence processes of member companies.

14.10 Best Practices for MFIs

In spite of recent steps to stop the fraudulent acts in MFIs, there appears to be pockets of these acts that tend to engulf MFIs now and then. Generally, fraud flourishes in an environment with complex processes and high volume of unsystematic transactions. In order to prevent such fraudulent acts, all activities connected with MFI's operations ought to be guided by policies and procedures without leaving unreasonable grey areas for manipulation. The abuses of the MFI principles have dented the image of the MFIs as many operators are seen as fraudsters. There is, therefore, the need to instil public confidence in the MFI but this would very much depend on the policy direction of the regulator, the BoG, as well as a thorough self-introspection by members of the microfinance institutions. Notwithstanding this, it can be said that the MFI concept still stands as a force to be reckoned with and given the necessary push, it can and must be able to contribute effectively to Ghana's socio-economic development.

At best, the management of these MFIs should not be dominated by family and friends or be run by family fiefs lacking any knowledge of business activities. People with the requisite skills that can transform the workings of these MFIs should be made to run these MFIs. Currently, one of Ghana's universities, the University of Cape Coast, has started programmes in microfinance to help in building up the technical capacities of prospective microfinance workers. This could help bring to the fore a new breed of practitioners well versed in the trade and also ensure the snags of the sector are done away with. MFIs would also need to appreciate the support of the use of appropriate prudential management tools like proper accounting practices or tools, hiring qualified human resources, good governance, among others, in order to give maximum buoyancy to the sector.

One of the major challenges facing the Ghanaian financial sector is the lack of credit referencing bureaus that banks and other financial institutions can rely on for customer credit data. The information or database on borrowers, their credit history, and repayment records has not kept pace with the growth of the microfinance sector and this has been a serious drawback. It is expected that this would ease in the future as the BoG provides licences to reputable firms keen to work in that direction. The lack of common benchmarks, methods for measuring and information sharing further inhibits the performance of the sector hence the need to embrace the credit bureau mechanism as much as possible. There is currently, an attempt though to develop a national data bank on microfinance. It is, meanwhile, suggested that the management of MFIs should spend much time in assessing the creditworthiness of their clients to minimise over-indebtedness. It is also important to ensure that the security and protection of deposits or savings of clients are guaranteed. At least, for now, there is a measure in place in that regard.

Another area that needs to be looked at is the need for the management of MFIs to design sound risk management frameworks to identify, monitor and control risks of the MFIs. Alongside these, employees should also be trained with service delivery mechanisms whilst the internal control systems need to be investigated periodically to assess whether the operations are being conducted appropriately.

A major challenge which MFIs face in Ghana is that of establishing a proper governance system, a point which has already been alluded to, earlier on, in the chapter. Indeed, sound corporate governance can enhance the quality of a business (Branch and Baker 1998). As Thomsen (2008) indicates, there is adequate evidence in the financial literature that supports the view that good corporate governance enhances the performance of a firm and also reduces risks. In line with this, the BoG, should ensure its background checks on directors are thorough enough in order to prevent unscrupulous persons from holding positions in the microfinance sector. Although it is a requirement that directors submit their personal details as part of the application for licences, more often than not, not much detailed checks are carried out on such personalities hence people with questionable characters sometimes find their way into the microfinance set-up.

Notwithstanding the difficulties that the MFIs are facing, it is quite realistic to state that they are still relevant in the Ghanaian financial landscape. It is, therefore, pertinent that they are nurtured appropriately so that they can play their roles quite effectively. What is needed is an effective regulatory approach to ensure sanity within that sector. The sector also needs appropriate responses to its numerous challenges. Improvements in the quality of human resource in the microfinance sector, for instance, can help with operational improvements.

The BoG has played a key role in promoting the microfinance sector by putting in place the necessary laws, regulations, and guidelines for the licensing, prudential regulation and effective supervision of the sector. But it still faces a difficult task of trying to monitor the rising numbers of MFIs. At the moment, the supervisory capacity of BoG is a huge challenge. Although the BoG has vowed to be more stringent in its regulatory oversight of MFIs (Wampah 2014), it must show clear evidence to that effect in order for the public to be certain of that stance.

For now, there is some evidence of progress in the MFI set-up. The sharply improving fortunes of the MFI sector derive from a combination of three broad factors. One is the enhanced diligence and closer attention of the BoG as the industry's regulator. Another is the microfinance institutions' desire to lend themselves to better corporate governance and more prudent financial management. The third is more caution and circumspection by the general public which has learnt the hard way to be cautious.

14.11 Conclusion

The chapter provided an insight into the financial sector in Ghana. Its focus, however, was on the MFIs and the challenges within the sector. It brought to the fore the enormous challenges the sector faces in terms of its infrastructural inadequacies, its poor governance structure, the lack of qualified personnel to drive the concept forward and the doggedness of the central bank to halt the abuse in the MFI system. Notwithstanding the afore-mentioned issues, the chapter noted that with proper regulatory interventions and commitment of other stakeholders to the core mission of microfinance operations, its challenges can be addressed and its prospects enhanced forthwith.

Further research within the microfinance sector, however, is essential to strengthen its evolution, quantify its impact and provide new frontiers for its development. Therefore, providing innovative approaches and bringing the latest advances and new technologies to practitioners will considerably contribute to the progress of the microfinance sector. In the light of this, it is proposed that scholars strive to provide better understanding of microfinance initiatives by looking into critical areas like the impact of governance mechanisms on MFIs performances and the interplay between board and management, both of which are essential for the successful evolution of the MFIs, in terms of strategy and operation, and how these can be marshalled to bring about the needed changes within the sector. Given the revealing results of financial performance as a determinant of better corporate governance practices, more analyses ought to be made too in determining how corporate governance policies and guidelines can be formulated in a way that does not undermine the financial objectives of MFIs.

References

Ackah, C., & Asiama, J. P. (2014). *Financial regulation in Ghana: Balancing inclusive growth with financial stability*. ODI Working Paper 410, November.

Adams, D. W., & Fitchett, D. A. (1992). *Informal finance in low-income countries*. Boulder: Westview.

Adombila, M. K. (2017). Banks pay 11.9% but charge 33.4%. *Graphic business*, 28 February. Accessed February 28, 2017, from http://www.graphic.com.gh/business/business-news/banks-pay-11-9-but-charge-33-4.html

Amesimeku, E. K. (2014). Ghana: Microfinance calls the shots. *Africa business*. Accessed February 27, 2017, from http://africanbusinessmagazine.com/african-banker/ghana-microfinance-calls-shots/#sthash.oGE1PaV1.dpuf

Antwi-Asare, T. O., & Addison, E. K. Y. (2000). *Financial sector reforms and bank performance in Ghana*. London: Overseas Development Institute.

Appiah, P. (2016). *Ghana Association of Microfinance Companies calls for clear-cut policy to define micro-finance operations in Ghana*, 13 January. Accessed March 7, 2017, from http://www.myjoyonline.com/business/2016/January-12th/gamc-calls-for-clear-cut-policy-to-define-micro-finance-operations-in-ghana.php

Armendariz, B., & Morduch, J. (2000). Microfinance beyond group lending. *Economics of Transition, 8*(2), 401–420.

Aryeetey, E., Baah-Nuakoh, T., Duggleby, T., Hettige, H., & Steel, W. F. (1994). *Supply and demand for finance of small enterprises in Ghana.* World Bank Discussion Paper No. 251.

Asiama, J. P. (2016). *Address at 'Fifteen years of Ghana Banking Awards: Enriching a healthy competitive landscape in the drive for consumer relevance banking,'* 26 August, 2016, Accra.

Asiama, J. P. (2017). Address at the 4th edition of AB and David's Crystal Ball Africa 2017 held under the theme: *Bank of Ghana's Monetary Policy in 2017*, 11 January, Accra.

Bank of Ghana. (2017). *Licensed Microfinance companies in operation as at 31 July 2016.* Accessed April 14, 2017, from BOG website https://www.bog.gov.gh/privatecontent/Banking_Supervision/LICENSED%20MFCs%20IN%20GOOD%20STANDING%2031-07-16.pdf

Basu, A., Blavy, R., & Yulek, M. (2004). *Microfinance in Africa: Experience and lessons from selected African countries.* IMF Working Paper No. 4/174. International Monetary Fund, 1–24.

Belnye, F. (2012). Financial inclusion and regulatory policy: The case of Ghana's informal and semiformal financial institutions. *Fletcher School Leadership Program in Financial Inclusion:* Ghana Policy Memo Innova*t*ions, *6*(4), 17–21.

Branch, B., & Baker, C. (1998). *Overcoming governance problems: What does it take?.* Paper presented at the Inter-American Development Bank (IDB) conference on credit unions, Washington, DC: IDB, March.

Brownbridge, M., & Gockel, A. F. (1996). *The impact of financial sector policies on banking in Ghana.* Institute of Development Studies WP 38.

Business Day. (2015). 18 million Ghanaians don't trust banks. *Ghanaweb*, 1 April. Accessed February 12, 2017, from http://www.ghanaweb.com/GhanaHomePage/business/artikel.php?ID=352668

Collins, D., Morduch, J., Rutherford, S., & Ruthven, O. (2009). *Portfolios of the poor – How the world's poor live on 2$ a day.* Princeton: Princeton University Press.

Conroy, J. D. (2003). *The challenges of micro financing in Southeast Asia.* Singapore: Institute of Southeast Asian Studies.

Diaz-Serrano, Luis; Sackey, Frank Gyimah (2015). *Is rationing in the microfinance sector determined by the microfinance type? Evidence from Ghana.* IZA Discussion Papers, No. 8999.

Field, E., Holland, A., & Pande, R. (2016). *Microcredit: Points of promise.* HKS Faculty Research Working Paper Series. Accessed May 4, 2017, from https://research.hks.harvard.edu/publications/workingpapers/Index.aspx

Ghate, P. (1990). *Informal finance: Some findings from Asia.* Economic and Development Resource Centre, Manila: Asian Development Bank.

Glisovic, J., Mesfin, S., & Moretto, L. (2012). *Microfinance investment in sub-Saharan Africa: Turning opportunities into reality.* CGAP brief. Washington, DC: World Bank. Accessed March 6, 2017, from http://documents.worldbank.org/curated/en/360871468194352693/Microfinance-investment-in-Sub-Saharan-Africa-turning-opportunities-into-reality

Issahaku, A.-N. (2016a). BoG Governor's Address at the inauguration of the Sunyani Regional Office Building of the Bank of Ghana, 30 June, Sunyani.

Issahaku, A.-N. (2016b). BoG Governor's Address delivered at the commissioning of the Services Integrity Savings and Loans Limited Head Office Building, 1 December, Accra.

Kendall, J., Mylenko, N., & Ponce, A. (2010). *Measuring financial access around the world.* World Bank Policy Research Working Paper 5253.

Moyo, J., Boaz, N., Oduor, J., & Simpasa, A. (2014). *Financial sector reforms – Competition and banking system stability in sub-Saharan Africa.* Paper presented at the joint RES-SPR conference on macroeconomic challenges facing low-income countries. Washington, DC, January 30–31. Accessed February 26, 2017, from http://www.imf.org/external/np/seminars/eng/2014/lic/pdf/Moyo.pdf

Munyambonera, E. F. (2013). Determinants of commercial banks' profitability in sub-Saharan Africa. *International Journal of Economics and Finance, 5*(9), 134–147.

Opare, N. D. (2001). Commercial banks must help micro-financing. *Daily Graphic*, October 29, 33.

Otero, M. (1999). *The evolution of non-governmental organisations toward financial intermediation*. West Hartford, CT: Kumarian Press.

PWC. (2016). 2016 Ghana banking survey – How to win in an era of mobile phone.

Quartey, P., & Afful-Mensah, G. (2014). Financial and monetary policies in Ghana: A review of recent trends. *Review of Development Finance, 4*(2), 115–125.

Robinson, S. M. (2001). *The microfinance revolution – Sustainable finance for the poor*. Washington, DC: The World Bank and Open Society Institute.

Roy, A. (2010). *Poverty capital: Microfinance and the making of development*. London: Routledge.

Senbet, L. W., & Otchere, I. (2006). Financial sector reforms in Africa – Perspectives on issues and policies. In F. Bourguignon & B. Pleskovic (Eds.), *Annual world bank conference on development economics – Growth and integration* (pp. 81–119). Washington, DC: The World Bank.

Sowa, N. K. (2003). Financial sector reform policies and poverty reduction. Accra: CEPA. Accessed April 14, 2017, from https://cepa.org.gh/researchpapers/Financial-Sector-Reform-Policies-and-Pove25.pdf

Spencer, S., & Wood, A. (2005). Making the financial sector work for the poor. *Journal of Development Studies, 41*(4), 657–675.

Srinivas, H. (2016). 14 Reasons why the informal credit market is used by the poor: Policy implications for microcredit programmes in developing countries. *GDRC research output*. Accessed May 4, 2017, from https://www.gdrc.org/icm/14reason.html

Thomsen, S. (2008). *An introduction to corporate governance – Mechanisms and systems*. Copenhagen: DJOF Publishing.

Wampah, K. H. A. (2014). BoG Governor's speech at the 14th annual working luncheon of the Ghana Association of Bankers, 16 July, Accra, Ghana.

World Bank. (2000). *World development report 2000/2001*. Washington, DC: World Bank.

Part III
Responsible Investment

Chapter 15
Socially Responsible Investment and Fiduciary Duties of Mutual Funds

Anna Doś and Monika Foltyn-Zarychta

15.1 Mutual Funds Fiduciary Duties in Times of Socially Responsible Investment

The role of the intermediaries in the financial market evolves and becomes increasingly important as the financial institutions' share in the public equity ownership increases. Mutual funds are vehicles that pool money from many investors and invest it in stocks, bonds, short-term money-market instruments or other securities to diversify investors' portfolios in order to limit the stand-alone risk level. A large part of mutual funds is affiliated with banks, which makes a bank a single depositary having general oversight over the assets. In such case, the bank is a single point of reference for both the fund managers and the investors. Thus, the main mutual funds governance challenge is to adopt mechanisms safeguarding investors' interests.

Enhancing the level of investor's protection is justified by a serious agency problem between individual investors and mutual fund companies arising out of delegated portfolio management. Placing managers' own interests ahead of the interests of the principals they represent (for example by excessive risk taking or negligence), as well as abandoning traditional principles of long-term investing are typical examples of agency costs borne by investors. These costs result from the asymmetry of information and limited control over portfolio managers. Such damages are believed to represent a type of a market failure and therefore the relationship between investors (principals) and managers (agents) is regulated by law. The basic rule applied in the case of the relationship between mutual funds and investors is the fiduciary duty, often recognised as one of the pivotal pillars of

A. Doś (✉) • M. Foltyn-Zarychta
University of Economics in Katowice, Katowice, Poland
e-mail: anna.dos@ue.katowice.pl; monika.foltyn-zarychta@uekat.pl

B. Díaz Díaz et al. (eds.), *Corporate Governance in Banking and Investor Protection*, CSR, Sustainability, Ethics & Governance,
https://doi.org/10.1007/978-3-319-70007-6_15

corporate governance within the financial sector (Macey and O'Hara 2003). However, a fiduciary duty is a complex concept and comes under legal, regulatory, economic and ethical debate.

Article 24 of Markets in Financial Instruments Directive (MiFID 2) requires an investment firm to "act honestly, fairly and professionally in accordance with the best interests of its clients". This requirement expresses the general understanding of mutual funds' fiduciary duties. The proper legal definition of the fiduciary duties is provided by Smith (2014), who states that "the fiduciary duty of loyalty is a distinctive legal obligation that adheres only to fiduciary relationships and is designed to regulate the exercise of fiduciary power", which essentially means "no man can serve two masters". However, Smith (2014) notices also that fiduciaries exercise their power or discretion in the face of incomplete contracts and thus beneficiaries in fiduciary relationships are always vulnerable to opportunism. The regulatory bodies being aware of "elusive" character of fiduciary duties focus on safeguarding "honesty, fairness and professionalism" by introducing a number of practical requirements (proxies for the fulfilment of fiduciary duties). These requirements, together with the governance and conduct policies adopted by financial institutions, create a set of mechanisms which actually govern fiduciary relationships. Presently, the governance mechanism enhancing fulfilment of fiduciary duties in the investment includes most often: custody of assets, hiring policies, remuneration schemes, due diligence, disclosure of portfolio information, licensing, certification, recovery funds, fee structures, standards in security selection, monitoring, selection of board members, ethics codes and codes of conduct, etc.

In the investment context, the fiduciary duties are traditionally interpreted as ensuring the highest return with the lowest possible risk for the beneficiaries. Therefore, the mechanisms mentioned above are aimed at securing the fund's financial performance in terms of risk and return. However, there is a new challenge on the horizon, which is—to define how sustainability issues should be embedded in the investment policies of mutual funds, and how this affects the fulfilment of fiduciary duties and the governance mechanisms to secure loyalty and care towards investors who aim to obtain financial returns whilst having goals that add a non-financial dimension.

"Socially responsible investing" (SRI), also described as "social investing," "socially aware investing" or "ethical investing", refers to the integration of environmental, social and corporate governance considerations (ESG) into the investment process. Thus, an SRI investor will avoid investing their savings in stocks of companies whose impacts on the society, environment and applied business practices are recognised as contemptible, and will favour stocks of those companies that positively affect the society and the environment (e.g. by providing education) and are properly governed. It is therefore believed that SRI can contribute to the sustainable development (Berry and Junkus 2013).

The origins of the socially responsible investing date back to the eighteenth century when Quakers who settled in North America refused to invest in weapons and slavery. The modern roots of SRI can be traced back to the social and environmental movements of the 1960s and 1970s. Since the financial collapse caused by the subprime turmoil, SRI has been seen as an investment style which helps to reduce negative social externalities and unethical business practices. Presently, the aims of socially responsible investors generally fall under one or more of the three categories: investing in keeping with certain values (the root cause for SRI), investing to balance risk and opportunities arising from non-financial aspects (fostered by financial distress faced by companies violating social norms) and investing to make a positive impact on the society, environment and business practices (the newest one). The strategies supporting SRI have evolved noticeably and at this moment there are several approaches to allocate capital for social and environmental benefits across the economy (including for example best-in-class investment, exclusion or ESG integration). For the past decade SRI has been growing constantly across all styles and almost all continents. In US at the end of 2015 $8.73 trillion of total assets under management was invested using one or more sustainable, responsible or impact investing strategies (US SIF 2015). In Europe, total assets committed to sustainable and responsible investment strategies reached $12.04 trillion in 2015. In Asia $52.1 billion in assets were identified as socially responsible investment (GSIA 2016). SRI has turned from a niche phenomenon into a financial market feature.

As a natural consequence, SRI-related background activities increased as well. Branch associations for the promotion and advancement of SRI (US SIF, EuroSIF), think-tanks, market indices (Dow Jones Sustainability, FTSE4Good), consultation papers, press releases, research, rating agencies for corporate social performance, workshops, conferences, and increasingly favourable legal frameworks all contribute to the growing importance of SRI. Companies massively issue integrated reports communicating financial, environmental and social performance to satisfy investors' growing information needs. Such trend modifies the financial landscape and makes traditional rules of the game outdated. However, the main force that drives the rise of SRI market is the will of an individual investor: their preferences, where ethical concerns become more and more pronounced (Nofsinger and Varma 2014).

SRI is an approach to investing that can be adopted both by individuals and institutions. Numerous banks worldwide offer socially responsible pooled investment products (mutual funds). In order to be reliable, all SRI products providers should establish a policy to fulfil their fiduciary duties as to the SRI product management. However, a question can be raised: how to understand fiduciary duties in times of socially responsible investment?

Institutional investors respond to the sustainability challenge in delegated portfolio management by cutting the challenge to the old ways of thinking that is in terms of risk and return. Namely, they found out that sustainability issues correlate to some extend with fund's financial performance. First, it was noticed that many institutions have become "universal owners" who own a small but representative fraction of most of the companies in the economy (Hawley and Williams 2002). In that case, the ability to satisfy traditionally understood fiduciary duties depends heavily on overall macroeconomic performance because portfolios are inevitably exposed to external costs from environmental and social damage (Mattison et al. 2010). The second observation was that risks and costs associated with unsustainable corporate policies may adversely affect corporate stock market value. Therefore, investing in financial instruments issued by responsible companies is believed to outperform conventional investment in the long-term perspective. Number of studies confirm that socially responsible investment funds perform better than conventional ones (e.g. Lean and Nguyen 2014; Lean et al. 2015; Nofsinger and Varma 2014; Friede et al. 2015).

The old way of thinking about fiduciary standards constrained the value-driven SRI (Troyer et al. 1985). Three powerful arguments rationalise limiting the understanding of the duty of care and loyalty to safeguarding retail investors' incomes. The first argument is that investors' ethical profile and values are substantially heterogenic (Sandberg et al. 2009). What is desirable from one retail investor's point of view is unethical from another retail investor's perspective (a good example is: a catholic investor for whom abortion is a murder, and a pro-choice investor who puts value on a freedom to choose). It is therefore very difficult to adopt a mutual fund's investment policy to satisfy shareholders' heterogenic preferences. However, certain attempt to overcome this problem can be done by applying well-established social conventions to serve as proxies for the will of the beneficiaries (Sandberg 2011). The second is that the social screening of stocks for ownership is a political act (Pan and Mardfin 2001). Therefore, the fear is that trustees might use the assets of mutual funds to promote self-interested ethical beliefs, personal, political or sustainability agendas or that they might fall under the influence of politicians or lobbyists (Lydenberg 2014). The third argument is that SRI requires investment managers to overlay a qualitative analysis of corporate policies, practices and impacts onto the traditional quantitative analysis of profit potential. This mixture of quantitative and qualitative goals results in a complex multi-criteria decision setting, where well tested models do not apply any more. Thus fiduciary duties may become an extremely "blurred" idea. For reasons shortly described above, many experts claim that fiduciaries should focus solely on the financial criteria while managing delegated funds.

However, an ongoing debate about SRI revealed that conceptually, a "benefit" to beneficiaries need not be limited to financial values (Richardson 2009). The first argument is that unsustainable investment decisions of mutual funds may create externalities which harm beneficiaries (e.g. air pollution). Fund managers' duty is to preserve or enhance their beneficiaries' assets and income in the context of the financial, economic, social, and environmental systems within which their beneficiaries live (Lydenberg 2014). The second argument is provided by Eccles (2012), who argues for redefining utility from the risk-return optimization aim to the "responsible behaviour" goal. He sees the challenge in formulating a new fiduciary duty paradigm that would—apart from financial gains—"restore the ethical capacity" of investing pursuit. In case the utility function of an individual is multi-attribute, it is prudent for fiduciaries to take into consideration the environmental, social and governance (ESG) issues (Lydenberg 2014). The rationale behind the multi-attribute investment utility function is provided below.

15.2 Individual Investor's Utility Function in the Context of SRI

The predominant model of investment decision making is based on the neoclassical Markowitz theory, a widespread paradigm for evaluating portfolio performance. It is based only on two characteristics: return and risk, sometimes described as the expected returns–variance of returns (E–V) rule. The model assumes that self-centred, rational investors maximize their utility by optimizing return to risk relation and by diversifying their portfolio (cf. Nilsson 2008). The investor's utility function concentrating solely on the financial performance is depicted by the formula (Markowitz 1952):

$U = f(E, V)$

where:

U—investor's utility,

E—expected return on investment,

V—investment risk, variance of returns (average squared deviation of return from its expected value).

The approach, concentrating on self-centred return-risk maximization, forms a baseline paradigm not only for individual investor's decision making but also for institutions managing the funds on behalf of the individuals.

The attempts to include non-financial performance into Markowitz theory have not developed yet into a single theoretical framework that would link social responsibility of an investment to an investment's returns depicting the optimal trade-off between social and financial performance (Berry and Junkus 2013). However, simple two-attribute utility function seems to be insufficient to explain the decisions made by SRI investors (Richardson 2009). The rationale to extend the basic model is that the investor is not a narrow-minded "rational man" but a "reasonable person" able to include the full range of motives, inducing fairness or environmental quality (Krosinsky et al. 2012).

The theoretical framework is supported by strong empirical evidence on differences between the conventional and the socially responsible investors. It has been revealed that some investors are willing to give up certain amount of their financial performance to achieve better results in social responsibility area. Borgers and Pownall (2014) confirm that pension funds beneficiaries are willing to give up some of the financial profits to change their portfolios into more socially responsible ones. Barreda-Tarrazona et al. (2011) show that some groups of investors invest mainly in SRI even though the financial performance is unsatisfactory. Apostolakis et al. (2016) investigating pension beneficiaries in Europe assume that they are consumers of investments with certain social and financial features, concluding that ¾ of them are willing to pay more for environmentally friendly products and thus suggesting a trade-off between the financial returns and the social effects.

Investors also differ in their decisions when they compare SRI and conventional investment. Saraiva and Tan (2013) find that when participants face two risky investments where only one has socially responsible attributes, the level of consistency in their decisions decreases. However, when they choose between two socially responsible investments, they make more consistent choices. Glac (2009) finds that although the majority of SR investors are interested in financial performance, they have higher acceptance for return differentials for the screened investments than for the conventional ones. This suggests deriving utility from the investment's characteristics other than the financial ones.

Non-financial factors that shape investors' decisions are not a recent phenomenon. Such motives (avarice and ambition) are mentioned in Smiths' work: "The Theory of Moral Sentiments" (1759). Keynes (1936) mentioned avarice and pride as drivers of investors' behaviour. The discussion may be also backed up with the attempts to extend narrow utilitarianistic view to include moral principles (Sen 1979; Sen and Williams 1982; Hausman and McPherson 2009). Hahn (1982) indicates that while the utility in its classical form is perceived as a pleasure of self-regarding activities, it can be enhanced to the concept of deriving pleasure from other-regarding activities. He also argues to include factors that would not be of consequentialist nature into the utility function. The extensions of the utility function are developed by several other researchers, i.e. Becker (1996) or Altman (2005).

Referring to investors' decision making, multi-attribute functions are usually extended from two (risk-return) to three dimensions, where the third one describes some general non-financial factor: personal values, degree of social responsibility (i.e. measured by ESG ratings) or share of SRI in the portfolio (cf. Saraiva and Tan 2013; Barreda-Tarrazona et al. 2011; Utz et al. 2014; Beal et al. 2005; Apostolakis et al. 2016). However, we advocate to split the third factor into three elements.

The first element is formed by investors' values. Values are commonly identified as "beliefs that a specific mode of conduct or end-state of existence is personally and socially preferable to alternative modes of conduct or end-states of existence" (Rokeach 1973). It is recognized that values serve as a moral compass that directs motivation and potential decisions (Schwartz 1992). The very first SRI practices were clearly value-driven (SRI origins date back to 1758 when Quakers decided not to participate in the slave trade).

The values refer to deontological perspective, where the utility is derived from the way the consequences are achieved. Hahn (1982) argues on this question pointing out that: "Not only the consequences matter (consumption), but also the way they are achieved". Values most commonly related to SRI are environmentalism (Vyvyan et al. 2007), religiosity (Gambling and Karim 1991; Lodi-Smith and Roberts 2007; Jaufeerally 2012; Peifer 2014) and ethicality or moral concerns (Anand and Cowton 1993; Clark-Murphy and Soutar 2004; Revelli 2016; Park 2005). The approach may be depicted i.e. by SRI investing strategies based on exclusions of gambling or pornography (EuroSIF 2016). Values are included in some examples of investors' utility function extensions: Beal et al. (2005) construct the investor's utility function with return and its deviations accompanied by the third factor: the degree of ethicalness of an investment. Apostolakis et al. (2016) propose a four-variable model with two value-related explanatory variables: concerns and attitudes.

Non-financial performance can be related to the impact that is created by SRI. A proxy of this impact can be given in extended utility functions by referring to ESG scores (cf. Barreda-Tarrazona et al. 2011; Utz et al. 2014). However, we argue that those impacts should be split into self-regarding and other-regarding outcomes, since they are driven by different motives.

Self-regarding SRI impacts are related to the influence SRI have on the whole economy, and—consequently—on beneficiaries' welfare. Lydenberg (2014) stresses that portfolio is not a "safe-box" unlinked to external conditions. European Commision (2014) also argues that: "environmental and resource efficiency issues can be financially material to either investment returns or risks" directly (resource-efficient production gives the companies competitive advantage) and indirectly (environmental or social degradation adversely affects the economic growth).

Finally, other-regarding preferences are related to investors' altruism. Altruistic acts are defined as"costly acts that confer economic benefits on other individuals" (Fehr and Fischbacher 2003). Altruistic preferences toward other people are backed by vast philosophical and ethical literature. They are analysed as an issue of allocating agents' resources between their own current and delayed consumption and the consumption by other people (cf. Simon 1995; Parfit 1984; Becker and Barro 1986). In case of SRI, altruistic acts are "costly" due to the fact that investors are willing to give up some of their return (Pasewark and Riley 2010), and "other-regarding" due to impacts created by companies included in SRI portfolio. The companies that fulfil environmental, social and corporate governance standards can improve i.e. environmental quality or the position of women in the job market (cf. Jansson and Biel 2014; Bauer and Smeets 2015; McLachlan and Gardner 2004) and by this way they create additional utility for investors (cf. Saraiva and Tan 2013).

To sum up, while classical Markowitz's investor utility function would be self-regarding return-risk maximization, the modern paradigm that could be derived from contemporary literature suggests that it is justified to include several additional factors: value-based deontological variable, and the investment impact levels on the investor's own welfare as well as the welfare of others.

$$U = f(E, V, D, IA, IE)$$

where:

D—values (deontological parameter), not related to the outcome of the investment, but the way of achieving it (i.e. the level of portfolio ethicality),

IA—impact altruism—positive impacts or avoided negative impacts of SRI on others via markets or outside markets (externalities),

IE—impact egoism—self-regarding positive impacts or avoided negative impacts of SRI on an investor via markets or outside markets (externalities).

Nevertheless, it must be noted, that an act of doing something good (altruistic preferences) is sometimes blurred with "warm glow" effect, defined as personal satisfaction from the very act of giving (Andreoni 1989, 1990; Chilton and Hutchinson 2000). This requires additional research and is not described in the chapter.

Additionally, disturbed preferences, bounded rationality, inconsistent decisions coupled with heuristics must also be perceived as limitations of extending the basic E–V return rule. For example Nofsinger and Varma (2014) claim that holding SRI may be related to the Prospect Theory due to the fact that SRI funds perform better in times of financial turmoil, and investors value their utility on losses more heavily than on gains. However, while those issues are well described (cf. Tversky and Kahneman 1975; Gowdy 2004; Assenza et al. 2014; Apostolakis et al. 2016), it must be noted that such problems apply in similar extent to trustees' "business-as-usual" (non-SRI funds) and therefore are not important when discussing the extension of fiduciary duties' relationship.

Ethical, environmental and social values together with investment impact are all important motives for socially responsible investment and could level the willingness to sacrifice financial return for pursuing non-financial goals. Therefore, they should be recognized as determinants of how to understand investors' interests that must be served by fund managers. From the legal point of view there are no obstacles to adopt a wider definition of fiduciary duties (Sanders 2014). Then, the issue of inclusion of investors' moral interests into fiduciary standards depends on whether the governance mechanisms, which support prudent fund management, will be appropriately selected and implemented. Establishing an appropriate policy in the area is an extremely compelling issue for the modern banks offering socially responsible pooled investment products. The next part of the chapter identifies the best practices in managing socially responsible investment for satisfying investors' financial and non-financial goals adopted presently in different banks across the globe.

15.3 Best Practices for Prudent Management of Value-Driven SRI

Since there is some utility that investors put at funds' non-financial performance, this value should be managed prudently. This is not an easy task. Barber (2007) points out: "Once considerations other than wealth maximization are relevant for investors, aligning the interests of portfolio managers and investors becomes extremely difficult". The de Larosière Report states that the corporate governance systems within financial institutions provided weak incentives for consideration of long-term sustainable investment policies (de Larosière et al. 2009). The improvement is thus necessary. It can be achieved twofold: firstly, by the wider adoption of good practices that are already developed within the industry, and secondly—by detecting which areas are neglected and require improvement.

To recognise good practices in prudent management of socially responsible mutual funds, the authors conducted a robust desk research of web-sites, statutes, reports, prospectus and other documents issued by mutual funds, institutional investors' advisors and consultants as well as consortia and associations for promoting sustainability in capital markets. The research focused not only at bank-affiliated mutual funds but on all possible types of mutual funds. That is because mutual funds that are not affiliated with banks provide a wide set of good practices which can be adopted in the banking sector.

The distinction between what is “a good practice” and what is not was made upon two considerable assumptions. The first assumption is that the good practices respect a retail investor’s ability to make an informed decision on how to locate their money in line with their preferences (regarding both: financial and non-financial outcomes). Therefore, for example the best-in-class strategy for SRI, which comes under a serious criticism from ethical point of view (best-in-class fast food companies would be included in the portfolio, no matter they spur obesity) is acknowledged as a good practice as far as the investor is informed about the strategy type and is aware of the idea of the strategy. It may be his goal to invest in such company to start changes in this type of a sin industry. Additionally, building appropriate comprehension of social and environmental goals and investment strategies is necessary to avoid cases of mis-selling. The assumption entails recognizing all practices reducing the asymmetry of information with respect to sustainability issues as good practices. The second assumption is that since retail investors are interested in being socially responsible, it is prudent for the fiduciary to exploit its capacity to support sustainability by efficient cooperation with companies, whose stock are held by the fund, as well as by pushing SRI agenda forward within the financial industry. In this way, the costs of reorientation towards sustainability are lowered and the financial performance of socially responsible investment may increase. Therefore, practices enhancing strategic perspective on sustainability as well as practices fostering cooperation with companies oriented at improving their environmental and social footprint are recognized as good practices here. The list of good practices identified under the study together with examples of successful adoption of the practices is provided in Table 15.1.

It was noticed that socially responsible mutual funds had already developed several practices helping retail investors to achieve financial goals whilst caring for social and environmental outcomes. First of all, the good practices listed in Table 15.1 enhance communication between the retail investors and mutual funds and the mutual funds and companies. Smooth and intense communication fosters informed decisions, lowers the costs of conflicts and may contribute to the alignment of goals of all parties involves (investors, mutual funds, companies), including the non-financial goals. Provided the communication is well-managed, the concord between an investor’s goals and a mutual fund investment policy is safeguarded. Moreover, the companies may adjust their operations towards capital market expectations. In this way the investors’ social and environmental goals can be achieved more easily and cheaply. Secondly, the practices listed in Table 15.1 comprise of learning on sustainability and promoting sustainability within the financial institution and the financial sector. Learning and promoting sustainability is driven by the strategic approach of financial institutions towards sustainability. It may improve the resilience of SRI market, which is crucial for providing investors with products which fit investors’ complex preferences.

Table 15.1 Good practices in managing sustainability issues by socially responsible mutual funds

Area	Practice	Examples
Managing relations with clients	Promoting responsible investment strategies among clients	– Nordea Bank, – Triodos Bank
	Informing in a detailed manner about SRI strategy in fund's prospectus, avoiding using poorly defined terms or phrases like "give consideration to" without guidance on what appropriate consideration looks like	– Oppenheimer ESG – Revenue ETF – Calvert Socially Responsible Funds – BNP Paribas Investment Partners – Desjardins Group
	Advising clients on identifying financial and non-financial goals and selecting SRI strategy which fits clients' preferences	– BlackRock Investment
	Allowing clients to ask for more information about incorporating ESG strategy	– BNO Paribas Investment Partners
	Reporting on ESG impacts of financial significance (risk profile)	– Calvert Investments on Calvert VP SRI Mid Cap Portfolio
	Informing about strategy and governance (SG) of an organisation—revealing organisation's overall approach to responsible investment (i.e. governance, responsible investment policy, objectives and targets, resources allocated to responsible investment and approach to collaboration on responsible investment and public policy-related issues) and the incorporation of ESG issues into asset allocation	– Citi Group – Desjardins Group
	Providing investment structuring and advisory services to clients	– J.P. Morgan Asset Management
	Informing clients about exploiting advisory and/or consultancy when it comes to ESG criterions in portfolio management	– Danske Bank – IA Clarington
	Informing about adoption of stewardship codes for SRI and compliance with the adopted codes	– Kiltearn Partners LLP
	Providing publicly disclosed and easily available (on-line) information about proxy voting policies	– American Century Sustainable Equity – Pax Global Environmental Markets Fund – Trillum Asset Management
	Providing easily available (on-line) record on how the fund voted their share on sustainability issues	– Aspiration Reedwood Fund

(continued)

Table 15.1 (continued)

Area	Practice	Examples
SRI strategy	Collaborating with advisors who proactively raise ESG issues within the advice that they provide (like for example ISS-Ethix, Mercer Investment Consulting)	– Danske Bank
	Aligning monitoring procedures, performance indicators and incentive structures with financial and non-financial objectives of SRI fund	– Triodos Bank
	Aiming at long-term persistence in the ESG-scores or other SRI strategy	– Parnassus Investment
	Not outsourcing proxy voting	– Kiltearn Partners LLP
Managing relationships with companies	Increasing dialogue between companies and investors. Direct talks with management on issues of ethical concern before going the resolution route are recommended. The preferable outcome is a negotiated settlement to avoid unnecessary costs	– Walden Asset Management – Servus Credit Union – The Ethical Funds Company Canada – Trillium Asset Management
	Exerting pressure on companies through shareholder resolutions if necessary	– Christian Brothers Investment Services
Strategic perspective on sustainability	The culture that sees the SRI as issue of substance which needs to be measured and appraised rather than neglected and treated with a 'tick box'	– Deutsche Bank – Amundi Asset Management
	Commitment to research, education, programs and strategic partnerships for increasing individual investors knowledge on SRI	– Trillium Asset Management – Morgan Stanley Investment
	Anticipating the most efficient ways of integrating ESG criteria in the investment range and keeping abreast of changing trends in SRI/ESG processes that best combine financial and extra-financial performance	– Edmond de Rothschild Asset Management
	Leadership in pushing SRI agenda forward within the industry	– TIAA-CREF Social Choice Equity

Source: Own elaboration

However, the practices listed in Table 15.1 are not all widely adopted among SRI mutual funds, including the bank-affiliated ones. The description of mutual funds SRI strategy is often slapdash. Quite frequently, SRI mutual funds inform perfunctorily about how their strategy may influence financial performance. They rarely use professional advisors with noticeable experience, knowledge and focus on sustainability, and they tend to rely on an over-simplified exclusion which instead omits value-driven investors' preferences. They tend to outsource proxy voting or they do not provide information on proxy voting. Given the ownership structure of mutual funds can change, the SRI strategy persistence is endangered. Some of them adopt stewardship codes, however, they do not inform about the compliance and since the violation of rules is not penalized this turns into window-dressing. Imprudent management of investors' non-financial goals may result in a noticeable disappointment of investors turning even into the withdrawal of funds from the capital market.

Additionally, some new solutions could improve fulfilling fiduciary duties. A few useful propositions are made in joint consultation paper launched by the European Supervisory Authorities (ESA 2017). They include:

- necessity to demonstrate to retail investors the relevance of ESG criteria for the whole value chain of investment, so that to avoid ESG criteria having little significance compared to how investment is made;
- specifying in detail the scope of the environmental or social objectives as well as the constraints the retail investor will have to accept to meet these objectives (for example, in terms of risk/return, time horizon, liquidity);
- educating retail investors on possible SR investment goals and approaches and providing information which would enable retail investors to place a product in the context of a universe made up of several major generic approaches;
- adopting high level of due diligence in developing and implementing investment strategy.

It is recommended to consider also the five propositions made by authors:

- to recognize the importance of the investors' preferences in terms of financial, social and environmental goals and to use this information for structuring products and for advising clients. Multi-criteria decision methods acknowledged for their soundness can be exploited for recognizing the importance;
- to inform the investors what the asset structure of SRI fund is (equities, fixed income, alternatives) and how holding different types of assets shapes the mutual fund's capability to influence company's behaviour and the socio-economic system as a whole;
- to inform investors about which type of SRI strategy (ESG incorporation, active ownership, impact investing) it provides with the most noticeable social and economic results and then to position fund's strategy against the ranking;
- to provide incentives for the fund's managers to improve its social and environmental performance. It has been proved, that bank managers are usually over-incentivised when it comes to reaching financial goals, and under-incentivised when it comes to reaching qualitative goal (e.g. customers' satisfaction) (Bénabou and Tirole 2016). For this reason, some SRI funds may only appear to be socially responsible;
- to respect the heterogeneity of investors' preferences by providing diversified products. Presently well-established social conventions serve as proxies for the will of the beneficiaries. However social norms are country- and culture-specific. It is possible to recognize it and tailor investment policy to the more realistic investors' profile.

There is a need of a policy fostering the adoption of already tested good practices and new solutions that may accelerate mutual funds commitment to care for the retail investor's non-financial goals. There are important examples of a sound and successful strategic approach towards sustainability of capital market investment, which may contribute to the diffusion of good practices. The diffusion may be also reinforced by some regulation. Policy recommendations may be derived from the recognition of already well-tested solutions and propositions of their advancements made above.

15.4 Conclusion

Socially responsible investment is gaining unprecedented attention in the financial markets. The phenomenon comprises of a complex set of goals of investment: financial performance accompanied by non-financial targets related to sustainability (natural environment protection, social equality and fair business practices). Some of SRI funds are invested directly by individual investors. However, the majority of funds are managed by financial institutions, where fiduciary duty issue emerges. The clash of the traditional aim of maximizing financial performance with as little risk as possible involved is then challenged by the non-financial beneficiaries' goals. The chapter argues that such extension of fiduciary duties towards caring for value-driven investors' non-financial goals is justified and feasible.

Theoretical research supported by some empirical studies shows that the extension of the basic risk-return Markowitz model is possible. We argue for extending the basic Markowitz model by three non-financial variables: depicting investor's deontological values, self-regarding indirect SRI impacts and other-regarding non-financial effects. Therefore, SRI mutual funds, which manage delegated money, should prudently care not only for investors' financial interest but also for their social and environmental interests. This constitutes a new dimension of mutual funds fiduciary duty. We then advocate that the feasibility of extending the traditional way of thinking about fiduciary duties depends on applying practices enhancing communication related to ESG issues and a strategic approach of mutual funds towards sustainability. Communication is the cornerstone of managing mutual funds for reaching financial and non-financial targets. It allows the alignment of goals between investors, mutual funds and companies. Learning and promotion of sustainability improves SRI market resilience.

Among the SRI mutual funds there are pioneers who have established and adopted a number of good practices, which enhance prudent management of relations with value-driven clients, responsible investment strategies as well as relationships with companies. However, the diffusion of recognised good practices is limited. It requires not only the industry self-regulation but regulations designed and implemented by the governments.

References

Altman, M. (2005). The ethical economy and competitive markets: Reconciling altruistic, moralistic, and ethical behavior with the rational economic agent and competitive markets. *Journal of Economic Psychology, 26*(5), 732–757.

Anand, P., & Cowton, C. J. (1993). The ethical investor: Exploring dimensions of investment behaviour. *Journal of Economic Psychology, 14*(2), 377–385.

Andreoni, J. (1989). Giving with impure altruism: Applications to charity and Ricardian equivalence. *Journal of Political Economy, 97*(6), 1447–1458.

Andreoni, J. (1990). Impure altruism and donations to public goods: A theory of warm-glow giving. *The Economic Journal, 100*(401), 464–477.

Apostolakis, G., Kraanen, F., & van Dijk, G. (2016). Examining pension beneficiaries' willingness to pay for a socially responsible and impact investment portfolio: A case study in the Dutch healthcare sector. *Journal of Behavioral and Experimental Finance, 11*, 27–43.

Assenza, T., Bao, T., Hommes, C., & Massaro, D. (2014). Experiments on expectations in macroeconomics and finance. In *Experiments in macroeconomics* (pp. 11–70). Bingley: Emerald Group Publishing.

Barber, B. M. (2007). Monitoring the monitor: Evaluating CalPERS' activism. *The Journal of Investing, 16*(4), 66–80.

Barreda-Tarrazona, I., Matallín-Sáez, J. C., & Balaguer-Franch, M. R. (2011). Measuring investors' socially responsible preferences in mutual funds. *Journal of Business Ethics, 103*(2), 305–330.

Bauer, R., & Smeets, P. (2015). Social identification and investment decisions. *Journal of Economic Behavior & Organization, 117*, 121–134.

Beal, D. J., Goyen, M., & Philips, P. (2005). Why do we invest ethically? *The Journal of Investing, 14*(3), 66–78.

Becker, G. S. (1996). *Accounting for tastes* (p. 157). Cambridge: Harvard University Press.

Becker, G. S., & Barro, R. J. (1986). Altruism and the economic theory of fertility. *Population and Development Review, 12*, 69–76.

Bénabou, R., & Tirole, J. (2016). Bonus culture: Competitive pay, screening, and multitasking. *Journal of Political Economy, 124*(2), 305–370.

Berry, T. C., & Junkus, J. C. (2013). Socially responsible investing: An investor perspective. *Journal of Business Ethics, 112*(4), 707–720.

Borgers, A. C., & Pownall, R. A. (2014). Attitudes towards socially and environmentally responsible investment. *Journal of Behavioral and Experimental Finance, 1*, 27–44.

Chilton, S. M., & Hutchinson, W. G. (2000). A note on the warm glow of giving and scope sensitivity in contingent valuation studies. *Journal of Economic Psychology, 21*(4), 343–349.

Clark-Murphy, M., & Soutar, G. N. (2004). What individual investors value: Some Australian evidence. *Journal of Economic Psychology, 25*(4), 539–555.

De Larosière, J., Balcerowicz, L., Issing, O., Masera, R., McCarthy, C., Nyberg, L. et al. (2009). Report of the high-level group on financial supervision in the EU. European Commission, Brussels.

EC. (2014). Resource efficiency and fiduciary duties of investors. European Commission, Brussels.

Eccles, N. (2012). New values in responsible investment. In *Responsible investment in times of turmoil* (pp. 19–34). Dordrecht: Springer. https://doi.org/10.1007/978-90-481-9319-6_2.

ESA. (2017). *Joint consultation paper on PRIIPS with environmental or social objectives, European Supervisory Authorities (ESAs: EBA, EIOPA and ESMA)*. Accessed June 19, 2017, from https://esas-joint-committee.europa.eu/Publications/Consultations/JC_2017_05_CP_EOS_PRIIPs_final.pdf

EuroSIF. (2016). *European SRI study*, http://www.eurosif.org/wp-content/uploads/2016/11/SRI-study-2016-HR.pdf

Fehr, E., & Fischbacher, U. (2003). The nature of human altruism. *Nature, 425*(6960), 785–791.

Friede, G., Busch, T., & Bassen, A. (2015). ESG and financial performance: aggregated evidence from more than 2000 empirical studies. *Journal of Sustainable Finance & Investment, 5*(4), 210–233.*e, 48*, 180–193.
Gambling, T., & Karim, R. (1991). *Business and accounting ethics in Islam*. London: Mansell.
Glac, K. (2009). Understanding socially responsible investing: The effect of decision frames and trade-off options. *Journal of Business Ethics, 87*, 41–55.
Gowdy, J. M. (2004). Altruism, evolution, and welfare economics. *Journal of Economic Behavior & Organization, 53*(1), 69–73.
Hahn, F. (1982). On some difficulties of the utilitarian economist. In A. Sen & B. Williams (Eds.), *Utilitarianism and beyond* (pp. 187–198). Cambridge: Cambridge University Press. https://doi.org/10.1017/CBO9780511611964.
Hausman, D. M., & McPherson, M. S. (2009). *Economic analysis, moral philosophy, and public policy*. Cambridge: Cambridge University Press. https://doi.org/10.1017/CBO9780511754289.
Hawley, J. P., & Williams, A. T. (2002). The universal owner's role in sustainable economic development. *Corporate Environmental Strategy, 9*(3), 284–291.
Jansson, M., & Biel, A. (2014). Investment institutions' beliefs about and attitudes toward socially responsible investment (SRI): A comparison between SRI and non-SRI management. *Sustainable Development, 22*(1), 33–41.
Jaufeerally, R. Z. (2012). Islamic banking and responsible investment: Is a fusion possible? In *Responsible investment in times of turmoil* (pp. 151–163). Dordrecht: Springer.
Keynes, J. M. (1936). *The general theory of employment, interest and money*. London: Macmillan.
Krosinsky, C., Robins, N., & Viederman, S. (2012). After the credit crisis – The future of sustainable investing. In *The Next Generation of Responsible Investing* (pp. 9–25). Dordrecht: Springer.
Lean, H. H., & Nguyen, D. K. (2014). Policy uncertainty and performance characteristics of sustainable investments across regions around the global financial crisis. *Applied Financial Economics, 24*(21), 1367–1373.
Lean, H. H., Ang, W. R., & Smyth, R. (2015). Performance and performance persistence of socially responsible investment funds in Europe and North America. *The North American Journal of Economics and Finance, 34*, 254–266.
Lodi-Smith, J., & Roberts, B. W. (2007). Social investment and personality: A meta-analysis of the relationship of personality traits to investment in work, family, religion, and volunteerism. *Personality and Social Psychology Review, 11*(1), 68–86.
Lydenberg, S. (2014). Ethics, politics, sustainability and the 21st century trustee. In *Socially responsible investment in the 21st century: Does it make a difference for society?* (pp. 197–213). Bingley: Emerald Group Publishing.
Macey, J. R., & O'Hara, M. (2003). The corporate governance of banks. *Economic Policy Review, 9*(1). Available from SSRN: https://ssrn.com/abstract=795548
Markowitz, H. (1952). Portfolio selection. *The Journal of Finance, 7*(1), 77–91.
Mattison, R., Trevitt, M., & van Ast, L. (2010). Universal ownership: Why environmental externalities matter to institutional investors. *UNEP Finance Initiative/PRI Association*.
McLachlan, J., & Gardner, J. (2004). A comparison of socially responsible and conventional investors. *Journal of Business Ethics, 52*(1), 11–25.
Nilsson, J. (2008). Investment with a conscience: Examining the impact of pro-social attitudes and perceived financial performance on socially responsible investment behavior. *Journal of Business Ethics, 83*(2), 307–325.
Nofsinger, J., & Varma, A. (2014). Socially responsible funds and market crises. *Journal of Banking & Finance, 48*, 180–193.
Pan, P. G., & Mardfin, J. K. (2001). *Socially responsible investing*. Legislative Reference Bureau.
Parfit, D. (1984). *Reasons and persons*. Oxford: Oxford University Press.
Park, H. (2005). The role of idealism and relativism as dispositional characteristics in the socially responsible decision-making process. *Journal of Business Ethics, 56*(1), 81–98.

Pasewark, W. R., & Riley, M. E. (2010). It'sa matter of principle: The role of personal values in investment decisions. *Journal of Business Ethics, 93*(2), 237–253.
Peifer, J. L. (2014). Fund loyalty among socially responsible investors: The importance of the economic and ethical domains. *Journal of Business Ethics, 121*(4), 635–649.
Revelli, C. (2016). Re-embedding financial stakes within ethical and social values in socially responsible investing (SRI). *Research in International Business and Finance, 38*, 1–5.
Richardson, B. J. (2009). Keeping ethical investment ethical: Regulatory issues for investing for sustainability. *Journal of Business Ethics, 87*(4), 555–572.
Rokeach, M. (1973). *The nature of human values* (Vol. 438). New York: Free Press.
Sandberg, J. (2011). Socially responsible investment and fiduciary duty: Putting the freshfields report into perspective. *Journal of Business Ethics, 101*(1), 143–162.
Sandberg, J., Juravle, C., Hedesström, T. M., & Hamilton, I. (2009). The heterogeneity of socially responsible investment. *Journal of Business Ethics, 87*(4), 519–533.
Sanders, W. (2014). Resolving the conflict between fiduciary duties and socially responsible investing. *Pace Law Review, 35*, 535.
Saraiva, P. P., & Tan, J. H. (2013). *Individual preferences for (socially responsible) investments under risk.* http://www.webmeets.com/files/papers/res/2014-phd/223/Job%20Market%20Paper%20Paulo%20Peneda%20Saraiva.pdf
Schwartz, S. H. (1992). Universals in the content and structure of values: Theory and empirical tests in 20 countries. In M. Zanna (Ed.), *Advances in experimental social psychology* (Vol. 25, pp. 1–65). New York: Academic Press.
Sen, A. (1979). Utilitarianism and Welfarism. *The Journal of Philosophy, 76*(9), 463–489. http://www.jstor.org/stable/2025934
Sen, A., & Williams, B. (Eds.). (1982). *Utilitarianism and beyond* (pp. 1–21). Cambridge: Cambridge University Press. https://doi.org/10.1017/CBO9780511611964.
Simon, J. L. (1995). Interpersonal allocation continuous with intertemporal allocation binding commitments, pledges, and bequests. *Rationality and Society, 7*(4), 367–392.
Smith, A. (1759). *The theory of moral sentiments.* London: A. Millar.
Smith, D. G. (2014). Contractually adopted fiduciary duty. *University of Illinois Law Review* 1783. Available from SSRN https://ssrn.com/abstract=2571646
Troyer, T. A., Slocombe, W. B., & Boisture, R. A. (1985). Divestment of South Africa investments: The legal implications for foundations, other charitable institutions, and pension funds. *Georgetown Law Journal, 74*, 127.
Tversky, A., & Kahneman, D. (1975). Judgment under uncertainty: Heuristics and biases. In *Utility, probability, and human decision making* (pp. 141–162). Heidelberg: Springer.
US SIF. (2015). Report on sustainable and responsible investing trends in the United States. Washington, DC.
Utz, S., Wimmer, M., Hirschberger, M., & Steuer, R. E. (2014). Tri-criterion inverse portfolio optimization with application to socially responsible mutual funds. *European Journal of Operational Research, 234*(2), 491–498.
Vyvyan, V., Ng, C., & Brimble, M. (2007). Socially responsible investing: The green attitudes and grey choices of Australian investors. *Corporate Governance: An International Review, 15*(2), 370–381.

Index

B. Díaz Díaz et al. (eds.), *Corporate Governance in Banking and Investor Protection*, CSR, Sustainability, Ethics & Governance,
https://doi.org/10.1007/978-3-319-70007-6

MIX
Papier aus verantwortungsvollen Quellen
Paper from responsible sources
FSC® C105338

Printed by Books on Demand, Germany